American Power after the Berlin Wall

American Power after the Berlin Wall

Thomas H. Henriksen

First published in 2007 by
PALGRAVE MACMILLAN™
175 Fifth Avenue, New York, N.Y. 10010 and
Houndmills, Basingstoke, Hampshire, England RG21 6XS
Companies and representatives throughout the world.

PALGRAVE MACMILLAN is the global academic imprint of the Palgrave Macmillan division of St. Martin's Press, LLC and of Palgrave Macmillan Ltd. Macmillan® is a registered trademark in the United States, United Kingdom and other countries. Palgrave is a registered trademark in the European Union and other countries.

ISBN-13: 978–0–230–60094–2
ISBN-10: 0–230–60094–8

Library of Congress Cataloging-in-Publication Data

Henriksen, Thomas H.
    American power after the Berlin Wall / by Thomas H. Henriksen.
      p. cm.
    Includes bibliographical references and index.
    ISBN 0–230–60094–8 (alk. paper)
      1. United States—Foreign relations—1989– 2. United States—Military policy. 3. United States—History, Military—20th century. 4. United States—History, Military—21st century. 5. World politics—1989–
    I. Title.

E840.H435 2007
327.73009′045—dc22   2007005493

A catalogue record for this book is available from the British Library.

Design by Newgen Imaging Systems (P) Ltd., Chennai, India.

First edition: November 2007

10 9 8 7 6 5 4 3 2 1

Printed in the United States of America.

Transferred to digital printing in 2007.

CONTENTS

ACKNOWLEDGMENTS

No work written under the auspices of the Hoover Institution should fail to laud the remarkable facilities and support provided by this unique institution. Its director, John Raisian, and his able lieutenant, Richard Sousa, along with their staff shoulder the administrative duties so others like us have the ultimate luxury—time to think and write. I am grateful and obligated to my Hoover colleagues for their stimulation and comments. Two non-Hoover commentators, Colonial William C. Hix (U.S. Army) and Irving Louis Horowitz provided many valuable insights on the manuscript, although I am solely responsible for the ultimate interpretation.

Over the years, I have been blessed with many first-rate assistants who contributed to my research, which formed the background of this work or helped directly in its preparation. Among the former are Margit Grigory, Jeanene Harlick, John Holzwarth, Kristin Gustavson Miller, Wendy Preuit, and Piers Turner and among the latter are Shawn Howard, Iva Naffziger, Dulcie Contreras, Janet Yang, and, most recently, Tristan Abbey and Diane Raub. The errors, of course, remain my own despite the many suggestions and assistance.

None of my efforts would have succeeded if not for the support and encouragement of my wife Margaret Mary and our family Heather, Damien, Thor, and Preston.

Introduction

THIS VOLUME IS INTENDED TO FILL TWO GAPS WITHIN INTERNATIONAL STUDIES LITERATURE since the Berlin Wall's collapse. First, it provides a single-volume description and analysis of the major—and many minor—American interventions in the post-Wall era. The background information, narrative, and discussion will acquaint an unfamiliar reader with the main international events that ensued after the Berlin Wall crumbled, which symbolically ended the four-decade Cold War and began a new chapter in America's global role.

Despite the fact that there are obvious "carry-forwards" from the Cold War era, which still cast giant shadows on the contemporary world, it is also true that world politics are vastly different since the Berlin Wall tumbled. To be sure, nuclear weapons and arms control agreements dating from the Iron Curtain epoch still impact the current strategic landscape. Communist governments still rule in China, Cuba, North Korea, and Vietnam. Yet the post–Cold War stretch has also bequeathed some new crises, which form the subject of this volume. Some of these events are fleeting and fade quickly from our consciousness. Yet, in reality, they impact our thinking and our policies today. America's setback in 1993 Somalia, for example, influenced the U.S. response toward the ouster of Jean-Bertrand Aristide in Haiti or toward the genocidal massacre in Rwanda. The first Persian Gulf War laid the groundwork for second conflict known as the Iraq War. This single-volume account, it is hoped, will help draw together and illuminate the connections as well as contribute to the reader's understanding of a tumultuous span of nearly two decades.

Second, the volume offers an explanation why the United States chose to intervene in a host of disparate crises. After the fall of the Berlin Wall, American power reached further and became more transformative than during much of the previous era, when the Soviet Union constrained U.S. actions. Official minds in Washington saw it within American interests to stabilize political turbulence in a host of areas that lacked oil or other vital resources. If instability spread, then it would endanger U.S. alliances, allies, and eventually economic and strategic interests. This helps explain why the United States intervened in Haiti, Bosnia, or Kosovo, none of which were economically important to American prosperity. Instability, for example, in southeastern Europe, spelled trouble for the United States first for its premiere alliance, NATO, and, perhaps ultimately, for Continental stability as happened with the outbreak of World War I. When jihadi terrorists struck the Twin Towers and Pentagon, the United States plunged into the lands east of the Mediterranean Sea to stabilize threats radiating from Afghanistan and Iraq.

A bit of historical reflection on the importance of stabile frontiers is instructive. Persistent attacks by invading barbarians over time weakened and then contributed to ancient Rome's collapse as these vandal hordes ravaged the empire's revenue-producing provinces. Later, Britain worried for centuries about the stability of the Low Countries because they could serve a launching pad for a sea-borne invasion of its islands, if a dominant power marched into Belgium and the Netherlands. In the British Empire, the imperative of stable frontiers assumed enormous significance. Writing about the "men on the spot" in India, Malaya, and South Africa, Professor John S. Galbraith chronicled the deep fear that turbulent frontiers generated among British officials and their defensive expansion against threats.[1] All states, not just empires, look with apprehension on volatile borders.

America's own Continental expansion stemmed, in part, from the necessity to tame its turbulent borderlands. Proponents of territorial expansionism pointed at threats from Native Americans or even Mexico to rally the nation for a push across the Continent. Later, the Monroe Doctrine sanctioned gunboat diplomacy in the Caribbean to contain instability so as not to invite European meddling in the U.S. backyard. During World War II, the United States fought to defeat threats emanating from Western Europe and East Asia. After the conflict, it stationed huge military forces to stabilize these areas and defend their borders from Soviet expansion. Thus, America's new frontiers became even more distant from its Western Hemisphere homeland. The aftermath of the 9/11 terrorist attacks, once more, witnessed American expansion, this time into Central Asia and the Middle East, to stabilize even more remote regions.

In and of itself, stability is not a bad thing for the world. It permits life to continue amid peace, makes possible conditions for economic growth and commerce, and promotes peaceful resolutions of disputes. It checks, or attempts to limit, wars, genocide, ethnic cleansing, and even the deleterious impact of natural disasters. When the United States did not act to stabilize violent outbursts, such as in Rwanda, Darfur, or the Congo, horrific tragedies occurred. Moreover, the United States, as this volume makes plain, embraced not the status quo but democratic transitions from authoritarianism.

Promoting freedom had long been a staple of American foreign policy. In the period after the Berlin Wall, nonetheless, the stability-cum-democracy approach assumed an even larger role in the visions of U.S. policymakers. America moved away from its stability-first policies of the Cold War that stressed political order against Soviet expansionism and toward a democracy agenda. It called into question its reliance on the "friendly tyrant" option to preserve stability. Authoritarian regimes were seen as breeders of violent ideologies that contributed to terrorism. Thus, democratic governance became interpreted as the best means to ensure peace and security.

America's interventions were not always predicated on imposing democracy by force of arms on turbulent lands as took place in Afghanistan and Iraq. In many prior instances, Washington left the actual implementation of a democratic process in local hands after a conflict or regime change operation. In a supreme irony, its reliance on democracy through military occupation to stabilize countries from the Suez Canal to the Himalayas backfired on its foreign policy mandarins. To confront terrorism and conflict in the Middle East and elsewhere the United States will have to find a new grand strategy.

CHAPTER 1

END OF THE BERLIN
WALL AND THE
AMERICAN COLOSSUS

There is nothing more difficult to take in hand, more perilous to conduct, or more uncertain in its success, than to take the lead in the introduction of a new order of things.

Niccolò Machiavelli

The reputation of power is power.

Thomas Hobbes

AN OBSERVER OF THE 1989 OCTOBER REVOLUTION PARADE IN MOSCOW'S RED SQUARE would have concluded that the Soviet Union was a formidable power with assured longevity. Against a backdrop of the hammer and sickle flags, the serried ranks of immaculately dressed Red Army troops goose-stepped in precision across the cobblestones. Row upon row of T-80 tanks rolled passed the Kremlin where Soviet President Mikhail S. Gorbachev gazed atop Lenin's Tomb. Road-mobile SS-20 ICBMs with their nuclear-tipped rockets aimed skyward followed the tanks. The Soviet arsenal paraded for the world to see, and it was an impressive display of military strength. The showy spectacle, however, masked the fact that this same Red Army—the victors of Stalingrad—had retreated from Afghanistan in defeat after a nine-year guerrilla war against Islamic warriors just months before the October commemoration. That defeat held immense import for any invasion, no matter how powerful, which came to transplant a foreign ideology and institutions on the Muslims lands between the Suez Canal and Kabul. But the historical significance of this Soviet debacle was obscured by the martial pomp in the Moscow streets until nearly 20 years later.

Little did the spectators realize on the sunny seventy-second anniversary commemorating the Bolshevik Revolution that the proud procession marked the denouement of the Marxist experiment in Russia and in the Soviet-controlled lands to its west. A small crowd of protestors in the shadows of the multicolored onion-shaped domes of St. Basil's Cathedral was the harbinger of Soviet Union's foundering, not the posturing Red Army. One large banner carried ahead of the alternative parade of 5,000 demonstrators read "72 Years Leading Nowhere." This was a searing indictment on this all but sacred day genuflecting to communist orthodoxy. Yet, the dissenters were neither apprehended, nor their signs seized, possibly the most revealing tremor of the impending geopolitical earthquake. Stalin or his immediate political heirs would have summarily shot or imprisoned them as "counterrevolutionaries" in the Siberian chain of Gulag camps. Days after the October martial pageantry, the Berlin Wall came down, heralding the Soviet Union's disintegration, the Cold War's end, and the singularity of American power in a turbulent world.

America thus stood at its zenith, without commensurate rival or overriding threat. Its strength derived not only from surviving the Soviet challenge but also from its military primacy, economic dynamism, technological prowess, scientific achievements, and seeming diplomatic indispensability to resolve nearly every global problem. Its world-class universities and media industries contributed to its powerful impact worldwide. As such, America's strength rested on a broad base, distinguishing it from militaristic empires of bygone eras. Its unparalleled power seemed to ensure military victory anywhere and to guarantee the export of democracy even to uncongenial environments to serve U.S. interests.

No onlooker of the Kremlin parade, or even the most farsighted seer in Washington, predicted that the coming Soviet dismemberment would result in the widespread application of more U.S. military power around the world, not less, in pursuit of an American age of democracy-induced stability. The tumbling of the Berlin Wall, in fact, meant that United States went from being the leader of the Free World to the earth's paramount power, with seeming global duties to shape and safeguard the world order in its own democratic image. To the official minds in Washington, implanting democracy became the best means to eliminate instability in the very same region that had ejected the Red Army in 1989. Unstable countries threatened regional peace, possibly dragging in the United States to protect alliances or allies, or they jeopardized America's commerce, access to resources, and even its own security.

America's arrival at the pinnacle of seeming omnipotence predisposed it to seek preservation of the existing order by deterring potential rivals, diminishing dangerous players, and transplanting democracy. Since America's global rise to prominence came not from territorial conquest like ancient Rome or from colonial expansion like Britain, it lacked ambition for traditional imperial dominions. Its idealistic impulse conditioned it to promote liberty, even by force of arms, and blinded its democracy enthusiasts to the animus their aims provoked in the Middle East, which had long resented non-Muslim penetration; however, that outcome lay years beyond the fall of the Berlin Wall. Before its reckoning east of the Mediterranean Sea, things went well for the United States. Stability-cum-democracy became tantamount to American security and prosperity among official minds in Washington when the new era dawned.

A glimpse of its future role arose from within the George H. W. Bush administration's Defense Department as it mulled over a post-Wall strategy just a few months after the Soviet Union's disintegration. A draft of the 1992 Pentagon's Defense Policy

Guidance propounded as a first objective the prevention of the "reemergence of a new rival," as a replacement "Soviet Union." Although the 46-page classified document called for addressing "sources of regional conflict and instability in such a way as to promote increasing respect for international law," it also envisioned U.S. unilateral action if necessary. "The United States should be postured to act independently when collective action cannot be orchestrated."[1] It advocated confronting "sources of regional conflict and instability . . . and encourage[d] the spread of democratic forms of government."[2] The draft provoked a public outcry after being leaked to the media. Its bellicose strategy elicited charges of imperialism and hegemony. Senator Joseph Biden (Democrat from Delaware) labeled the draft document as prescription for "literally a Pax Americana."[3] The political furor forced a rewrite of the Pentagon draft to smooth its sharp edges.

Harder in concept than the prevailing early 1990s outlook, the policy guidance document still did not really anticipate the coming exuberant exercise of American power around the globe to confront rogue states, terrorist networks, insurgencies, or humanitarian tragedies, but it did clearly envision the defense of "the established political and economic order."[4] This desire for stability was fused with democracy promotion as the post–Berlin Wall era lengthened. A democratic order assumed a strategic role in Washington's official thinking as American power was transformed by the Soviet Union's eclipse.

At first, the United States looked for security by negotiating nuclear arms control treaties with the Soviet Union, reuniting Germany, turning to economic globalization, and undertaking humanitarian operations to preserve order. Instability had long been an American concern. The United States' expansion across the American continent was, in part, motivated by an impetus to calm its turbulent frontiers. In the early twentieth century, it watched for instability in the Caribbean, lest European powers perceive an opportunity to meddle despite America's warnings in its Monroe Doctrine. During World War II, the United States defeated enemies in Western Europe and East Asia, where it remained afterward to stabilize potential threats and halt Soviet expansion. After the Berlin Wall, the concern manifested itself with stabilizing operations in Panama, Somalia, Haiti, and the Balkans. The 9/11 terrorist attacks, once again, propelled the United States on another offensive. Just as the Pearl Harbor bombings shattered the United States' isolation from overseas troubles and flung it politically and militarily into the heart of Europe and the western rim of Asia, so too did the Twin Towers collapse drive it into the Middle East and Central Asia to transmute and democratize these explosive societies, only to experience the hostile recoil from the Islamic world.

This pattern of traversing from disengagement out of world affairs back to hyperactivism was not unfamiliar terrain for the United States. At a different pace, such a trajectory had been repeated after both world wars. Following each of these major conflicts, and even the Vietnam War, the United States wearied of international burdens and retired from its duties only to be jerked back into action by an attack on its Pacific fleet or by apprehensions of Soviet expansionism. In each counterattack, democratization of former foes was an integral component of America's stability-first strategy so long as it did not jeopardize U.S. security or commercial interests.

THE SOVIET DECLINE

By 1989, the Union of Soviet Socialist Republics verged on bankruptcy. The military spectacle on the Day of the Great October Socialist Revolution was real enough. But like the idealized 1930s Potempkin villages, designed to persuade credulous visitors of Soviet Russia's prosperity, the parade fostered false assumptions about the true condition of the communist state's battered economy. Professor John Lewis Gaddis compared the Soviet Union to the formidable prehistoric triceratops that for all its "bristling armaments" was possessed of "digestive, circulatory, and respiratory systems" that kept "shutting down."[5] The martial procession, in reality, resembled a cracked mirror; some images were clear and accurate but the overall picture of comprehensive power was badly distorted.

The George H. W. Bush government initially moved cautiously toward the failing Soviet Union and its troubled domination of Central Europe. For all its difficulties, the Cold War bequeathed a stable, even somewhat predictable, international environment for the United States. It dealings with the Kremlin had gradually taken on a somewhat established pattern. The 1962 Cuban missile crisis had sobered both mega powers about the risk of thermonuclear war. Although there were other storm clouds in Soviet-American relations, none ever again edged the two superpowers toward the brink of a nuclear exchange as had Moscow's bid to place nuclear missiles on the Caribbean island. Afterward, negotiations and arms control agreements engendered a rough symmetry and equanimity that fostered restraint between the two reigning atomic behemoths.

With the assumption of Mikhail Gorbachev as the secretary general of the Communist Party of the Soviet Union in 1985 to reinvigorate the state's ailing economy, the USSR looked less a stabile counterweight to the United States. Like Martin Luther, Gorbachev sought to reform the corrupt and decrepit centrally run system, not create something new. His call for perestroika (restructuring) and glasnost (openness), however, further jolted the political and economic apparatus that defined the Soviet state.[6] Events themselves in short order washed over the Soviet leader like a political hurricane. However commendable, even the best of Gorbachev's specific measures were but small upward steps on a fast-moving downward escalator. The Soviet Union's internal plight soon raised questions about viability of the decades-old East-West rivalry. At the twilight of Ronald Reagan's presidency, British Prime Minister Margaret Thatcher, in fact, asserted, "We are not in a Cold War now."[7] A few months later, Reagan's vice president of eight years succeeded him in the White House without any clear understanding that his administration would preside over the liquidation of the Soviet imperial enterprise.

THE ACTION SHIFTS TO CENTRAL EUROPE

Soon after George Herbert Walker Bush's inauguration in January 1989, Central Europe was convulsed in political turmoil. Protestors took to the streets in several capitals demanding to be rid of the Red Army's occupation, the deadening communist rule, and repression from homegrown secret police. Poland, the most restive Kremlin satellite, had experienced a decadelong resistance from Solidarity, a workers' movement. So agitated had the Polish political landscape become that the communist regime of General Wojciech Jaruzelski opted to hold partially free elections in June. The voters rewarded Solidarity with 99 of the 100 open seats. This victory convinced Solidarity to form a coalition government with smaller parties and name Tadeusz Mazowiecki as Poland's next prime minister. This independent leadership represented the first democratic government in Central Europe since the Iron Curtain fell over Central Europe, and it served as a regionwide beacon to aspiring democratic figures and movements.

The Bush White House was convinced that a new political order was at hand, when the Gorbachev regime publicly advised its Warsaw protégés to acquiesce in the transfer of power. Instead of marching Soviet troops into Poland to put down a nationalist revolt, the Kremlin, in effect, scrapped its self-declared Brezhnev Doctrine that justified the suppression of noncommunist rulers. Earlier, the Red Army had ruthlessly cracked down on rebellions in Berlin (1953), Hungary (1956), and Czechoslovakia (1968). But in 1989, Gorbachev sidelined Soviet tanks and went along with the political shift in Poland.[8]

As Poland erupted, Hungary followed suit. The Hungarians defied Gorbachev's Russia on two significant fronts. Like the Poles, they first held elections in which the disbanded Communist Party tried to resurrect itself as the Socialist Party to garner only 9 percent of the votes. As a consequence, the triumphant noncommunist movements formed an independent and democratic administration. Next, the Hungarians breached the Iron Current by dismantling the barbed-wire fence along its border with Austria, permitting thousands of Central Europeans to stream westward to freedom. Metaphorically, this act was the finger out of the dike that led to fall of the Berlin concrete barrier months later.

Juxtaposed to the snowballing of triumphant democracy movements in Central Europe was the severe setback to political freedom in China in June 1989. Alarmed about national impact of prodemocracy protestors in Beijing's Tiananmen Square, the Chinese Communist Party bloodily suppressed the demonstration with the People's Liberation Army's tanks. The heavy-handed repression shocked Washington and other Western capitals. American observers had come to see the birth of democracy as the natural outgrowth of China's decadelong economic liberalization begun by Deng Xiaoping to modernize and develop the Chinese economy.

Rather than joining the West European chorus at the G-7 (the world's major industrial powers) summit in Paris calling for sanctions against Beijing, the United States' prized its stabile relations with the burgeoning global economic engine. President Bush deflected a stiff response because he held that the "stability of the US-Chinese relationship was too important to world peace to sever it completely."[9] Instead of punishment, Bush and his lieutenants secured a moderate reprimand by withholding additional World Bank loans to China and, in effect, warning Beijing about future transgressions. Confronting China offered U.S. policymakers scant prospect of harmonious Sino-American relations or of integration of the Asian giant into the international system. Bush's handling of the crisis offered a lesson in statecraft. Democracy could not be forced from abroad; it has to well up from within a people over time.

Back in Europe, on the other hand, the United States enjoyed greater leverage to pry Soviet forces out of their bases in the Warsaw Pact countries, reunite the two

Germanys, and secure nuclear arms control agreements with Moscow to reduce the atomic threat posed by massive arsenals and intercontinental ballistic missiles. During the second half of 1989, the Bush White House redoubled its attention on Central Europe. It did so cautiously wanting to further moderate headway without triggering a Soviet backlash that could upend the march toward political freedom. Change within a stable environment was the objective.

Reacting to the democratic upsurge in Poland and Hungary, George Bush uttered in Mainz, Germany, after the NATO summit on May 29–30, 1989 what became a rallying cry east of the Elbe River. The American president said the West's goal was "to let Europe be whole and free." He then added that the 1975 Helsinki Accords, which both United States and the Soviet Union signed, must be extended to "promote free elections and political pluralism in Eastern Europe," a declaration he repeated during high-profile stops in Warsaw and Budapest to massive crowds later in the summer.[10]

By mid-1989, East Germany, or the German Democratic Republic (GDR), succumbed to the same political upheavals that pulsed through Poland and Hungary. Voting with their feet, East Germans swarmed across the open Hungarian border into Austria and then finally into the freedom of West Germany or the German Federal Republic (FDR). Next, East Berlin crowds cheered Mikhail Gorbachev's October visit perceiving the Kremlin leader as embracing change that their leadership did not mirror. In fact, however, the Soviet head warned his East German counterpart to implement perestroika reforms or risk his position. As the political ground slipped beneath his feet, Erich Honecker turned his back on change and did, in fact, fall from power when the German Communist Party deposed him to save its own skin.

The internal security minister Egon Krenz was Honecker's replacement. He tried half measures to preserve the communist regime but only made matters worse when his government opened the Berlin Wall on November 9, 1989. Instead of relieving pent-up pressure among East Germans, the crack in the stone fence propelled them and their West German brethren to break down the Wall in a carnival atmosphere. No other single incident has so graphically symbolized the end of the Cold War as has the destruction of the Berlin Wall. It signaled dramatically the dawning of a new era, one promising German reunification and European wholeness.

The political turning points in East Germany, Poland, and Hungary cleared the way for other Central European nations to make their transitions. As elsewhere, street protests and strikes toppled the communist government in Czechoslovakia. Longtime dissident Vaclav Havel, the renowned Czech playwright, took office in late 1989 from which he scheduled free elections for June. Havel's Civic Forum Party won a strong plurality enabling it to form a coalition government with another non-communist party.

The anticommunist tide washed eastward over Bulgaria, Romania, and Yugoslavia where noncommunists or communists-turned-socialists ran in elections and won political office. Democracy seemingly sprang from the woodwork. The old communist bosses fell like kingpins in relatively violence-free elections. Only in Romania did the reactionary ruling clique of Nicolae and Elena Ceausescu set its face against the rising wave of reform with their notorious secret police, the Securitate, while the country sank into economic stagnation. Before it switched sides to join the antiregime protestors, the Securitate shot down demonstrators in the streets. Once their secret police prop crumbled, the Ceausescus found themselves before a firing squad on Christmas day in 1989 when they fled for the Romanian border. The irenic transition in Yugoslavia, though initially bloodless, far surpassed other communist changeovers in turmoil and bloodshed. The Yugoslavian catastrophe is narrated below, but its quiescent turnover fooled none of the keen observers that trouble lay around the corner in the deeply divided country.

American Strategic Goals in the Emerging Order

The George Bush government recognized that the Soviet Union was unable and unwilling to intervene to halt the political disintegration of its satellites. The evolving political landscape in Central Europe favored the United States while it demanded little from U.S. officials to sustain the momentum. In fact, the rapidity of events spurred American officials into action. With strategic winds blowing in its favor, Washington resolved to push for nuclear arms reductions with its Cold War nemesis so as to ensure American security and a lower nuclear equilibrium. Thus began a process where the Bush White House walked a line between stabilizing a strategic threat to America and retaining Gorbachev's hold on power as long America made gains.

Washington resurrected the Strategic Arms Reduction Treaty (START) talks from the previous Reagan administration. Secretary of State James Baker brought Soviet Foreign Minister Eduard Shevardnadze to his ranch in Jackson Hole, Wyoming, in a move that smoothed the way to complete the negotiations. Two years later in July 1991, the United States and the Soviet Union signed the START I agreement that reduced the nuclear warheads to 6,000 held by the two signatories, a reduction of nearly half for each atomic titan. The treaty also cut back the delivery systems of each to 1,600, whether intercontinental ballistic missiles (ICBMS), submarine-launched ballistic missiles, or long-distance bombers. The reductions rendered the United States more secure and the nuclear duel more stable.

The signing ceremony in Moscow's St. Vladimir's Hall afforded the President Bush an occasion to journey to the Russian capital as means to defuse Soviet military and party opposition to Gorbachev's conciliatory treaty with the United States. But Russian pride resisted the gesture of American president coming to the heart of the Soviet Empire rather than the Kremlin chief venturing to Washington. George Bush's trip was also memorable in a manner that demonstrated America's post–Cold War priorities for order.

On August 1, 1991, the presidential delegation left Moscow for Kiev, the Ukrainian capital, at a time when there was much political ferment in the East European nation. The American president addressed the Ukrainian Supreme Soviet, in what the media and pundits dubbed the "chicken Kiev" speech. His remarks about "suicidal nationalism," intended to tamp down extreme nationalism, fell on unreceptive ears. He spoke of a "democratic stability" when he declared, "Americans will not support those who seek independence in order to replace a far-off tyranny with a local despotism."[11]

Bush's comments struck Ukrainian nationalists as out of sync with their nationalistic aspirations to break decades of Soviet subjugation. Later, Brent Scowcroft, the president's adviser and alter ego, refuted the judgment of Bush's timidity by holding that America's forty-first chief executive meant to pour water on the raging fires of ethnic extremism in Yugoslavia and Moldavia as well as Ukraine.[12] In actuality, George Bush reflected an American desire for stability over fragmentation of the Soviet polity. Instability could well imperil Gorbachev's shaky rule, jeopardize Soviet troop withdrawals, and undermine current and hoped-for arms agreements. If political disorder erupted, then it might require U.S. commitments or even military intervention to set things right. Recall that the United States had just wound down the first Persian Gulf War at this time in mid-1991, which will be discussed in chapter 3. Another serious overseas engagement roused deep misgivings. Secretary of State James A. Baker III played the same status quo tune to rebellious republics in Belgrade just prior to Yugoslavia's breakup with the same lack of success as did Bush in Kiev. None of the aspiring nationalists wanted to place stability over local sovereignty.

The growing political restiveness on the Soviet periphery convinced the U.S. government to redouble its arms control initiatives while the getting was good. As he prepared to leave office after losing the November 1992 presidential election, George Bush committed the United States to START II. This second arms control treaty slashed active nuclear weapons by two-thirds—3,500 American warheads and 3,000 Russian warheads. Four years later the U.S. Senate ratified START II, and the Russian Duma, or legislature, took yet another four years to approve it. The nuclear arms control push attained other major strides. The Cooperative Threat Reduction program, which was a U.S. Senate initiative, allocated funds from the Defense Department to dismantle Russian nuclear and chemical weapons, lest they wind up in the wrong hands. Next, James Baker, America's top diplomat, convinced the newly independent Belarus, Kazakhstan, and Ukraine to agree to the Lisbon Protocol in May 1992 that eliminated their nuclear arsenals inherited from Moscow during the Cold War, when they were Soviet republics.[13]

GERMAN REUNIFICATION WITHIN NATO

American progress in comparatively weakening its old foe's nuclear arm capacity was at least equaled on the ground. Less than a month after the Berlin Wall tumbled, American and Soviet principals met face-to-face on shipboard off the coast of Malta. President Bush chose the venue as consciously reminiscent of the storied encounter between Franklin Roosevelt and Winston Churchill near Newfoundland in 1941, which recorded the birth of the Atlantic Charter, a joint declaration on the goals for the war against fascism.

Although the Malta summit resulted in no similar resounding proclamation, it represented a defining round of talks between George Bush and Mikhail Gorbachev. Carried out below decks of U.S. and Soviet warships amid blustery weather, the negotiations helped foster a personal bound between the two leaders and led to a number of understandings, if not hard-and-fast agreements. President Bush offered incentives to the economically hard-pressed Soviet delegation, including most favored nation trade status, financial credits, and pledges to work for observer status for Moscow at the General Agreements on Tariffs and Trade. Gorbachev welcomed the proposals, which would buttress his perestroika reforms to lessen the grip of the Soviet centrally controlled economy. The Kremlin leader reciprocated by promising to stop arms transfers to El Salvadoran rebels and, significantly, to renounce interference in Nicaragua's free elections set for February 25, 1990. The voting unexpectedly recorded the election of Violeta Chamorro, a nonrevolutionary figure, to the presidency, which constituted a political victory for U.S. policies in Central America.

The grand prize—German reunification—temporarily eluded the American negotiators off the Maltese seacoast. Reflecting their history, the Soviet delegates were reluctant to contemplate a reconstituted Teutonic power on their doorstep after being on the receiving end of two bloody German invasions in the twentieth century. A divided and weakened German nation suited them just fine. On the German question, Moscow was as behind the political curve as it was on its own wheezing economy. Events on the ground raced inexorably toward German unity. As the Soviet economy spiraled downward, the Germans took matters into their own hands. Germans in each zone pushed to reunite. In the Federal German Republic, Chancellor Helmut Kohl shaped policies and offered funds to the East Germans. In the German Democratic Republic, the agitation for unity came from the bottom up rather than the top down.

By this time, the United States was well into its "beyond-containment" approach to the USSR. Its goals now embraced a withdrawal of the Red Army from Central Europe and the Baltic states, a less nuclear-threatening Soviet Union, and a reunited Germany within the North Atlantic Treaty Organization, America's premiere alliance with several West European countries and Canada. To accomplish this grand design, American policy evinced less emphasis on reforming Soviet society. In fact, it favored Gorbachev's retention of the CPSU general secretaryship enabling him to further American desiderata for the post-Wall era. This orientation earned George Bush opprobrium as a foreign policy "realist," that is to say a statesman interested only in international power relationships and not the domestic political alignment within states. Rather than pushing democratic reform in the tottering Soviet edifice, the Bush White House opted for attainable ends. In retrospect, it seems highly unlikely whether Washington could have made meaningful liberalizing headway against entrenched political and military institutions, burgeoning corruption, and a calcified communist structure in the sprawling Soviet construct.

The United States concentrated on achievable priorities to enhance stability in Europe, the scene of two major American military interventions during both world wars and much worry in the course of the Cold War. Anticipating the Red Army's redeployment from Central Europe, the West Wing planned next to reunite Germany. U.S. officials considered the division an anachronistic settlement deriving from the immediate post–World War II period. Left to fester politically, it might well destabilize the Continent in the new era. Secretary of State Baker and his lieutenants advanced reconciliation negotiations by the "Two-Plus-Four" talks, in which the two German states served as the principals in arranging unity and the four World War II victorious powers—Britain, France, Soviet Union, and the United States—functioned as coprincipals to establish borders and security arrangements, which embodied NATO membership.

These deliberations began after the East German election and amid accelerating political change in East Germany. By early 1990, the GDR no longer operated, as its command economy squeaked and creaked toward dysfunction. Its citizens stopped paying taxes, flocked into the streets to demonstrate against the regime, and demanded reunification with their West German brothers. Seeking to calm the swirling turbulence, Berlin agreed to speed up the elections from May to March 18, and Moscow realistically acquiesced.

The results from the East German voting stunned the German Communist Party and the Kremlin, for they foresaw a political victory in the first free election in the eastern zone since 1932; instead, 48 percent of the populace endorsed Chancellor Kohl's Christian Democratic Union's Alliance for Germany. The Social Democratic Party captured 22 percent, while the former Communist Party scored only 16, with smaller parties taking the rest. The two top vote-garnering parties were offshoots of the major West German parties and entered into a coalition government. That government quickly struck an economic and monetary merger with the FDR that ensued on July 1, 1990, just eight months following the Berliners assault on the Wall.

The polling outcome reverberated within the power corridors in Washington, Moscow, London, and Paris. Such a resounding victory for the forces of reunification meant that even the reluctant British and French resigned themselves to the inevitability of one powerful Germany astride the Continent. Both nations, along with the Soviet Union, initially resisted American pressure for German unity. Each government wanted the United States to maintain a strong military and diplomatic presence in Europe to avoid a repetition of the 1930s American isolation that contributed to German aggression. Washington used its strong hand to haul them toward its agenda.

Aversion, therefore, gave way to acceptance on how best to enfold the new German entity within the European comity of states to neutralize any potential recurrence of Teutonic militarism. France, the country that suffered three German invasions in a 70-year span, worked hardest to enmesh Germany in a web of Continental political and economic alliances. Aware of its neighbors' apprehensions, the Kohl government lessened the opposition by agreeing to borders and security provisions.

Meeting in Dublin on April 28–29, 1990, the European Community (EC) endorsed the process for the reunion of the two Germanys. More significantly, the member states moved forward on a Franco-German initiative for a political union beyond the looser EC grouping that promised to embed the enlarged German entity within its ranks. This summit breathed life into the unionization process that resulted in the Maastricht Treaty signed in 1991. The treaty brought forth the European Union from the European Community. European apprehensions of a strong German state, in fact, contributed to the Continental political union. For its part, America encouraged the union to foster peace and stability among nations known for their savage wars.

In the meantime, Gorbachev's Russia grew more determined, first, to thwart German reunification and, then, to block the new nation from membership in NATO. A divided, and hence weaker, Germany suited Moscow's defensive posture better than a possible return of a Germanic powerhouse in *Mitteleuropa*. After the

March election, the German reunion looked as if it was a foregone conclusion, and Helmut Kohl moved quickly with his economic and monetary integration strategy. Thus Moscow stiffened its fight against German entry into NATO as a fallback position. It raked up not only Germany's Nazi past but also the neo-Nazism that lurked on the fringes of the German youth culture as justification for international monitoring. This was something the Germans, with four decades of proven democracy behind them, found insulting. Allusion to the darker side of Germany's twentieth-century history angered the Bonn government and spurred it toward reunion, which formally took place on October 3, 1990.

After the East German election, the United States redoubled its drive to unite Germany and place the larger polity in the Atlantic alliance as the best means to stabilize the Continent. Moscow dug in its heels at the prospect of NATO advancing toward its border. It called for either a neutral Germany or one tied to the Warsaw Pact as well as NATO. The dissolution of the Warsaw Pact along with its pro-Soviet regimes removed that option from consideration by mid-1990. As for German neutrality, the United States rejected that approach. It argued to Soviet officials that a freestanding Germany would likely oscillate unstably between East and West, or, more likely, it would draw smaller states into its own orbit like a magnet attracts iron filings. Such a grouping might take on an anti-Russian orientation, inciting European instability. Washington negotiators argued it was far better for Moscow to have Germany moored in the democratic and peaceful Western alliance. The United States also reasoned that German participation in NATO served as another hedge against any resuscitated Russian designs on westward expansion.

At the time, the Bush government's logic proved helpful but not decisive. What tipped the Kremlin's decision toward the American position was its desperate economic plight. Mikhail Gorbachev made it known to Secretary Baker that the Soviet Union required $20 billion in funds and credits to cover its communist-to-capitalist industrial conversion. Financial resources were also needed for debt repayment, consumer goods, and plant retooling from military to civilian manufacture. American aid was modest, because the White House believed that assistance would simply "go down the rat hole" in a centrally planned economy.[14] Chancellor Kohl's Germany, on the other hand, stood ready to grease the skids for a rapid Red Army retreat from East German soil and for NATO membership. He offered Gorbachev DM 12 billion and interest-free credit of an additional DM 3 billion.[15]

America's assertiveness to reunite and to put a reunited Germany in NATO belies the conventional image of George Bush as a kinder, gentler, and less risk-taking president when compared to his predecessor. Soviet, French, and British reluctance to a reunited Germanic powerhouse athwart the Continent was overcome by American perseverance. President Bush behaved more unilaterally and less conciliatory than is often perceived toward three powers in the outer ring of the Two-Plus-Four formula. He believed that the U.S.-proposed European settlement was best for Continental harmony despite its partners' hesitation. He thought that U.S. policy was "too important . . . to review with the allies in the usual way."[16] The three other members of the "Four" in Two-Plus-Four also desired to keep U.S. military forces in Europe as the stabilizer and protector of the status quo. Later, Mikhail Gorbachev recorded in his memoirs that he had "made several attempts to convince the American President that an American 'withdrawal' from Europe was not in the interest of the Soviet Union."[17]

American power in Europe, in the last analysis, assuaged Russian, French, and British fears. At that time, the United States stationed some 315,000 troops in Europe. The German-European reconciliation proved so successful that by 2005 America had reduced its commitment to less than 100,000 military personnel on the Continent, which attained a flowering of democracy that the United States and its West European allies inspired and aided but did not impose by force of arms.

In a muted ceremony in a Moscow hotel, rather than the Kremlin, the six foreign ministers of the Two-Plus-Four arrangement signed the Treaty on the Final Settlement with Respect to Germany on September 12, 1990. The treaty constricted the new Germany by making it renounce aggression, by limiting the Bundeswsehr to 370,000 troops, and by committing it to the Nuclear Non-Proliferation Treaty, which the West Germans had already signed. In return, Moscow promised to vacate the Red Army from its East German garrisons before 1995; in reality, it did so two years earlier. The Bundeswsehr was allowed to move into the former Eastern zone but without nuclear arms. Significantly, the treaty entitled the new sovereignty to enter any alliance. Finally, it dissolved the Four Power framework that had overseen Germany since the end of World War II. The signing itself lacked any of the drama that accompanied the breach of the Berlin Wall nearly a year earlier, but it did contractually reconcile a long-divided Europe.

THE SOVIET UNION'S DISSOLUTION

For the United States, the treaty signing brought little respite in its worried focus on the Soviet Union and its embattled Gorbachev. The centrifugal forces tearing at the country intensified. A description of these events would take us too far beyond account of U.S. policies after the Berlin Wall. Suffice it to note that Moscow's bloody suppression of Lithuania's independence movement in mid-January 1991 marked a turning point for Gorbachev's political survival. Denying prior knowledge or responsibility for the crackdown later cost the Kremlin chieftain support from his security forces. In late August, some elements within the Red Army and KGB, the secret police, staged a coup that temporarily removed Gorbachev from power, thereby enfeebling him irretrievably after his restoration. Other factors eroded Gorbachev's standing as well.

During the months after Soviet clampdown in Lithuania but before the coup, Gorbachev compounded his missteps by going along with the drafting of the misnamed Union Treaty advanced by Boris Yeltsin, at the time the chairman of the Supreme Soviet in the Russian Republic, the dominant republic in the USSR and the emerging rival of the Kremlin boss. The treaty, in fact, was a recipe for the Soviet Union's dissolution and the last straw for Soviet hard-liners, because it devolved political and economic power to its constituent republics. The Soviet rear guard resolved to act when it learned that Gorbachev intended to sign the Union Treaty with Kazakhstan's president on August 20, 1991.

The plotters sprang their coup while Gorbachev vacationed in his dacha in the Crimea. They dispatched armored vehicles and soldiers into Moscow's streets while sequestrating Gorbachev. Despite the show of armed power, the ringleaders lost their nerve, and soldiers refused to shoot the demonstrators. Questions still remain about the half-baked takeover attempt, but its outcome is clear: it speeded up the Soviet breakup.[18] In the aftermath, the Soviet military establishment, KGB, and upper echelons of the CPSU were discredited and distrusted within the country and beyond. After Gorbachev's return to power, Azerbaijan, Estonia, Kyrgyzstan, Moldova (once known as Moldavia), Ukraine, and Uzbekistan declared their independence from the USSR. Other republics followed suit. The dissolution of the USSR was an accomplished fact by late 1991, and it deprived Gorbachev of a political office. His rival, the loutish Boris Yeltsin as head of Russia, loomed even larger in American thinking after the August coup.

Before the Soviet Union's disintegration, the United States weighed its options in dealing with the revolutionary changes exploding in the sprawling country. The August coup clarified the Soviet dysfunctional reality and sparked a reassessment of U.S. policies. What would happen if a second ouster occurred and installed a Soviet general or political reactionary who sought to roll back American gains in Central Europe? Just as important, would a splintered USSR really be a bad outcome for the United States? The answer to both questions was Yeltsin. Since he had opposed the August coup, he was likely to honor Gorbachev's decision on the German question and oppose the restoration of the Soviet order that old-line military and party officials dreamed. Moreover, he was serving as a catalyst for the Soviet Union's collapse. Thus, President Bush and his closest advisers might personally lament Gorbachev's downfall, but they were more than prepared to accept Yeltsin's ascension so as to protect American diplomatic and arms control victories. George Bush and later Bill Clinton did, in fact, consolidate American gains after Yeltsin ascended the presidency of the Russian Federation. Yeltsin replaced the USSR with the Commonwealth of Independent States that grouped many of the successor republics into a looser, volunteer, and much-attenuated structure. It proved a weak reed for Kremlin superpower nostalgia.

AN AMERICAN ACHIEVEMENT

Washington's handling of German reunification and the Soviet unraveling strengthened America's global paramountcy. The arms control agreements, Central European freedom from the Red Army, and the Soviet Union's disintegration—all left the United States stronger than before the Berlin Wall passed into history. The East Germans, Poles, Czechs, and Hungarians themselves played a starring roles in the dramatic events leading to their returned sovereignty. A Kremlin leader other than the reforming Mikhail Gorbachev, nonetheless, might have attempted to turn the clock back by ordering in Russian armed forces to crush the revolts in Central Europe as his predecessors had. Still, the United States figured indispensably in the outcome. It assisted in the German reunification, the withdrawal of the Red Army from the "captive nations" of Central Europe, and the scaling down dramatically of U.S. and Soviet nuclear arsenals. In retrospect, these dramatic events look almost inevitable but President Bush's foreign policy team worked astutely, flexibly, and imaginatively to bring about conciliation and stability to a vast volatile domain east of the Elbe

River. To attain Germanic unity, the United States also had to bring along Britain, France, and a fearful Soviet Union, which all wanted to avoid a return to a powerful Central European state.

The Cold War's termination spawned a not-unexpected paradox in international relations in that it undermined the long-standing Euro-American alliance. There are no immutable laws in history, but one recurring phenomenon is that after victory the former defensive coalitions lose their validity. This also happened initially to NATO after the Soviet Union broke apart. Without the common Soviet threat, the Atlantic alliance lost its purpose and frayed before the war on terror. This true state of affairs was not widely recognized until the approach of the Iraq War, when transatlantic relations sank amid acrimony, only gradually mending over time. Before that healing, American power seemed to reach a pinnacle, having vanquished its longtime nemesis.

The triumph of U.S.-endorsed democracy in Central Europe and even temporarily in post-Gorbachev's Russia constituted a heady brew for Washington governments over time. The receptivity to democracy within the former "evil empire," in fact, began a process in which the official American mind believed that consensual government would always promote stability and American interests. As time would tell, it was a false faith when spread by military force in Muslim lands east of the Mediterranean Sea.

America's diplomatic success was also accomplished at a time when Washington had a full plate of troubles elsewhere. In August 1990, Iraq invaded neighboring Kuwait raping the tiny sheikdom and threatening Saudi Arabia with a similar attack. Until the following March, the White House was preoccupied by the extraordinary military buildup, air campaign, and ground war in the Persian Gulf, which will be subsequently narrated. Coping with two major crises, which has rarely been America's strong suit, unfolded well for the Bush foreign policy lieutenants, particularly with the Soviet Union's collapse. Their management of Euro-Russian relations surpassed the debacle that followed World War I with the aborted League of Nations and U.S. isolation. Even after World War II, when the United States established a raft of diplomatic, economic, and military measures to contain Soviet expansionism, the world faced a 40-year Cold War.

The peaceful winding down of the East-West competition after the Wall vanished, on the other hand, remains a crowning attainment, except for two missteps. During the early 1990s, the United States let slip two political convulsions that seemed merely sideshows compared to the main events in Europe and Persian Gulf. It undertook no adequate measures to quell Yugoslavia's brewing civil war or to tame the engulfing anarchy in Afghanistan that a decade later bred a terrorist menace that so devastatingly struck America's preeminent financial and military landmarks in Manhattan and Washington. Both trouble spots, as will be described, metastasized into full-blown threats that gnawed at stability in their arenas. Before those developments, the United States restored harmony in its own hemisphere.

CHAPTER 2

ᵣ INTERVENTION AND DEMOCRACY IN CENTRAL AMERICA

We, the Panamanians, will sit along the banks of the Canal to watch the dead bodies of our enemies pass by.

Manuel Noriega, December 17, 1989

Power consists in one's capacity to link his will with the purpose of others, to lead by reason and a gift of cooperation.

Woodrow Wilson

WHEN GEORGE H. W. BUSH UTTERED that America's purpose "is to make kinder the face of the Nation and gentler the face of the world" at his inauguration on January 20, 1989, he seemed to be charting a new national path.[1] Later, the one-term president appeared to confirm this direction with calls for a "new world order." His critics berated him for promoting what they believed was a fuzzy internationalism that subordinated American interests to an expansive United Nations global agenda. But America's forty-first chief executive, in practice, subscribed to advancing U.S. interests by using UN auspices or other international coalitions whenever possible to subdue disorder when it threatened American priorities. His embrace of an internationalist rubric did not exclude a healthy dose of America's objectives, including the advancement of democracy.

THE UNITED STATES AND NICARAGUAN CONTROVERSY

President Bush inherited two conflicts in the Western Hemisphere from the preceding administration—one in Nicaragua and another at home with the U.S. Congress over Washington's policies toward the Central American country. The new Oval Office occupant resolved to douse both infernos that engulfed the Reagan presidency. For the Reagan government, Nicaragua cast a long shadow in the global struggle with the Soviet Union. In 1979, a tinhorn dictator named Anastasio Somoza

Debayle was ousted in a civil war at the hands of the Sandinista National Liberation Front (FSLN), which was aided by Cuba. Marxist in orientation, the FSLN, or simply the Sandinistas, captured headlines with the bloody overthrow of Somoza. Cuba's Marxist leader Fidel Castro flew to Managua to celebrate the first anniversary of the Sandinistas' victory and strengthen ties with a fraternal regime. The Sandinistas proclaimed themselves a people's vanguard and looked to the Soviet bloc for aid and inspiration.

Until the Sandinistas seized power, Cold War tensions in this hemisphere were focused on Cuba, which spread subversion in Africa and Latin America. To Washington, the Sandinistas now threatened Central American states. Like the Vietnam War, the Nicaraguan upheaval divided American opinion, however. Academics, politicians, and religious figures often interpreted the Sandinista regime through an idealized prism of Marxist-inspired peasants ruling on behalf of the downtrodden masses to build a socialist, classless, workers' paradise. Instead, the Sandinistas forged a close dependency with the Soviet bloc, built up the largest army and security apparatus in Central American history, aided like-minded guerrillas in El Salvador and Honduras, and erected a statist, confiscatory economy, which enriched the leaders and their cronies.

Washington could not turn a blind eye to Nicaraguan developments. President Jimmy Carter, who grew painfully aware of Moscow's expansionism after the Soviet invasion of Afghanistan in late 1979, wanted to live with the Sandinistas so long as their human rights violations remained hidden to the outside world. But the flood of Nicaraguan refugees into the United States made it impossible to ignore this repression. The prospect of Soviet high-performance jets appearing in Nicaragua concerned the incoming Reagan government, which decided to combat Managua.

This counteroffensive formed part of the Reagan Doctrine of which the anti-Soviet campaign in Afghanistan figured as the centerpiece and the one in Angola as almost a sideshow. Through covert means, the Central Intelligence Agency trained, armed, and equipped Nicaraguan exiles in nearby Honduras. Reagan officials acknowledged the secret campaign to put pressure on but not overthrow the Sandinista regime headed by Daniel Ortega. Hardly anyone read this fine-line distinction as genuine, for the Nicaraguan rebels, or contras, waged a bloody guerilla campaign against the Sandinista rulers. The contra rebellion claimed some 30,000 Nicaraguan lives from 1981 to 1990.

Revelations about Washington's covert assistance to the Nicaraguan contras provoked a congressional firestorm. On December 8, 1982, the House of Representatives overwhelmingly passed the Boland Amendment, so named for its sponsor Congressman Edward Boland, a Massachusetts Democrat. This legislation banned the Department of Defense or the CIA from supplying weapons or military instruction for the objective of overthrowing the Managua regime. To comply with U.S. laws, the contras fought ostensibly to force the Sandinista to hold fair and free elections. In reality, their ultimate goal was to oust Sandinista leader Daniel Ortega.

The Reagan White House tried to block the spread of Sandinismo into Honduras and El Salvador, both of which requested U.S. support as the conflict spilled over their borders from Nicaragua. El Salvador suffered a bloody civil war with leftist guerrillas that claimed 75,000 lives from 1979 to 1992. Honduras escaped heavy casualties with about 140 deaths but still noted the disappearance of a reported 184 individuals of varying nationalities from its territory.[2]

When it came to light in early 1984 in a *Wall Street Journal* story that the CIA secretly mined Nicaraguan harbors, opposition to the White House's Central American policy erupted on Capitol Hill.[3] In October, Congress passed the third Boland Amendment, which reaffirmed two earlier versions to block aid to the contras. But this time the lawmakers also mandated an end of support not only from the United States but also from any country cajoled by Washington to help the contras. This meant the Reagan officials could not find third-party states (Saudi Arabia and Brunei had channeled help) to fund or supply arms to wage a covert war against the Sandinista regime. Without such assistance, the anti-Sandinista forces were severely hobbled. What followed led to one of the most sensational political scandals of the twentieth century.

Mid-level officials within the White House embarked on a rogue operation to circumvent the law of the land. Members of the National Security Council plotted to skirt the Boland Amendment forbidding military aid to the contras. This involved a complex and devious scheme. Secret arms sales to Iran were undertaken, which was locked in a life-or-death war with Iraq during most of the 1980s, in return for the release of American hostages in the Middle East. Since Iran backed terrorist networks in Lebanon, it was believed that Tehran was in a position to spring the captives. Proceeds from the purchase were then funneled to the Nicaraguan rebels. What made the back-channel deal especially controversial was the adversarial relationship the United States shared with the theocratic regime in Tehran. Since the 1979 takeover of the American Embassy in Tehran and the detention of the 52-member staff for over a year, Iranian-American relations had been at daggers point.

How much Ronald Reagan actually knew of the transfer-of-funds scheme is still disputed. He denied any knowledge of it. The president was certainly determined to win the release of U.S. hostages. The NSC staff members definitely wanted the money accrued from the arms sales to underwrite the Freedom Fighters, as Reagan termed them, in Central America. Some held the president responsible.[4] Others imagined the whole caper as a modern-day version of overzealous knights murdering Thomas Becket not on the verbal order of Henry II but rather responding to the English monarch's innermost wishes.

In any event, Washington was rocked by the revelations about arms-for-hostages and under-the-table funds for the contras in November 1986. As the details filled the nation's newspapers and airwaves, the White House came under withering political fire from the other end of Pennsylvania Avenue. Congress held hearings to denounce and probe Ronald Reagan's role. For months, the Reagan presidency hung in the balance. Though he survived the ordeal, Ronald Reagan endured relentless accusations about the Iran-contra episode.[5] Congressional relations remained frayed, especially over Central American policy, as George H. W. Bush won the election to the White House two years later.

Newly elected President Bush harbored powerful reasons to put the Nicaraguan controversy behind his fledgling administration. While George H. W. Bush's role in the Iran-contra scandal was much less central than others, the record makes clear that he participated in some of the meetings about the weapons-hostage swap. He and his own Secretary of State James A. Baker III (who once served as Reagan's Chief of Staff) had advocated military assistance during the Reagan presidency to the contras as the soundest means to pressure Managua to halt the export of revolution in Central America and to hold free and fair elections. Politics also dictated putting a contentious issue between the executive and the legislative branches well behind an incoming president. Besides, the pragmatic Bush, unlike Ronald Reagan, embraced a less than visceral approach to combating communism in Central America.[6]

Other political considerations arose as well. The new Bush administration knew that an agitated congressional opposition to arming the contras precluded U.S. military support for the anti-Sandinista forces. James Baker embarked on his secretaryship amid tense negotiations—not with a foreign power but ironically with the U.S. Congress over Washington's policy in Nicaragua. America's top diplomat characterized his Capitol Hill diplomacy as "intense, partisan and frequently acrimonious."[7] Like most incoming administrations, the Bush inner circle hoped to start off on a note of bipartisanship with Congress, especially since the Democrats held majorities in both houses and even the congressional Republicans felt bruised by the Iran-contra scandal. In seeking a way out of the Central American imbroglio, the White House looked to strengthen the budding peace process in the region.

Costa Rica's President Oscar Arias Sanchez persevered in his goal of a durable diplomatic solution. He reconvened the four other Central American presidents in early 1989 in Costa del Sol, El Salvador, after which it was announced that the Ortega regime acquiesced to holding a presidential election by late February 1990. Few impartial foreign observers put much faith in a fair and free vote in Sandinista-controlled Nicaragua. But the agreement served as a timely pretext for the recently inaugurated President Bush to fashion a new Central American policy.

The fledgling Bush foreign policy team resolved to firm up Arias' Central American agreement, although the United States was not a signatory. The White House also lobbied the factious anti-Sandinista resistance to unify behind a single candidate to oppose Ortega. It pressured the United Nations, European Community, the Organization of American States, and even former president Jimmy Carter's policy center in Atlanta to inundate Nicaragua with observers prior to the election. To assist Violeta Chamorro and her Union Nacional Opositor in the uphill electoral struggle against the entrenched Sandinista regime, Washington enlisted the National Endowment for Democracy to direct voter registration and to furnish technical expertise to the challenger.

These efforts paid off. Strange as it may seem to outsiders, the Nicaraguans voted out Ortega and put Chamorro in office. The stunning communist electoral defeat engendered repercussions well beyond the Central American country. It dealt a serious blow to the *norteamericano* sympathizers of the Marxist regime on U.S. campuses and in Washington advocacy offices, who for years protested that the Sandinistas represented the will of the Nicaraguan people. It vindicated the bipartisan accord that the White House forged with Democrats on Capitol Hill. More importantly, it brought stability, peace, and democracy to a war-battered region, as the rural conflicts ended first in El Salvador and then later in Guatemala. The Soviet hand was also thwarted in the Western Hemisphere, although Moscow continued to provide aid, albeit on a vastly decreased scale, to Cuba.

Even more emphatically for an understanding of the post–Berlin Wall policies of the United States, the Nicaraguan settlement accomplished two feats. First, it foreshadowed America's trust in democracy to bring stability to conflict-ravaged countries or areas. The Bush White House and its succeeding residents subscribed to the conviction that reasonably free and fair elections brought peace and moderation to strife-filled zones by channeling political grievances from bullets to the ballot box. Second and significantly, it set a contemporary precedent of using elections to dampen down a raging conflict. The examples of democracy bringing stability in postwar Germany, Japan, and Italy came after their decisive defeat and nearly unconditional surrender to the Allied powers. The Nicaraguan case took place amid a civil war, a far more dramatic proof of democracy's efficacy in bringing peace and order. Later, the same democratic antidote to poisonous turmoil was applied in other arenas to foster stability. The U.S. military intervened in Panama, changed the regime, installed a democratic government, and stabilized the country. It would also be tried in such turbulent cases in Haiti, Bosnia, Kosovo, Liberia, Afghanistan, and eventually Iraq. What worked elsewhere did not predict a similar outcome in Middle East, which historically fought against non-Muslim intrusions; however, first Nicaragua and then Panama helped condition Washington to put its faith in American-imposed democracy to bring peace and steadiness in turbulent places.

THE U.S. INTEREST IN PANAMA

North American interest in Panama stretched back more than a century. After the United States acquired California from Mexico, transportation to the West Coast ballooned in the nation's commercial priorities. California's gold rush in 1849 motivated thousands of migrants to cross the Panamanian isthmus to prospect the West Coast's new El Dorado. The Panama Railway first linked the Atlantic and Pacific oceans in 1855 across the isthmian peninsula with rapid transport. It also whetted the appetite for a transoceanic waterway as the ideal solution to ship-borne commerce. French investors leapt ahead by negotiating with Colombia, which at that time governed Panama, to obtain a concession to dig a canal. But French construction under Ferdinand de Lesseps stumbled as the company went bankrupt and workers died in droves from malaria and yellow fever. The enterprise's default paved the way for the United States century-long preoccupation with Panama and its two-ocean passage.

By guile rather than gunfire, Washington wrested control of Panama from Colombia. Theodore Roosevelt, who wielded a big stick while talking softly, coveted the Isthmus of Panama to build his transoceanic canal. He tried first by fair means to convince the Colombian parliament to ratify its own government's treaty permitting a slice of territory for a Canal Zone for the seaway channel. Failing at diplomacy, President Roosevelt turned to foul means. He encouraged an indigenous Panamanian revolt against Colombian rule. Three days after the start of the rebellion in 1903, Washington diplomatically recognized the infant Republic of Panama. It deployed warships to block Bogotá from landing troops to crush the uprising and bribed the

Colombian admiral to steam his small flotilla away. The new country lost little time in leasing the Canal Zone, a 10-mile strip on either side of the proposed waterway, to its North American benefactor. Not long afterward, the United States resumed the Canal construction.

The opening of the Panama Canal on August 15, 1914 led to prosperity for those living within the confines of autonomous zone, which benefited from the spending of U.S. military bases. But life in greater Panama changed little. The Canal transit fees benefited the political elite. Panama came to represent the quintessential banana republic (for the most of the first three-quarters of the twentieth century) replete with poverty, political instability, repressive dictatorships, widespread corruption, and, of course, reliance on the main export of bananas. The authoritarian stability associated with General Omar Torrijos Herrera from 1968 to his death in 1981 contributed to modest economic growth. After his passing, civilian leaders put on a fig leaf to the outside world behind which military strongmen held the reins of power.

Deemed a strategic "choke point" by the Pentagon, the United States was loath to hand over the Canal Zone to Panamanian sovereignty despite local pleas until Jimmy Carter moved into the White House. President Carter pushed through Congress the 1977 Panama Canal Treaty granting a return of the Canal Zone to Panama by 2000, with both states guaranteeing the Canal's neutrality. Neither the impending unmooring of the Americanized zone nor the winding down of the U.S. covert intrusion against the Sandinistas entailed the slackening of Washington's strategic interest in Panama. Internal misdeeds riveted Washington's attention only insofar as they endangered Panamanian stability and U.S. interests. It was for this reason that the United States peered uneasily at local political activities in the late 1980s. During that period, Manuel Antonio Noriega concentrated power in his hands. Capital flight, foreign debt, and budget deficits marked Noriega's tenure. General Noriega's rise to power and fall from American grace formed the pivot on which U.S. policy turned. As a young officer in the Panamanian Defense Force (PDF), Noriega received cash from the CIA as a paid agent. Later, he also received payments from the Colombian-based Medellin narcotics cartel in return for allowing Panama to serve as a conduit for the drug dealers to reach their North American market and as a money-laundering service for the cartel's lucrative profits from sales within the United States.

The Reagan administration had relied on Noriega to channel military supplies to the contras. It initially "turned a blind eye to Noriega's" ties to Latin American drug lords because of his usefulness in "airlifting military supplies to the Contras after Congress had banned the direct provision of US military aid to them."[8] Despite his past collaboration with the spy agency, Noriega eventually became an American bête noire, even to the hardheaded Reagan foreign policy team, who discerned his hand in the death of Hugo Spadafora, a human rights activist. At this point, things went from bad to worse. Noriega instigated the overthrow of ex-Sandinista supporter Nicolas Ardeta Barletta, when he investigated charges that Noriega had political rival Hugo Spadafora beheaded. The coup stripped the political cover from Noriega. He was no longer the power behind the throne but he openly and illegally held the reins of government. A Florida federal court issued an indictment for the arrest of Panamanian despot in early 1988 on drug-trafficking charges. By this time, Reagan's advisers wanted to be rid of him. Ruling out military force, they turned to a spate of measures, including engineering a coup, imposing economic sanctions that aggravated Panama's economic blight, and even wooing him to step down by quashing the court's indictment so he could take up exile in Spain.[9] Nothing worked. Noriega refused to budge, and Reagan handed over the problem to his successor.

WASHINGTON PUTS NORIEGA IN ITS CROSSHAIRS

With the receding of the Cold War in Central America, Noriega had outlived his political usefulness. Possessed of thug-like cunning, the autocrat lacked the long-range savvy to cut a deal and his own losses while he still had room to maneuver. Like Saddam Hussein and Slobodan Milošević, the Panamanian dictator underestimated the relative increase in American power as the Soviet Union declined, conferring greater latitude on Washington to punish its bogeymen without fear of triggering an East-West confrontation. In the post–Berlin Wall era, dictators no longer had a ready international patron to come to their assistance the way that the Soviet Union nurtured authoritarian figures in Damascus, Havana, and Pyongyang. Nor were right-wing autocrats any longer needed to stem the advances of local communist movements. Despots were slow to recognize the new realties of ascendant U.S. power and Washington's predisposition to exercise it. Like the Iraqi and Serbian strongmen, Noriega taunted the United States in words and in deeds, which disturbed his neighborhood.

Strategic reasons also dictated a change in course toward the Panamanian tyrant. Under terms of the Carter-era Panama Canal Treaty, the United States agreed by the start of 1990 to replace the head of the Canal Commission with a Panamanian, selected by the government of Panama, as a step toward the final turnover of the waterway to local sovereignty. The prospect of a Noriega man as commissioner pained official Washington. The approaching deadline concentrated Bush's attention, even though negotiations with the Soviet Union preoccupied him during the first years of his presidency. He wanted to stabilize Panama before handing over the Canal.

George Bush also had a personal reason for standing tall against the dictatorship in Panama. During his years as Ronald Reagan's vice president, he lived in the shadow of the popular president, much admired by movement conservatives for his toughness toward the Kremlin. To counter the appearance of an anemic persona, Bush strove to sound and act resolute. As vice president, he had publicly rejected plans to cut deals with Noriega. After his election, Bush laid down a tough line that "Noriega must go."[10]

Like Reagan before him, Bush initially did not place the use of military force at the top of his option list to resolve the Panama dilemma. He pinned his hopes on the May 10, 1989 Panamanian elections to remove Noriega. The president buttressed his long-shot bet with $10 million to help the anti-Noriega campaign. James Baker urged former president Jimmy Carter and the Carter Center in Atlanta to observe voting in Panama. Carter's accounts together with those from other sources documented pervasive fraud before and during the voting. Even so, Noriega openly hijacked the election by barring his opponent from office, which shook the isthmian state.

The Bush government signaled a tougher policy as a result of Noriega's stealing the election from Guillermo Endara, who won the presidency with 62 percent of the vote. The Panamanian general simply refused to recognize Endara's political victory. The next day George Bush asserted to the media that "the days of the dictators are over."[11] He backed up his rhetoric by announcing the recall of Arthur Davis, the U.S. ambassador to Panama, by reducing the embassy staff by two-thirds, by withdrawing Americans not living in the protected Canal Zone, by deploying an infantry brigade to strengthen the already present 12,000 military personnel in U.S. Southern Command (SOUTHCOM) at that time based in Panama, and by stepping up the number of troop exercises so as to intensify the psychological war against the Noriega regime. Bush and Baker also concluded that General Frederick Woerner, SOUTHCOM's commander, lacked sufficient toughness toward Noriega and indeed betrayed a sense of "clientitis" with Panama's tyrant. Hence, the administration replaced him with the gung ho General Maxwell Thurman, setting the stage for military action.

The United States, however, first took its diplomatic case to the Organization of American States (OAS) meeting in Washington in mid-May. As it turned out, the OAS proved to be a weak reed on which to lean because of its ingrained distrust of the Colossus of the North. Fear and resentment of U.S. interference south of the Rio Grande undercut Washington's diplomatic efforts to get Latin American governments to deal with the Noriega headache. Instead, the OAS stood on its long-standing principle of noninterference into the internal affairs of the member states. Little did the South Americans realize that the days of inviolable sovereignty were passing, as became readily apparent in the humanitarian-cum-military interventions into Somalia, Bosnia, Haiti, Kosovo, and East Timor during the next decade.

Still, Secretary Baker believed "it was important to give the OAS a chance—if for no other reason than . . . the United States had exhausted every peaceful, diplomatic alternative."[12] For a hundred years, the United States' southern neighbors learned to be wary of the American eagle's predatory gaze. The U.S. top diplomat tried in vain to gain Latin America's cooperation or at least its acquiescence. By this time, military plans were afoot, nonetheless, because the Panamanian's misdeeds worried his onetime benefactors.

Turning the screws on Noriega exacerbated his tendency to reach down rather than up the scale of human conduct. Baker wrote that Noriega "was becoming increasingly radicalized" by this time. He received Libyan financial assistance and Cuban arms along with training for his paramilitary "Dignity Battalions," little more than street thugs. Noriega also funneled weapons to erstwhile enemies such as the Nicaraguan Sandinistas along with El Salvadorian guerrillas. Panama's behavior in drug trafficking and gun running fit the profile of the rogue states that emerged in the 1990s. The secretary of state's characterization of Noriega as the "Muammar Qaddafi of Latin American" confirmed Bush officials' tendency to judge him in the same category as the Libyan troublemaker. None of his actions improved Noriega's standing in Washington or Panama; it instead put him in U.S. gun sights.

Yet, the administration wistfully hoped for an internal coup rather than external intervention, sparing the United States from openly ousting a corrupt caudillo. After the fraudulent May elections, it sent stern messages to Noriega to decamp soon or risk a forceful ouster. The United States let it be known that its ire was directed at

Noriega alone and not the PDF or the Panamanian people. It was a calculated strategy to separate the dictator from his military prop, rendering him vulnerable to a coup. This destabilization tactic worked only to a degree, due to Washington's unreadiness.

In early fall 1989, Washington got wind of a coup in the making but dismissed it as yet one more rumor of which there had been many. It turned out to be the genuine article, if somewhat farcical in its execution. The wife of Moises Giroldi Vega, a Panamanian army major and former Noriega loyalist, revealed plans of a plot to overthrow the dictator to a SOUTHCOM intelligence agent on October 1. Alas, Major Giroldi's timing was bad. Both General Thurman and Colin Powell, the incoming chairman of the Joint Chiefs of Staff, were brand new to their respective postings and unprepared to take advantage of the windfall. Moreover, no one believed Giroldi's wife except the president, who argued the morning after learning of the impending coup, "If someone's willing to do one, we have to help him."[13] Bush stood alone among his advisers, whose skepticism prevailed over the president's instincts.

In the end, the Bush administration vacillated, and the plotters, who had actually seized Noriega, lacked crucial American military assistance on the spot. But the coup's instigator, with a comical Gilbert and Sullivan touch, bungled the enterprise, allowing the captured dictator to summon his rescuers. Moreover, Giroldi mouthed nothing about restoring democratic rule to Panama, something that Bush and his lieutenants judged essential. Returning democracy to the Panamanian "thugocracy" ranked high among the president's rationales for toppling Noriega. Giroldi's grievance with the country's Bonaparte ran to the parochial interest of withheld pay to PDF troops. Noriega escaped with his life and repaid the coup perpetrators' mercy by having Giroldi and other plotters tortured and executed. He also purged one-quarter of the PDF troops to get rid of suspected Giroldi sympathizers. The ill-fated ouster erased any possibility of another coup.

Republicans as well as Democrats in Congress roundly criticized the White House's mishandling of an opportunity to take advantage of what Bush had instigated for in the past several months—an internally orchestrated coup. A year later, President Bush repeated same error on a grander scale when he encouraged Kurds and Shiite Iraqis to rise up and toss out Saddam Hussein in the wake of the first Gulf War. Rather than the repetition of history being a farce, it was a tragedy as Hussein's army and secret police murdered thousands of the regime's opponents. At all events, the United States was back to square one in Panama, left to resort to its own devices in light of the brutal end to the Giroldi affair. No internal revolt could be expected. Yet, George Bush persisted in the will-o'-the-wisp pursuit of a covert operation to overthrow his villain. Despite the president's personal antipathy for Noriega, he authorized the CIA to spend a paltry $3 million to recruit Panamanian military officers and exiles to topple the Panamanian caudillo. In a rendition of tragedy repeating itself as farce, the administration's tentative plans came to light in the press in mid-November.[14] At the time and in retrospect, the effort looked puny to Noriega foes. Thereafter, Washington abandoned plots to unseat the Panamanian dictator. Instead, it turned to direct military action to impose stability and restore democracy.

U.S. MILITARY INTERVENTION

Late in 1989, the United States finalized its plans for an armed intervention to seize Noriega and to scrap the PDF as a debased and bullying institution that propped up dictators. A policy to eliminate the PDF reflected a significant and healthy change, for it was a big part of the antidemocracy impediment in Panamanian society. Operation "Blue Spoon" formulated to deal with Noriega was resuscitated and revved up. The Pentagon deployed 10,000 soldiers in the XVIII Airborne Corps to reinforce 13,000 SOUTHCOM troops already in Panama.

When Noriega's paramilitary Digbats (Dignity Battalions) shot and killed a U.S. Marine officer riding in a jeep on December 16, 1989, Washington decided to put its game plan into play. Before it launched its attack, members of Noriega's puppet National Assembly declared war on the United States. A hastily convened meeting of key Bush advisers concluded that military force constituted the only appropriate response to yet another provocation in Panama. They agreed that Noriega's henchmen would kill more Americans even if no invasion took place. Heads or tails, the United States lost; it was better to take casualties in an invasion and be rid of the Panamanian tyrant than passively wait for more American deaths and still have Noriega in power. His threats and provocations unsettled the isthmian country at a time when the United States faced a transfer of the Canal's authority.

The presidential advisers considered whether they had ironclad justification for military action. Briefly, they laid out their reasons—Noriega's notorious contempt for democratic government, his lengthy drug-trafficking record and subsequent indictment, the threat he presented to an orderly transfer of the Canal to a duly constituted Panamanian authority, and finally the murder of an American trooper. "Let's take them up on their declaration of war," General Powell advised.[15] In spite of the president's expressed concerns about American casualties, the stakes in his mind were high enough and he decided, "Okay, let's do it."[16]

Critics of the Panama invasion believed Washington skated on razor-thin legitimacy. They argued that Bush's rationale smacked of a replay of the Monroe Doctrine power politics, casting a sphere of influence over Latin America and punctuating it with twentieth-century gunboat diplomacy—Caribbean style. To detractors, breaching a nation-state's sovereignty because of its internal practices represented a violation of international jurisprudence as it evolved after the Treaty of Westphalia in 1648. Noriega might be a despicable tyrant but he was, after all, Panama's own tyrant—legitimately or illegitimately. By personalizing the struggle against Noriega, Bush, in effect, boxed himself in a corner making his fight with Noriega a mano a mano contest. Not to oust the Panamanian leader, it was argued, confirmed the Bush wimp factor to Ronald Reagan stalwarts.

Washington stood on firm legal grounds, however. The Canal treaties authorized actions by the United States to deal with internal threats as well was external ones. The PDF's mounting rampages against U.S. forces, their dependents, and civilians were deemed hostile acts against the United States. The dictator's threat to "sit along the banks of the Canal to watch the dead bodies of our enemies pass by" underlined the peril that he and his thugs posed. On December 15, the Noriega-dominated National Assembly declared that "the Republic of Panama is in a state of war for the duration of the aggression unleashed against the Panamanian people by the U.S. Government."[17] Noriega's illegitimate rule provided further justification.

Originally code-named Blue Spoon for security reasons, the operation's name was changed by the Pentagon to the much more inspirational-sounding Operation Just Cause. The Panamanian assault went more or less like clockwork and was a tactical surprise in spite of many indications of an impending attack. CNN began broadcasting live feed of warplanes taking off from Pope Air Force Base in North Carolina, which tipped off viewers that an attack had been launched. U.S. troops rolled out from their Canal Zone bases at Fort Amador as paratroopers descended from the sky to capture key points in Panama City and environs in early morning on December 20, 1989. Paratroopers from the 82nd Airborne Division flew from their base at Fort Bragg and parachuted over Torrijos International Airport east of the city. Along with other units, they entered the city of Colón, encountering stubborn defenders. Army Rangers also took to their parachutes to land west of the airport where they struck at PDF units at the Rio Hato barracks, which in the past had suppressed antiregime forces. The high-tech, radar-evading F-117A stealth Nighthawk fighter participated in its first combat deployment by raining down bombs just moments ahead of the Ranger airdrop. Light infantry troops from the California-based 7th Infantry Division arrived soon after by aircraft to restore order in the countryside. The Marines seized the Bridge of the Americas over the Panama Canal paving the way for U.S. ground forces to enter the capital.

American forces quickly struck and virtually gutted the Commandancia, the PDF headquarters, which severed its communications with the Panamanian defenders elsewhere. The 4,000 PDF soldiers and especially the Dignity Battalions initially surprised the U.S. forces by putting up an unexpected stiff resistance during the first 18 hours. But the Panamanian units proved no match for the 26,000 U.S. troops, the largest military deployment since the Vietnam War and the biggest parachute operation since World War II. Fighting and looting lasted seven days rather than the predicted three. It, however, required Washington to deploy additional troops to put down rioters and patrol the streets than it had been originally planned in an eerie foreshadowing of postinvasion of Iraq. A pro-Noriega guerrilla movement operated for several months before being quelled, in a sort of preview of what lay in store for U.S. forces in post–Saddam Hussein Iraq after the second Persian Gulf War.

Elite units played a role that foreshadowed their use in the Persian Gulf War, the Balkans, and, most prominently, Afghanistan. The ultrasecretive Delta Force rescued Kurt Muse, an American hostage, who the CIA pinpointed in the Modelo Prison. The Navy SEALS secured Patilla Airport and private airfields, denying Noriega an aerial getaway. The Special Forces were assigned the nettlesome, and ultimately frustrating, task of locating and apprehending Noriega himself. To facilitate their task, Bush offered $1 million reward for information leading to Noriega's apprehension—a technique to be used frequently later against anti-American terrorists.

The Panamanian strongman temporarily eluded capture by hiding out for five days before seeking sanctuary with the papal nuncio. After protracted and complex negotiations engaging the nunciature, Vatican, Panamanian authorities, and local U.S. military commanders, Noriega surrendered to the United States on January 4, 1990 rather than face the mob of 20,000 outside the Vatican Embassy demanding his head. The reward money played no part in his capture. Panamanians greeted Noriega's departure with relief and jubilation; thousands took to the streets to celebrate, banging pots and pans and setting off firecrackers. After being placed in the custody of DEA officers in Panama City, Noriega was flown to Florida where he stood trial in federal court for drug trafficking. In full-dress military uniform, he pleaded immunity as a political prisoner. The court found him guilty of drug and racketeering violations and sentenced him to 40 years in prison on September 16, 1992.

Operation Just Cause amounted to a case study in well-executed military intervention. Far more went right than wrong, but it did eerily anticipate the short-falls in other U.S. combat insertions afterward. "The overwhelming success of JUST CAUSE must be attributed to the fact that the PDF simply did not put up serious or sustained resistance."[18] Most deserted, leaving small bands of die-hard elements to battle the well-armed invaders. Even without dogged opposition, problems surfaced to confront the attackers.

First and foremost, the planners of the Panama invasion sorely underestimated number of troops for the postattack stage because of a temporary breakdown in law and order. When the PDF disintegrated, Panamanians from poorer neighborhoods poured into downtown Panama City and Colón to loot and ransack stores. The spectacle of unruly mobs produced public relations problems for the Pentagon, until it deployed an additional 2,000 infantrymen. The lesson that an occupation demands more armed personnel than an assault was lost on Washington officials a decade later in the months preceding the Iraq War.

Another difficulty arose with the "guns for money" effort to remove weapons from civilian or former combatant hands, because initially U.S. soldiers adminis-tered it, which made it dangerous for would-be sellers to approach out of fear of being mistaken as aggressors. Moreover, American units had no cash ready to buy the pistols, rifles, and grenade launchers when offered for exchanged. Standing up a successor to the PDF also ran into more serious drawbacks. The U.S.-installed Panamanian government stood up its own civilian police force, the Público Fuerza, to restore order but had to rely on rank-and-file PDF manpower while it also weeded out the officers and worst criminal perpetrators. During the first days of patrolling, U.S. troops accompanied the novice policemen, something that American GIs resented. They considered this duty as police work, not soldiering, and some also felt uneasy cooperating with men who just days before had shot at them.

The civil-military operations that came in the wake of the almost flawlessly synchronized attack constituted "the most conspicuous lapse in the planning of the U.S. military operations in Panama City."[19] The invasion force had neither the proper training nor the prepared psychological outlook to transition from combat to civic-type missions to stabilize a badly disrupted society, even one where the vast majority of the population favored the toppling of General Noriega's authoritarian regime. Operation Just Cause demonstrated in spades that the United States could project its military force just about anywhere in the post–Berlin Wall era. But it also signaled that Washington was prone to underestimate the required number of forces in postinvasions environments and to underprepare for after-combat operations. As one student of Just Cause concluded, "[T]he greatest flaw in planning UO (urban operations) in Panama was the failure to coordinate the combat with the stability operations."[20] This conclusion echoed in future assessments as the United States intervened in other trouble spots.

POLITICAL AND DIPLOMATIC FACTORS

The political side of Just Cause actually preceded the start of military operations. Less than an hour before the intervention, U.S. officials transported the duly elected President Guillermo Endara and two vice presidents to Fort Clayton, near the Pacific opening of the Canal, where they were sworn into office by the head of the Panamanian Commission on Human Rights. They remained at the fort while the worst fighting raged. Endara's taped address to his countrymen was broadcast by Costa Rican radio, because Noriega loyalists still held Panama's radio stations. A suitable replacement government constituted a key aspect of Operation Just Cause for returning democracy to the country. It did more than fulfill a pledge to restore popular rule: it provided limited political cover from Latin American aversion to the United States' meddling in countries within the Southern Hemisphere. Washington also quickly announced the lifting of sanctions and the unfreezing of some of Panama's financial assets held in American banks as part of its normalization of relations. In many respects, the U.S. intervention was a showcase study of the integration of military and political phases in a manner so sadly absent 15 years later in Iraq. Getting the post-war political piece in place before the guns fired meant that the troops came home earlier and the victory was consolidated.

Despite attempts to pave the way diplomatically, U.S. intervention provoked fierce Latin American and international condemnation. On December 21, 1989, 20 member states of the Organization of American States passed a resolution in Spanish "deeply deploring" the U.S. invasion, with six abstentions and one negative vote—that of the United States. This censorious judgment represented a landmark in the OAS' 42-year history. Never before had the United States suffered such a verdict. Panamanian President Endara voiced opposition to the OAS condemnation. He argued that the will of the people must count as an expression of self-determination and not an "outmoded view" about an unsanctioned sovereignty-breaching intervention. He believed that the May 1989 election results legitimated his government and Washington's intercession to seat him in the presidency. Striking back at a century-long tradition of U.S. "gunboat diplomacy," Latin American nations heaped scorn on the United States for reverting to its once-discarded practice of militarily intercession into the smaller countries to its south.

The controversy spread from the Western Hemisphere to the United Nations. The Soviet Union and the People's Republic of China predictably sponsored a resolution in the Security Council condemning the United States and calling for an immediate troop withdrawal. Although London and Paris voted with Washington to veto the proposal, they could not head off a General Assembly debate and passage of a resolution labeling American actions as a "flagrant violation" of international law and demanding redeployment of U.S. military forces from Panama by a lopsided 75 to 20 votes, with 40 abstentions.[21] To sum up, America's withdrawal, Panama's return to democracy, and the passage of time dissipated the anger but not Latin American memories of Washington's high-handedness.

Judging by previous military engagements to Operation Just Cause, U.S. casualties were light, lower than expected. American deaths numbered 23 soldiers and three civilians. By comparison, the terrorist truck bombing of the 1983 Beirut Marine Corps barracks alone cost 241 lives, and the much-smaller Grenada sea-and-air invasion just days afterward resulted in the deaths of 19 U.S. service personnel. Controversy surrounded the number of Panamanian casualties because of disputed accuracy of the figures. The United States officially reckoned that 324 of Panama's soldiers and 220 civilians died in the conflict.[22] Rumors circulated for years about mass graves with huge numbers of dead but no substantiation came to light. Larger death rates were avoided as PDF commanders surrendered rather than confront certain annihilation. U.S. offers of cash for arms also convinced holdouts to turn in some 50,000 weapons. The destruction of property was great due to the conflict and the looting by the Panamanians themselves. The Chorrillo district next to the Commandancia suffered severely from the attack and resulting fires. Ten blocks were destroyed, leaving 18,000 people homeless.

The Endara government estimated reconstruction costs alone at $1.5 billion. Strangled by two years of American-imposed sanctions, the economy spiraled downward, with some 150,000 unemployed. Over the next two years, Washington provided slightly over $1 billion in emergency economic aid, reconstruction funds, loans, and guarantees. This was far less than needed, but America's aid to Panama competed with funds for Nicaragua and Central Europe together with other longer-term U.S. beneficiaries with stronger clout in Congress.

REGIME CHANGE AND DEMOCRACY

On balance, America's military sweep uprooted the entrenched caudilloism and set Panama on the path to democracy. Military rule, dictatorship, and oligarchy had marred the country's political past. Thus, the conflict, in effect, gave the democratic elements a fresh and powerful start. Five years later, the country held its first truly democratic and competitive elections. The intervening years held many economic and social problems but democracy endured, even when in 1997 SOUTHCOM decamped for Florida, taking with it a hefty source of U.S. currency. The accusation that Bush manufactured the invasion's justifications—the promotion of democracy, protection of American lives, safeguard of the Canal, and apprehension of Noriega—to retain possession of the waterway turned out to be bogus. The United States relinquished control of the waterway on December 31, 1999, as specified in the Carter agreement. Although Panama saw Martin Torrijos, the son of long-term dictator Omar Torrijos, legitimately elected president in May 2004, Panamanian democracy owed its restoration to U.S. power. Like the 1983 Grenada intervention, Panama proved that democracy can be promoted through the barrel of gun, when an authoritarian clique obstructed free and fair elections. But in neither case did the United States engage in a lengthy occupation as in postinvasion Iraq. Instead, it quickly handed over the reins of power to indigenous politicians and left the countries to find their own democratic way.

Although American soldiers did die at the hands of Noriega's poorly armed and trained Digbats, the Panama campaign brought back some of the mystique to the armed forces that had been lost since the Vietnam War and compounded by a string of dismal armed operations—the deeply flawed Desert One rescue mission into Iran, the gaffe-packed Grenada invasion, the bombing of Marine headquarters in Lebanon, and the wrongful downing of an Iranian airliner. The doubts created by these setbacks about the American military and its civilian leadership led Colin Powell earlier to reflect: "We have got to win cleanly next time."[23] The outcome was never in doubt. For the United States, a superpower, the execution had to be near flawless, however. Operation Just Cause went a long way to reclaim the U.S. military's luster and Washington's reputation for competently projecting power into politically difficult environments.

President Bush's aim of returning democracy and subduing a lawless country, detractors charged, amounted to no more than a masquerade for American global domination—criticisms that did not hold up in light of the many demands for the military support of humanitarian interventions that followed during the 1990s. Naysayers countered that use of force to rescue a massacred minority could be employed because it rested only on selfless motives. The legitimate resort to military action for national interests was, ipso facto, rebuked by antiwar critics of the 1960s. Later in a reversal of roles, the traditional proponents of military operations developed a case of the jitters when Bill Clinton advocated humanitarian missions. During the next decade, advocates and critics of military intrusions switched positions. Defying ornithological categories, doves metamorphosed to hawks and vice versa.

Much more significantly, the Panama intervention pointed to the new dynamics of the post–Berlin Wall era, when the United States wielded its considerable military might to oust odious leaders, who threatened American interests, humanity itself, or stability of their arenas. Regime change in Panama marked the latest and muscular version of a well-established U.S. pattern of dispatching unfriendly or inimical governments. Dating from Spanish-American War, Washington made several stabilization forays into the Caribbean region to advance its purposes and protect its security. The Cold War bore witness to the expansion of the U.S. regime-change methods beyond America's Caribbean backyard, usually to head off Marxist rule. U.S. presidents engineered or backed coups in 1953 Iran, 1960 Congo, 1963 South Vietnam, 1973 Chile, and 1986 Philippines along with interventions closer to home in 1954 Guatemala, 1961 Cuba, and 1965 Dominican Republic, besides the Grenada invasion. In the case of the Philippines, the Reagan government pressured pro-American dictator Ferdinand Marcos to accept exile paving the way for a democratic stability after much political turmoil on the islands.

The term "regime change" did not gain widespread currency until the end of Bill Clinton's presidency. By then the United States was taking action against run-of-the-mill dictators, not the Kremlin's presumed clients. Regime change became an almost accepted enterprise so that George H. W. Bush, William J. Clinton, and George W. Bush instigated ousters about once every 18 months, as will be noted subsequently, to secure political tranquility. Until the Iraq War, regime-change operations went relatively smoothly thereby perhaps contributing to the notion of their ease. Knocking off a dictatorial regime was one thing but staying around to implant democracy was quite another, as the United States was to learn in post–Saddam Hussein Iraq.

Other states engaged in regime-change business too. The Soviets did it in abundance, and so did the Germans during World War II and the British in the course of ruling an empire. Installing compliant rulers is a luxury, commonly reserved for weighty military players. Yet, many middle- and even light-weight powers have engaged in regime-change ventures. For instance, France deposed the Central African Republic's "Emperor" Jean Bedel Bokassa, renowned for cannibalism, in 1979. Vietnam invaded Cambodia in 1978 to rid it of the notorious Pol Pot regime, and Tanzania marched into Uganda in 1979 to oust its bloodthirsty tyrant Idi Amin, who took up exile in Saudi Arabia. In each of these three latter cases, the regime changers acted without prior United Nations approval. But in each instance, the regime changers returned power to the local politicians rather than proselytizing democracy as the United States unwisely attempted when it ousted the Iraqi regime years later.

For the United States, regime change contributed to the accusation that it acted as an imperial power in the image of Rome or Britain. But conquest provides no sound explanation for such endeavors are passé in an era of globalization, where comparative economic advantage renders martial subjugation useless. An empire for profit does not explain America's Panamanian intervention or subsequent invasions; they are far too expensive in blood and treasure. But security and stability—whether achieved by democracy, containment, or invasion—do offer a strong explanation. By sustaining an age of stability the United States could avoid costly wars, attain access to resources and markets, and rely on its own economic engine for growth. Protracted overseas ventures have been internally divisive in America's history, as vividly demonstrated by the conflict in Iraq. Before that, America's first Persian Gulf War enjoyed more popular support because it was short, victorious, and stayed clear of a lengthy occupation to install Western, multicultural democracy in the teeth of Muslim resistance.

CHAPTER 3

THE PERSIAN GULF WAR

I was convinced that the best way was to shape opinion not by rhetoric but by action.

George H. W. Bush, September 1990

If man does find the solution for world peace, it will be the most revolutionary reversal of his record we have ever known.

George C. Marshall

AMERICA WENT TO WAR AGAINST IRAQ under the United Nations' Charter to repel Saddam Hussein's 1990 invasion of Kuwait. As head of an international coalition, it also defended Saudi Arabia and the West's access to the region's oil. In brief, the United States fought to preserve the status quo in the Persian Gulf. If Hussein's conquest stood, then it would have upset the Middle East's political order. The war confirmed America's superpower status that its eclipse of the Soviet Union had earlier announced. Most strikingly, it reinforced America's bent to act as a global stabilizer and set the stage ultimately for the imposition of a Western multiconfessional democracy by military occupation in a region fiercely resentful of a non-Muslim presence.

For George Herbert Walker Bush, the Persian Gulf War defined his presidency in a way that no other enterprise on his presidential watch, domestically or internationally, did. The initial Iraq war still stands out as *the* pivotal feature in a crowded field of global crises he handled. Had the war toppled Saddam Hussein, leaving Iraq a benign and pacified, even if not a democratic, state, then the historical judgment might have paralleled the Panama intervention, which is largely forgotten outside of Latin America. But the first Gulf conflict merely restored the status quo ante, leaving a wounded and resentful Hussein who unsettled the Middle East. Just as World War I led to World War II, the Persian Gulf War laid the groundwork for the Iraq War.

The first Gulf War's inconclusiveness overshadowed so many of America's superb foreign policy achievements in managing the disintegration of the Soviet Union and reintegration of a reunited Germany into NATO. Yet, by not pushing into Iraq to oust Hussein, George H. W. Bush, like the mythical Daedalus, escaped the fate of Icarus, who did not follow his father's advice and flew high into the Mesopotamian sun, only to see his waxed wings melt and crash. Years later, George W. Bush's Icarian flight pitched the United States not only into a second war with Iraq but also into a gargantuan effort to restabilize the Middle East. It greatly departed from his father's more practical stabilization operation.

BACKGROUND TO A BELLICOSE DICTATORSHIP AND A U.S. WAR

Iraq's political birth as a modern-day state is recent. Its progenitor, Mesopotamia (Greek for the region "between the rivers"), had antecedents reaching back over three millennia. Mesopotamia, most of which is contained within the boundaries of contemporary Iraq, was the home of some of the earliest, if not *the* earliest, civilized communities as exhibited by its advances in urbanization and literacy. Lying along two of the world's most chronicled rivers, the Tigris and the Euphrates, this fertile region gave birth to a series of ancient civilizations in Sumer, Assyria, and Babylonia. Saddam Hussein often referred in speeches to the past glories of his country's history. In modern times, its oil reserves gave it strategic importance. Alone among Arab states, modern-day Iraq has both oil and water, endowing it with wealth and prominence. Its geographical location was less fortuitous. Mesopotamia was often caught in the crosscurrents of invading armies and empires prior to the Ottoman Turks' conquest. The Ottomans ruled it for over 300 years until it came under British governance at the end of World War I.

Britain, acting under a mandate from the League of Nations, merged three provinces over which the Ottomans based their administration—Mosul, Baghdad, and Barsa—into one political entity. These provinces more or less conformed to the country's three major enthoreligious groups, which are subdivided into clans and tribes. Mosul, in the north, is home to the Kurds, who yearned for their own sovereign states, for hundreds of years. The Kurdish people form less than 20 percent of the country's population of some 26 million people. Baghdad, roughly in Iraq's midsection, contained about 20 percent of the population who made up the Sunni branch of Islam. Basra, the southernmost zone and name of its principal city, holds some 60 percent of the people, who make up the Shiite followers of Islam, some of whom look to the Islamic Republic of Iran for material assistance and spiritual guidance. British rule encountered bitter resistance. In a bid for unity, British officials placed Emir Faisal from Saudi Arabia, the field commander of the Arab Revolt against the Turks in World War I, on the throne before the country's independence in 1932.

Iraq's monarchy succumbed to the same political furies that swept over other Middle Eastern states. Beginning in the 1950s, a new generation of military officers, impatient with the fledgling parliamentary institutions or wastrel monarchs, toppled the old order to install a radicalized vision of progress that ended in authoritarianism. The Iraqi military tossed out the British-installed, Westward-leaning throne in a bloody pro-Soviet coup in 1958 that killed King Faisal II and other members of the royal family and snuffed out Iraq's fragile democracy. Led by Brigadier Abd al-Karim Qasim, the usurpers established a military dictatorship that was marred by political turmoil until his overthrow in 1963. What followed Qasim's leftist regime turned out to be more an interregnum than a genuine political consolidation until Saddam Hussein took the reins of power in 1979 as the head of the Baath Party and Iraq's government. Hussein's path from a dirt-poor birth near Tikrit, just north of Baghdad, in 1937 to the pinnacle of a ruthless, one-party state was marked by assassinations, exile in Egypt, conspiracy, and Stalin-like machinations to take over the country's security apparatus.[1]

Brief though Qasim's dictatorship was, it sill redefined Iraqi international relations. He withdrew from the U.S.-blessed, anti-Soviet Baghdad Pact (with Britain, Iran, Pakistan, Turkey) and entered into a close relationship with Moscow and its Soviet bloc. Thus began Iraq's dependency on the Soviet Union for arms that Saddam Hussein enjoyed up to the Persian Gulf War. Observing Iraq's switching sides through a Cold War lens, Washington considered Iraq simply a radical, pro-Soviet client until 1979, when two momentous events transformed America's fortunes in the Persian Gulf theater.

The Iranian revolution abruptly redrew the Middle East's political map. Until the overthrow of Shah Mohammed Reza Pahlavi, Iran advanced U.S. interests in the region by fulfilling its role as a regional "policeman" under the Nixon Doctrine. The shah relished his role as a staunch friend in the volatile arena. After the shah's ouster, the Islamic Republic implacably defied the United States. A second blow to America's equanimity in the Middle East stemmed from the Soviet Union's invasion of Afghanistan. Moscow feared the loss of influence in the mountainous country where a Marxist government tottered on the brink of collapse. Soviet armed forces tried to prop up the regime but instead sparked a rebellion. No single act did more to light the deadly fuse of extremist Islamic resentment toward the West than the Red Army intervention. Before that crisis fully unfolded, Washington awoke to the fears of a Soviet thrust southward toward the petroleum fields and warm water ports in the Persian Gulf.

As part of the newfound realities, President Carter vowed to defend pro-Western governments in the Gulf. This Carter Doctrine took operational form in the Rapid Deployment Joint Task Force. That organization evolved into United States' Central Command during the first Reagan administration. CENTCOM geographically encompassed the Middle East and Southwest Asia. Much enhanced, it was CENT-COM that later carried out both Gulf wars and swept the Taliban from power in Afghanistan. Before those conflicts, in 1980, the United States watched as Iraq invaded Iran.

The Iraq-Iran War lasted eight years, the longest conventional conflict of the twentieth century, and cost hundreds of thousands of lives and billions of dollars. Yet, the outcome was inconclusive. Tehran agreed to a UN-brokered cease-fire only when Baghdad threatened greater reliance on chemical weapons than it had already used in nerve agents and mustard gas attacks on Iranian trenches. Convinced that he might have lost to the mass wave assaults by thousands of suicidal Iranian youth, Saddam Hussein resolved to step up Iraq's pursuit of a full range of weapons of mass destruction (WMD), including nuclear and biological in addition to chemical arms. This decision was to put him crosswise with the United States and its allies. Well before that occurrence, the Iraq-Iran War bred another conflict that triggered American entry into its first Gulf War.

By 1988, and the end of the fighting with Iran, the Hussein regime found itself financially strapped and in debt for an estimated $60 billion to the Gulf states, principally Kuwait and Saudi Arabia. They had supplied funds to halt the expansion of Iran's brand of Shiite fundamentalism. Rather than expressions of gratitude, Hussein demanded cancellation of the debt to repay Iraq's sacrifices. In his mind, the sheikdoms owed him for their safety. Failing to convince Kuwait to drop its claims, Iraq turned to armed conquest to restore its financial house.[2] Hussein's regime coveted Kuwait's oil that when combined with Iraqi holdings totaled about 20 percent of the proven global oil reserves, a figure that would give Baghdad a decisive influence in the petroleum market. Baghdad also held revanchist claims to Kuwaiti territory dating from the colonial era and wanted access to the kingdom's shoreline for deepwater ports.

THE UNITED STATES EXTENDS AN OLIVE BRANCH

The incoming George H. W. Bush government initially adopted the conciliatory line of its predecessor toward Saddam Hussein only to face Iraq's aggression. The Reagan administration perceived Saddam Hussein as a moderating strongman. It also saw Iraq as counterbalance to Iran's theocratic regime, which sponsored terrorism in Lebanon and against Israel. As Soviet problems mounted, Moscow's clientage of Iraq slipped, providing Washington a freer hand toward Baghdad. President Bush's national security principals accentuated this "realist" approach to statecraft and saw Iraq as a power package to be counterpoised against America's declared adversaries in Tehran. This was a Cold War way of doing business, when Washington buttressed unsavory dictators so long as they were anticommunist. In Iraq's case, it opposed congressional sanctions on Iraq for its appalling human rights abuses. Instead, the United States extended credit guarantees for American grain exporters to Iraq. At first, Bush's engagement of Iraq paid off. For example, Baghdad offered to pay compensation to the families of sailors killed on the USS *Stark*, which Iraq struck with an antiship missile during its war with Iran.

As the 1990s dawned, the Hussein regime, however, repeatedly flashed warning signals that its moderating period was dead. Throughout the spring of 1990, Saddam Hussein made inflammatory speeches, taking up the Palestinian cause, demanding the withdrawal of the U.S. Navy from the Gulf, and urging brother Arab states to reactivate the 1970s oil embargoes against the West. On April 2, in one particularly shrill rhetorical outburst, Hussein announced the fabrication of advanced chemical weapons and threatened their use "to make the fire eat up half of Israel with chemical agents, if this nation [Israel] becomes involved in an attack against Iraq."[3] His anti-American and anti-Israeli rhetoric recast him into a sort of savior of the Palestinian cause. Hussein's fiery speeches elevated his standing in the Arab world to Nasserite levels. Not since Gamal Abd Nasser, Egypt's late president, had there been an Arab leader whose inflammatory oratory stirred Arab passion to such heights.[4]

By springtime, the United States did begin to pay slightly more attention to an escalating Iraqi arms buildup. It foiled an illegal scheme to purchase nuclear-triggering devices, denied components for a "super gun" artillery piece, and blocked the sale of tungsten furnaces useful for Iraq's illicit nuclear weapons program. In May 1990, the administration suspended its commodity credits to Baghdad to purchase $500 million worth of American grain. Washington realized that Hussein was abandoning his cloak of moderation. Yet, it neglected to embark on deterrent steps, and Iraq pressed ahead.

At this time, the Bush foreign policy team suffered from crisis fatigue. They had become overrun by a slew of international hot spots. Prior to Iraq's storming into Kuwait, senior Bush officials were absorbed by the revolutionary changes taking place within the Soviet Union, the reawakening of nationalism in Central Europe, the aftermath of Panama intervention, and the massacre in Tiananmen Square. Such a full plate led Secretary of State Baker to pen in his memoirs that before Iraq struck Kuwait "it was simply not prominent on my radar screen, or the President's."[5] Still, the United States missed an avalanche of warnings, as Hussein fulminations zeroed in on Kuwait over grievances about Iraq's debts, their joint border, and oil prices. He accused Kuwait and the United Arab Emirates of thrusting a "poisoned dagger" into Iraq's back by flooding the crude market to sustain their revenues amid falling world demand. His Revolutionary Day speech on July 17, 1990 sounded much like a "public case" for invasion into Kuwait.

Little time was lost in speculation about Saddam Hussein's next move. First, he nullified Iraq's wartime debts to Kuwait. Then on July 24, Hussein's Soviet-supplied T-72 battle tanks rumbled up to the Kuwaiti border and stopped just short of crossing. His boldness was breathtaking because he ordered the march toward Kuwait one day after the Pentagon announced that it had acceded to the UAE's request to send a tanker and cargo planes to the Gulf to participate in joint military exercises. Moreover, a senior administration official publicly declared that the aircraft deployment was intended "to bolster a friend and lay down a marker for Saddam Hussein."[6]

The State Department's muddled signals, on the other hand, conveyed vacillation rather than resolute deterrence. The border tension precipitated an unexpected summons from Saddam Hussein to U.S. Ambassador April C. Glaspie. At the famous meeting on July 25, the Arabic-fluent ambassador spoke alone with the Iraqi leader. What information has come to light from this encounter has been much analyzed. Interpretations of this well-studied exchange were a decidedly unfavorable assessment of the American envoy. After listening to Hussein's hyperbolic exposition about Iraq's grievances, Glaspie, to her critics, sounded too sympathetic to the despot. The ambassador drew no line in the sand. Instead, she uttered "diplomatic speak" by stating "as you know, we don't take a stand on territorial disputes."[7] By this, she meant that the squabble over the Iraqi-Kuwaiti border was not Washington's concern. Her detractors argued that such a statement represented a veritable green light to Hussein aggressions. By her account, she also voiced American resolution to defend its allies and access to oil in the region. In diplomacy, as in seduction, silence does not necessarily mean consent, but it can easily be so construed. It is unknowable whether a tougher statement would have deterred Hussein. Judging by his subsequent behavior, it seems doubtful.

A SHIELD IN THE DESERT

Midnight came for the Cinderella country of Kuwait when Baghdad launched its violent offensive on August 2, 1990. Kuwait's leap from desert poverty to petroleum-lubricated opulence afforded the tiny Gulf kingdom neither military security nor diplomatic status, just importance to Western consumers. Iraq's thrust onto Kuwaiti soil and its rape of Kuwait City riveted world attention on a region vital to the global economy. Television cameras beamed footage of startling street scenes of bloodshed and anguish from Kuwait's capital city. Iraqi soldiers failed to capture the emir, Sheikh Jaber al-Ahmed al-Sabah, who fled to Saudi Arabia, but killed a younger brother, Sheikh Fahd. In four days, Iraq crushed the faint resistance and conquered the tiny state. The Iraqi forces carried out mass arbitrary detentions, torture, and extrajudicial executions of hundreds of civilians. Iraqi forces also swept up American and British citizens, trundling them off to Baghdad, along with 605 still-unaccounted-for Kuwaitis. They also began a seven-month-long looting binge, stealing 29,000 private automobiles, hundreds of paintings and art objects, and, most significantly, all of the country's essential state documents such as international treaties and historical papers relating to its political birth. Next, they turned to firebombing museums, palaces, and power stations. The cost of destruction, including the torching of Kuwaiti oil installations totaled some $173 billion, according to the Public Authority for Assessment of Damages Resulting from Iraqi Aggression, a Kuwaiti commission set up in May 1991 to tally the costs of Iraq's "reannexing" the so-called breakaway province.[8]

The prostrate sheikdom appealed for outside intervention to repel the invaders, as its small defense force disintegrated. An emergency meeting of the UN Security Council passed Resolution 660, which condemned Iraq's aggression and demanded a withdrawal and negotiation of the dispute. Even the Soviet Union endorsed the resolution, and only Yemen abstained. The Security Council's censure cut no ice with the Iraqi dictator. Nevertheless, it did afford Washington legal and political cover for its spearheading of a military campaign to expel Iraq from Kuwaiti territory. The Bush government likened Iraq's aggression to the Third Reich's territorial conquests, which had to be turned back.

Two broad courses of action presented themselves. Either the United States could implement a sanctions policy to hurt Iraq over a long period of time or unleash a military counterattack to roll back Iraq's aggression. Embargoes raise havoc with a target nation's economy but almost never bring down dictatorships, which deflect the economic hardships to their hapless citizens. Mounting an armed counterassault risked international opposition, alienation of pro-American states in the Middle East, and American lives in combat. The menace posed by Hussein to Saudi Arabia and to the broader region, nonetheless, made the latter course the only feasible alternative. Otherwise, the Gulf would have descended into a chaotic tailspin as Iraq threatened its neighbors.

General Norman Schwarzkopf, commander-in-chief of Central Command and the officer responsible for executing a military response in the Gulf, briefed the U.S. civilian leadership about Iraq's large but decrepit armed forces. Reflecting America's bitter experience in Vietnam, Schwarzkopf's recommendations were in line with those of Chairman of the Joint Chiefs of Staff Colin Powell, who expressed reluctance to a war. If any military action did take place, they wanted overwhelming force applied against Iraq. Their plans envisioned initially 100,000 troops for the mission; this figure later augmented fivefold.

In weighing military action, Bush and his top aides had an array of concerns. Strategically, they worried that Baghdad now dominated 20 percent of the world's oil reserves and they fretted about Hussein regime's hints at a further drive into eastern Saudi Arabia, which held another one-fifth of the planet's known oil deposits. Domestically, the White House was concerned about the American public's abhorrence of casualties, that much of the Saudi oil flowed to Japan, and that restoring the Kuwaiti monarchy ran counter to America's democratic ideals. Externally, the United States was on the line, as the offshore heavyweight, to respond in some fashion to naked aggression. The heads of Muslim states such as Egypt and Turkey telephoned President Bush to express their determination that Iraq's assault could not be left unopposed. Aside from Jordan, Yemen, and Yasir Arafat's Palestinian Liberation Organization, Iraq stood alone in the Muslim world. Turkish President Turgut Ozal told Bush that the Iraqi dictator "must go" because "Saddam is more dangerous than Qaddafi."[9] Saddam Hussein's grab for oil and territory unnerved his neighbors. As a precedent to settle grievances, it opened a Pandora's box of other territorial disputes between Syria and Turkey, Egypt and Libya, Yemen and Saudi Arabia. Hussein's invasion stood to destabilize Middle East.

The Bush foreign policy team, stiffened mainly by Secretary of Defense Dick Cheney and National Security Adviser Brent Scowcroft's hawkish outlook, decided almost immediately that the defense of Saudi Arabia stood out as *the* key issue. Should Saudi oil and its revenues fall into Saddam Hussein's hands, then the strategic balance would be tipped against the United States and its allies in the Middle East. Convincing the hesitant Saudis proved more troublesome than warranted by the imminent peril they faced. Riyadh, however, fretted about a large U.S. military presence since it would excite anti-American sentiments among the Saudi population, who regarded their country as the cradle of Islam and protector of its two most holy shrines. In this dire assessment, the Saudi rulers were proved to be correct, because Osama bin Laden, a little-known dissident, seethed over the defilement of Islam's birthplace and sanctuary by the arrival of infidels or "Crusaders" as the businessman-turned-terrorist characterized U.S. soldiers. The royal family's decision, more than any other factor, ignited bin Laden's anti-American and antimonarchy fury, as the world was later to learn.

Even though he set the war wheels turning, Bush feared the Saudis would seek a deal with Saddam Hussein rather than accept Washington's offer to defend them militarily by the only reliable means available—ground troops. The palpable threat posed by the expanding number of Iraqi-armored units proximate to the Saudi border finally clinched Riyadh's decision about the necessity of U.S. forces to shield it from Iraq but not before Washington dispatched a high-level civilian and military delegation to the desert kingdom. Headed by Cheney and Schwarzkopf, the team had both to persuade the Saudi royals that Iraq presented a clear and present danger to them and that the United States had the resolve to see the crisis through until Hussein was defeated. After its hasty departure from Lebanon in the wake of the terrorist assault on the U.S. Marine Corps barracks, America appeared an unreliable partner. The delegation succeeded in both quests. Next, Washington deployed the 82nd Airborne Division and two U.S. Air Force tactical fighter squadrons as a temporary shield and as a vanguard of a much larger force that amassed on Saudi territory in the coming months.

DIPLOMACY BEFORE THE STORM

Diplomacy was an integral part of the U.S. anti-Iraq strategy, although it had to compete with Washington's attention on the Central Europeans' break for freedom from Moscow. The United States struggled to pull together a coalition of military partners and to gain the United Nation's imprimatur, feats that garnered George H. W. Bush lasting acclaim as a statesman. The president's internationalist bent predisposed him to pursue coalition warfare rather than unilateralist conflict against Iraq. Saudi Arabia's green light to a large-scale American garrison smoothed Washington's coalition building with Arab and Muslim states. President Bush pursued coalition building by telephoning world leaders, seeing them personally in Washington or his vacation home in Kennebunkport, Maine, and dispatching James Baker around the world. Once King Fahd agreed to U.S. forces on his soil, Washington conjured up the fiction of a genuine Saudi-American partnership by splitting the military commands as a sign of unity. U.S. Commander Norman Schwarzkopf was to preside over the U.S., British, and other ground forces, while Prince Khalid Bin Sultan al-Saud would lead the Arab contingents and smaller non-Arab forces.

If the Saudi Arabian embrace of the U.S. deployment made possible the coalition building among Arab states generally, it did nothing to alleviate pressures felt by America's foremost ally in the region—Israel. Indeed, coalition building aggravated Israel's isolation because Washington's diplomatic wooing necessitated Tel Aviv's exclusion from the coalition and its forbearance when Baghdad fired Scud missiles at the Jewish state. Later, Bush wrote, "The Israelis understood this point intellectually, although it was emotionally difficult for them to stand aside."[10] Long in Saddam Hussein's gun sites, Israel went on a defensive war footing.

If hit by Iraq's Scud missiles, Tel Aviv promised to strike back, which would fracture the multistate coalition when the Arab states pulled out because of any Israeli participation in an assault on a brother Muslim nation. To offset Israel's vulnerability to aerial bombardment, the United States dispatched Patriot batteries in September 1990 during the course of the military buildup in the Gulf. It was revealed later that Washington exerted all its political leverage to restrain the Yitzhak Shamir government when Hussein's Scuds rained down on Israeli cities, producing little serious damage but killing two citizens.[11]

Like Napoleon and Hitler, President Hussein possessed serious doubts about the steadfastness of any coalition ringed against him. Dictators are wont to see divisions among their adversaries, which they can exploit. By their nature, coalitions are inherently unstable. The member states are often as wary of their partners as they are of their declared enemy. The Iraqi dictator did his utmost to drive wedges between coalition members. He tried to curry favor with France by releasing some 250 French hostages in October. He floated "peace initiatives" throughout the autumn of 1990. These stratagems proved unavailing, however. Despite occasional intracoalition tensions, the alliance hung together until the war's conclusion.

Pressed against the wall, Saddam Hussein even sought to paper over the bitter relations with his erstwhile bête noire, Iran. In mid-August, he offered Tehran a peace settlement. Iraqi troops decamped from over 1,000 square miles of Iranian territory that Baghdad had seized in the 1980s war. As it turned out, Iran, in fact, largely sat on its hands during the Gulf War. When Baghdad dispatched its warplanes to Iranian airfields for safekeeping, the government in Tehran simply seized them, effectively putting them out of commission. Threatened by a powerful Iraq, Ayatollah Ruhollah Khomeini, Iran's political and spiritual leader, indulged in a bit of schadenfreude as his nemesis suffered a severe thrashing by the U.S.-led forces, although he and other mullahs grew apprehensive over the widening U.S. foothold in the Persian Gulf.

American efforts to forge a broad-based coalition against Iraq got a boost from the United Nations, when it went along with Washington's urgings to stand against the invasion. Article 51 of its charter spelled out the "inherent right of individual or collective self-defense if an armed attack occurs against a member of the United Nations." But the Security Council's authorization to defend Kuwait all the same constrained American power by limiting Washington's objectives to merely expelling Hussein's army from the Gulf sheikdom. Invading Iraq and ousting the Baath regime was not part of the UN resolution. Before the negative postmortems arose about the wisdom of letting Hussein escape punishment for his misdeeds, the United Nation's approval of the Gulf War was hailed as the wave of the future and endorsed by President Bush as such.

Another critical link in the chain tightening around Iraq was the Soviet Union, whose shadow still fell across the Middle East. Long a patron of its Iraqi client, Moscow initially resisted the U.S. agenda. The Mikhail Gorbachev government already beset by Central European political ferment was confronted with internal political opposition over its flaccid response to America's aggressive posture toward Iraq. Yevgeny Primakov, chairman of the USSR Supreme Soviet and close Gorbachev adviser, was both architect and advocate of the traditional Kremlin policy in the Middle East and sought to let Saddam Hussein off the hook, perhaps with a separate Soviet peace settlement. In October, Primakov flew to Baghdad to induce Hussein to withdraw from Kuwait; but the Iraqi despot wanted too many concessions, and the Soviet envoy's deal-making trip came to naught. Bush and his Secretary of State Baker eventually persuaded Gorbachev to acquiesce to the U.S. hard line against Iraq.

The controversy over military means came to head in late August when five Iraqi oil tankers steamed toward Yemen. How to block their passage became an issue. Security Council's Resolution 661 laid down an economic embargo on Iraq. Bush advocated enforcing the UN sanctions with military action, but the Soviets wanted to let the ships sail and give diplomacy another chance to de-escalate the crisis. The French argued that without the word *force* contained in the resolution, the United States could not fire on the vessels. The Franco-Soviet interpretation prevailed. In retrospect, the Paris-Moscow axis was the tiny cloud on the horizon indicating stormy relations in the future for the United States over its subsequent Iraqi policy.

Reluctantly, Bush allowed the vessels to proceed and granted the Soviets three days to convince Saddam Hussein to leave Kuwait, a failed labor and a decision opposed by Margaret Thatcher. It is when Bush called the British prime minister to inform her of his decision that the Iron Lady uttered her famous rejoinder to the president: "Well, all right, George, but this is no time to go wobbly."[12] The "go wobbly" anecdote took on a life of its own, casting doubt over George Bush's resolve. In fact, Bush did not go "wobbly," and America with its over 30-nation coalition went on preparing for war, while its government tried to shore up its case for a military option at home and abroad.

Internationally, the White House sought financial assistance from governments unlikely to commit combat units to the coalition. It realized that financial costs were prohibitive, particularly as the American economy was mired in a steep downturn. Moreover, Europe and Asia depended on Middle East oil much more than did the United States. Thus, Washington reasoned that other states, whose history or constitutional restrictions precluded them from deploying military forces, should pay their fair share. Both Germany and Japan—wealthy, oil-dependent, and pacifically orientated nations—stood at the top of a listing of possible financial contributors. Secretary of State Baker directly passed the "tin cup" during his trips to foreign capitals as early as August. He first got a $15 billion pledge from Saudi Arabia and then the same amount from the exiled emir of Kuwait. Japan and Germany also chipped into the war chest. Eventually, the United States raised $67 billion, roughly five-sixths of the total $87 billion expended in the Gulf War. It was to be a war on the cheap, a venture probably never to be repeated.

President Bush and his foreign policy aides resolved to pursue a dual-track approach toward Baghdad. First, they made an international appeal to increase pressure on Iraq to retreat. If they failed at the United Nations to obtain authorization to expel militarily Iraq's army, the Bush White House intended to assemble an ad hoc coalition of willing partners, much as George W. Bush ultimately did in 2003. General Powell set January 15, 1991 as the deadline for completion of the military buildup in neighboring bases. That date became the deadline for diplomacy to work as well. The second track lay through the Security Council, which as it turned out passed Resolution 678 on November 29 that sanctioned "all necessary means," that is, the use of military force, should Iraq not withdraw by January 15. But just as allied troops and arms flooded into the Gulf region, so too did the home-front opposition increase to a war policy.

The Oval Office encountered stiff domestic opposition to a war almost from the start of Baghdad's invasion. President Bush addressed a joint sessions of Congress to build domestic support for his overseas policies on September 11. He recounted his ongoing talks with Gorbachev and how Soviet-American progress on Central European issues contributed to "historic cooperation" to grapple with the crisis in the Persian Gulf. More significantly, the speech also broached Bush's much-criticized concept—a *new world order*, in which a new era can arise "free from threat of terror, stronger in the pursuit of justice, and more secure in the quest for peace." Bush defined this new international ordering as "a world in which nations recognize the shared responsibility for freedom and justice."[13] Detractors scored the concept a mushy multilateralism. Shrouded in lofty terms, few saw it for what it really was—a call for international support of America's desire for stability.

America's forty-first president returned to the "new world order" theme in a high-profile address before the UN General Assembly after the Gulf War. On September 23, 1991, he declared, "I see a world of open borders, open trade, and . . . open minds, a world that celebrates the common heritage that belongs to all the world's people, taking pride not just in hometown or homeland but in humanity itself."[14] Traditional Republicans took issue with what they interpreted in excessive internationalism moving the United States into a world government with the United Nations and sending American soldiers abroad in blue helmets on endless wars and peacekeeping missions.[15] Placed on the defensive, Bush jettisoned the notion with its trappings of Wilsonian idealism. But the theme, if not the phrasing, was resurrected by his successors as means to accomplish America's stabilizing goals in turbulent corners.

To counter the domestic opposition to a possible war against Iraq, George Bush mobilized an international lineup behind his pistols-cocked brand of diplomacy before taking up challenge on Capitol Hill. The White House particularly courted the United Nations for the legitimacy to expel Iraq from Kuwait. As we shall see later, this approach turned out to be a reverse order of priorities from Bush's son, George W. Bush, when he challenged Iraq's purported threat from weapons of mass destruction. Bush, the son, first solidified his congressional base before turning his full attention to the recalcitrant Security Council.

Congressional adjournment on October 28, 1990 for the midterm elections brought some respite for the embattled White House, but it still faced rearguard objections to war from Capitol Hill. Since Congress was not scheduled to return until early January, it appointed an 18-member team to consult with the West Wing on the Iraq question. Senate majority leader George J. Mitchell (Democrat from Maine) joined House Speaker Tom Foley (Democrat from Washington state) in placing a provision in the adjournment resolution allowing the congressional leaders to reconvene in case the Bush administration decided to go to war without the legislative branch's authorization. Many House and Senate members vigorously opposed the Oval Office's military buildup in the Gulf as precluding the use of sanctions and diplomacy alone against Iraq.[16] This opposition enjoyed broad support within the democratically controlled Congress as well as within a large segment of the public. The possibility of another Vietnam War suffused political discourse, as did the intractable nature of Middle East politics to any Western-introduced military resolution.

Members of both houses reminded the White House that the U.S. Constitution reserved the power to declare war to Congress. This debate replayed a stormy chapter in American history, when the legislative branch tried to constrain the executive office from waging war in Southeast Asia and passed the 1973 War Powers Resolution over President Nixon's veto. That legislation limited the president's foreign policy options by directing the White House to consult with Congress prior to "introducing United States Armed Forces into hostilities."[17] Should the president commit forces without approval, perhaps in an emergency requiring immediate intervention, the law forced the president to withdraw them, unless congressional authorization was obtained within 60 days. Talk of the War Powers Resolution contributed to the administration's thinking that congressional consent would be needed before a large-scale conflict could be staged. But it embarked first on obtaining the Security Council's approval.

Capitalizing on the United States' turn in the rotating presidency of the Security Council during the month of November, Secretary of State Baker obtained passage of Resolution 678 by 12 votes, three more than necessary so long as none of the five Permanent Members vetoed the resolution. China abstained. Resolution 678 called for the use of military force against Iraq unless it withdrew from Kuwait by

January 15, 1991. Thus, the United Nations voted for war if Iraq refused to comply with its resolutions. The last time it endorsed military action had been to defend South Korea from invasion by the North in 1950.

Pressure to find a peaceful resolution intensified from congressional leaders and from the UN Secretary General Javier Perez de Cuellar in the weeks preceding the January deadline. So remote did a favorable outcome appear to Bush insiders that they discussed whether to strike Iraq even if the administration lost the vote in Congress. Meanwhile, Perez de Cuellar's arm-twisting compelled President Bush to attempt a last-chance meeting with Baghdad. He dispatched Baker to Geneva to meet with Iraq's foreign minister and Hussein confidant Tariq Aziz on January 9. The face-to-face parley with the suave, cigar-smoking Iraqi officials presented risks for the United States. What if Iraq suddenly made an apparent concession? Such a tactic might upend the unity of the coalition, energize legislative opposition to the White House, and allow Hussein to somehow preserve his hold on Kuwait.

To forestall a trick, Baker carried a letter from George Bush intended for the Iraqi president. This letter set forth a stern warning. Bush wrote that the "United States would not tolerate the use of chemical and biological weapons or the destruction of Kuwait's oil fields or installations." It threatened "the strongest possible response," which implied a resort to nuclear weapons.[18] In subsequent years, much has been made of Bush's tough language as a credible deterrent that convinced Hussein to foreswear the use of weapons of mass destruction in the Gulf War. No chemical, biological, or nuclear shells fell on the advancing coalition. Be that as it may, the Iraqi dictator was not dissuaded from destroying the Kuwaiti oil patch, an environmental catastrophe along with evaporating about 3 percent of the Gulf kingdom's known reserves before U.S. firefighting teams extinguished the flames.

Moreover, it is uncertain what exactly Aziz told Hussein about the U.S. warning because the foreign minister refused to take the letter, after reading his personal copy. This stubborn gesture was emblematic of the Iraqi dictatorship. In the final analysis, Iraq's willfulness played into the Bush administration's hands. Washington worried that a serpentine Saddam Hussein might wiggle out of its Kuwaiti predicament by conditioning its withdrawal on quasi-plausible terms. But Hussein's recklessness paved the way for his militarily defeat and expulsion from Iraq's so-called nineteenth province.

Meanwhile, at home opponents still bucked the White House's march toward war. They called for sanctions to bring Saddam Hussein's regime to heel. They belittled the president's strategy to rescue an outdated monarchy. They overestimated by order of magnitudes the number of American dead and wounded. James Schlesinger, a former Cabinet secretary of defense and energy predicted several tens of thousands of U.S. casualties. But the White House pushed ahead.

On January 8, 1991, President Bush formally requested congressional action on a resolution authorizing the use of force in line with the Security Council's Resolution 678. After three days of somber debate, both houses voted to back the presidential call to arms. The House passed it with a comfortable margin of 250 to 181 votes, while the Senate did so by a 52 to 47 vote, historically the slimmest margin ever on a war vote. Beyond the momentous decision to go to war, the vote held another political significance. Due to the Gulf conflict's overall successful outcome and its favorable resonance among the American public, it later made opponents of the second Gulf War hesitant to defy George W. Bush's call to arms in fall 2002.

Had four more senators voted against the resolution—assuming the president opted to avert a constitutional crisis and comply—Iraq might have been subjected merely to porous sanctions. Baghdad would have emerged from the Kuwait crisis to dominate Persian Gulf. The Iraqi sphere would have extended over Saudi Arabia, Bahrain, the United Arab Emirates, and other Gulf microstates as well as Kuwait. Drawing on revenues from its vassals, Baghdad's power would have transformed the region just as had ancient Babylon. More frighteningly, this new Babylonian Empire would have assuredly acquired nuclear weapons, already under development in Iraq's laboratories at Tuwaitha, Al Athir, and other facilities that were bombed in the course of the U.S.-led counterattack and dismantled by the UN inspections only made possible by America's victory. One prominent Iraqi scientist Jaffar al-Jaffar predicted that Baghdad was "three years away, give or take a year" from producing atomic weaponry when the coalition attacked.[19] The United States might have been able to deter a regional Iraqi powerhouse from some adventures with America's vast nuclear arsenal, but a nuclearized Iraq would also have been capable of deterring the United States from interfering in Baghdad's newly acquired sway over the Persian Gulf littoral. Thus, the United States preserved its regional nuclear monopoly, its strategic dominance in the Gulf, and its role as stabilizer of the volatile Middle East.

OPERATION DESERT STORM

The winter sky high above the date palm groves, mosques, and minarets lighted up with futile antiaircraft tracer rounds fired upward as the American and British warplanes unloaded their deadly cargoes. Orange and red flashes arched into the air as vividly as the swirling spectacular scenes reminiscent of the animated classic Fantasia. Another war had come to the historic land of Mesopotamia, a crossroads in ancient and modern conflict, but it differed from chariots and phalanxes of earlier times.

The United States unleashed Operation Desert Storm using ultramodern arms against Saddam Hussein's trench-bound troops and dug-in tanks. Wave after wave of U.S. F-15E bombers, F-117 Stealth fighters, and British Tornados lifted off carrier decks or desert airfields in Saudi Arabia. Eisenhower-era B-52s flew from Diego Garcia Island thousands of miles to the south in the Indian Ocean. Their bombs, 9 percent of which were either laser-directed or satellite-guided devices, fell one payload after another on Iraqi targets. Tomahawk Land Attack Missiles zeroed in on military installations and surface-to-air missile sites. Launched from warships hundreds of miles away, these cruise missiles got their first wartime baptism of fire in the Persian Gulf War, often striking targets within meters from their computer-programmed coordinates. Onboard cameras recorded the pinpoint accuracy of the precision munitions, which struck on the crosshairs of a headquarters building or zoomed down bunker ventilator shafts.

Death from the heavens rained down unconditionally. The Iraqi ground units could not run let alone hide from the unremitting aerial killing machines. Never had such state-of-the-art military power been leveled at such a hapless force since English archers let fly arrows from their longbows into the French-mounted nobility at Crécy at the start of the Hundred Years War. Never before were images of precision-strike bombs and missiles beamed into American living rooms via television footage. The futuristic systems gave a picture of the battlefield that resembled a video game, not a killing field. Push-button warfare looked remote, even antiseptic (except for those targeted) and reasonably safe for the bombers, many of them jetting at 3-mile-high altitudes.

Every war is unique, but the Persian Gulf War was more unique than most. It witnessed the first unveiling of America's information-age weaponry that seemingly rewrote military history. The lengthy, uninhibited military buildup in the lands neighboring Iraq by the coalition, the lopsided outcome, the disparity in weapons, tactics and generalship, and yet its political inconclusiveness that inevitably led to another war—all made the conflict distinct. The purpose of the following summary is to draw out the key points of the war, not to refight the battles with pushpins standing in for army divisions on grid maps. How the Gulf War precipitated a redux, served as a first counterproliferation campaign, and a case study for possible clashes with other so-called rogue states made the initial war with Iraq of international importance. It also shaped U.S. diplomacy for well over a decade.

The war began on January 17, 1991 with an aerial bombardment that soon incapacitated Iraq's military. The 39-day air campaign preceded the land operations. Saddam Hussein threatened the "mother of all battles" to defeat the multinational coalition arrayed against him. Instead, he saw the birth of a new form of warfare for which his forces were woefully unprepared. For Iraq, it was worse than a rout; it was a humiliation of towering proportions. Baghdad suffered an unmitigated calamity. The coalition won an unalloyed victory. Conditioned by the eight years combating Iranian-massed suicidal waves and static trench warfare reminiscent of World War I, Iraq collided with techno-American power.

Dubbed "Nintendo warfare" after the popular video game, the "smart" weaponry boasted a much-ballyhooed revolution in military affairs. This so-called watershed in the art of warfare announced a new era in human conflict that promised push-button wars whereby enemy combatants were eliminated without miring young men in the mud and close combat. A decade later, the post–Iraq War insurgency, nevertheless, provided a necessary corrective to the *Star Wars* scenarios as U.S. Marines and Army soldiers fought insurgents in alleyways and gutted buildings, with classic infantrymen tactics of one step back for every two forward.

The ground-war phase of the Gulf War commenced on February 24 and lasted a mere 100 hours. American armored forces, long trained to smash the mighty Red Army across European plains, rolled over the Iraqi tanks, leaving decimated iron hulks, dead bodies in the thousands, and demoralized adversaries in their wake. So overawed were the Iraqi soldiers that they surrendered en masse to whomever they encountered, even Western journalists. Along with a half million American troops, there were 160,000 non-U.S. coalition troops from 34 countries, with Britain and France fielding the largest contingents of combat troops. Despite the multinational flavor of the anti-Hussein coalition, the United States spearheaded the offensive and carried the greatest load.

The set-piece battles gave rise to a dangerous myth that was not dispelled until the second Gulf War. In conventional force-on-force firefights, the Iraqi Republic Guards acquitted themselves abysmally. They lacked up-to-date armaments and realistic training exercises. As a conventional military force, they disintegrated under the American blitzkrieg warfare of coordinated air and ground fire from rapidly maneuvering 70-ton Abrams main battle tanks and Bradley Fighting Vehicles. Yet as insurgents in a guerrilla war, the Iraqis later proved far tougher to eradicate in the postconflict phase of the Iraq War. This complicated subject deserves to be treated separately, but for the purpose of this chapter suffice to note that the resounding Iraqi defeat in the Persian Gulf War misled the civilian planners in the George W. Bush administration about the nature of Iraqi society and its deep hostility to non-Muslim occupiers 12 years later.

A BULLET DODGED

Washington officially halted Operation Desert Storm because the U.S.-led coalition accomplished its UN-mandated mission—the expulsion of Iraq from Kuwait. To intervene in Iraq was judged as a violation of that authority. Moreover, the American public and their political representatives signed on for a war of ejection, not occupation. Calling off the war was also seen as politically astute because sending masses of Iraqi soldiers to their graves would detract from the victory itself, poisoning the atmosphere in the Middle East. Prolonging the fighting meant the decimation of the fleeing Iraqi troops along the Kuwait-Basra road. General Powell said it succinctly: "We don't want to be seen as killing for the sake of killing."[20]

Geopolitical reasons also justified a cessation of fighting. Bush's closest advisers argued that a politically viable Iraq, even under Hussein, served as a military counterweight to Iran and Syria, two other fiercely anti-U.S. regimes in the region. The president and his inner circle reckoned that without a strong hand at the helm of a defeated Iraq, the country was likely to fragment along ethnic and religious lines, leaving two or even three ministates. Iraq's neighbors might be tempted to fill the political vacuum. At the time, these reasons persuaded most commentators. The intervening years, nevertheless, dealt that rationale hammer blows, as Baghdad persisted in threatening transregional stability. In time, Bush's triumph was equated with a squandered victory to rid the world of a menacing tyrant, but history is a greater seat of irony than this judgment.

By not invading Iraq in 1991, the United States spared itself large-scale grief, as became so evident in the aftermath of the 2003 invasion, where guerrilla insurgency, factious politics, and decrepit infrastructure met the victorious American and British liberators. That outcome almost makes Bush's 1991 decision seem prescient, although it left Hussein in power. Officials in the George H. W. Bush administration did anticipate the turmoil that dispatching Saddam Hussein would entail. The president himself reflected that in his memoirs: "Had we gone the invasion route, the United States could conceivably still be an occupying power in a bitterly hostile land."[21] General Powell wrote favorably about George Bush's decision to halt the war: "He had promised the American people that Desert Storm would not become a Persian Gulf Vietnam, and he kept his promise."[22] Secretary of Defense Cheney explained the decision against regime change by stating the following: "Once you've got Baghdad, it's not clear what you do with it. It is not clear what kind of government you would put in place of the one that's currently there now. . . . How much creditability is that [non-Hussein] government going to have if it's set up by the United States military when it's there?"[23] By not lunging toward Baghdad in 1991, the United States concluded that it had dodged a political bullet. In the final analysis, the United State used its immense power to restore the status quo ante. It reinstalled the medieval monarchy in Kuwait, merely expelled Iraq from Kuwaiti soil, and left a resentful Saddam Hussein in power to continue to make mischief.

Finally, the Bush administration desired to shift its diplomatic focus to the Madrid Conference and the resolution of the Israeli-Palestinian conflict. It reasoned that with a checkmated Iraq a new day had dawned on the Middle East peace process. A lingering occupation of Iraq conflicted with this goal by needlessly entangling the United States in an arduous pacification of one of the Middle East's major states. Such a turn of events would further undercut Washington's role as a neutral mediator in the long-standing Israeli-Palestinian dispute. The meeting in the Spanish capital in October 1991 did revive the Middle East process. It laid the foundation for the Oslo accord between Israelis and Palestinians during the Clinton administration that lifted peace hopes so high before crashing them on the shoals of terrorists within the Palestinian population.

The Persian Gulf War transformed the region and, in many ways, the international terrain of the post–Cold War world as the United States strengthened its stabilization agenda. The war crowned America's peaceful triumph over the declining Soviet Union. Moscow's internal disarray was so pronounced by 1991 that it sidelined itself from discord in the Middle East. Indeed, Washington and Moscow officially cooperated for the first time in a major overseas war since World War II. The Gulf War swept away any lingering doubt about America's claim to sole global superpowerdom through its dazzling array of high-accuracy weaponry.

Total American combat casualties numbered 147 deaths, which stood substantially lower than the 18,000 estimated by Pentagon planners. Another 235 troops died in accidents and other noncombat deaths. By comparisons to battles in World War II or even Vietnam, for instance, these figures were exceedingly light. Tens of thousands of mostly American and British service members, however, suffered from mysterious illnesses later identified in some cases as Lou Gehrig's disease that could have been brought on by the toxic mixture of inoculations, sarin gas, burning oilfields, and depleted uranium shells that gave off radioactivity.[24] Iraqi casualties were more difficult to determine due to the chaos and Hussein's desire to cover up his defeat. Estimates placed the numbers at 3,500 civilian deaths and between 20,000 and 26,000 military personnel.[25]

Saddam Hussein dismissed his catastrophic defeat and brushed aside the thousands of deaths among his population. He proclaimed victory. His propaganda organs manufactured a triumphal account for his cowed countrymen, claiming that his severely mauled Republican Guards had actually beaten the Washington-led armies, which stopped short of entering Baghdad out of fear. It later came to light that President Hussein attributed his survival to his arsenal of chemical, biological, and nuclear weapons. This belief reinforced the lesson that he took away from the earlier Iran-Iraq War when Baghdad's nerve gas shells threw back the massed Iranian offenses. Twice these prohibited armaments, in his mind, saved the Baathist regime. Henceforth, the acquisition or just the pretense of stockpiles of mass-death weaponry was the warp and woof of Hussein's self-preservation apparatus. Inside and outside the police state, everyone came to believe that Baghdad had hidden away vast quantities of atomic, biological, and chemical arms. It took a foreign occupation more than a decade later to prove otherwise.

AFTEREFFECTS

The conflict interjected American power into the Persian Gulf littoral on an unprecedented scale. Thousands of U.S. troops, airmen, and sailors flocked into Saudi Arabia and its neighboring states. They constructed air bases, improved harbors, and mingled with the local people. They also grated on the Arab mores and Islamic beliefs. Their presence bred resentment and anti-Americanism among segments of the population, particularly the fundamentalist Islamic communities, who believed that the presence of Western nonbelievers defiled Islam's most holy shrines. This antagonism fueled a virulent Islamic extremism that found its expression in terrorist acts against the West in general and the United States in particular. Thus, the war constituted a bridge between two eras—the old Soviet-American competition in the Middle East and the new global-pecking order with the United States perched on the top but detested by large numbers of Muslims.

The Gulf War also foreshadowed the U.S.-led armed humanitarian interventions that so characterized the disorderly global landscape of the 1990s. In each, Washington harnessed willing allies to confront some form of aggression and to restore order by complex diplomacy accompanied by military force. This multilateral approach, portended by the Gulf conflict, became a byword for world problem solving. But the UN's imprimatur did not erode the American belief as expressed by President Clinton's Secretary of State Madeleine Albright that the United States constituted the "the indispensable nation" to resolve the world's troubles. Deputy Secretary of State Lawrence Eagleburger put it more aptly when confronted with Hussein's Kuwaiti invasion: "It is absolutely essential that the U.S.—collectively if possible but individually if necessary—not only put a stop to this aggression but roll it back."[26] Even the UN's imprimatur left it up to Washington to marshal the wherewithal to handle a crisis. Like the Old West sheriff, the United States then corralled a posse of willing states against desperados in the Balkans, Haiti, Sierra Leone, or East Timor, who spread conflict and turmoil.

As a curtain-raiser on military operations in the service of humanity, the United States ordered returning naval forces from the Persian Gulf conflict to assist cyclone-ravaged Bangladesh. A flotilla of eight U.S. warships arrived off the port of Chittagong in mid-May 1991 to disburse food, water, and medicine to victims of a devastating storm the previous month. "We went to Kuwait in the name of liberty, and we've come to Bangladesh in the name of humanity," said Major General Henry Stackpole, the leader of the task force.[27] The Bangladesh operation set a precedent for expeditionary forces deployed to aid tsunami and earthquake victims elsewhere in South Asia years afterward in the cause of stability.

Also in the Gulf War's immediate aftermath, the outcome appeared to banish Vietnam malaise from the American psyche. The Vietnam War specter had, in fact, haunted successive American presidents, who feared bogging the nation down in another bloody, protracted conflict of indeterminate outcome as took place in Southeast Asia from 1961 to 1973. Politicians wrung their hands about "body bags" returning from foreign engagements. Ironically, the high-tech, low-casualty war against Iraq, in fact, reinforced the Vietnam syndrome. It re-etched a baseline in the American consciousness for short-duration wars with miniscule U.S. deaths that affirmed the immanence of the Indochina ghost, not exorcised it from the nation's memory bank.

To spare needless killing on the "highway of death" leading from Kuwait City to Basra, American political leaders and military brass ceased firing and allowed the retreating Republican Guards to escape with their arms. Even Robert E. Lee's less-vanquished army was relieved of its artillery and rifles by General Ulysses S. Grant at the famous Appomattox courthouse surrender, which ended the American Civil War. Confederate soldiers kept only their horses and officers their sidearms. But in the Gulf War, far too many Iraqi units left with much of their armaments intact. The disinclination to neutralize the retreating tank and troop columns ensured Hussein's political survival when the Kurds and Shiites rebelled.

Despite CIA predictions of Saddam Hussein's imminent downfall in the wake of a military defeat, the Iraqi tyrant clung to power. In fact, Hussein suppressed the Kurdish rebellion in the north and the Shiite revolt in the south that arose, in part, due to George Bush's comments at a press conference announcing on March 1, 1991 the cease-fire talks to be held at Safwan, inside the Iraqi border. The president repeated his call for rebellion: "In my own view, I've always said it would be—that the Iraqi people should put him [Hussein] aside and that would facilitate the resolution of all these problems that exist, and certainly would facilitate the acceptance of Iraq back into the family of peace-loving nations."[28] Following President Bush's call for Iraqis to "get matters into their own hands" at another occasion, the Iraqi Shiites and Kurds rebelled.[29]

During this rebellion, the Bush administration stood aside as the Republican Guards, many of whom the coalition had just spared from annihilation on their pell-mell exodus, savagely suppressed the rebels. To make matters worse, General Schwarzkopf blundered by permitting the Iraqi armed forces to retain their helicopters, which they put to deadly use as gunships against the rebels.[30] Hussein's Republican Guards and death squads killed as many as 300,000 people from the rebelling Shiite and Kurdish communities, and Washington passed up an opportunity to assist the rebels in destabilizing the Hussein dictatorship.

Once securely back in control, the Iraqi president became virtually immune from internal threat, except for an occasional assassination attempt. The Baath Party's Argus-eyed security apparatus functioned with a Stalin-like brutality, arresting, torturing, and executing suspected dissenters. The bulk of Hussein's Sunni henchmen hailed from the west-central region radiating from his birthplace outside Tikrit and belonged to the ruling party. The Tikriti-Baathist axis kept Hussein in power, and he looked out for its interests in return. Together, they terrorized the population to hang onto power and privilege.

WARLIKE CONTAINMENT

Despite its decisive military victory, the United States could not extricate itself from the Iraqi problem. Instead, the Bush government laid the cornerstone of what became a "hot containment" policy toward Iraq for the next 12 years, spanning the last months of its governance, all the Clinton years, and into the George W. Bush administration. Washington turned toward covert methods and internationally mandated economic sanctions to destabilize Saddam Hussein's regime or, at minimum, to pressure it to conform to the cease-fire agreement and many UN resolutions.

Disturbed by waves of Kurdish refugees fleeing into Turkey to escape the Republican Guards' repression, the United States established a "safe haven" in the northern tier that became known as Kurdistan. It had two motives. First, Turkey already felt under siege by its restive Kurdish minority in the country's southeastern corner. A surge of Iraqi Kurds across their common border spelled further trouble for Turkey's slow-burning rebellion. As a NATO ally, Turkey's plight registered keenly in Washington, London, and other Atlantic alliance capitals, which sought to relieve Ankara's predicament.

Second, something had to be done to shield the Kurds from a vindictive Hussein. Using Security Council Resolution 688 that called upon Iraq to halt its repression of the country's population, Washington, London, and Paris acted without further explicit UN authority to establish the Kurdish sanctuary and a "no-fly zone" above the thirty-sixth parallel, which they dubbed the northern zone. The United States sent lightly armed infantrymen and CIA agents into northern Iraq as Operation Provide Comfort. In time, this northern tier developed a measure of autonomy from Baghdad. The allied commitment to Kurdistan nurtured democracy and economic growth over the 1990s, a political breakthrough among the 5 million Kurds that has often been underappreciated by the outside world. This democracy fostering in the heart of the Middle East foreshadowed a dramatic turnabout in U.S. policy on the heels of the Iraq War, when America backed democratic movements where once its stability-first policy had acquiesced toward authoritarian rule.

The United States did not duplicate this protectorate in the southern reaches of the country where the Shiite community had staged a failed sectarian revolt against the Sunni-dominated Baath regime. Acting with Britain and France, the United States erected just a southern "no-fly zone" below the thirty-second parallel in August 1992, which afforded little genuine security to the Shia who were hunted down and killed by Hussein's thugs.

America initiated what became a standard, even routine, response to Baghdad's provocations—the resort to air strikes to enforce compliance. Along with British and French warplanes, American jets flew almost daily sorties in the twin air exclusionary zones. Just before the start of Operation Desert Fox, the four-day bombing campaign, on December 15, 1998, France suspended its participation in the southern "no-fly zone."

Afterward, the Anglo-American air fleets alone patrolled the two zones until the outbreak of Iraq War, when they shifted to all-out combat operations. Their patrols fired on Iraqi planes and hurled air-to-surface missiles at radars when they "locked on" the allied planes. Some 350,000 sorties were flown by the start of the Iraq War in 2003, and by that time the cost of militarily hemming in Saddam Hussein had reached an estimated $30 billion.

The Bush government's multilateral approach to Iraq's invasion of Kuwait translated into a larger role for the United Nations in the post–Gulf War Iraq. The Security Council set down the cease-fire terms following the conflict in Resolution 687. The resolution, among other things, demanded that Iraq pay for war damages to Kuwait and recognize its border with that country. It also formed the UN Special Commission (UNSCOM) to ferret out and destroy any Iraqi weapons of mass destruction stockpiles or production capabilities. The UN resolution compelled Iraq to comply with the WMD searches until their completion before the Security Council would lift its 1990-imposed sanctions.

Washington's well-founded apprehensions about Baghdad's nuclear ambitions had caused it to unleash air strikes early in the war against the sprawling complex at Tuwaitha, 12 miles southeast of the capital.[31] At the tail end of the fighting, conclusive proof was uncovered about Iraq's covert atomic program. This discovery threw serious doubt on the efficacy of the UN's atomic agency. The Vienna-based International Atomic Energy Agency (IAEA) failed to discover the extent of Iraq's nuclear program before the Gulf conflict. This failure made Washington leery of relying on IAEA assessments about the status of clandestine nuclear efforts in North Korea and Iran. In the case of Iraq, American insistence led to the formation of UNSCOM as a rival to the IAEA so as to detect and dismantle any future Baghdad programs to manufacture WMD. Fears of secret WMD facilities gave birth to a dread that blossomed into "Iraqnaphobia" as the decade lengthened.

Additionally, the United States also authorized $15 million for covert operations to oust Saddam Hussein. Congress later bumped the sum to $40 million.[32] The CIA was placed in charge of fomenting an insurgency or coup against the Baath regime. Nothing came of these clandestine activities, except the conviction that an externally induced regime change was at best a million-to-one shot. The Baath regime shot scores of would-be usurpers who acted on their own to overthrow President Hussein.

In summary, the outgoing Bush White House installed a four-pronged containment formula—airpower-enforced no-fly zones in the north and south, internationally authorized sanctions, arms inspections, and covert support for internal opposition to overthrow the Iraqi autocrat. None worked. Hussein persisted in destabilizing the region by his actions and threats, suppressing the populace, and fanning anti-Israeli terrorism. A much greater application of U.S. power was required to realize a Hussein-less Iraq. Before America's second war against Iraq, Washington tried to stabilize the Gulf arena by holding Iraq in check.

Just before George H. W. Bush vacated 1600 Pennsylvania Avenue in January 1993, after losing his bid for reelection, Saddam Hussein decided to test American and UN resolve by hindering the UNSCOM inspectors. His regime chafed under the economic sanctions and intrusive weapons inspections. The Security Council held Iraq in "material breach" of Resolution 687, the so-called cease-fire resolution, and set in motion plans for military attacks. The Hussein regime dismissed the UN warning. The White House ordered U.S. pilots to take action along with British and French flyers in a 100-aircraft armada against Iraqi air defense systems, in what became in time a typical target of subsequent Anglo-American assaults.[33] After the intensive three-day aerial assault, Iraq declared a "cease-fire" allowing UN inspectors to resume their searches.

The United States thus began a policy of relying on air attacks in pursuit of a gun-barrel diplomacy, a war in the time of peace so to speak. Under a UN aegis, the United States initiated a decadelong form of shooting diplomacy that was unprecedented. The Anglo-American air operations cleared Iraqi planes from huge swaths of their own airspace and bombed ground targets repeatedly without any serious international challenge, or even substantial critical Western comment, to this strategy. Looking back, this use of allied power in a warlike containment of Iraq was an extraordinary chapter in the annals of international relations as a means to promote stability. In retrospect, nonetheless, it constituted a much wiser course of action than invasion, occupation, and democracy transplanting in an arena militantly intransigent to non-Muslim interference.

CHAPTER 4

GLOBALIZATION, SOMALIA, RWANDA, AND HAITI

O brave new world, That has such people in't.

Shakespeare's *The Tempest*

Within the next hundred years, nationhood as we know it will be obsolete: all states will recognize a single, global authority.

Deputy Secretary of State Strobe Talbott
during the Clinton administration

WHEN WILLIAM JEFFERSON CLINTON RODE INTO THE WHITE HOUSE ON A WAVE OF ECONOMIC OPTIMISM, he and his fellow citizens hoped to look inward to resolve America's problems. Declining economic indicators, national unemployment at 7.5 percent, and rising federal budget deficits defined the months preceding his election. The Democratic Party nominee painted his rival as a "foreign policy president" and out of touch with America's domestic troubles. The Arkansas governor pledged to "focus like a laser" on improving the country's economic health. International issues seemed to evaporate with the dust from the Berlin Wall's destruction.

The national campaign was not devoid of international content, however. Contrary to much of the conventional wisdom about the presidential race, Bill Clinton campaigned as a candidate with an assertive foreign policy agenda. Despite the pervasive slogan of his platform, "it's the economy, stupid," Clinton did not restrict his focus to internal problems. Nor did his inexperience with the international issues inhibit him from staking out firm positions, although George Bush made light of his limited global credentials.

Candidate Clinton berated President Bush for his pragmatism and realpolitik in conducting the nation's overseas affairs. He derided the incumbent for selling out American ideals in post–Gulf War Iraq and in China after the crackdown in Tiananmen Square on prodemocracy protestors. Clinton promised that, if elected, he would "link China's trading privileges [with the United States] to its human rights record and its conduct on trade and weapons sales." He faulted the White House occupant for "coddling the old communist guard in China."[1] He believed economic sanctions were an appropriate response to China's violation of human rights. In short, the young governor portrayed the internationally experienced president as too much a "realist," without American idealism and a belief in spreading democracy abroad.

Settling into the White House with no real foreign policy experience, Bill Clinton looked to others to help him gain his sea legs. The president-elect chose Warren Christopher as his secretary of state because of his experience in Jimmy Carter's State Department. Christopher had served in the campaign as head of the vice presidential selection committee, from which Al Gore emerged as Clinton's running mate partly because of his work on arms control issues in the U.S. Senate. Except for his choice of Congressmen Les Aspin as secretary of defense, Clinton's front-rank picks for foreign and security posts drew heavily from the Carter administration that left office in 1981. In addition to Christopher, these other foreign policy principals included Anthony Lake (National Security Affairs adviser), Madeleine K. Albright (U.S. permanent representative to the United Nations), and R. James Woolsey (director of Central Intelligence). Samuel "Sandy" R. Berger served as Lake's deputy and succeeded him in 1996, when he left to take up a professorship at Georgetown University.

In his inaugural address, Clinton once again gave voice to an expansive international role for the United States. He used the now-standard phrase that Washington would resort to military means when "our vital interests are challenged." Yet, additionally, the forty-second president interjected a Wilsonian notion by conflating a challenge to American interests with global concerns when he added "or the will and conscience of the international community is defied, we will act, with peaceful diplomacy whenever possible, with force when necessary."[2] By this declaration, the incoming president seemingly committed the United States to act as a global police officer on behalf of the international community.

President Clinton's interests, in reality, rested with internal concerns. Generally, he tended to avoid foreign affairs in the initial years of his tenure. Because his heart lay in domestic issues—economic revival, health care, and welfare reform—he delegated more latitude to his subordinates than was the case in formulating home front policy.[3] Both Christopher and Lake shared the same assignment to "keep foreign policy from distracting the President from his domestic agenda."[4] As will be abundantly clear, the president's lieutenants had as much success in walling off international troubles as Canute did in stopping the incoming tide.

Foreign issues did come into clear focus for Bill Clinton when they contributed to improving the nation's economy. He believed that the post–Cold War period afforded an opportunity to invigorate the economy through international commerce. This approach mutated into his globalization agenda that formed one of Clinton's legacies. Integrating the globe's economies and currency flows and promoting the movement of labor and data across international borders got a huge boost under Bill Clinton when he won passage of the North American Free Trade Agreement in Congress. Although President Bush initialed the free-trade zone pact with Canada and Mexico, he left office before the legislative branch could pass it. Clinton's victory on Capitol Hill provided political momentum for U.S. membership in the World

Trade Organization (WTO), which is the primary international center dealing with global trade rules among nations.

To the Clintonian officials, the WTO would further globalization, which in turn would spur economic growth worldwide, leading to peace and stability as populations experienced higher living standards. Years after radicalized Islam bred the scourge of terrorism, globalization was seen as one factor inviting a bloody backlash against global commerce, Western values, and universal democracy, because it endangered the tenets of Islamic extremism.

AN INTERNATIONAL SCENE "WITHOUT FORM AND VOID"

The Cold War's termination gave rise to an inward turn among many citizens. Americans longed for the "peace dividend" due the country after four decades of their tax dollars spent on defense. The United States' early 1990s introversion conformed to historical patterns. After every major international engagement, the country hungered for a return to normalcy and business as usual. This happened decidedly after both world wars and, even to a degree, the Vietnam War. Besides, the post–Berlin Wall trouble spots looked less frightening and more amenable to resolution in unison with other capitals than had the existential threat posed by the Soviet Union's massive atomic weaponry.

The incoming Clinton foreign policy aides, in fact, shared George Bush's anxiety about the continued threat of the Russian arsenal, which still had enough nuclear-tipped intercontinental ballistic missiles to wipe out the United States several times over. Thus, they too pursued arms control agreements with Moscow. They worked harder than the Bush government at moving Russia down the democratic path, at the end of which they vainly hoped for a stabile democracy unlikely to challenge American interests. But they fell to the same tendency as their predecessors by personalizing relations with the Russian leader. While Bush and his senior advisers pinned their hopes on Mikhail Gorbachev, the Clinton foreign policy team embraced Boris Yeltsin, even helping his 1996 reelection campaign.[5] Russia was just one piece in the post–Berlin Wall geopolitical puzzle, however.

Across the Pacific, a prosperous Japan had arisen to rival American capitalism under Washington's defensive umbrella during the Soviet-American confrontation. The United States beheld a Japan resplendent in globally appealing consumer products, high-tech manufacturing plants, innovative management techniques, and bushels of cash to buy up American architectural icons such as Rockefeller Center or swank golf courses such as Pebble Beach. Presidential aspirant Paul Tsongas remarked in the 1992 New Hampshire primaries that the Cold War was over and Japan had won. Japan's economic prowess even contributed to misanalyses of the danger it posed to the United States. One widely selling book *The Coming War with Japan* even advanced the far-fetched notion that Washington and Tokyo were predetermined to resume war over a similar set of incompatible interests in Asia as in World War II.[6]

Other big theory books captured the uncertainty in the American mood without the Soviet competition in every sphere of life from possible Armageddon to the Olympics. Francis Fukuyama, for example, postulated that the evaporation of the Soviet Union conjured up a sort of "end of history" and left liberal democracy as the only unassailable model for societies, with no genuine political competitors.[7] Islamic theocracies and rogue state dictatorships soon offered an unforeseen defiance to liberal governments. Alone among the 1990s "big think" books, Fukuyama's work was the most optimistic about the future. Others prophesied dire events.

Chief among the prophets of doom for the Clinton policymakers was the journalist Robert Kaplan who looked apprehensively at the turbulent third world. He predicted in a widely noted 1994 *Atlantic Monthly* article a coming anarchy fueled by a resurgence of ethnic violence, environmental scarcity, overpopulation and disease, and expanding criminal enterprise.[8] His antiutopian perceptions gained du jour currency among policy wonks, for abundant evidence appeared already at hand in Africa, Asia, and even in European fringes. These apocalyptic calamities threatened planetary order in a way that would drag the United States into militarized rescue operations or even wars unless it checked disorder.

While the planet's periphery did breed horrible man-made disasters of starvation and massacres, the danger to the United States came, in part, from a clash between civilizations, not within failing nation-states. Harvard Professor Samuel Huntington wrote first an article and then a book, *The Clash of Civilizations and the Remaking of World Order*, which attracted much notoriety.[9] While the Washington political establishment saw the forces of global economic convergence bringing the world closer to political harmony, Huntington presciently forecast that modernization does not equal Westernization. Indeed, pushing the universality of Western culture and enlightened secular democracy was dangerous because it "could lead to a major inter-civilizational war" between political cultures, which possess vastly different ideals and norms, particularly the Muslim world. Largely obscured by lesser crises, the Huntingtonian proposition gained a new lease on life after the 9/11 attacks and the Iraqi occupation.

Why did these commentator's perceptions matter in a world now devoid of the Soviet Union? The short answer lies in the observation that ideas have consequences in the formulation of a nation's policies. A longer explanation rests at the heart of the discussion of Bill Clinton administration's actions overseas. Whereas George H. W. Bush came to office with a worldview inherited from previous Oval Office occupants stretching back to Harry Truman and the containment doctrine, no such ready framework greeted Clinton's national security principals. They faced an international landscape radically transformed by the Soviet Union's splintering. All the struts had been kicked from beneath the foreign policy establishment's *Weltpolitik*. But from the Cold War era, it carried forward and reinforced the objective of preserving stability, which had become so much a part of the Soviet-American duel. Official Washington gradually started to turn away from its stability-first policies to espouse ideals such as spreading democracy. The nascent government acted hesitantly on this principle, even though it spoke with more than one voice about the country's direction.

The senior Clinton officials laid out several agendas nine months into their tenure in an effort to answer the question as to what was America's purpose after the Berlin Wall fell. Warren Christopher, America's top diplomat, focused his remarks on resolving the standoff between Israelis and Palestinians. Madeleine Albright, Washington's representative to the United Nations, attempted to clarify America's participation in multilateral approaches to overseas crises by stressing defined objectives, adequate resources, and termination points so as to address critics of her "assertive multilateralism."[10]

Anthony Lake's contribution to the policy-by-speech approach ("From Containment to Enlargement") sketched out an ambitious goal at Johns Hopkins University in his remarks that both drew on American traditions and foreshadowed President George W. Bush's approach a decade later. Lake advocated a policy of democratic enlargement because "the addition of new democracies makes us more secure because democracies tend not to wage war on each other or sponsor terrorism."[11] In commending a strategy of "enlargement of the world's free community of market democracies" as a successor to the Cold War doctrine of containment, the National Security adviser anticipated U.S. policy of advancing democracy for peace and stability after 9/11 attacks. Events confirmed that pushing democratic governance via military invasion was the wrong prescription for political order or even America's vital interests but that revelation was a decade hence.

On September 27, 1993, Bill Clinton delivered the final speech in the series. He spoke at the United Nations and addressed two audiences with different messages. To international observers, he reassured doubters about America's continued overseas leadership. He insisted, "The United States plans to remain engaged and to lead." But to his domestic constituency, the president sought to dampen apprehensions about wading into the deepening Bosnian crisis or other trouble spots abroad. Clinton, therefore, added, "If the American people are to say 'yes' to UN peacekeeping, the United Nations must know when to say 'no'" to too many commitments.[12] A week afterward, the Somali upheaval tested Washington's own peace-support mission and sharpened the debate about how the United States would use its immense power in world affairs.

SOMALIA: THE ROAD TO HELL IS PAVED WITH GOOD INTENTIONS

Of the many flash points in the immediate post–Berlin Wall world, Somalia hurtled the most meteorically across the political firmament and then just as quickly sank again into obscurity. While it streaked briefly into Bill Clinton's consciousness, it left an indelible imprint on his thinking. Somalia became *the* sole prism through which other political traumas in faraway places were judged. Such a political watershed was an unlikely outcome for an enterprise initiated simply to feed a destitute population in a desiccated northeastern African land, where most people lived nomadic lives with their cattle and camels. It, in retrospect, should have served as a red flag to subsequent Washington policies to invade, occupy, and impose democracy on Muslim populations.

George H. W. Bush had ordered the humanitarian intervention into Somalia out of altruism in the twilight of his presidency. Presidential aspirant Bill Clinton endorsed Bush's decision. Television images of starving children in wretched conditions plucked at American heartstrings. This so-called CNN factor, as it came to be known, accounts in large measure for Washington's extension of succor to a starving African population. Before leaving office, Bush interpreted the alleviation of hunger as accomplishing the goal of the Pentagon's Operation Restore Hope and a sign to wind down the humanitarian intervention. On the eve of Bill Clinton's inauguration, Bush's Pentagon staged a symbolic withdrawal of several hundred U.S. Marines as prelude to eventual UN control of the mission. Many other U.S. military units left during the following months. The official turnover to the United Nations took place in May 1993 under the Clinton administration. The Pentagon transferred command of the international force to the United Nations Operation Somalia (UNOSOM) and pulled out all but some 5,000 U.S. troops who made up a part of the total UN force of nearly 30,000.

The Clinton government initially went along with the disengagement plans of its predecessor. Secretary of State Christopher noted the completion of the Somalia mission in a June 1993 cable to all U.S. ambassadors as one of the new administration's nine accomplishments abroad, including "unflinching support for President Yeltsin" of Russia and "stepped up support for Iraq's democratic opposition." He also wrote, "We have phased out the American-led mission in Somalia, and taken the lead in passing responsibility to the United Nations peacekeeping force."[13] This pronouncement turned out to be greatly premature.

Instead of decamping from Somalia, the United States deepened and broadened its commitment to the "failed" state to halt the spreading anarchy. Washington embraced a multinational, UN-sponsored peacekeeping operation to salvage the beleaguered Somali society from civil disorder. It also entertained the notion of "nation building" to restore order under UN auspices. Somalia's lack of natural resources, democratic traditions, or even a homogeneous population posed just some of the problems. Armed clans pushed the society to the brink of anarchy as they jockeyed to rule the parched and desolate land. Split by clan feuds, Somalia was a dangerous place because both Moscow and Washington had flooded it with small arms during the height of their East-West competition. Warlords armed to the teeth menaced the country with their militias. These "technicals" prowled Mogadishu's streets in vehicles brisling with machine guns and rocket-propelled grenade launchers.

The United States could deliver food to Somalia and be tolerated by the warring factions, but to impose order and pluralistic institutions called for nothing less than a full-scale pacification campaign. It was beyond the means of the small external forces to secure political reconciliation and democratic governance in clan-torn Somalia. These conditions did not sober the enthusiasm in the nascent U.S. government for a multilateral role in nation building. It believed the Soviet Union's downfall ushered a malleable era of promise. During Clinton's first summer as president, his administration reversed course in Somalia. Christopher announced the following in a cable to the diplomatic corps on June 7: "[F]or the first time there will be a sturdy American role to help the United Nations rebuild a viable nation state."[14] It constituted a turning point in relations with the United Nations as well as with a fractured country on the Indian Ocean. The secretary's cable thus pointed the United States into unchartered waters.

American forces, therefore, started down the path of "mission creep" from a temporary distributor of relief to urban counterguerrilla warfare in the course of just a few months. The story is not a sinister plot but rather a tale of improvisation deriving from poorly thought-through plans on how to stabilize Somalia. This evolution deepened Washington's commitment to the UN's campaign to root out warlord opposition and reform Somali society. The American response also involved UN blue helmet forces in offensive operations and led to U.S. forces fighting, if only nominally, under a UN commander—both activities broke long-held precedents.

An uneasy Congress held hearings to question the administration's redeployment of U.S. military units for stepped-up combat operations sanctioned by the United Nations. It fretted about the recurring reports of street skirmishes. Madeleine Albright traveled from her UN post in New York City and testified on June 24, 1993 before a House subcommittee. Her statement that "assertive multilateralism" served U.S. interests became a lightening rod for detractors of humanitarian interventions. She justified U.S. military participation in UN operations against Somali clan lords as necessary for "rebuilding Somali society and promoting democracy in that strife-torn nation."[15]

A series of violent actions crystallized the redirection in U.S. policy. These events intensified from small-scale but bloody military raids to the citywide uprising in Mogadishu in early October. UN officials, especially Boutros Boutros-Ghali, and retired U.S. Admiral Jonathan Howe, who was the secretary general's special envoy in Somalia, held a jaundice opinion of the Habr Gidr clan and its leader General Mohamed Farrah Aidid. The secretary general, a former Egyptian deputy foreign minister knowledgeable about Somalia, reviled Aidid for overthrowing the Somali despot, Siad Barre, formerly backed by Cairo. Both saw the warlord for what he was—the most ruthless kingpin among many corrupt and cruel clan chieftains. For his part, Aidid resented UN interference and feared that it sought to restore his rival clan, the Darod, to power. Aidid had ousted Siad Barre and his Darod faction two years earlier. Sharing power with other clan chiefs, as the United Nations insisted, held no interest for him.

The UN officials decided to destroy Habr Gidr and remove its head as means to bring peace and order to Somalia. In pursuit of this goal, the UN authorized a series of assaults on Aidid's clan during the summer. The raids ignited reprisals from Aidid and his Somalia National Alliance (SNA), the political/military arm of the Habr Gidr. The most damaging SNA counterattack killed 24 UN Pakistani soldiers in June. The clashes induced the United States, at Howe's urging, to deploy elite military units to pacify the population and hunt down Habr Gidr's higher-ups. Defense Secretary Aspin and the Joint Chief's General Powell approved the request, despite misgivings about the direction of U.S. policy in the escalating lethal environment. Not to do so would have let down the local commander Major General Thomas Montgomery, who asked for reinforcements for his expanding mission.

THE BATTLE OF MOGADISHU

The arrival of U.S. Army Rangers and the Delta Force, a supersecret commando unit, in the capital city thoroughly militarized the UN's relief campaign. These forces undertook manhunts to capture Aidid and his lieutenants. Swooping down from the sky in MH-60 Black Hawk helicopters in six smoothly executed operations before the climatic firefight on October 3, the elite Army units killed or kidnapped many Somalis in the name of restoring order. The street fighting fed reprisals against the American-manned Quick Reaction Force leading up to the deadly confrontation. On August 8, a remote-controlled mine killed four U.S. soldiers riding in a Humvee.

This stiffened the soldiers' resolve to settle scores against the Skinnies or Sammies, as the troops called the Somalis.[16] A climax came in the escalation of combat assault on a hot afternoon on the first Sunday of October in the sprawling seaside capital.

The fateful snatch operation aimed to apprehend Aidid's confidants at a meeting in the center of town near the landmark Olympic Hotel. Task Force Ranger ran into trouble when one and then a second Black Hawk helicopter (three others limped back to the American base) were brought down by ground fire to the dusty and violent streets. The city rose up against the downed aircraft crew and the encircled U.S. troops. Mog, as the American soldiers called it, was awash in handheld weapons, which transformed the citizenry into a virtual levee en masse. Women and children joined the battle as scouts, weapons retrievers, and even actual combatants. Fighting continued into early hours of the next day before a makeshift column of Pakistani and Malaysian tanks and armored personnel carriers driven by Americans could reach the vastly outnumbered Rangers and Delta operatives and escort them out of the fury.

The 15-hour Battle of Mogadishu claimed 18 American lives and possibly 500 Somali fatalities. Seventy-three Americans were wounded and an estimated 1,000 Somalis. By body count alone, the trapped U.S. troops gave much better than they got. They nabbed two of Aidid's top men and a further 60 followers. When the improvised rescue column finally reached the Ranger contingent, the combined force fought their way out of downtown with their captives in tow. Tactically, it was an American victory, for the troops accomplished their mission and displayed enormous courage under withering crossfire from every street corner. But battlefield success is measured by nonmilitary factors as well.

Politically, the murderous gunfight in Mogadishu's teeming streets represented a setback for all parties. The White House suffered a political blow among a bewildered American population who believed that the United States was doing good in a far-off and needy land. This episode reinforced the perception that Clinton was over his head in foreign policy as well as grossly distracted from the formulation of the nation's security agenda. Somalia also endured a defeat because of the subsequent U.S. withdrawal and international loss of interest in the country's plight.

On a wider scale, Washington delayed or avoided responding to other humanitarian tragedies while it distilled the bitter lessons of peacekeeping gone awry in Somalia. As a consequence, many people were killed, maimed, or lost their homes in civil conflicts in Rwanda and Bosnia while Washington and other capitals debated the costs and benefits of rescuing them by intervention, lest the mission sustain casualties and become "another Somalia." U.S. power looked hollow, particularly in the Middle East, where Iraq's dictator and Islamic extremists concluded that America lacked resolve.

For the Somalis, the Battle of Mogadishu was a catastrophe. The fighting decimated and demoralized General Aidid's militiamen. His supporters were appalled at the desecration of the American dead, a violation of Islamic tenets. Some feared massive reprisals from the United States; they contacted UN officials to negotiate before the Americans struck back. Many simply packed their belongings and got out of town in anticipation of a counterattack.[17] No military retribution took place but, even more destructive, the United States simply abandoned Somalia to its dismal history.

Rather than hitting back, Clinton did the reverse. He had no stomach for further combat operations. The United States deserted the country and exacted no revenge against the Aidid. His jubilant fighters drew conclusions about Washington's irresoluteness, a judgment that was broadcast around the world. Other ramifications stemmed from the "Black Hawk down" incident. Before the 2003 U.S.-led invasion into Iraq, Saddam Hussein's Fedayeen trained themselves to reenact a series of "Mogadishus" against their occupiers.[18] Years after the Mogadishu firefight evidence came to light confirming the suspicion that Osama bin Laden, the terrorist mastermind, had assisted Aidid's militias preceding the firefight. America's cut and run from Somalia strengthened bin Laden's standing in the Middle East and encouraged him to undertake more daring operations.[19]

As Americans recoiled at the graphic television images beamed from Somalia of their dead soldiers scourged and dragged through the hot streets amid cheering crowds, immediate repercussions were felt in the highest government circles. Away from the capital in California to promote health care reform, President Clinton expressed anger at his subordinates for not keeping him fully informed of risking ventures in Mogadishu. He demanded of his advisers, "How could this happen?"[20] The president recognized that the Somali mishap had to be reined in, or it would impact prospects of deploying U.S. ground units in Bosnia to enforce an agreement when it was reached as well as placing at risk his domestic programs.

CLINTON'S ASTUTE DEFENSE

Representatives of both political parties grilled Clinton officials beginning the day after the misfired Task Force Ranger foray. The administration's foreign policy team endured more harsh censure when it came to light that General Montgomery had made unanswered requests for AC-130 gunships and battle tanks. Secretary of Defense Aspin's inaction on Montgomery's appeal cast doubt on the administration's competency in security matters. But the U.S. Congress' growing disenchantment with the militarization of Somali policy during the summer of 1993 resulted in the administration's reluctance to grant its local commander all the firepower he requested. One close student of the Mogadishu firefight questioned the likelihood that the heavier weapons would have been actually deployed in the October 3 force package, since the request did not come until September. Moreover, the snatch operation called for light and mobile troops striking quickly into the market area.[21] Whatever the case, the Somalia venture represented another example of the United States injecting inadequate military forces into a dangerous environment. This predilection persisted after Somalia, with severe consequences in Iraq.

The Oval Office got beyond the crisis by blaming the United Nations, whose reputation was further tarnished. It was disingenuous to hold the United Nations responsible for the shortcomings of Task Force Ranger or the larger Quick Reaction Force. Never had the U.S. commando operations come under the UN's control. The United Nations commanded only a 2,700-person logistical contingent. The United States controlled its own combat missions. For an undersiege White House, it was clever politics. Never blame yourself until all other possibilities are exhausted, as Mark Twain advised.

President Clinton also undertook other damage control measures when putting in motion a plan to withdraw U.S. forces. The best defense being a good offense, he ordered a boosting of troop strength in Somalia with 1,700 soldiers in the country and a further 3,600 Marines on ships offshore to act as a reaction force. The aircraft carrier USS Abraham Lincoln served as the flagship of the flotilla, with 10,000 sailors and airmen on duty. The reinforced contingent numbered 20,000 personnel. Counterintuitive as it appeared—to deploy more force to extricate fewer soldiers—it made good public relations sense. Moreover, the Pentagon wanted an adequate standby force, should fighting break out in the seething port city before the scheduled withdrawal of all U.S. troops in five months.

Bill Clinton also dropped the armed pursuit of the warlord Aidid and vowed to help the Somalis "reach agreement among themselves so that they can solve their problems and survive when we leave."[22] Two months after the Ranger raid, Secretary of Defense Les Aspin resigned in the wake of a U.S. Senate report that blamed him and the president for the Somali debacle. It was no secret that Clinton wanted rid of the ineffectual and digressive Aspin. William Perry, a former Pentagon official and Aspin's deputy, assumed the top civilian post in a badly shaken Defense Department. Finally, the White House returned Robert Oakley, the former U.S. ambassador to Somalia, back to Mogadishu to work on a political settlement to end the turmoil. Thus, the Clinton White House put the best face on what was in reality a "cut-and-run" maneuver.

The Reagan administration had done much the same thing after the 1983 suicide bombing of the U.S. Marine barracks in Lebanon, which killed 241 American troops. But it added a twist. Just hours afterward, Ronald Reagan ordered a sea and airborne invasion against the Marxist regime on the Caribbean island of Grenada. Thus, a retreat in one part of the world was obscured by an attack elsewhere. Reagan's Secretary of State George Shultz credibly argued that the Grenada decision had been made before the terrorist assault on the Marines.[23] Nevertheless, the timing was fortuitous in the public relations sense. Clinton studied the Reagan precedent but decided not to copy it.[24]

In the final analysis, the Battle of Mogadishu represented a lose-lose outcome. The U.S. military won a tactical victory, but Washington lost a political battle. The administration looked as if it had fallen asleep at the wheel while trying to reform and stabilize a fractured society. Most significantly, the State Department evinced Pollyannaish optimism about what 400 elite U.S. soldiers could accomplish in clan-split Somalia. Adequate force is a prerequisite to establish order, as the United States was to relearn many times.

Somali warlord Mohamed Farrah Aidid claimed his clan had beaten the world's mightiest military machine in an urban battle. He also took credit for America's dis-engagement from his country. But Somalia lost not only Washington's assistance but also the world's interest in helping it rebuild. Two months after the Ranger raid, the United Nations ended its hunt for Aidid and released eight of his compatriots. The Security Council indulged in a face-saving gesture by setting up a special commission to determine those responsible for the deaths of the UN and U.S. peacekeeping forces in Somalia—a useless endeavor. General Aidid died as he lived, amid gunfire in 1996. Yet, his death brought neither peace to the violence-prone territory nor massive assistance that had preceded the bloody fight in the ancient African city. The international community, led by the United Stated, no longer cared.

By the time the last American soldiers departed on March 25, 1994, some 100,000 U.S. troops had served in Somalia. Operation Restore Hope had cost 30 American lives and left 175 wounded. Had the sacrifices been worth the effort? Estimates of the number of Somalis saved from starvation ran from 100,000 to 250,000 lives. This praiseworthy record may have led Warren Christopher to over-state Washington's contribution to the Horn of Africa country: "We leave the country in a lot better shape than [when] we went in."[25] The semblance of order that preceded the exodus was more mirage than reality. This was not America's fault alone, however. No other state or combination of states rushed to fill the vacancy left by departing GIs. But the U.S. withdrawal left an unstable country that later facilitated terrorist operations by Al Qaeda against American embassies in Kenya and Tanzania in 1998. Eight years afterward, Somalia endured conflicts with Islamist factions eroding still further any American hopes for tranquility in the Horn of Africa.

Somalia chastened the Clinton administration's exuberance for the introduction of U.S. forces in unstable countries. Nevertheless, it did not eliminate elite opinion for an American role in crisis intervention to clamp down on violence in Haiti, Bosnia, Kosovo, and elsewhere. President Clinton, however, hesitantly tiptoed toward calls for placing U.S. soldiers in harm's way to the point of seeming indifference to the fate of the wretched in faraway corners. Rwanda became the first victim of the Clinton avoidance because it was judged peripheral to America's need for stability.

RWANDA: GENOCIDE AND APATHY

That April is the cruelest month was confirmed in the Central African country of Rwanda, a lush, mountainous, and coffee-growing state. Violence flared there as well as in Bosnia, Angola, East Timor, and the Nagorno-Karabakh region of Azerbaijan in the post–Berlin Wall period. It was a particularly bloody stretch of history, but in Rwanda the gates of hell truly opened. Just days after American forces completed their withdrawal from Somalia, on April 6, 1994, Rwanda leapt into the genocidal abyss. On that date, Juvénal Habyarimana, the Rwandan president, was killed when a ground-fired missile struck his plane as it approached the suddenly darkened Kigali Airport. The downed aircraft also took the lives of several government officials returning from negotiations in Tanzania where bordering states expressed their alarm about the multiplying killings between Rwanda's Hutu and Tutsi communities. The Tanzanian meeting drove home the point that if a Hutu-Tutsi civil war resumed, it would spill across borders, engulfing Rwanda's neighbors.

Under pressure in Tanzania, Habyarimana pledged to incorporate more of the minority Tutsi in his one-party government to alleviate the brewing tensions. His party, Mouvement Républicain National pour le Dévelopement (MRND), had resisted power sharing. With outside pressure, especially from France, a peaceful transition might have been possible well before the April 1994 plane explosion. Paris gradually had replaced Brussels as the Kigali government's main benefactor in financing and supplying arms to the Habyarimana regime after it took power in 1975. French backing made the president impervious to international demands to move toward a consensual government.[26] At the start of his presidency, he had subdued the volatile Maryland-sized country of 7 million. In time, the peaceful exterior revealed a dictatorship and exclusion of the Tutsis from the political process.

Interethnic conflict was not something new to Rwanda, a former Belgian colony. Violent clashes killing thousands had broken out repeatedly before and after Rwanda achieved its independence in 1962. This bloody history prompted outside states to attempt to head off another harrowing explosion. In August 1993, the Arusha Accords were signed between the Hutu government of Habyarimana and the Tutsi-dominated Rwanda Patriotic Front, with elections scheduled within 22 months. The UN Security Council adopted Resolution 872, creating UN Assistance Mission for Rwanda (UNAMIR) in October. Canadian Brigadier General Raméo A. Dallaire with a battalion of Belgian troops took command of UNAMIR. Another 800 Ghanaian soldiers and 900 Bangladeshi personnel also joined the peacekeeping mission.

All through early 1994, General Dallaire informed UN headquarters in New York City of impending bloodshed, pleaded for reinforcements, and requested permission to conduct arms seizures to no avail. Within Rwanda, the genocidal demons had been cultivated and organized by extremists among the Hutu population, who homicidally connived to block implementation of the Arusha Accords. In all likelihood, Habyarimana's own army shot down his plane because the president appeared to be assenting to demands for Tutsi inclusion. Radio Rwanda, the official government radio station, and private studios, especially Radio Mille Collines, labeled all Tutsi and tolerant Hutu as enemies of the country. These broadcasts instilled fear, incited violence, and fingered moderate Hutu and all Tutsis for elimination. Extremists referred to the Tutsi as "cockroaches." The uneducated and unemployed were mobilized into militias, not unlike the Brown Shirts during Germany's Weimar Republic. Of these, the Interahamwe became notoriously effective killers; they were attached as a youth wing to the ruling MRND. It organized disciplined cadres nationwide that gave rudimentary military training to street toughs, criminals, and other dregs. The Interahamwe became the Hutu killing machine.

The day after the downing of the presidential plane, systematic bloodletting started against opponents of the MRND regime, prodemocracy Hutus, and the Tutsis in Kigali. One of the first moves of the Interahamwe militia, as it embarked on a genocidal campaign, was to kill 10 Belgian UN soldiers. In response, France sent troops but they merely evacuated French and other European citizens. On April 21, 1994, the 15 ambassadors in the Security Council passed Resolution 912 that withdrew the majority of the peacekeepers despite General Dallaire's protests and pleas for between 5,000 and 8,000 troops to quell or at least retard the unfolding horror all around him. Hundreds of thousands of Tutsis made a mass exodus into Tanzania, straining the existing skimpy food, health, and sanitation facilities.

What took place during the next couple of months was an orgy of insensate cruelty, human suffering, and crude barbarity. Although some victims were shot or blown to bits by hand grenades, the vast majority of people were hacked to death, face-to-face, by hate-crazed youths armed only with machetes. Hutu militias and freelance killers burned Tutsis alive in churches, killed them as they fled, and slaughtered men, women, and infants in designated assemblages. They flung bodies in rivers, left them along roads, and disposed of them in garbage trucks assigned for the task. The killings went forward unhindered for three months while the world sat up and took notice but did nothing. Estimates of the carnage place the figures at about 800,000 deaths during the 100-day rampage that was carried out with mad jubilation.

By May first, the top echelon of the Clinton administration discussed how to organize and pay for military intervention by states bordering Rwanda. The decision makers rejected any U.S. deployment to halt the killing. As the UN Secretary General Boutros-Ghali spoke louder about the frenzied killing in Rwanda, Washington rushed for cover. President Clinton offered his assessment: "Lesson number one is, don't go into one of these things and say, as the U.S. said when we started in Somalia, 'Maybe we'll be done in a month because it's a humanitarian crisis.' . . . Because there are almost always political problems and sometimes military conflicts, which bring about these crises."[27]

The Rwandan Patriotic Front (RPF) rallied its forces and turned the tables on the Hutu militias by mid-July 1994. The RPF swept into Kigali and put to flight the perpetrators of the Tutsi mayhem along with the greater Hutu population. Another humanitarian nightmare ensued. Fearing retribution, the Hutus fled across the Zaire border (Democratic Republic of the Congo) and into improvised camps in Goma and Bukavu, breaking records for the largest and fastest exodus. Immense suffering took place as the latest batch of refugees succumbed to exhaustion, starvation, and cholera. Mass graves, stacks of dead corpses, and some 4,000 orphans presented scenes of appalling horror among the overcrowded and filthy camps.[28]

Given the public uproar, the United States was unable to continue to stand on the sidelines. Washington deployed some 4,000 troops to the Zaire camps and mass airlifted water and supplies that cost an estimated $400 million. Nevertheless, the U.S. troops stayed clear of any duties that might be construed as peacekeeping operations. They confined themselves to humanitarian activities of distributing food, water, and shelters to the destitute people. With the Somalia case still fresh, the Defense Department counseled against a military role to interdict the mass killing. The Pentagon even refused to jam the extremist Hutu radio broadcasts that guided the militias, fearing a first step down the slippery slope to involvement. America's stance toward Rwanda was a policy of nothing ventured, nothing lost, except for hundreds of thousands of lives in a distant land.

The defining scandal of the Clinton administration was not the Monica Lewinsky tryst in the White House but rather its callous disregard of luckless souls in Rwanda. The United States abdicated political responsibility and shirked moral leadership in order to avoid "another Somalia." Additionally, Washington stalled and frustrated United Nations reactions to the genocide. It downplayed the crisis and inhibited the Security Council from mounting an effective countering operation. The president and senior officials in the State Department treated the Rwanda catastrophe as a "peacekeeping headache to be avoided" not a "human rights disaster requiring urgent response."[29] Political order in Rwanda fell outside American concerns about stability in an obscure African precinct.

To be sure, other states, particularly European countries such as France that had cultural and political ties to Rwanda, also behaved abysmally. At the same time as the

Rwanda genocide commenced in April, the European nations similarly watched as the Serb forces attacked the U.N.-mandated "safe areas" of Gorazde in Bosnia. The Western middleweight powers simply marched lockstep behind the United States, even when it was in retreat. America's political preeminence demanded that it lead. Instead Washington shrugged. Later, after Washington recovered its bearings, the Clinton government prodded the United Nations and European states to intervene to stop the bloodshed in the Balkans, because stability in Europe was more prized than in Central Africa.

If anyone wants to glimpse a world without a superpower to intervene on behalf of helpless people, then the Rwandan slaughterhouse offers such an example of a power vacuum, as historian Niall Ferguson observed. Such a political universe is reminiscent of the Dark Ages after the fall of the Roman Empire, when anarchy, marauders, and deadly plagues "stalked the world of Charlemagne."[30] The Rwandan genocide overlapped with a crisis closer to the United States, however.

HAITI: WHERE THE PAST IS PROLOGUE

Five hundred miles from the Florida coast sits the island of Hispaniola, on the western third of which lies the Republic of Haiti. It shares two distinctions from the rest of Latin America. It is the Western Hemisphere's poorest state and it ranks second, only to Cuba, in possessing the most tortured historical relationship with the United States. Soon after the American colonies won their freedom from King George III, Haiti imitated its northern role model in the 1804 slave revolt that won independence from France. Despite its similar birth as the future United States, Haiti's political evolution diverged from its powerful northern neighbor. For 200 years, the small urbanized and predominately mulatto elite has lorded over the majority black peasantry. Haitian history is replete with turmoil, violence, political corruption, and despotic rule. Underdeveloped and economically backward, Haiti became one of the worst-case studies among third world's impoverished and authoritarian countries. Mother Theresa, no stranger to destitution, is said to have characterized Haiti as the "fifth world."

Haiti enjoyed a sorry interaction with the United States prior to the Clinton presidency. It suffered from neglect to subjugation, followed again by inattention. President Woodrow Wilson dispatched armed forces to the Caribbean nation in 1915, ostensibly to restore order, bolster democracy, and protect access to the newly opened Panama Canal. After an occupation spanning five presidencies, Franklin Roosevelt ended direct governance and pulled American troops from Haiti in 1934 as part of his Good Neighbor policy toward Latin America. The modest progress in political stability and economic progress made during 19 years of U.S. military rule receded with the return of homegrown tyrants. Thereafter, Haiti slipped in and out of Washington's political consciousness until early in the 1990s.

From Port-au-Prince's slums, Jean-Bertrand Aristide, a young Catholic priest, emerged as a charismatic opponent of the junta. As the head of the Lavalas Movement (from the Creole tongue for a flash flood that destroys everything in its path), Aristide championed the poor and disenfranchised. His election with 67 percent of the vote in December 1990 hastened the fall of military rule and led briefly to short-lived expectations for political reform. Once in power, Aristide's inflammatory rhetoric against the "bourgeoisie" and contempt for parliamentary or constitutional niceties aroused fear among the wealthy elite and top army officers. He showed himself to be no Haitian version of a Jeffersonian Democrat. In fact, the new president's espousal of liberation theology resulted in his being defrocked by the Vatican. His high-handedness in pursuit of a societal reordering alarmed the privileged circles, which orchestrated Aristide's overthrow in 1991.

The George H. W. Bush administration dealt minimally with the Haitian military coup. It declared Aristide's ouster a threat to democracy, extended asylum to its deposed president and his coterie, and turned back the Haitian boat people who fled to U.S. shores from political repression and economic hardship. Washington, along with most other capitals, refused to extend diplomatic recognition to the usurpers. It also froze Haitian financial assets in American banks in a lame effort to convince the coup plotters to return to democracy.[31] The Bush government released about $1 million a month to Aristide for expenses while in exile from Haitian funds at the U.S. Federal Reserve Bank.

None of these small-scale measures proved effective in curbing the junta's power or in convincing it to relent. As such, they opened the administration to charges of neglect, racism, and inappropriate priorities. The United States, critics charged, employed military force to overthrow a Marxist regime in Grenada during the early 1980s but turned a blind eye to rescuing a democracy on another Caribbean island. The Bush government, its detractors added, intervened in Panama to oust its drug-lord-run government but demurred in restoring a black, democratically elected president.

Presidential candidate Bill Clinton criticized Bush's dawdling in the 1992 presidential campaign. In a preelection speech to the Los Angeles World Affairs Council, the presidential contender said that he would seek to "buttress democratic forces in Haiti, Peru, Cuba, and throughout the Western Hemisphere." During the presidential race, Clinton frequently faulted President Bush for playing "racial politics" by repatriating Haitian asylum seekers. Clinton passionately pronounced, "I wouldn't be shipping those poor people back."[32] His pronouncements implied a welcome mat to Haitians fleeing poverty and political persecution; he would soon feel the consequences of his invitation.

Once in the presidency, Bill Clinton, in fact, reversed his campaign position and tightened his predecessor's restrictions on Haitian emigrants because of the growing domestic opposition to the inflow, particularly into the state of Florida, which received the lion's share of the boat people. As governor of Arkansas, Clinton learned a sobering political lesson from the 1980 Mariel boatlift from Cuba. Governor Clinton helped President Jimmy Carter, his fellow Democrat in the White House, by allowing the fleeing Cubans what he thought was just a temporary home. But the federal government kept the refugees in Arkansas past the state's gubernatorial election date. Governor Clinton thought the Cuban refugees played a role in his defeat at the polls, when voters became disenchanted with him after the newcomers in Fort Chafee rioted against their incarceration. Fearing a repetition, President Clinton promptly instituted a naval blockade off Haiti's coast to stem the waves of refugees while his administration searched for solutions to the Haitian predicament.

Espousing negotiations as the best option for dealing with the Haitian junta and restoring political order, the new president convened talks on New York City's Governors Island. Clinton pressed for a UN agreement and endorsement by the Organization of American States. Concluded on July 3, 1993, the settlement called for democratic elections, modernization of the security forces, and the return of the deposed Aristide as the lawful president by October 30. It failed in any judicial accounting of the junta for its seizure of power, nor did the abuse of human rights receive attention in the accord. In fact, the Lavalas role in government stood to be reduced.

The United Nations Mission in Haiti (UNMIH) was established to oversee the agreement but the UN mission did not take up its peacekeeping duties until after Clinton militarily intervened 15 months later. Afterward, UNMIH was extended to 1996 under which 24 countries contributed military personnel.[33] Before that, General Raoul Cédras, the chief Haitian strongman, accepted the UN-brokered plan for a return of the ousted president but soon reneged on it. Betwixt the cup of Clinton's good intentions and the lip of his reluctance to wield military power, there were to be many slips.

USS HARLAN COUNTY FIASCO

In advance of the deadline for restoration of democracy, the Governors Island agreement called for landing 1,300 UN police and military advisers to retrain the Haitian army for a nonpolitical stabilizing role in a democratic society. A contingent of 200 lightly armed American soldiers and Canadian Mounties steamed into the Port-au-Prince harbor on board the *USS Harlan County* on October 11. Before the amphibious ship could land at the Haitian capital's docks, it was defied by a rowdy crowd of demonstrators, who had been orchestrated by the Haitian military leaders. The protestors chanted "Somalia, Somalia" to draw a parallel to the recent American debacle in the African country. News of a superpower's setbacks travels fast even to remote islands such as Haiti. No further evidence is needed to prove that the world's autocrats took note of Washington's balking in face of conflict in Somalia or elsewhere.

Rather than disembarking the advisers and facing down the demonstrators, the U.S. government stopped the operation. Two days later, it ordered the *Harlan County* to sail away. That a mob of dockside thugs could stare down the reigning superpower spoke volumes about its shortage of resolve. Madeleine Albright later reflected in her autobiography that the naval vessel's beating a retreat was "a low point in Clinton administration foreign policy."[34]

Reacting to the black eye, Clinton reimposed sanctions that had been lifted when it seemed Haiti was moving toward honoring the Governor Island's agreement. He also froze Haitian state assets and restricted travel to the Caribbean island, as had his predecessor. The junta-choreographed rebuff of the *Harlan County* ensured that General Cédras would not live up to the Governor Island negotiations. Even worse, Washington was caught flat-footed without a fallback option.

Coming just a little more than a week after the bloody Ranger foray in Mogadishu, the administration's decision makers were loath to run into "another Somalia." Les Aspin's Pentagon was especially reluctant to put lightly armed military and police personnel in harm's way as well as to embark on an open-ended commitment to another failing state. The Director of Central Intelligence Woolsey also warned of the dangers of landing troops in Haiti. Prior to Aristide's presidency, the CIA had been paying Rauol Cédras, Philippe Biamby, and other coup plotters under the table. They had overthrown the Marxist cleric-turned-politician and now ran the Haitian regime. Understandably, intelligence community was less than thrilled to intervene on Aristide's behalf.[35]

Politicians joined the chorus opposing the dispatch of ground troops to the small island nation. Bob Dole, the Senate minority leader, threatened legislation against the White House if it deployed U.S. forces except to meet a national security emergency. The Kansas Republican pitched his stand as a constitutional one of protecting the legislative branch's prerogatives against an overweening executive. Even some Democratic lawmakers took a dim view of deploying U.S. forces, lest they encounter another Somali-type reception. Isolationist impulses gripped both parties in the immediate post–Cold War years. Partisan politics was also a factor, however, as Republicans hoped to take advantage of Clinton's troubles, while he sought a modicum of normalcy in Haiti.

The U.S. government turned once again to the United Nations to resolve the Haitian stalemate. Urged by Clinton's UN representative, the Security Council imposed wide-ranging sanctions on Haiti. The Pentagon deployed warships to enforce the oil and arms embargo. The Cédras-headed regime was unimpressed and refused to fulfill its July pledge to step aside for Aristide's return. The sanctions exacted a heavy toll on the Haitian people. Light industry withered. Tourism dried up. Unemployment spiked to 70 percent. Electricity in the cities disappeared. Imported food vanished. The sanctions reportedly caused a thousand deaths a month among children under five years of age according to a study released in November 1993 by the Harvard Center for Population and Development Studies.[36]

Haiti's worsening economic straits quickened the flight of refugees from hunger as well as persecution at the hands of the regime's "attaches." An unknown number perished at sea in flimsy crafts trying to reach the Florida coast. Washington responded by rescuing boatloads of desperate people. It placed them in temporary quarters at the U.S. naval base on Cuba's Guantanamo Bay and in military bases in Panama to avoid a political backlash within the United States. The junta and its cronies were isolated from material want by their horde of American dollars. If anything, the U.S. embargo furnished an opportunity for the Haitian rulers and their allies to cash in on sales of black market goods. Contraband, even small gasoline containers, was smuggled over the border of the neighboring Dominican Republic. The ruling troika colluded with their military counterparts in Santo Domingo to make millions of dollars by breaking the oil embargo.

President Clinton promised even harsher sanctions if General Cédras refused to relinquish power by January 15, 1994. When the deadline passed without a regime change, both Cédras and Aristide concluded that the administration's threats amounted to mere bluffs. Searching for an alternative, Washington concocted a scheme that called upon Cédras to resign his army command and for Aristide to name a new prime minister, someone more palatable to the junta. Additionally, the plan envisioned the Haitian parliament to pass an amnesty law protecting the army officers who staged the anti-Aristide coup, as another inducement to facilitate cooperation. Aristide and Cédras greeted it with distain.

Aristide, who set up a prince-across-the-water court in Washington, denounced the administration's refugee policy as "racist" and "criminal." Since Clinton had doubled the monthly amount of money paid from Haiti's frozen funds to Aristide and allowed the former president to receive some $2.5 million in royalties paid per month by international carriers of long-distance telephone calls operating in Haiti, the exiled president had funds to buy influence.[37] Aristide paid high-priced lobbyists and law firms to work on his behalf to generate media attention. His appearances took on celebrity trappings. He served as best man at the wedding of Bobby Kennedy Jr., the son of the slain 1960s political icon and brother of John F. Kennedy. High-level Clinton officials courted Aristide to conciliate him. On one occasion, the Pentagon accorded him a 21-gun salute, followed by a briefing from Secretary of Defense Perry. On the political offensive, Aristide circulated a statement to the United Nations and the Organization of American States in which he compared Washington's turning back asylum seekers to a "floating Berlin Wall."[38]

The White House's irresolution incurred criticism legislators, particularly the Congressional Black Caucus in the House of Representatives. Joined by liberal Democrats in both Houses, the Black Caucus pushed their case with growing headway, impelling the administration to edge glacially toward armed intervention. The Oval Office recognized the political importance of the liberal wing of the Democratic Party and especially the Afro-American community to its party's fortunes in the November 1994 congressional election and his own second-term prospects. One participant in the UN Security Council inner circle later wrote, "Military intervention in Haiti derived in part from a need by the Clinton Administration to demonstrate domestically that the USA retained the will and capacity to act decisively on the international level."[39]

The Clinton government returned to the United Nations and obtained the Security Council's unanimous vote to impose a near-total embargo (with the exception of food and medicine) on May 6, 1994. With this vote, the administration adopted the sanction policy long favored by Aristide despite concerns that a stringent economic ban would merely deepen the plight of ordinary Haitians without hastening the departure of the Haitian military rulers. Sanctions made a poor country even more desperate. Sanctions, however, enabled Washington to claim to have discharged a responsibility without resolving a problem. In short, by slapping on sanctions, it did "something."

Unfazed, the junta was prepared to endure sanctions regardless of the privations its citizens suffered. The downtrodden voted with their feet, or rather with unseaworthy craft, to flee the repression and privation. Some 5,000 fled each week during the early summer. Between August and the first week of September, the figure surged to 30,000 asylum seekers. Haiti's political turmoil was directly impacting the United States. Next the administration shut down U.S. commercial air links with Haiti, cut off travel visas to the United States, and froze the U.S. assets of Haitian citizens, marking the first time that Washington froze individual assets of another country's nationals since the Vietnam War. Still, the Haitian generals stood steadfast. Washington had to up the ante or else suffer another embarrassment about tolerating instability in its backyard.

TOWARD INTERVENTION

At the end of July, Clinton sought and gained Security Council authorization for a multinational force in Resolution 940 to "use all necessary means" to eject the Haitian junta and return Aristide to the presidency. The UN vote represented a first time for such authority in the Western Hemisphere. It also protected the president's political flank from adverse opinion. Once obtained, the authorization signaled that the military intervention was a near certainty unless the Haitian junta departed. The Security Council resolution set no deadline for an incursion but called for "the restoration of democracy and prompt return of the legitimately elected President."[40]

Caught between the anvil of the Black Caucus and the hammer of refugees deluging on Florida shores, President Clinton resolved to lance the Haitian boil with the only means available—military power. But first he tried, as a last-ditch effort, a covert operation aimed to bring down the three-man junta. The CIA launched a $12 million "secret enterprise" to buy "friendly elements" in the Haitian armed forces with cash and supplies weapons and communications equipment. The agency got no takers.[41] With all other options expended—negotiations, sanctions, and covert action—the White House chose intervention.

By mid-September, the president acknowledged that the United States had "exhausted diplomacy" to calm the island's turbulence. Yet, the Clinton administration chose diplomacy one last time, although a U.S. military invasion was in the immediate offing. It dispatched three emissaries—former president Jimmy Carter, former chairman of the Joint Chiefs of Staff Colin Powell, and Senator Sam Nunn (Georgia Democrat)—to parley with General Cédras in Port-au-Prince. Washington let it be known that its threesome would discuss only the "modalities" for the departure of the ruling clique, not further delays. The three interlocutors touched down in Haiti on September 17 with 36 hours to convince the junta to allow for a peaceful military entry. As U.S. warplanes lifted off their runways, General Cédras and two other junta leaders agreed to relinquish power, leave the island, and accede peacefully to what was described in Pentagonese as "a permissive invasion." It was a good deal for the triumvirate, for they kept their ill-gotten gains from the sanction-busting schemes. Still, Carter termed them honorable men as they decamped for exile in Panama. The Port-au-Prince agreement averted a fight between the junta's puny army and police and the U.S. combat forces.

In one crucial dimension, Bill Clinton both continued the policy of his immediate predecessor and his successor; he engaged in regime change and imposed democracy for stabilization. George H. W. Bush tossed out Panama's General Manuel Noriega, and George W. Bush ousted Iraq's Saddam Hussein. Getting rid of troublesome dictators was becoming the American way of doing business. Haiti constituted President Clinton's first regime change, but it was not to be his last. Half a decade afterward, a more confident Clinton agitated successfully to rid the Balkans of Serbian President Slobodan Milošević but much blood would flow before that.

On September 19, 1994, the American-led military invasion met no resistance from the ragtag Haitian armed forces of only 7,000 (including police) poorly armed and trained men. The Haitians lacked military tanks, aircraft, warships, or even armed helicopters.

Off Haiti's coast, two aircraft carriers, the *USS America* and the *USS Dwight D. Eisenhower*, cruised with a complement of 2,000 Army and Special Operations troops and 50 helicopters. Twenty thousand U.S. troops parachuted or disembarked on the western edge of Hispaniola Island to take up another stabilizing occupation with the expectations of a better life among ordinary Haitians. And to jump ahead of this narrative, once more, little would survive the military pullout. Less than a month after intervention, on October 15, Washington returned Aristide to the presidency amid cheering Haitian crowds.

Operation Uphold Democracy was almost anticlimactic after several months of Hamlet-like indecision in the White House. Clinton's irresolution, in fact, detracted from what might otherwise have been a triumph of presidential decisiveness and burst of American might in pursuit of a worthy cause. Instead, a sigh of relief rather than pride characterized the mood among students of American power still haunted by the "Mogadishu syndrome."

President Clinton never relished drinking from the cup of battered states. In Haiti's case, he feared it would descend into a low-intensity battleground reminiscent of Somalia. He feared accusations that he would be deploying young Americans into a type of combat that he had skipped in the Vietnam War. Political calculations also swayed policy decisions. Casualties could jeopardize the president's standing in the polls, his domestic agenda, and his party's prospects in the November congressional elections. His apprehensions were justified as the Republicans retook control of the House of Representatives after almost three decades of minority status. But the causes of this political realignment had more to do with a broad array of domestic issues, among them the failed jobs bill and health care reform, than the Haiti question.[42]

Yet Bill Clinton wanted to salvage at least a modicum of foreign policy success from his Haitian initiative in light of the Somali setback and the Bosnian impasse (to be discussed in the next chapter). Seven months after the intervention, he flew to the island republic. In a made for photo opportunity, a radiant Clinton posed with jubilant crowds and celebrated "bringing back the promise of liberty to this long-troubled land."[43] Almost a year later as political slayings marked the Haitian elections, Clinton still portrayed the Haitian intervention as triumph in his 1996 State of the Union address, where he prematurely proclaimed that "the dictators are gone, and democracy has a new day."[44]

Fortunately for the West Wing, media scrutiny on the continuing Haitian troubles lapsed soon after the introduction of troops and the return of Aristide. Other pressing issues, such as bleeding Bosnia, captivated interest. Political violence, long a staple of Haitian life, persisted under the newly repatriated government. U.S. operations in Haiti totaled $1.2 billion by March 1995, when Washington officially handed the Haitian mission over to the UNMIH. The transfer did not sever Washington's involvement, however. Twenty-five hundred U.S. troops remained in the UN contingent of nearly seven thousand peacekeepers and police officers from 30 countries. The U.S. expenditures finally reached $3.2 billion by the end of Washington's training and development programs. When possible, the Clinton administration preferred to funnel its financial aid through nongovernmental organizations, wary that money directed to the Haitian government would be siphoned off to private accounts. But however commendable, even the best of these specific measures were but footprints on the beach.

Within Haiti the political waters reverted to their familiar deadly and corrupt crosscurrents after its 1996 presidential election. Because the constitution barred Aristide another term, his handpicked successor, Réné Préval, a member of the outgoing president's Lavalas movement, came to office shackled to his predecessor and compromised by a corrupt electoral process and by widespread violence. Préval slipped into the presidency with only 28 percent of the electoral population voting. Soon after, the familiar patterns of the Duvalierist dictatorship returned. Opponents suffered the loss of life, limb or property for speaking out against the regime. Lavalas loyalists prospered from government largesse or inside contacts. The poor suffered as they had before Aristide's rise to power. Wisely, however, American policy was informed by a pragmatism that dictated a hands-off approach to Haitian governments. Micromanaging an American brand of democracy, as tried in Iraq, was prudently avoided. Better to leave the Haitians to manage themselves than having outsiders do it and reaping a whirlwind.

In November 2000, Aristide won reelection as president in a vote marred by irregularities and violence. Returned to power, Aristide's governance was marinated in corruption. These events disabused even the most ardent optimists of Haitian recovery. The United Nations, as a consequence, shut down its Haiti mission and withdrew from the country in February 2001. The reversion to past times was complete. The climax of Aristide's story did not play itself out, until he fled into exile on board a U.S. airplane to Africa during the George W. Bush administration, when Washington tried again to stabilize the unruly republic. Well before the United States engineered Aristide's regime change, the Bosnian crisis obsessed Washington.

CHAPTER 5

BOSNIA: WAR AND INTERVENTION

The purpose of all wars is peace.

St. Augustine

The foundations of empire are often occasions of woe; their dismemberment, always.

Evelyn Waugh

You can always count on the Americans to do the right thing after they have exhausted all other possibilities.

Winston Churchill

THE CONFLICT IN BOSNIA AND HERZEGOVINA DIFFERED in two major ways from the Somali and Haitian strife for American foreign policy mandarins. First, Bosnia lay within the heart of Europe and, second, it sprung from the political disintegration of a whole nation-state. Lying close to the boundaries of America's foremost alliance, the North Atlantic Treaty Organization, the Yugoslavian violence demanded resolution or it threatened to engulf southeastern Europe. The crisis became *the* central international issue of President Clinton's first term.

If Somalia made Americans circumspect about militarized humanitarian enterprises, then the violent Bosnian disorder prompted many, even antiwar opponents, to be uneasy about standing on the sidelines of history, while a brutal dictatorship such as Slobodan Milošević's in Serbia promoted the mass killing of its Muslim population. The Bosnia dilemma crystallized the debate on interventions as no other trouble spot in the first half of the 1990s. However disinclined Bill Clinton initially felt about entering an interethnic civil war, his ultimate decision resulted in military, political, and diplomatic ramifications far removed from the operation itself. It reversed the slow-moving U.S. disengagement from Europe after the Berlin Wall's crash, clinched the expansion of NATO eastward, and led to a much more militarily intrusive operation on behalf of the Muslims living in Kosovo province four years afterward. More fundamentally, the Bosnia intervention acutely raised the issues of regional stability and nation-building endeavors to a prominence unmatched by the earlier crises. America's hand in reconstructing civic order in the Balkans even surfaced in the 2000 election and exploded in the George W. Bush presidency because of the example it set for Afghanistan and Iraq.

BACKGROUND TO THE BALKAN CRISIS

The multinational Yugoslavian entity was a creation of the winds of national self-determination that blew fiercely in the Balkans at the turn of the twentieth century. The vintage term *Balkanization* meant small quarrelsome states and derived from the tortured legacy of the region. Only the ramshackle Austro-Hungarian Empire managed to bring a semblance of peace to a rebellious arena and then for only a time. And as every schoolchild knows, the Serb student's assassination of the Austrian Archduke Ferdinand in Sarajevo in 1914 ignited the fuse leading to World War I that saw the breakup of the Austro-Hungarian kingdom. Balkanization re-earned its meaning in the 1990s, when history and political ambition again veered the Balkans into the heart of darkness.

Cobbled together after 1918 from lands within the defunct Austro-Hungarian and Ottoman empires, Yugoslavia was a mélange of nationalities each with distinct religion and culture. After the declaration of the Kingdom of Serbs, Croats, and Slovenes as a constitutional monarchy in 1921, Yugoslavia, as it was renamed in 1929, endured as an independent kingdom until it was overrun by Nazi forces in World War II. During that war, interethnic killings ripped at the fragile fabric of society as the country sunk into several smaller civil wars. These conflicts within the greater war planted seeds of hatred that bore unusually bitter fruit. The memories of collaboration with the Nazi occupiers or communist resistance against the Third Reich stayed fresh among the population and shaped attitudes as the Berlin Wall crumbled.

Following the German defeat, the country fell within the Soviet bloc and under the leadership of the communist partisan leader Marshal Josip Broz Tito and his guerrilla bands. Under Tito's presidency, Yugoslavia split with Moscow in 1948 and pursued an independent "road to socialism." In 1963, it promulgated a new constitution establishing a socialist federal state made up of six republics: Croatia, Bosnia and Herzegovina, Montenegro, Macedonia, Slovenia, and Serbia, the latter of which encompassed two semiautonomous regions—Vojvodina and Kosovo. Intrarepublic cohesion eroded after Tito's death in 1980 as separatists and independence tendencies reawakened.

Replaying their historical role, Russia, Turkey, Greece, Germany, France, and Britain bolstered specific nationalities in the early 1990s simmering turmoil as they had during the nineteenth century. Moscow held the Serbs dear, since they were Slavic peoples who shared the Eastern Orthodox belief. Athens, a center of the Orthodox faith, also backed their coreligious brethren. Remembering their Serb allies against the Nazis, London and Paris initially evinced a reluctance to confront Belgrade no matter how egregious its behavior. Later in the decade, both became fed up with Serbian atrocities. Germany's partiality belonged to the Croats with whom it had been allied in World War II. In addition, a sizable Croatian minority existed within Germany. The Germans were also pro-Slovenia because of a shared

Roman Catholicism and because Germany's Slovenian minority held an affinity to its homeland.

The 2 million Bosnian Muslim community was the odd man out in Europe; it aroused little sympathy in the Continent's chancelleries. But the Balkan Muslims, despite being largely secularized and Europeanized, did arouse sympathy in the Middle East, particularly from Turkey, Saudi Arabia, and Iran. Their deaths and rapes at the hands of Serbs or Croats also struck a humanitarian chord in the United States, the perennial champion of the underdog, which equated Muslim survival with the region's stability.

The Serb-Muslim animosity threatened to reignite the Turkish-Greek enmity that existed for centuries. An overriding reason to contain and squelch the Balkan violence stemmed from the widespread concern that the ethnic infighting would eventually pull in Turkey on the side of the Muslims and Greece and Russia on the side of the Serbs. While this worst-case scenario never materialized, the possibility existed. As such, it eventually concentrated minds in Washington on halting the conflict before it triggered a wider conflagration.

A symbolic turning point in Yugoslavia's contemporary history took place on June 28, 1989, when several hundred thousand Serbs gathered at the Field of Blackbirds outside of Priština, the capital of Kosovo, to commemorate the 600-year anniversary of the Battle of Kosovo Polje. At the site in 1389, Serbian knights led by Prince Lazar fell to the Turkish invaders. The epic anti-Muslim struggle, in Serb minds, ushered in five centuries of darkness and misrule. In Serbian lore, the conflict attained a cataclysmic, even quasi-sacred, image of heroic resistance to the Ottoman Empire and, by extension, to any foreign interference. Over the centuries, Kosovo Polje gained a mystical hold on the Serbian imagination.[1] It gave rise to the cult of Serbian victimization that justified putting other nationalities to the sword. Six centuries afterward, the demagogic Slobodan Milošević manipulated and exploited the imagined glory of the historic struggle to whip up a Serbian nationalistic fever in his campaign speeches.

On December 9, 1990, Milošević rode this ethnic passion to the presidency in Serbia's first multiparty elections since World War II. A product of the communist bureaucracy, Milošević and his wife and political ally, Mirjana Marković, capitalized on Serbian nationalism to clinch their hold on power and strengthen the authoritarianism that they had grown accustomed to from their party membership. History in Yugoslavia, as Faulkner reminded us of the American South, was not dead; it was not even past. Moreover, demagogues could always rekindle a people's worst impulses. Milošević's ambition to make Serbia the dominant player in the Yugoslav federation of nearly 24 million people precipitated the country's spiral into disunity and warfare.

Neither Slovenes nor Croatians wished to live in a Serb-dominated Yugoslavia under an authoritarian Milošević, and they rebelled. Belgrade struck back through its auxiliaries. These Serbian militias battled other nationalities in territories they regarded as ancestral lands to hack out exclusive Serb entities and link them to form a Greater Serbia. They mounted systematic campaigns of atrocities, employed summary executions, and widespread rape as means of intimidation. Made up of common criminals, violence junkies, and other societal misfits, these militiamen relished their grisly territorial grab. The Serbs, in turn, fell victim to this "ethnic cleansing" as the Croatians and Muslim adopted the same macabre practices in the latter stages of the war to regain historic territory.

THE UNITED STATES STEPS AWAY FROM
THE BOSNIAN *CAULDRON*

The George H. W. Bush administration did its utmost to stay clear of becoming militarily entangled as the slaughter worsened in southeastern Europe. In the words of Secretary State James Baker, Washington "felt comfortable with European Community's taking responsibility for handling the crisis in the Balkans."[2] Judging by how U.S. interests were tied to political equanimity, Washington missed the importance of the brewing Balkan conflict. American thinking was still conventionally rooted in seeing threats only from other states, such as the Soviet Union, not from the disorder that bred terrorist sanctuaries or internal instability that could draw the United States into a vortex. As Baker picturesquely phrased his view, "We don't have a dog in this fight."[3] Although a cavalier statement, it set the direction for the Bush policy. Influential Republicans, including former president Ronald Reagan, joined the stentorian voice of Britain's Margaret Thatcher in criticizing George Bush's coldhearted realpolitik for shrugging off American ideals and ignoring Europe's historical inability to solve its own problems.

For once, an American administration was not split among itself on a major foreign policy question involving the potential use of military power. The Defense Department, having just finished the Persian Gulf War, firmly opposed another military intervention, especially one that carried overtones of a Vietnamese civil war. The State Department, which often took a different tack from the Pentagon, refrained from dissent. Secretary Baker readily agreed with his president's decision that the United States should not "fight its fourth war in Europe in this century," referring to the two world conflicts and the Cold War.[4]

Europe, in fact, asserted its own prerogative on resolving the trouble in the center of its Continent. Luxembourg's Foreign Minister Jacque Poos, whose country held the rotating presidency of the European Community, threw the post–Berlin Wall's European sentiment into sharp relief with his emphatic declaration: "This is the hour of Europe, not the hour of the Americans."[5] The Western European Union (WEU)—the European Community's defense arm—represented an independent apparatus from the U.S.-dominated NATO and a military instrument, if Europeans chose that option. The raging Balkan inferno offered a test case for this newfound European unity, one that produced an abdication from any decisive action.

Given these constraints and its preferences, the Bush foreign policy team pursued a diplomatic solution rather than a military one for the unfolding conflict in the Continent's southeastern quadrant. Secretary Baker visited Belgrade on June 21, 1991 to meet with the heads of each of the six republics in the Federation Palace, a Soviet-era monstrosity. His message included, first, a plea for preserving Yugoslavia's territorial integrity and, second, a warning against unilateral declarations of independence. He said the United States would withhold diplomatic recognition of any self-declared independent states. Consensual modifications of borders were acceptable, if all parties agreed. All this fell on deaf ears.[6]

The spark that exploded the tinderbox came just days after Baker's failed Belgrade trip. The parliaments in Slovenia and Croatia each unilaterally declared independence from Yugoslavia unless all the republics reached a new compact. The central government dispatched tanks and helicopters to quell Slovenia's bid for freedom. Contrary to expectations, the Slovenes outfought the Serb-dominated Yugoslav National Army (JNA), seizing 2,000 prisoners in a 10-day clash. Negotiations resulted in a release of the captured troops and Belgrade's recognition of Slovenia's independence.

Rather than licking its wounds, Belgrade stepped up its ultranationalistic propaganda and on-the-ground agitation elsewhere. Two months later, Serb militias commenced fighting in Croatia. They were joined by regular JNA units to "ethnically cleanse" lands they claimed as Serbian. Ratko Mladić, one of the JNA officers, was at the time an obscure lieutenant colonel. During the course of the Balkan fighting, he rose to general and acquired notoriety for overseeing atrocities that earned him an indictment by the War Crimes Tribunal in The Hague. In December, the local Serbs declared independence for the Krajina region, which made up almost a third of Croatian territory.

The Croatian murders or deportations at gunpoint sparked international opprobrium. Austria, Belgium, Britain, and France introduced a motion to the UN Security Council to place an arms embargo on all of Yugoslavia. The United States concurred. On September 25, 1991, the UN Security Council unanimously passed Resolution 713, imposing an arms ban on the entire Yugoslavia to dampen down the violence by curbing the influx of weaponry. In retrospect, embargoing arms deliveries held disastrous consequences for the very people that the policy sought to protect—the Bosnian Muslims and Croats who bore the burnt of the Serb onslaught. The Serbs already possessed the bulk of the federal Yugoslav National Army's armories, the munitions plants, and the established weapons pipelines abroad. In short, the ban left the Croats and Muslims naked to Serb tanks and artillery. Rather than reducing the level of violence, the embargo abetted Belgrade's ambitions. Had the victims been able to defend themselves, then a progression from deterrence, stalemate, and armistice could have emerged, with peacemaking in their train.

Another adverse circumstance flowed from the European Community countries petitioning the Security Council. It linked the EC and the United Nations in such a manner as to give the New York-based organization political authority in the fragmenting Yugoslavia. Thus, Europeans and Americans looked to the United Nations to resolve the Balkan mess. Events on the ground conspired to demonstrate repeatedly that the world body was ineffectual in this role, because the major powers seating in the Security Council disagreed among themselves. Russia, Serbia's de facto patron, refused to countenance resolutions against Belgrade. Britain and France also evinced Serbian sympathies. Alone, the United States gravitated toward the Bosnian Muslims.

This intracouncil wrangling defied the immediate post-Wall expectations that the United Nations was destined to assume a prominent international influence once the Soviet-American standoff ceased among the 15 nation members seated around the Council's horseshoe-shaped panel. The UN's shortcomings sidelined it not only in Bosnia but also in other crises. As the world body stumbled, America gradually expanded its role of international arbiter and global stabilizer.

Meanwhile, Belgrade took advantage of the political vacuum. Serbian forces unleashed a three-month siege of the historic Dubrovnik in October 1991, a Croatian seacoast architectural treasure. By shelling the medieval buildings from the sea and shore, they cut off the city from water or land connections. The brazen bombardment of the historic Old Town and a defenseless population again outraged international opinion against Serbia. Far worse atrocities were committed against Vukovar, where Serb artillery razed the inland city before the Serbians entered to massacre hospital patients in their beds. Some 5,000 inhabitants lost their lives to Serbian militia during the last months of 1991. These Serb sieges roiled the Balkans.

Recognizing the gravity of the escalating violence, the Bush administration pressed the Serbians and the Croatians to demilitarize Dubrovnik on the Adriatic coast, to accept the deployment of UN peacekeepers, and to welcome special envoys approved by the Security Council. Javier Pérez de Cuéllar, the secretary general, selected Cyrus Vance, who had been former president Jimmy Carter's secretary of state, for the position. Vance worked with the EC's special envoy Lord Carrington, who negotiated the transfer of white rule to the African majority in Rhodesia (Zimbabwe) in the 1970s. Carrington favored a loose federation. Neither Slovenia nor Croatia would accept this plan. Nor would Serbia's ambitions have been satisfied under such an arrangement.[7]

In late November 1991, Croatia and Serbia did agree to the demilitarization of Dubrovnik and to the deployment of UN peacekeepers. Thus began the flawed deployment of UNPROFOR (UN Protection Force) into the Balkan morass. UNPROFOR often served as hostages to the Serbs rather than protectors of desperate victims. A 12,0000-strong UNPROFOR took up posts in February 1992 to stop the violence between Croatian and Serbian units fighting in Croatia's Krajina territory with its Serb majority. Later, UNPROFOR fielded troops to protect encircled Muslim communities. Serbia's spreading aggression alarmed another political entity at this time.

Bosnia and Herzegovina—a Yugoslav republic that last enjoyed full sovereignty as a medieval kingdom—awakened to the new realities of the splintering Balkans. Forty percent of Bosnia's prewar population comprised so-called Slavic Muslims, who were overwhelmingly European in custom and secular in religious orientation. Croats and Serbs made up the balance of the populace. Fear of Serbia's domination and hope of independence prompted the Bosnia Muslims and Croats to seek their own country.

Bosnia's President Alija Izetbegović, a Muslim political activist, held a republicwide referendum on independence. It won a landslide victory of 99 percent among the enclave's Croats and Muslims. The Bosnian Serbs boycotted the voting, arguing that it was illegal. Although Izetbegović's role was not "blameless" in promoting trouble, his action did not carry a "moral equivalence," as Professor Timothy Garton Ash wrote.[8]

The referendum's outcome became the equivalent of a declaration of war for Serbia. In retaliation, the Bosnian Serbs proclaimed their own republic, made Pale its capital, and sought to tie it to Serbia. Radovan Karadžić, the Republika Srpska leader, espoused a radical Serb nationalism that justified murdering and deportation of non-Serbs from their lands. In time, the International War Crimes Tribunal indicted him for war crimes as well.

When the three newly sovereign states of Slovenia, Croatia, and Bosnia-Herzegovina joined the United Nations, Serb retaliation was swift in coming and it fell mainly on Bosnia-Herzegovina. Slovenia and Croatia had extracted themselves from the crumpling Serb-dominated Yugoslav edifice, although fighting persisted in eastern Croatia between Croatians and Serbs over the possession of the Krajina pocket. The fate of Bosnia, particularly the encircled Muslim-dominated city of Sarajevo, overhung Europe and Euro-American relations for the next three years.

Sarajevo's international pleas for intervention to save the city and its environs from Serb retaliation went unanswered in Washington or European capitals. Meanwhile, the fighting and atrocities in Bosnia became a modern-day Inferno. Amid the growing gloom, a fascinating incident took place with implications for the future. A little-known mujahideen (holy warrior) from the Afghanistan resistance to the Soviet invasion, Osama bin Laden, journeyed to Sarajevo in 1994 and offered the assistance of his former guerrillas to Izetbegović. Weapons and fighters also came from Saudi Arabia, Libya, Iran, and Kuwait. This Muslim channel stirred concerns in the West, which the Serbs did their best to fan as evidence of the birth of a radical Islamic state in Europe. When the cessation of fighting finally occurred, the agreement did much to eliminate the conditions that produced an extremist Taliban regime in Afghanistan in the late 1990s. But before the Dayton Accord, there remained much bloody fighting, macabre scenes of atrocities, and ineffectual diplomacy as well as apprehensions of Islamic extremism.

WASHINGTON AND EUROPE PASS UP AN OPPORTUNITY

Due to American fence sitting under presidents Bush and Clinton until mid-1995, European actors held center stage, even if at times their efforts were more theatrics than substance. The script underwent profound changes when the United States spearheaded the bombing of Serb targets in 1995. Then the lead diplomatic and military role fell decidedly to Washington.[9] But before that dramatic reversal, America stood in the wings.

The Europeans injected themselves into a flurry of bureaucratic and diplomatic responses to cope with the spreading violence in the Balkans. The European Community (now known as the European Union) and the Conference on Security and Cooperation in Europe (now known as the Organization for Security and Cooperation in Europe) as well as individual Continental states—all went into a high gear of meetings, consultations, and conferences to stanch the flow of blood in the Balkans. They stepped away from the one ready military force that could have acted decisively: NATO.

Paris, Brussels, and London at this early stage did not want to engage NATO, for this would bring the Americans in through the side door of the transatlantic alliance. Both sides of the Atlantic shared the view that NATO was an anti-Soviet alliance. Over time, NATO assumed a broader perspective. Before that sea change, Washington deferred to the EC arrangement for similar reasons; it shrank from military action in Balkan conflict under the NATO flag, for it would invariably lead to America assuming ultimate responsibility for management of the crisis. The United States wrongly deferred to the Europeans, who proved incapable of squelching the Balkan tragedy. All the foot dragging simply encouraged Serbian aggression. To follow in detail the European diplomatic meanderings would be a lengthy task—and in terms of this book a distorting one. It must be enough to sketch an outline of Euro-American interactions.

A fragmenting multinational Yugoslavia was an unwelcome prospect for the possible instability in Europe itself and for the repercussions it might have on U.S. priorities with the Soviet Union over German reunification, Germany's NATO membership, and nuclear arms agreements with an undersiege Mikhail Gorbachev. President Bush's aides realized the dangers in southeastern Europe. National Security Adviser Brent Scowcroft and soon-to-be Secretary of State Lawrence Eagleburger (who replaced Baker in mid-1992) had both served in Belgrade earlier in their careers and understood that Yugoslavia's dismemberment meant unleashing the dogs of war. After leaving office, Scowcroft and Eagleburger acknowledged that the bloody Balkan odyssey might have been averted on their watch by preemptive military intervention.[10] The United States wanted peace in Yugoslavia but not enough to head off the gathering storm.

Along with European capitals, Washington contented itself with condemning all the parties for the outbreak of fighting. It held that a resort to force by the Balkan players violated the 1975 Helsinki Principles, which guaranteed the inviolability of borders established at the end of World War II. In reality, the United States wanted Europe to step up to the plate and deal with the messy Yugoslav disintegration. Yet, it desired that the Continent look across the Atlantic for guidance. For example, the Bush policy team urged the Europeans not to recognize the sovereignty of the various Yugoslav republics.

In December, Germany, succumbing to domestic pressure, broke the transatlantic consensus and unilaterally recognized Croatia and Slovenia. Since the EC needed German assent for its Masstricht treaty to create the European Union, it acquiesced to Germany's importuning and recognized as well the sovereignty of the two breakaway republics in mid-January 1992. Both actions represented setbacks to Washington's diplomatic initiatives.

To compensate, the United States granted diplomatic recognition to Bosnia-Herzegovina in April 1992 when it normalized relations with Slovenia and Croatia. However, it backed off exchanging ambassadors with another breakaway province, Macedonia, from the Yugoslav rump, because of intense lobbying from Greek-Americans and Greece itself. Athens objected to the seceding republic calling itself "Macedonia" because it might make territorial claims to northern Greece, where the name also applied.

Thus, it promised a veto if Macedonia applied for recognition from the European Community. Greece in addition placed an embargo and political pressure on the impoverished southern Balkan country until it agreed to call itself the Former Yugoslav Republic of Macedonia in 1995 in return for diplomatic recognition.

THE BOSNIAN HORROR SHOW

President Bush's last year in office recorded an enormous catastrophe in the Balkans. Beginning in April 1992, the Serbians laid siege to Sarajevo to lash back at the international recognition of Bosnia's statehood. The very brazenness of the attack was not lost on anyone who reflected on the fact that this cosmopolitan city of a half million inhabitants hosted the 1984 winter Olympics. From the mountainous fortifications surrounding Sarajevo, Serb snipers gunned down Sarajevans, while UN peacekeeping troops stood by powerless to halt the killings. Once again the CNN effect on television sets projected images of suffering and heartache around the world. Led by President Izetbegović, the Bosnian Muslims expounded a platform of their enclave's "unique character as a multi-national, multi-religious republic" that appealed intensely to American elites.[11]

The Serbian blockade of Sarajevo gripped the city for 44 months in a bloody strangulation. It turned the historic Bosnian city into Dantesque hell. Human rights groups reported that more than 11,000 people, including 1,500 children died in Sarajevo siege. The residents were often short of food, water, electricity, and medical treatment. Disadvantaged on battlefield, the Sarajevans eventually emerged as victors in the all-important propaganda contest in large measure because their plight captured international sympathy. To Americans, it was a David-versus-Goliath struggle, but in this case David lacked even a decent slingshot.

The advent of the Sarajevo siege convinced Washington to prod the European states toward collective action against Serbia for aggression. To the Europeans, U.S. policy assumed a one-dimensional perspective, seeing only Bosnian Serbs and their patron Serbia as the aggressors. Britain and France interpreted the fighting as a civil war, for which Americans—politicians and pundits—accused them of a pro-Serb bias, dating from their wartime collaboration during the 1940s. Cynical Europeans, on the other hand, saw the Bosnian Muslims as cleverly exploiting American sympathy for their own agenda of creating a nonviable ministate ringed by hostile nations, which could set a precedent for their own minority populations to hive off independent countries that threatened a Continentwide fragmentation.

Washington did win passage of UN Resolution 757 in the Security Council that imposed an economic embargo on the Serbia in May 1992. At the G-7 summit in June, Washington gained backing for additional measures "not excluding military means" to deliver humanitarian relief to encircled Bosnians. This idle threat of military action was followed by an equally idle call for joint action. Speaking at the July meeting of the Conference on Security and Cooperation in Helsinki, George Bush called for doing "all we can to prevent this conflict from spreading."[12] But no preventive measures ensued.

That summer the United States shifted into nonstop presidential campaigning, and Baker left his post to manage Bush's failed election bid. America diverted its attention to the national election, evermore loath to enter into a hornet's nest in the months preceding a close presidential race. The new secretary of state perpetuated the Bush-Baker foreign policy team's assessment that no external force could resolve the factional conflict. In September 1992, Eagleburger emphasized, "Until the Bosnians, Serbs, and Croats decide to stop killing each other, there is nothing the outside world can do about it."[13]

The outgoing Bush government did undertake a massive airlift to Sarajevo and also airdropped supplies to communities outside the city limits in December 1992.

This one bright spot on the dark diplomatic landscape came in response to estimates of some 100,000 deaths from starvation and exposure among the hungry and displaced Bosnians. Washington also pushed relief supplies of food, fuel, and shelters along ground corridors from Croatia and even Serbia. For all its considerable good in saving thousands of lives, the air operations were a mere stopgap. They impeded no ethnic expulsions. Serbs steadily pushed their offense to conquer an enlarged national homeland.

As the Bush government departed from office, Serb domination was approaching three-quarters of the Bosnia-Herzegovina territory that would mark its furthest gains. Facing no genuine international threat, the JNA and its local auxiliaries closed in on Sarajevo and other Muslim enclaves in the war-torn republic. Ethnic cleansing was in full furry to bring about a Greater Serbia. The United States and its European allies stood by as Bosnia writhed. The Serbs drew the conclusion during 1992 that they had a free hand, unhindered by international interference. Protecting the UN blue helmets and ensuring the erratic relief supplies (more often than not interrupted by Serb thugs) took the place of forceful initiatives. The transatlantic community needed a realistic approach, but none was to come for years.

BILL CLINTON AND BOSNIA

By the time the Clinton administration took office in late January 1993, it faced a much shrunken Bosnia from what it had been a year earlier. It also confronted an exceedingly unworkable plan by Cyrus Vance, the UN envoy, and David Owens, the European Community's emissary, who replaced a disillusioned Carrington. The Vance-Owen peace solution envisioned 10 quasi-autonomous provinces within Bosnia-Herzegovina, nine of which would fall under specific nationalities.[14] Muslims, Croats, and Serbs would govern Sarajevo, the tenth area. The fledgling Clinton White House greeted the Vance-Owen plan skeptically, despite European endorsement. Rightly, it assessed the scheme as impractical and unenforceable, while it rewarded Serb aggression.

What put Washington in an awkward position was that it had no meaningful alternative to offer. Instead, it adopted what was termed a humanitarian-diplomatic initiative, using carrots and sticks to convince the warring parties to make peace. This approach mimicked the Bush administration's do-nothing-of-consequence toward the Balkan imbroglio. Not long after Bill Clinton's inauguration, he had backpedaled from the previously tough campaign rhetoric about Bosnia. Warren Christopher initiated the new line when he avowed on an April 1993 CBS's "Face the Nation" broadcast: "[T]he United States simply doesn't have the means to make people in that region of the world like each other."[15]

As in the contemporaneous Somali and Haitian crises, the Clinton administration looked to the United Nations and, in the Bosnia case, also to the European Community to resolve the strife. Multilateralism without American leadership was chasing a dangerous fantasy. Palming off responsibilities to international organizations offered an escape from shouldering the burdens and expenses of a forward foreign policy. President Clinton did speak out against the carnage in the fragmenting Balkan state. During a photo op with Czechoslovakia's President Vaclav Havel on April 20, the president stated, "The United States should always seek an opportunity to stand up against—at least speak out against—inhumanity."[16] Such statements gave Clinton's friends or skeptics little confidence in the new administration's ability to wield power. The themeless policy drift toward Somalia, Haiti, and Bosnia was condemned "ad hocism" by commentators at the time.

Alarmed by the spreading conflict, Clinton's innermost circle looked to U.S. air-power, America's weapon of choice, to check the Serb advances. They ruled out deploying land forces. Colin Powell, the chairman of the Joint Chiefs of Staff, adamantly opposed placing American GIs in harms way until the United States "had a clear political objective." Grounded in the hard knocks of the Vietnam War, the Army general worried about potential mismatch between military means and fuzzy political goals. Madeleine Albright, then the U.S. representative at the UN, hit back in what became a much-quoted retort: "What's the point of having this superb military that you're always talking about if we can't use it?" Powell's rejoinder made the point that the American armed forces consisted not of "toy soldiers" to be "moved around on some sort of global game board." To him, "tough political goals" had to be set first, and then they "would accomplish their mission."[17] But the Clinton Cabinet agreed that the deteriorating situation endangered political tranquility in Europe.

The United States therefore came around to the plan to dispatch Christopher to Europe and Moscow to broach a hastily conceived plan. The U.S. formula dubbed "lift and strike," which envisioned a lifting of the UN arms embargo to help the out-gunned Bosnian Muslims and the launching of air strikes to compel Serbian acquiescence to humanitarian relief deliveries, went no where with the Europeans. The British and French, who had most of the troops in UNPROFOR stationed in Bosnia at the time, believed that the Serbs would retaliate against their forces. London and Paris proposed that the United States first deploy its own soldiers before resorting to air attacks. Germany and Italy also objected, and the latter country's prime minister believed that the proposed American action "would be like throwing a log on a burning fire."[18]

Rather than trying to whip a dead horse, the U.S. government quietly ditched its "lift and strike" formula. Nonetheless, the ill-fated approach still served Bill Clinton who blamed the Europeans for not undertaking a stronger direction to the unfolding genocide in Bosnia. In response, the Europeans pushed through the United Nations the concept of "safe areas" in Bosnia-Herzegovina to protect the embattled Muslims. The Security Council passed Resolution 824 on May 6, 1993, declaring the Muslim-populated towns of Sarajevo, Tuzla, Zepa, Gorazde, Bihac, and Srebrenica to be safe areas "free from armed attacks and from any other hostile acts." But the UN resolution nimbly shied away from the use of the term "safe havens," which carried explicit connotations under international law of immunity for refuge seekers.[19]

Signing onto the resolution did two things for the United States: it papered over the earlier rift with Europe on Washington's "lift and strike" prescription and it led to another formula to finesse an exit for American leadership in addressing the Bosnian morass. Testifying before the House Foreign Affairs Committee, Christopher asserted that the factional war in Yugoslavia "at heart . . . is a European problem."[20] In spite of this Pilate-like observation, the United States could not so easily wash its hands of the matter, as events churned inexorably in the former Yugoslavia.

Spring 1993 proved a pivotal moment in the Bosnian turmoil. Not only did May witness the U.S. disengagement from an assertive policy but also the Bosnian Muslims realized that survival rested in their own hands, for they lost their only ally. The Bosnian Croats, who made up 17 percent of the ministate's population, turned on the Muslims in order to carve out their own exclusive mini-nation. As such, the Bosnian Croats served as a proxy force for Croatia proper, whose President Franjo Tudjman, like Milošević, acted as puppet master when things suited him. Later, he and Milošević cut the strings and let their puppets tumble.

For now, the Croats in the western reaches of the Herzegovina part of the embattled republic established Herceg-Bosna, a separate enclave with its own military and police forces, local government, and schools. Croatian paramilitaries also opened fire on the Bosnian Army in the multiethnic town of Mostar, about 40 miles southwest of Sarajevo. Croatian guns shelled the sixteenth-century Turkish bridge over the Neretva River in November. The arched Old Bridge, as it was known, had stood as metaphor for the web of community ties among the various religious groups in Bosnia-Herzegovina. Its destruction tore at the heart of Mostar. After the war, the Old Bridge was rebuilt using original Turkish blueprints and reopened in 2004 with Balkan music, folk dancing, and speeches about peace and reconciliation.

By the time the picture-postcard bridge fell, the fighting resembled a war of all against one. Yet, this portrayal is too simplistic, although mutual suspicion abounded. The Croatian and Serbian leaders met and most often agreed only on destruction of the Muslims, while Croatian and Serbian fighters carried on their slit-throat fights against each other in the trenches. They referred to each other by the hated World War II designations—the Croats were remembered as Nazi-aligned Ustashe (fascist police) who murdered non-Croats, and the Serbs were recalled as the procommunist Chetniks, who killed non-Serbs.

During 1993 and 1994, international diplomatic activity focused on two more negotiated settlements designed to bring peace to Bosnia before the United States brokered the Dayton agreement at the end of 1995. Both these diplomatic forays fizzled amid escalating violence and disorder, which prompted the United States to wield the threat of NATO airpower to protect the safe areas. The strongest warning to the Bosnian Serbs came in reaction to the infamous Bosnian Serb mortar shell that exploded in Sarajevo's open-air market on February 5, 1994 killing 68 people and wounding a further 200—an attack that represented the single most deadly incident in the three-year siege of the capital.

The bloody spectacle concentrated the Clinton government's attention on the looming chaos in Bosnia. The United States, backed by France, forced a decision on NATO member states. They got NATO to issue a 10-day ultimatum, threatening to bomb Bosnian Serb gun positions unless pulled from the high ground surrounding Sarajevo. The United States leaned on Moscow to use its leverage with the Serbs. After intense negotiations with Bosnian Serbs and the intervention of President Boris Yeltsin to place 400 Russian troops from UNPROFOR into vacated Serb trenches, the Bosnian Serb leader Karadžić gave into the demand. Also following the mortaring of the Sarajevo market, two U.S. F-16s jets flying under NATO colors shot down four Serb aircraft for violating the "no-fly" zone in central Bosnia that the United

Nations had declared in October 1992. The aerial combat constituted the first military action by NATO in its 45-year history.

Next, Washington persuaded its NATO partners to employ limited air strikes against the Bosnian Serbs who were attacking 65,000 people trapped in the city of Gorazde in April 1994. Ostensibly, the bombings were to protect the 12 UN peace-keepers inside the urban perimeter. But this was more of a cover story than the truth. These so-called pinprick bombings fell far short of halting the Serb advances. Still, President Clinton hailed the effort: "This is a clear expression of the will of NATO and the will of the United Nations."[21]

When the Clinton government redoubled its arm-twisting of NATO member states for robust aerial attacks, it nearly split the alliance as Britain and France opposed further escalation as did the United Nations. London and Paris even drew up plans to withdraw their ground troops, who constituted the bulk of the now 28,000 "blue helmets" on the ground in the event of any major air strikes. The United States acquiesced to Britain and France, which also argued that an escalation of NATO forces would pit the alliance against the United Nations.

THE UNITED STATES PUSHES FOR A RESOLUTION

The year 1994 witnessed the beginning of two major U.S. initiates that contributed to the Dayton peace gathering in late 1995. One action midwifed the rebirth of the Muslim-Croat cooperation, and the other marked the active participation of Russia in the diplomatic initiatives to resolve the Balkan conflict. U.S. diplomacy secured both breakthroughs, as federal lawmakers and elite American opinion pressed for a resolution to the fighting. Feeling congressional pressure to come to grips with the Bosnian crisis, the White House stepped up its efforts. Capitol Hill even passed a bill to lift the embargo on arms sales to Bosnia, which President Clinton vetoed in August 1994, because it amounted to "the wrong step at the wrong time."[22]

American diplomats in the Balkans carried on discussions from mid-1993 with the Croatians and the Bosnian Muslims to re-form the anti-Serb alliance. By combining threats to impose sanctions on Croatia with blandishments to integrate the new country politically and economically into the West, the United States pressured President Tudjman. It also persuaded Germany, Croatia's prime backer, to add its leverage to its own coaxing. The tactics worked, and Tudjman agreed to the cutting off of Zagreb's support for the Croatian mavericks in western Herzegovina and withdrew 30,000 Croatian troops from the Bosnian republic. Bosnia's President Izetbegović joined his Croatian counterpart in the White House to sign the Washington agreement on March 18. Both governments, therefore, escaped the economic and political ostracism that befell Serbia.

The U.S.-engineered Muslim-Croat Federation was hardly an alliance of bosom compatriots. Too much killing, animosity, and mutual suspicion existed for genuine trust. But despite its ups and downs, the federation lumbered along; its glue was their shared anti-Serb sentiments. Tensions persisted within the federation, but fighting ceased between the two former adversaries. The agreement enabled the Bosnians to receive military supplies through Croatia without the former "weapons tax" skimming off a high percentage of the arms that came from a highly unusual source.

Not until April 1996, months after the Dayton settlement, did it come to light that President Clinton himself approved two years earlier a covert arms pipeline through Croatia to the Bosnian Muslims from Iran. This authorization contravened international agreements and double-crossed American allies. But the clandestine enterprise helped to redress the imbalance of power on the ground, where the Serbs had held an arms monopoly.[23] When the operation was revealed, congressmen voiced disapproval about being left in the dark and raised concerns about expanding Iranian influence in the Balkans that resulted from Clinton's under-the-table assent. Realistically, Washington's decision on the flow of clandestine arms was far better than doing nothing in the face of the relentless carnage.

The second major American move on the Balkan chessboard brought Russia into the peace process together with the key European players. Without the Russians, who sided with the Serbs, no genuine agreement could be reached. If Moscow remained opposed to peace initiatives, then its resistance would lead anew to Cold War-type divisions in Europe. In spring 1994, the United States, Russia, Britain, France, and Germany established a five-nation Contact Group to resurrect an international peace process after over a year of diplomatic stalemate. Harkening back to the nineteenth century when the great powers imposed settlements, the Contact Group desired to set down boundaries to separate the combatants and to shore up stability in the Balkans.

Drawing lines on maps proved to be the easy part. Far more difficult was the task to maintain unity among the Contact Group members and the impossible goal at this stage to get assent from embittered protagonists themselves about national borders. Unveiling proposed boundary lines at a Geneva meeting in July 1994, the Contact plan demanded an up-or-down decision by the warring parties. It was an easy choice. They all rejected the Group's boundaries. Acceptance would have required the Serbs to surrender too much conquered territory and the Muslims to acknowledge too much lost ground while rewarding Serb ethnic cleansing and genocide. Stiffing the Contact Group held consequences for American policy, Euro-American relations, and the Serbs.

By spurning the Contact Group's solution, the Bosnian Serbs opened a division with their chief patron. Slobodan Milošević needed Pale's cooperation to end the international sanctions on Serbia and Montenegro, the two remaining republics in the old Yugoslavia. The Serb president began to pressure Radoran Karadžić, the Bosnian Serb leader, to embrace the new map. Milošević's arm-twisting, character defamation of Karadžić and even a hasty Belgrade-imposed embargo on Pale came to no avail. Karadžić refused to budge. His intransigence, however, hardened the split with Belgrade. This disunity became critical during the Dayton meetings.

TURNING POINTS

Other forces were also at work by 1995 compelling a policy switch for the White House. Domestically, the early stirrings of the presidential election campaign the next year also spurred the incumbent to protect his political flank from criticism. Well before announcing his candidacy for the presidency, Bob Dole, the Republican Senate leader, joined the parade of critics against the president's stand on the arms embargo, even if it meant breaking with Washington's European allies. The pressure bore results. Clinton relented and stated that the United States would no longer enforce the embargo, although it would not formally depart from the agreement.

Internationally, changes were afoot in Europe paving the way for a redirection in American policy in 1995. In France, Jacques Chirac assumed the presidency on May 17 from François Mitterrand. Outraged by Serb hostage taking of French peacekeepers serving in UNPROFOR (whose ranks suffered over 70 troops killed), Chirac embarked on a bid to refurbish French grandeur and in so doing espoused a tough line toward Serbia. Former president Mitterrand, who had recalled the Serbian alliance as hedge to German power, represented the World War II attitude of containing Germany. By contrast, Chirac was convinced that the intense violence in southeastern Europe endangered the dream of a unified and peaceful Continent far more than German economic strength. France's new government signaled an end to the three-year Euro-American roadblock impeding action in the Balkans. Despite previous warm feelings toward the Serbs as World War II allies or from shared anti-Muslim sentiments, Britain as well as France had become disillusioned with Serbian cruelties and sought a cessation to the war that could widen to include Russia, Turkey, Greece, and Bulgaria. These realignments pointed to a narrowing of the differences with Washington at a time when transatlantic relations were at rock bottom over Bosnia.

By far the greatest impetus for change, nonetheless, came from the calamitous destruction of the Muslim pocket in Srebrenica (the "place of silver") on July 10, 1995. The destruction of the UN "safe area" jolted President Clinton "to find a way to save Bosnia that restored the effectiveness of the UN and NATO" and politically stabilized the Balkans.[24] The White House occupant also realized that the Bosnian atrocities were a vulnerable pivot on which his reelection could swing.

For the United States and Europe, the hinge point of the Bosnian conflict was the catastrophic fall of Srebrenica in easternmost Bosnia-Herzegovina. The sheer scale of the carnage made it impossible to ignore. Srebrenica's prewar population of 8,000 had swollen to 40,000 refugees. Encircled by the Bosnian Serb militiamen and Serbian regular forces, the inhabitants endured hardships, unable to escape the siege or to live much above subsistence on scanty UN relief supplies. Less than 10 miles from the Serb-Bosnian border, its very existence constituted a perceived threat to Serbia itself. While the town was supposed to be demilitarized, the Bosnian Muslims persevered in launching counterraids against their oppressors. The besiegers used these counterattacks as pretext to overrun Srebrenica and massacre its male population.

Like Sarajevo, the Srebrenica "safe area" had become a symbol for both sides and especially for the powers that signed up to protect it. When news transpired to the outside world that the Bosnian Serb militia and Serbian policemen had mowed down the captured male population of 7,000, while 400 Dutch UN peacekeepers stood by helplessly, the diplomatic calculus was irrevocably changed. The atrocities resulted in an indictment of General Mladić by the International War Crimes Tribunal at The Hague. The Srebrenica tragedy was the biggest massacre in Europe since World War II atrocities, a colossal disgrace for the United Nations, and a signpost pointing toward greater transregional instability, if the fighting persisted.

Salt was rubbed in the UN's wound two weeks later, when Žepa, another "safe area" to the west of Srebrenica, also fell to local Serb fighters. Although Žepa's capitulation represented another Muslim defeat, it possessed the paradox of making peace more achievable. Previously, the frontiers resembled complex geometric configurations, with tiny land corridors linking the beleaguered enclaves to the larger Bosnian entity. Eradication of the enclaves left ethnically pure sectors; Serbs were generally in their exclusive sectors and Muslims were in their separate localities. The July 1995 battles produced nearly exclusive ethnic ghettoes, around which boundaries could be more easily drawn.[25]

Oblivious to adverse world opinion, the Serb militias believed they were on a roll and soon laid siege to the Muslim outpost of Bihac in the northwest corner of Bosnia-Herzegovina. What mattered about the Bihac enclave more than other Muslim "safe areas" in the southeast was that it could be reached in an hour by car from Zagreb, far too close for the comfort of the Croatian government. The Serbian militiamen overplayed their hand by moving on Bihac, for they provoked a Croatian counterattack, which by late summer washed them away. These harsh, even cruel, realities became important factors for the map drawers at the Dayton meetings that fall. In the meantime, the rape of Srebrenica set in motion a diplomatic counteroffensive.

At a summer NATO meeting the United States, bolstered by Britain and France, chartered a historic path for the transatlantic alliance that had hovered on the brink of irrelevance after the fall of the Berlin Wall. Momentously, the allied defense ministers decided that NATO, not the United Nations, would call the shots on whether to use airpower and to what extent in the defense of Gorazde, another UN "safe area." It is difficult to overstate the importance of this decision: it gave the old anti-Soviet alliance a new lease on life; it laid the foundation for NATO's Kosovo air campaign four years later; and finally it put NATO on the path leading to its deployment in Afghanistan after the U.S.-led coalition invasion in 2001.

Events on the ground once more dramatically altered the diplomatic realities when in early August Croatia unleashed a swift and merciless Operation Storm to defend Bihac against the local Serb militia and recapture the Krajina pocket. Unexpectedly, the Croatian army crushed the Serb paramilitaries who surrendered their putative capital, Knin, without resistance. Both the CIA and the Pentagon made no bones about their pessimistic estimates of the Croatian martial capabilities, but they were dead wrong. The Croatian forces next punched into western Bosnia, smashing Serb defenses in lighting and coordinated sweeps. Milošević did not lift a finger to help his embattled brethren because he wanted to hang onto power and to have the international sanctions lifted. For the first time since the Balkans war broke out, the Serbian forces suffered a major battlefield defeat. But the foray left gruesome atrocities and 170,000 refugees among the fleeing Serbian population in its wake. At the time, the West generally ignored the Croat war crimes in its desire to reach a settlement.

Croatia's revived military prowess derived from the instruction it received from a private American company, Military Professional Resources Incorporated (MPRI). Based in Alexandria, Virginia, MPRI advised the Croatian army prior to its offensive. Its instruction and training transformed a ramshackle collection of rifle-toting militiamen into a force that approached a modern professional army. The veteran instructors instilled the discipline and confidence that went a long way in preparing the Croatian troops to shatter the vaunted invincibility of the Serbs, a myth that they self-promoted among the Western media. The retired U.S. military officers and non-commissioned officers (NCOs) who worked for MPRI reconstituted the Croatians into an integrated force of airpower, artillery, and rapidly advancing infantry that has been described as a text for coordination and maneuver.[26]

Clinton's State Department licensed MPRI to instruct the Croatian military in NATO-style operations and training that began in October 1994. Because the Croatian blitzkrieg violated a UN cease-fire and sowed death, destruction, and hordes of refugees, the United States and MPRI came under scrutiny. The fact that some Croatian officers were indicted for war crimes committed during the counterattack was a noted failing. Both Washington and MPRI tried to distance themselves from their role in the preparation of Zagreb's countersweep, contending that the Croatians received instructions in democratic values and civil-military relations, along with orientation on battlefield strategy.[27] The pretense fooled no one. On the other hand, what else could the Clinton administration have done? It was reluctant to enter the fray with U.S. armed forces without widespread public support, which never materialized.

As an alternative, the use of a private firm proved effective and inexpensive in shifting the military and then diplomatic balance in the war after four years of running Serb victories. By first brokering a Croat-Muslim alliance to face off against the Serbs and then facilitating Croatia's combat preparedness, the United States engineered the turnaround in the Balkans. Aside from the squeamishness of antipower critics, the employment of a private company to implement a sound policy made—and makes—a lot of sense in this instance. The White House kept the appropriate congressional committees informed of its actions, thereby minimizing their aversion. Standing by watching helpless men, women, and children be mass murdered by Serb gangs was clearly wrong. At last, the Clinton administration chose to act correctly in good cause after monumental hesitations in the face of a return to European barbarity and spreading anarchy as the Continent wrung its hands.

All these factors—the horrors of Srebrencia and Žepa, the NATO summit, and the Operation Storm—combined to energize the United States to undertake a concerted effort to halt the war. Along with the State Department, Bill Clinton took an active role to forge a peace settlement. The confirmation of Richard Holbrooke, former U.S. ambassador to Germany, as assistant secretary of state for European affairs eight months earlier placed a relentless negotiator as Washington's point man in the Balkans. Holbrooke stepped up his shuttle diplomacy among the Balkan and European capitals, as conditions changed on the ground in mid-1995.

America's late summer initiatives gained additional momentum when the Bosnian Serbs committed a fresh act of barbarity by again firing a mortar round into a Sarajevo marketplace, killing 38 people on August 28. Washington interpreted the massacre as a direct affront because of its recently launched major diplomatic effort. It responded with renewed vigor in pressing for a NATO counterstrike. Two days after the marketplace massacre, an American-led NATO bombing storm struck Serb units encircling Sarajevo.

Operation Deliberate Force deployed 60 warplanes from Italian airbases and the aircraft carrier *USS Theodore Roosevelt* on station in the Adriatic Sea. They were joined by British and French artillery shelling from their Rapid Reaction Forces around the Bosnian Muslim capital. Tomahawk missiles also rained down on Serb positions. For two weeks, the U.S.-orchestrated NATO pounding destroyed Bosnian Serb fortifications, artillery emplacements, storage facilities, radar sites, and communication nodes.[28] The NATO assaults came at the time when the Croatian and Muslim counterattack was in full swing and functioned as its close-air support. All the same, General Mladić, the local Serb commander, dug in his heels, but Milošević knew better and pressed Holbrooke to halt the bombing.

These attacks marked a visible return of the United States to leadership of the Atlantic alliance, something that had languished during much of the Balkan crisis. This fresh resolve led to the final resolution of the raging conflict. Without it, the Europeans would have dallied and ducked from coming to grips with a Hobbesian state of nature, where civilization succumbs to barbarism. That turbulence might have acted like a suction pump drawing in neighboring states, perhaps even Russia, to restore order but actually widening the fighting and perhaps again making the Balkans a flash point leading to another World War I-type conflict.

The U.S.-led NATO foray also drove the wedge deeper between Pale and Belgrade. Milošević's growing public disenchantment with Karadžić since the unveiling of the Contact Group's settlement a year earlier now came into clear focus with Operation Deliberate Force. When Holbrooke visited Belgrade, he unexpectedly discovered that Milošević had corralled Karadžić and other Pale leaders into a "joint Yugoslav-Republika Srpksa delegation for all future peace talks." They signed what Holbrooke termed the Patriarch Paper; it granted Milošević "virtually total power over the fate of the Bosnian Serbs."[29] It was so named because Patriarch Pavle, the head of the Serbian Orthodox Church, had witnessed the signed document. Milošević would henceforth speak on behalf of all Serbs with the West, thereby mediating a settlement that put Belgrade's interests ahead of Pale's.

DAYTON DIPLOMACY

After years of frozen diplomacy, events in summer 1995 laid the groundwork for the U.S.-initiated Dayton peace settlement. Belgrade's concessions on a "Joint Agreed Statement of Political Principles" ensured that Bosnia had a legal existence "with its present borders," and "continuing international recognition." The Bosnian Muslims initially objected to recognition of a separate Serb entity, the Republika Srpska, but relented. At a Geneva meeting in early September, American diplomats next forged agreement on the size of the contested "statelets" with foreign ministers from Bosnia, Croatia, and Serbia. The Muslim-Croat Federation gained 51 percent of the former Bosnia and Herzegovina republic. The Republika Srpska got the remaining 49 percent of the territory. The exact boundaries were yet to be drawn. Before that, United States played a key role in guiding the course of the fighting.

Ground down by the U.S.-led NATO bombing, the Bosnian Serbs agreed to lift the siege of Sarajevo on September 14. But the ground war in the surrounding countryside raged unabated. Croatian and Muslim advances sent the Bosnian Serbs reeling, retreating from small towns in the western parts of Bosnia and Herzegovina.

When the attackers threatened Banja Luka, the second largest city and a Serb stronghold, Washington intervened to halt their advance.

The United States feared the political consequences as thousands of displaced Serbs from Banja Luka poured into Belgrade and inflamed their Serbian brothers' passions. One likely scenario from a fallen Banja Luka envisioned Milošević entering the war on behalf of his kinfolk to save his own skin. Otherwise, Serbian citizens would replace him with a genuine Serb patriot, and the Balkans would be reconvulsed. American diplomats wanted Milošević to stay sidelined in the war and to clinch an overall peace settlement. They sensed his desperation and willingness to negotiate away the dreams of the Bosnian Serbs in order to retain his power.

Washington instructed Zagreb to call off its support of the onslaught and return its troops to Croatian barracks. In return, Holbrooke pledged to President Franjo Tudjman that he would work for the restoration of eastern Slavonia into Croatian hands. As a result, the Croatian strongman withdrew his forces from the Bosnian battlefields. The United States also put the screws to President Izetbegović. He also agreed to break off the Muslim counterattacks, believing that a political victory was ultimately more important than military gains. By the time the guns fell silent, the boundaries had been drastically altered. Two months earlier, the Bosnian Serbs held about 75 percent of the territory. The Croat-Muslim juggernaut and U.S.-NATO airpower reduced these holdings to approximately half of Bosnia-Herzegovina. The military advances on the ground conformed at least in the rough allocation of the land, if not actual boundaries, to the Contract Group map drawers' outline.

Before the Dayton talks got underway, the United States grappled with how to include Russia, another piece in the perplexing puzzle that made up the Bosnian conflict. Without Moscow's agreement, Belgrade could hold out for a better deal. Washington, eager to build a special relationship with post–Cold War Moscow, desired to lessen anti-American feelings in Russia and to win over the Boris Yeltsin government by securing its blessing for a peace settlement. At a Waldorf-Astoria Hotel meeting in New York, Bill Clinton, himself, asked presidents Tudjman and Izetbegović to "do something for the peace process" by traveling to Moscow to meet with President Yeltsin before the Dayton negotiations. Clinton wanted this trip to enable the Russian leader to "send a signal to the Serbs, and to allow the Russian people to see that he is part of the [peace] process."[30] This signal would boost Yeltsin candidates in the approaching Duma, or lower house, elections. What was good for Yeltsin was good for the United States went the rationale since the Russian president often accommodated American plans. Neither the Croatian nor the Bosnian presidents were eager for the Moscow visit, but they went along with the American request.

Washington's diplomatic maneuverings assuaged Russia's concerns about a U.S. and NATO presence within its traditional sphere of influence. They also provided valuable lessons on how to cope later with Russian opposition to the eastward enlargement phase of NATO, which was formalized in 1996 with invitations for membership to Hungary, Poland, and the Czech Republic. In the immediate, it facilitated a Russo-American understanding on Moscow's deployment of peacekeeping troops to the Balkans, if an agreement was concluded at Dayton.

For the first time since their World War II cooperation, Russian and American soldiers agreed to operate under a unified command of the NATO-led Implementation

Force (IFOR). The Russian soldiers had their own reporting structure answering to a Russian general but had to accept subordination to the U.S. command structure, a fact that American "sugarcoating" disguised. President Clinton brokered this Russo-American understanding with Boris Yeltsin at Franklin D. Roosevelt's former residence at Hyde Park in mid-October. State Department officials chose the site because the Russian president, like many of his countrymen, revered Roosevelt as a close wartime ally.[31]

This joint peace-soldiering force marked three firsts for NATO. It would be NATO's first out-of-area deployment, its first post–Cold War mission, and its first joint operation employing non-NATO troops, Russians among other nonalliance personnel. The contentious negotiations among the Balkan factions opened in November 1, 1995 at the Wright-Patterson Air Force Base in Dayton, Ohio. The American delegation picked the site because of its remoteness from Washington so as to be relatively media leakproof. Representing the United States were Warren Christopher and Richard Holbrooke, the secretary of state's principal architect of the peace talks. Serbia, Croatia, and Bosnia each sent their presidents. Pale was without a place at the table. Even if the Serbian President Slobodan Milošević had not already cut out the Bosnian Serbs from direct participation in settlement discussions with his Patriarch Paper in August, Pale had dealt itself out of the game by its atrocities and by its stubborn refusal to enter give-and-take negotiations. Since President Karadžić and General Mladić were both indicted on charges of war crimes by The Hague, neither could travel anywhere beyond the Serb enclave for fear of arrest. The Europeans were nowhere to be seen.

For 21 days in a sealed-off environment, the principals and interlocutors squabbled over boundaries. The most tension arose from the 51 to 49 territorial percentages, previously adopted by the Contact Group. This allocation nearly brought the peace talks in the Hope Conference Center to an abrupt conclusion. In the end, the Bosnian Serbs held onto 49 percent of Bosnia and Herzegovina, even if some of the lands were desolate scrub and rock-strewn wastes. The Croat-Muslim Federation retained the balance in the divided country with a politically convoluted three-president government structure that lasted for a decade.

The Dayton Accord was formally signed on December 14, 1995 in the Élysée Palace in Paris. Europe's worst fighting since World War II was thus brought to a peaceful close but not before over 200,000 deaths and some 2 million people had been displaced from their homes. The worst war crimes in Europe since the Holocaust accompanied the disintegration of the former Yugoslavia. In an often-cited 1995 *Foreign Affairs* article, Holbrooke judged the Bosnian conflict as "the greatest collective security failure of the West since the 1930s."[32]

On December 31, 1995, the first American troops crossed the Sava River from Croatia into Bosnia to take up their duties to enforce the peace agreement for what was to be a one-year commitment. Before the deadline of December 20, 1996 lapsed, Washington extended it to February 1997 and then shifted it once again before eliminating it altogether. The NATO-led IFOR commanded some 60,000 soldiers, of whom 20,000 were from the United States, in what was a virtual army of occupation, not a traditional peacekeeping mission. IFOR was to enforce peace, not stroll amongst a reconciled population. The sheer size and heavy armaments of the IFOR prompted Secretary of Defense William Perry to label it "the biggest and toughest and meanest dog in town."[33]

This mission entailed disarming and separating the ethnic combatants. Enforcement of the *Pax* NATO was vigorous from its start. Unlike the Iraq occupation a decade later, the IFOR operation was well planned and well executed, with sufficient force in place to head off resistance from die-hard elements. In 1996, IFOR switched its name to the Stabilization Force (SFOR), better to reflect its mission. Violent incidents and overt hostility to foreign troop presence petered out over time. This outcome defied the worst fears generated by the press and pundits. Gradually the troop levels were reduced as the fears of violence abated, until the U.S. contingent numbered 700 soldiers in Bosnia, when NATO handed over its nine-year peacekeeping duties to the European Union on December 2, 2004. A couple hundred GIs remained to help the local officials in downsizing the Croat, Muslim, and Serb militaries and placing them in under a single command. The EU put in 7,000 troops to replace the NATO force.

The United States' ambivalence about nation-building enterprises was evident in Bosnia long before it became a deficiency in Washington's postwar Iraq plans. A clearer, more balanced understanding of the multifaceted dimensions of American power in the Balkans could have paid off less than a decade later. Perhaps a stronger, bipartisan endorsement in Bosnia would have yielded commitment, lessons, and skills that could have been readily applied in post-Hussein Iraq in 2003, where reconstruction and state-building activities stumbled badly from the onset.

There were problems with Dayton Accord, however. The agreement let Milošević off the hook by lifting sanctions on Serbia and by allowing him to escape punishment for his key role in instigating and perpetuating the Balkan bloodletting. More tellingly, it left him in power, unchecked and free to resume his ethnic cleansing agenda in Kosovo. Soon afterward, the United States passed up an opportunity to rid the Balkans of Milošević by not assisting local reformers. Crowds took to the streets of Belgrade and other Serbian cities in late 1996 and early 1997. The Serbian president's authoritarianism and corruption enraged his prodemocracy opponents. When he repudiated his opposition's electoral victories in 14 of Serbia's 19 largest cities, the prodemocracy reformers staged massive rallies in late 1996. By early February, support for the movement cut across nearly every segment of Serbian society. Key Milošević pillars abandoned the tottering regime. Army units stayed in their barracks, leaving the Ministry of the Interior's paramilitary units as the only reliable proregime force. Milošević clung to power by making some tactical concessions, and the protests subsided.

As a consequence of the orchestrated NATO deployment and the Dayton deal, the United States had recaptured its resoluteness. Its prior waffling and "ad hocism" seemed only a memory. American power ensured peace, economic betterment, and political stability in a war-shattered patch of Europe. The imposition of order, in fact, set the United States up for an even greater experiment in transplanting its version of stability in the vastly different venue of the Middle East less than a decade hence, with much less success.

The preintervention period marked one of the worst periods in Euro-American relations since the 1956 Suez Crisis. The end of the conflict salvaged President Clinton's reputation from complaints as being weak and ineffectual. Richard Holbrooke noted the turnaround: "Washington was now praised for its firm leadership—or even chided by some Europeans for *too much* leadership."[34] That America was faulted for too much influence in the Bosnian aftermath hinted at another rocky road ahead between the United States and Europe in resolving threats to security.

CHAPTER 6

KOSOVO: ROUND TWO IN THE BALKANS

In order for a war to be just, three things are necessary. First, the authority of the sovereign. Secondly, a just cause. Thirdly, a rightful intention.

Thomas Aquinas

FOR THE UNITED STATES, THE DAYTON ACCORD WAS MERELY A PRELUDE to another gathering storm in nearby Kosovo. Regarded as the birthplace of Serbian nationalism, the Kosovo province was left out of the negotiations at Dayton, Ohio, as a deal breaker. Since Slobodan Milošević and his compatriots regarded Kosovo with a quasi-spiritual attachment, the American interlocutors reasoned that it was better to reckon with Kosovo's resolution at another time than make it part of the overall settlement. Taking Kosovo off the table and leaving Milošević in power was a formula for a truce, not a durable peace or stable landscape.

Even though it did not take up Kosovo's cause at Wright Patterson Air Force base, the United States remembered it afterward. The Clinton government stopped the reentry of Federal Republic of Yugoslavia ([FRY] Serbia, Montenegro, and Kosovo) to membership in the World Bank and the International Monetary Fund, calling attention to Belgrade's persistent misrule in the Connecticut-sized territory. In effect, the Clinton policy maintained economic sanctions on the FRY by walling it off from financial credits from the two financial institutions and stunting its economic recovery from communism and war. To rebuild and retool, Belgrade desperately needed an infusion of funds. Instead, the United States froze out the FRY while the European Union recognized it. The EU held that the FRY could be politically opened up, and Milošević swept aside more quickly by bringing the isolated state back into the European fold.

FROM TRANQUILITY TO INSURGENCY

During the Bosnia fighting, Kosovo appeared a deceptively tranquil island in a violent sea, despite sharing the same historical pathologies as the rest of the Balkans. The early prevailed over the Kosovars until World War II. The German invasion shattered

Serbian rule and reignited ancient passions for independence as Kosovars and Serbs fought a bitter civil war within the larger conflict. After the war, Marshall Tito's communist regime took conciliatory steps toward the Kosovo enclave by granting it limited autonomy and by placing it on a par with the other republics in the federation. The Berlin Wall's fall reawakened Kosovo's longings for sovereignty.[1]

One manifestation of its blossoming nationalism took shape in the formation of the Democratic League of Kosovo (known by its Albanian initials, LDK) on December 23, 1989. Ibrahim Rugova, a professor of Albanian literature, was chosen by his academic colleagues to be its leader. The LDK, like the democratic movements forming in Central Europe at the time, aspired to a peaceful transition from the old order to sovereignty and political pluralism. The Serbian authorities, in turn, tolerated the LDK's passive politicking.[2] But Serb security forces cracked down hard on any armed or high-profile dissent to keep a tight lid on independence movements. Another manifestation occurred when riots at Priština University went from protests over living conditions to demands for Kosovo's independence.

The budding nationalistic fervor caused Kosovo's minority Serb population to emigrate. Although percentages of Albanians versus Serbs were in dispute, they were about 90 percent and to 10 percent, respectively, among the province's 2 million residents. With fewer Serb workers, Kosovo's government agencies underwent a further "Albanianization," which in turn contributed to more outflows of Serbian people who feared for their lives and livelihood. These factors set the stage for explosive politics.

Just as insecurity gripped Serbs living in Croatia at the time, so too did it manifest itself among Serbs residing in Kosovo. Into these swirling crosscurrents of ethnic nationalism stepped Slobodan Milošević, the onetime Communist Party hack turned ultranationalist. Ambitious, cunning, and corrupt, Milošević seized upon Serbian discontent, shaped it, and rode it power. In 1987, Ivan Stambolić, the president of Serbia, dispatched his understudy, Milošević, to reassure the uneasy Kosovo Serbs about mistreatment at the hands of their fellow Albanian citizens. His protégé instead stoked the fires of Serbian jingoism. With empathy, Milošević voiced what became an electrifying call to arms, "No one should dare to beat you again," at a rally held in the Field of Blackbirds.[3] This inflammatory sound bite struck an emotional chord with Serb resentment, and it was recycled repeatedly on Serbian television and spread by word of mouth. It vaulted Milošević to the pedestal of a cult figure, eclipsing Stambolić and allowing him to consolidate his own power base and win the Serb presidency. Years later, in 2005, a special court in Belgrade convicted Milošević's eight-man "liquidation unit" of assassinating Stambolić five years earlier, to eliminate him as a possible political threat to his former deputy. Gratitude was not one of Milošević's virtues. Once in the presidency, Milošević moved from rallies to action by usurping control in the two Serbian provinces of Vojvodina and Kosovo.

The United States, in fact, contributed to the province's placidity. It assessed Kosovo markedly different from Bosnia. Rightly, President Bush and later Bill Clinton feared that the spread of the Yugoslav conflagration into Kosovo would inevitably pit NATO allies against one another. If Serbia touched off fighting in Kosovo, it would in all likelihood inflame Albanian nationalism in Macedonia and Albania proper. Unless halted by the United States, a conflict could pull in the Greeks alongside the Serbs, which would, in turn, drag in Turkey and Bulgaria on the side of the Albanian nationalists. In short order, the entire Balkans would spiral into chaos and bloodshed unless something was done.[4]

Alarmed by Serbian repression in Kosovo, the George H. W. Bush administration during its waning days in office issued an uncharacteristically blunt threat to Belgrade. Known as the "Christmas warning," the United States sent a cable on December 24, 1992 to Milošević: "[I]n the event of a conflict in Kosovo caused by Serbian action, the United States will be prepared to employ military force against the Serbs in Kosovo and in Serbia proper."[5] Whether the stern notice succeeded or Serb attention diverted to combat already underway in Bosnia and Croatia, an uneasy calm descended over Kosovo until the end of the decade.

Beneath the tranquil exterior in the early 1990s, a clandestine political movement developed that was hostile to what it perceived as the LDK's sellout to Belgrade. Various small, secretive parties coalesced in mid-1993 to form what became known at the end of that year as the Kosovo Liberation Army or KLA (in the Albanian rendering it was the Ushtria Çlirimtare e Kosovës or the UÇK). The KLA's founding meeting took place in the Drenica Valley, northwest of Priština, a hotbed of anti-Yugoslav sentiments. While a few members of the KLA occasionally attacked the Serb police and their "collaborators," the tiny faction was obscure to most Kosovars until the Dayton terms became known.

THE OTHER SHOE DROPS

The Dayton agreement radicalized Kosovars' opposition to Serb control, for the settlement left them out in the cold. Their sense of injustice was heightened when the European Union diplomatically recognized the Federal Republic of Yugoslavia because such an acknowledgment carried with it the acceptance of the status quo of Kosovo's bondage to Belgrade. This awakened resentment matured slowly because Rugova's LDK had a near monopoly in politics and the media in the province.[6]

Events in neighboring Albania also reshaped Kosovo's political order. By 1992, the Albanians had overthrown their xenophobic communist rulers after 46 years of repression. As the world's most reclusive country, except for North Korea, its transition was far from easy, leaving the impoverished state on the Adriatic Sea prone to turmoil and plagued by powerful organized crime networks. Albania also underwent one of those untoward events that defy the elaborate mathematical models of Western game theorists to predict political events. In spring 1997, the Albanian government collapsed because thousands of its citizens lost their personal savings in a classic Ponzi scheme. So widespread was the financial ruin that the political repercussions undercut the government and precipitated chaos throughout the tiny country. During the bedlam, the nation's armories were pried open, flooding the market with cheap AK-47 assault rifles, ideal weapons for guerrilla warfare. This windfall enormously benefited the embryonic KLA, some of whose members in Albania bought up numerous weapons for a song.

Within Kosovo itself, events marched inexorably toward an insurgency. The KLA attacked Serbian police officers and recently arrived "colonists" who immigrated reluctantly into the province when their former homes in the Krajina pocket were overrun by Croatian troops in August 1995. Belgrade settled some 16,000 Serbian refugees to strengthen the government's hold in the volatile territory, but their welcome was less than friendly. Sporadic attacks had long been factor in the restive province, but the relocation of displaced Serb families exacerbated tensions and accelerated the KLA's armed resistance, as it tried to displace the passive LDK as the representative of the Kosovars.

When the insurgency crackled across the Kosovo landscape it carried its own blend of violent traits. Unlike the siege warfare of Sarajevo and other Bosnian strongholds, the Kosovo conflict represented a more fluid form of fighting without dug-in cannons, deep trenches, and set-piece engagements. Hit-and-run ambushes, burst-of-gunfire assassinations, and tit-for-tat killings characterized the battles. Like so many insurgencies, the guerrillas were not above killing their fellow countrymen if they presumed them collaborators or from other political factions, including LDK members.

The KLA insurgents relied on Albania for across-the-border bases to train, regroup, and gain provisions and arms. They struck and retreated, provoking the Serbs into disproportionate retaliations. This in turn generated recruits for the rebels. With heavier weaponry—armored vehicles and helicopters—Belgrade could stand and fight, but the insurgents relied on classic guerrilla tactics. They attacked and then melted into the countryside. The Serbs tried unsuccessfully to seal off the Albanian frontier to freeze the flow of KLA fighters and munitions. The Milošević regime, which during the Bosnian turmoil promised the West another Vietnamese quagmire if it intervened, now found itself ensnared in its own mini-Vietnam.

The Kosovo conflict bore some traits of the recent fighting to its north. Each side torched the farms and dwellings of the other community. Livestock were machine-gunned. Ethnic cleansing had become an equal opportunity employer by both sides. Lines of distraught refugees, both Serb and Kosovar, choked the roads as they fled to safety across the borders. Like a Greek tragedy, the actors at various stages had no choice but to take the next step in the blood feud. They raised the ante by multiplying the killings, with civilians on the receiving end of most of the gunshots.

INTO THE WORLD'S SPOTLIGHT

The spreading violence soon attracted Western media and diplomatic attention. This notoriety was one of the KLA's secondary goals so as to upstage Rugova and the LDK. Its primary objective was first to focus international scrutiny on Belgrade's misrule and then to alter the West's acquiescent posture toward Serb domination. The KLA's strategy was audacious and risky, but it worked completely. Nonetheless, the path to its ultimate victory was bloody and convoluted.

As much as there had been justifiable consternation in Washington over the Bosnian conflict drawing in neighboring states, so too there existed the distinct likelihood that the Kosovo fighting would destabilize the Balkan neighborhood. Heightening that fear were KLA pronouncements about a war of liberation for Albanians living in Macedonia and Montenegro to create a Greater Albania. In turn, the Serbs played up Western fears territorial volatility. They labeled the KLA a terrorist organization and a "front for a pan-Albanian ethnic movement" engaged in "international aggression."[7] Not surprisingly, the bluster about redrawing the region's boundaries, once again, riveted apprehension in foreign ministries on the Balkans and initiated diplomatic efforts to preserve stability.

The United States reestablished the Contact Group (which again comprised Britain, France, Germany, Russia, and the United States to deal with the earlier Bosnia crisis) and reviewed proposals for a sanction policy against Serbia. Although Moscow disapproved of even a limited embargo, it could not dissuade Western foreign ministries from slapping economic sanctions on the Federal Republic of Yugoslavia. Next, America explored initiatives for direct intervention into Kosovo to stanch bloodshed, but it ran up against the long-standing doctrine of sovereignty.

This international principle of sovereignty was said to have originated with the Treaty of Westphalia in 1648 that ended the Thirty Years War.[8] No mere fig leaf, the Westphalian stricture enshrined the international norm of the inviolability of state sovereignty that permitted a legal framework for the Belgrade regime to abuse the Kosovo population. Rulers within states are the arbiters of legitimate behavior. Intervention across borders constitutes aggression, and thus the international community hung itself up on the sovereignty principle, fearing that intervening to protect the Kosovars was, in fact, an act of war. For his part, Milošević drew comfort from the sovereignty precept.

Washington's entreaties for military operations against the FRY at first went nowhere with the NATO countries, which refused to take actions without UN authorization. Two veto-wielding powers—Russia and China—hinted at blocking such approval in the Security Council. Their obstruction pulled the United Nations out of any realistic solution to halt the atrocities within Kosovo. And it confirmed Belgrade's assessment of the West's disinclination to intervene in Kosovo.

Meanwhile back in Kosovo, the expanding insurgency sidelined Ibrahim Rugova, as the KLA guerrillas captured the limelight. Facing political irrelevancy by 1998, the LKD leader faxed a letter to Richard Holbrooke of Dayton fame, inviting the former diplomat to assume a mediator role in the conflict-torn province. At that time, Holbrooke had returned to the private sector in New York City. Later, in June the White House nominated him to be the U.S. representative at the United Nations. Holbrooke shuttled between Belgrade and Priština attempting to arrange a meeting between Rugova and Milošević. When it took place, the proceedings backfired on Rugova, who came off as an appeaser, boosting the rival KLA's standing.

THE UNITED STATES GETS TOUGH ON KOSOVO

At the urging of the United States, the NATO defense ministers convened in Brussels on June 11 and 12, 1998 and laid plans for military actions, if called upon to employ force against Serb units in Kosovo. The meeting's truculent agenda was intended to restrain Belgrade's hand in Kosovo, but it failed. Milošević remained steadfast because he had become inured to the West's lengthy agenda setting and its hesitancy in deploying force. The Serb strongman also banked on the Europeans' aversion to apply military power without a Security Council blessing as had been the case during the Bosnian crisis. The European Union governments did join the United States in prohibiting investments in Serbia and Montenegro and barring FRY flights from landing at their airports. But they still demurred from waging war against the Milošević regime.

Under U.S. prodding, NATO turned to a display of airpower to underline its warnings to Belgrade. Washington favored a robust show of force, whereas the Europeans preferred a nonthreatening warning. The whole dance resembled the desultory sidesteps and halting shuffles of the previous Bosnia crisis. Not appreciating the linkage between diplomacy and credible force, NATO fired the equivalent of a blank cartridge at Serbia, when it lofted some 80 warplanes into the Balkan skies on June 15, 1998. So as not to violate Serbian airspace, the flight plan stipulated that the aircraft skirt the FRY borders by jetting over Macedonia and Albania. Designated as Operation Determined Falcon, the NATO commanders wanted to overawe Serb ground forces with their aerial prowess. But the Serbian military and police paid it little heed as they persisted in their deadly operations. Determined Falcon had the unintended effect of demonstrating to NATO members that hollow gestures were useless against willful men such as Milošević.

But Determined Falcon sparked consternation in Moscow, which was already worried about a proposed expansion of NATO eastward toward the Russian border. Plans to incorporate Poland, Hungary, and the Czech Republic into the Atlantic alliance in April 1999 made Boris Yeltsin especially anxious about a Western military intervention into the former Soviet sphere and deepened his distrust of the United States, which was leading the charge for NATO enlargement as means to entrench European stability through wider membership in the alliance.

As for the United States, it sought to align Russia on the West's side in its bid to quell the spreading violence within the Kosovo province. President Clinton telephoned Yeltsin several times to bring him on broad. Soothing the Russians took time and money; earlier, the White House pushed along a $10 billion loan from the IMF to Moscow in 1996 just prior to presidential election, which saw Boris Yeltsin win a second term.

The American efforts paid off on another issue. On September 2, 1998, President Clinton met with his Russian counterpart in the Kremlin's Catherine Hall to sign security agreements on sharing information on ballistic missile launches and removal of weapons grade plutonium from the two countries' stockpiles. At the press conference, the U.S. president announced that he and Yeltsin "agreed that the Serbian government must stop all repressive actions . . . and pursue an interim settlement."[9] Both countries worried about instability in southeastern Europe, leading to a larger conflict.

A greater anxiety gripped the Kremlin in addition to its suspicions about NATO operating in its backyard. It theorized that air strikes on behalf of the Kosovars against the Serbs were little more than pretext for similar bombing operations against Russia for its battles against the separatists in Chechnya. Both Chechnya and Kosovo were made up of Muslim majorities. In each province, the populations boiled with independence passions from governments dominated by Slavs and the Orthodox faith. The parallels were too close for Moscow's comfort. The Russian Foreign Minister Igor Ivanov made just that point in a telephone conversation to Secretary of State Albright when he spoke, "Madeleine, don't you understand we have many Kosovos in Russia."[10]

Thus, Washington's forward policy in Kosovo could not be implemented in a vacuum. It had to take into account Russian sensibilities or it would encounter resistance from an agitated Kremlin. Two key threats stood out for Western policymakers. First, the Russians could conceivably aid the Serbs, rekindling Cold War-type tensions between East and West. The other and related danger centered on the adverse impact of inciting Russian nationalism, which benefited Yeltsin's right-wing opponents and hard-line army generals. Just as the previous Bush government strove to shore up a shaking Mikhail Gorbachev, so too the Clinton administration angled to bolster Boris Yeltsin for the same reasons—it benefited the United States. The American contradictions of pushing Milošević, a Kremlin client, and helping Yeltsin called for a balancing act.

What saved Washington was Milošević, who never passed up an opportunity to place himself on the wrong side of history. It was in Belgrade's interest to restrain Serb reprisals in the rebellious province. De-escalation in the violence stood to divide the United States from its more hesitant European allies and to facilitate Russian backing of the FRY's retention of Kosovo. Moscow desired to keep Kosovo off the front page of the world's newspapers. But within Kosovo, the Serb military and police did their utmost to make headlines by committing gruesome atrocities. A maverick client such as Milošević frustrated his Kremlin patron. In time, Moscow tired of the high maintenance associated with the Serbian strongman and simply abstained from confronting the West over its military action against him.[11]

America's policy, as shaped by Madeleine Albright, was decidedly anti-Milošević. The secretary of state regarded Milošević as the root of all evil in the Balkans. She quickly became the leading proponent among the top U.S. officials for using military force to topple him so as to bring peace to the region. In her mind, Kosovo was merely a repetition of Bosnian horrors in the early 1990s. Aligned against Albright's bellicosity were William Cohen, Clinton's third secretary of defense, and his Pentagon military chiefs. A moderate Republican Senator from Maine, Cohen took over the reigns of the Defense Department when Bill Perry returned to Stanford University. Cohen reflected the general's caution about sliding into a quagmire á la Vietnam. One senior military officer who saw eye-to-eye with Albright was General Wesley Clark, the Supreme Allied Commander in Europe (SACEUR) and thus military head of NATO military forces in Europe. Increasingly, Holbrooke also judged Milošević as an impediment to stability of the entire region. At this point, the hawks stood in the wings of the Kosovo controversy but events in due course would propel them to center stage and convince President Clinton that only force could bring steadiness to the Balkans.

Throughout 1998, and especially in the final months of that year, Albright and the whole U.S. foreign policy bureaucracy was sidelined by the cascading domestic crisis engulfing Bill Clinton. Implicated in a sexual liaison with Monica Lewinsky, a former White House intern, the president stood accused of perjury and obstruction of justice for which he faced impeachment. Judging by the polls and by the November off-year election when the Democrats gained five seats in the House of Representatives, Clinton's popularity held steady but he was on the political defensive for much of the year. While ultimately impeached by the U.S. House of

Representatives along mostly party votes on December 19, the U.S. Senate acquitted President Clinton of both charges on February 12, 1999. Before the Senate acquittal, the scandal transfixed the nation for months and hobbled its exercise of policy abroad.

During autumn 1998, the security climate worsened in Kosovo as NATO military and diplomatic activities multiplied. The Serb army shelled villages to retaliate against elusive guerrillas, and the KLA shot back with kidnappings and assassinations. In early September, NATO's Secretary General Javier Solana announced that the organization's planners finished its operational plan for a military intervention should it be required. A couple of weeks later on September 24 in Portugal, the NATO ambassadors meeting in the North Atlantic Council adopted the plan and issued a communiqué that outlined a stepping up of the "level of military preparedness" for the eventuality of an air campaign. The so-called OPLAN 10601, known in civilian parlance as Operation Allied Force, laid out a phased air campaign that entailed an escalation of bombing to ratchet up pressure until its ends were achieved. Allied Force set in motion the stationing of U.S.-based B-52s in Britain and the readying of aircraft already arrayed in Europe.

Before the NATO communiqué, the United States pressured the Security Council with partial headway, for it approved Resolution 1199 that evenhandedly demanded all parties "immediately cease hostilities" while reaffirming a commitment to "the sovereignty and territorial integrity of the Federal Republic of Yugoslavia."[12] Despite U.S. efforts, the resolution hewed to the UN's previous course of sparing Serbia a palpable threat. Upholding state sovereignty mattered more than humanitarian considerations not only to the Russians but also to the skeptics of establishing an interventionist precedent for meddling in a nation's internal affairs. The threat of a Russian (and perhaps Chinese who wanted to deal with autonomous Taiwan as a domestic issue) veto in the Security Council ruled out a forceful UN course of action. Then the cork came out of the bottleneck.

The full-bore U.S. approach unexpectedly won out at an impromptu meeting in the VIP lounge in London's Heathrow Airport on October 8 among the Contact Group foreign ministers and Richard Holbrooke. As expected, Igor Ivanov, the Russian foreign minister, stated that the Yeltsin government would veto a military-enabling resolution in the Security Council. Then the Russian envoy expressed a startling breakthrough to the stalemate. If NATO went ahead without UN approval, Moscow would just denounce the action. In short, Moscow was willing to stand aside and let NATO deal militarily with the FRY. Equivalent to a political wink and nod, the seismic Russian shift in direction was a turning point for American diplomacy. Since London and Paris had come round to Washington's position of using NATO against Serbia, Russia's acquiescing meant a formidable obstacle disappeared.[13]

Armed with this newfound consensus and the muscular Allied Force plan, Holbrooke returned to Belgrade in mid-October to face down the Serbian autocrat, at least so it was believed. Recognizing the American emissary's newly strengthened hand, Milošević outwardly assented to a series of measures toward stabilizing the conflict-torn province. First, he acceded to NATO flights over Kosovo to monitor events on the ground. Second, he allowed the intercession of unarmed OSCE observers, named "verifiers," in the violence-soaked enclave. Next, Milošević approved the right of return to over 100,000 displaced persons to their former homes. Additionally, he gave into the demand to scale back his security forces, and at the end of the month some 4,000 paramilitary police did pull out of Priština. Finally, he agreed to the start of a political process to determine Kosovo's future.[14]

Holbrooke and his European peers believed that the promise of a NATO bombardment had compelled Milošević to concede. They were wrong. The agreement held two advantages for the FRY chief: it spared Serbia bombing and it averted the deployment of Western soldiers into Kosovo. Milošević perhaps also expected NATO and the Contact Group to restrain the KLA, which did not happen. In fact, the guerrillas filtered back into positions abandoned during Serb summer offensive, which infuriated Belgrade.

On December 24, the Serb security forces activated Operation Horseshoe. A month later, by the end of January 1999, the Draconian offensive caused the total number of displaced people to reach half a million either within the province or across its borders in Albania and Macedonia. A particularly gruesome atrocity shocked the Western governments into a demand that both parties halt the killing and negotiate their differences. At the village of Račak, a firefight was followed by a Serb massacre of 45 civilians. The cold-blooded murders captured headlines and precipitated calls "to do something" about the reign of terror unfolding in Kosovo.[15] To paraphrase Talleyrand, the Račak murders were worse than a crime from the Serb perspective; they were a mistake.

Madeleine Albright seized on the international outrage over Račak to rally adherents to her long-held approach that diplomacy without military power was useless in the Kosovo maelstrom. Her entreaties now found receptive ears in London with the new resident at Ten Downing Street. In May 1997, Tony Blair of the Labour Party succeeded the cautious John Major as prime minister in a landslide election victory. Blair's exhibited little of his predecessors' disinclination to wade into the Kosovo fighting. His deeply held instincts for humanitarian intervention resembled Britain's great liberal politician William Gladstone of the late nineteenth century. Therefore, Her Majesty's Government made it easier for Washington to forge a military coalition against Serbia to restore order to the war-ravaged Kosovo enclave.

PEACE TALKS AT RAMBOUILLET

Out of necessity, the American secretary of state subscribed to the one-last-chance brand of diplomacy, not because she believed Milošević could be dealt with in a forthright manner. She did so predicting that his obstinacy would once and for all solidify the Europeans behind her position that only force, not diplomatic tangoing, would bring him to heel. She prevailed in debates within the Contact Group, which issued a summons on January 29 to the Belgrade regime and to the Kosovo combatants to convene at the negotiating table. Compulsion, not willingness to negotiate, was the key ingredient in bringing the sides together. If the Serbs failed to heed the cease-fire warning, they would be bombed. If the Kosovars remained impervious, they would be left isolated to face the Serbians alone. As a venue and date for the peace talks, the Contact Group chose the fourteenth-century chateau in Rambouillet, a town 30 miles south of Paris, on February 6, 1999.

Rambouillet attracted the Kosovar political elite. Ibrahim Rugova, the LDK president, came with his deputies, as did Hashim Thaçi, a founder of the KLA, and an indicted war criminal. The Kosovar delegates selected Thaçi as their head. The United States assembled a group of legal advisers to help make up for the Kosovar's lack of experience and expertise. On the other hand, the Serb delegation comprised lesser-known figures and was headed by Ratko Marković, Serbia's deputy prime minister. Decisions came from Belgrade, not the FRY delegates anyway. Fearing arrest for war crimes, Slobodan Milošević refused to leave Belgrade but interjected himself into the proceedings via telephone.

The European members desired a diplomatic solution to preserve the unity of the Federal Republic of Yugoslavia as the UN resolution set down. They believed that the creation of a separate, homogenous Kosovar Albanian nation represented a major departure from other multiethnic European states that could set a precedent for breakaway entities across the Continent. They wanted a trial period that allowed Belgrade to mend its ways in Kosovo by allowing the province a large measure of autonomy.

This approach satisfied neither combatant delegation. Each stuck to its guns, rejecting half-a-loaf offers. The Kosovar delegates looked askance at the postponement of an independence referendum three years into the future. They demanded immediate sovereignty. In addition, the KLA faction was adamantly against disarming its guerrilla bands. The Serb delegation embraced the wording in the documents about the territorial integrity of Yugoslavia, interpreting it as a guarantee barring Kosovo secession. But it and the string pullers in Belgrade strenuously resisted a NATO military presence in Kosovo, even if it meant disarming the KLA. The Serbs were willing to accept limited autonomy but not statehood for the province. On March 18 in Paris, Thaçi and the Kosovar delegation signed the Rambouillet accord in a brief ceremony that the Yugoslav delegation and the Russian negotiator boycotted.

The United States' eleventh-hour efforts were rejected by Belgrade, which interpreted the Rambouillet as an ultimatum and not an accord. The FRY refused to swallow the so-called Appendix B of the agreement that authorized NATO troops, "vehicles, vessels, aircraft free and unrestricted passage and unimpeded access through the Federal Republic of Yugoslavia," not just Kosovo. The FRY rejected this as an infringement of its sovereignty.[16] Milošević feared NATO forces would imperil his rule.

In light of the death and destruction endured by the FRY from NATO airpower for 11 weeks, the question should be asked: why did not Milošević cave in to American demands? Briefly, the FRY's president may have thought that NATO was bluffing or that Moscow would block the aerial bombardment and come to his rescue. Worried about the parallels between Chechnya and Kosovo, the Kremlin could conceivably lend the Serbs advanced missile systems, if not actually confront a NATO aerial onslaught. Milošević erred in his assessment of Yeltsin. Moscow made its own calculations and washed its hands of a troublesome client rather than defying Washington. The FRY chief may also have believed the boasting of his generals that their antiaircraft missiles could shoot down enough Western airplanes and capture enough pilots to wring a cease-fire from NATO. Besides, the Serb military thought by dispersing their armed forces into guerrilla bands they could wage another Vietnam for NATO's conventional units and tactics. What is also likely is that Milošević weighed the dismal record of American power as applied in Somalia, post–Gulf War Iraq, and elsewhere and found it wanting. He saw that Saddam Hussein survived the December 1998 bombings without great losses. In short, American ultimatums lacked credibility.

Washington also miscalculated in sending mixed signals to Serbia. As the Rambouillet negotiations pointed toward failure, the Pentagon redeployed the aircraft carrier *USS Theodore Roosevelt* from the Adriatic Sea, where it had been within striking range of Belgrade, to the Persian Gulf. It was the wrong signal, at the wrong time, for the wrong reason.[17] Belgrade no doubt breathed a sigh of relief as the warship sailed away.

During the weeks preceding the Paris signing ceremony, the Oval Office waged another campaign on Capitol Hill to ensure congressional authority for America's spearheading a NATO military action. Within the ranks of both political parties, legislators greeted presidential pleas for military authorization with skepticism. Detractors doubted that America, in their view, should be pursuing militarized social welfare work around the world, when in reality bringing order to chaotic province advanced U.S. interests. In any event, the White House succeeded. Just prior to Kosovars signing the Rambouillet accord, the House of Representatives voted 219 to 191 for approval of Clinton's plan for dispensing troops to implement a possible peace settlement. By a vote of 58 to 41 the Senate authorized the White House to join in NATO bombing operation.

A POST–BERLIN WALL CASUS BELLI

Two powerful explanations arose for the justification of going to war against a state, which never directly threatened its neighbors with aggression. One rational dealt with preventive warfare to spare a wider calamity and contain, if not defuse, instability. And the other reason revolved around the humanitarian interventions to protect peoples within a sovereign nation. Preventing a war by starting a small conflict seemingly defies logic. Yet a firebreak can contain a prairie fire. Prowar officials analogized from the firefighter's use of a "control burn" to contain a conflagration. In the Balkans, with its interlocking ethnic-nationalistic hatreds, the concept enjoyed more than a little plausibility because the smoldering ethnic strife in Kosovo could be fanned into a regional firestorm. As the bombing started, President Clinton's address to the nation noted the geopolitical perils: "Let a fire burn there in this area and the flames will spread."[18] America found itself, however reluctantly, again cast in the role of global stabilizer as the United Nations' shortcomings became evident.

Humanitarian reasons for war also gained enormous prominence in American elite circles. It became fashionable to advocate armed humanitarian interventions by citing the texts of St. Thomas Aquinas on just wars or by recalling failures to prevent the Holocaust. A reprise of genocidal killings helped morph the Vietnam War era doves into hawks. In a sharp departure from the cynicism of realpolitik, stability and humanitarian rationales for war added other two causes to the three sketched by Thucydides two millennia before—fear, honor, and interests.

The Kosovo bombing constituted a number of other firsts as well. NATO, an alliance established 51 years before to fight the Soviet Union, first employed its military against another European state, which did not attack its neighbors. A war was also waged to implement Security Council resolutions without obtaining specific UN authorization. This established a slender precedent for George W. Bush's subsequent attack on Iraq, where the United States cited nearly a score of Security Council resolutions, but failed to obtain a specific war-authorizing vote in the council. Finally, the Kosovo campaign witnessed the innovation of airpower alone, without ground troops, to attain a military victory.

Despite the divisions and unease within the Clinton government, the president came around to the position that the United States could not sit idly by while a second Balkans' tragedy destabilized Europe. As for Clinton himself, he was more comfortable with the idea of employing military force than had been the case during his first administration. The Bosnian and Rwandan crises attuned Clinton to the need for American military action as an antidote for the Balkan virus.[19] European stability, NATO's new post–Cold War role, and Russia's political evolution toward democracy—all would be set back if Washington allowed Milošević to spark a region-wide conflict. More experienced and more confident in international affairs, Clinton wanted to stabilize Europe, signal America's solidarity with NATO allies, and enshrine a legacy of an effective presidency.

The prowar faction, moreover, foresaw a short bombing effort to bring the autocratic FRY leader back to the bargaining table. They were in sync with NATO estimates that Belgrade would capitulate in a matter of days, not weeks, as had been the case four years earlier during the brief Bosnian air campaign. The first night of the shelling, the secretary of state appeared on a television news program and stated: "I don't see this as a long-term operation." The U.S. officer in charge of the NATO air campaign, Lieutenant General Mike Short, later concurred with Albright's prediction. He was told at the campaign's start: "This'll be over in three nights."[20] These forecasts proved to be a headache for the president and his senior staff, as the aerial pounding dragged on and civilian deaths mounted. In fact, the aerial campaign lasted a total of 78 days, much longer than any of the war planners envisioned. The ramifications of this prolonged shelling spilled over into intra-NATO squabbles, Russo-American tensions, and even disagreement within the Clinton government on how to bring harmony to a violent corner of southeastern Europe.

"MADELEINE'S WAR"

Rambouillet's failure to secure a peaceful Kosovo solution meant another example of Clausewitz's maxim that war is the continuation of politics by other means. NATO resorted to force to impose a political solution. Thirty-four hours after Washington's emissary, Richard Holbrooke, left Belgrade empty handed in his last-ditch search for concessions from Slobodan Milošević, NATO warplanes dropped their deadly ordnance on military installations in Belgrade's outskirts on March 24, 1999, beginning America's second martial intervention into the troubled Balkans at the head of a NATO coalition.

Militarily, the campaign's implementation was flawed. Students of airpower advocate a massive delivery of destruction from the outset. Instead, the NATO air assault incrementally increased, starting with some 400 planes before approaching 1,000, unlike the devastating opening punch of the first Gulf War when 2,700 planes struck in the initial week.[21] America's NATO allies flew 40 percent of the strikes, with France supplying almost a hundred aircraft, second only to the United States in its contribution. But it was the United States that furnished all the stealth aircraft and most of the refueling planes and electronic warfare assets. America dominated the planning of the air war because it alone possessed the intelligence gathering and analysis function along with the battle damage assessment capability. Ninety-nine percent of the target nominations originated with the U.S. intelligence. No Serb-flown MiG-29s lifted off the runways to fight the NATO warplanes. The United States suffered the only two NATO air loses to missiles, which downed a F-117A Nighthawk and a F-16 Fighting Falcon. The aircrews escaped harm in both cases.

Curiously, detractors of the three-mile-high bombardments believed the tactics somehow unfair, even unchivalrous, because the pilots placed themselves out of danger. It was unjust to kill, while not offering the enemy the opportunity to return the favor, because advanced technology allowed Western aircrews the luxury of delivering death with near-impunity. Warfare is never fair. Europe's mounted aristocracy decried the crossbow, for example. The lopsidedness of the fighting actually speeded the demoralization of the Serb civilian population, one of the goals of the bombing.

A far greater controversy took place within NATO over target selection. Sensitive targets, those of dual civilian-military use or located nearby noncombatant populations, required approval from alliance members, at least the American, British and French—the major three participants. France often blocked or at least delayed the process by raising objections that necessitated time consuming and frustrating appeals by NATO's supreme military chief, General Clark, to secure a go-ahead. France's pro-Serb sentiments were suspect, but Paris also embraced the belief that postwar reconciliation and reconstruction would be eased by less bombing damage. The United States worried that the a desultory application of power worked to the Serb advantage, by opening the door to intra-NATO factionalism and by giving running room to antiwar protests in Western states.

Another dispute revolved around the actual targets selected for destruction. Since World War II's strategic bombing, American airpower doctrine has stressed turning off the lights, water, and manufacturing capacity of a declared enemy along with pulverizing the typical military prizes of tanks and trenches. Selecting factories, bridges, and electrical power grids for demolition meant that mistakes occurred and noncombatants died in what was referred in a bureaucratic phrase as collateral damage. Serb propaganda made much of these errors, which hardened protests among the war's debunkers. The Federal Republic of Yugoslavia published a book, *NATO Crimes in Yugoslavia*, which gave graphic accounts of bombing victims, replete with grim pictures of charred and carbonized bodies. Estimates of civilians killed by NATO bombs ranged from 500 to 2000, plus 6,000 wounded. As such, the air campaign fell well short of an indiscriminate blitz.[22]

The most controversial bombing mishap took place when an American B-2 stealth bombers struck the Chinese Embassy in downtown Belgrade with five 2,000-pound, satellite-guided bombs on May 7. The attack killed three staff members and wounded another 20. The bombs were meant for the FRY's arms procurement center. The errant air strike amounted to a public relations disaster. China erupted in fury with huge, seething anti-American demonstrations. Rock-throwing rioters damaged the U.S. Embassy in Beijing and imprisoned Jim Sasser, the American ambassador, within its buildings. The mistaken embassy bombing played into the Chinese government's campaign to intensify nationalism as a substitute for waning communism.

Washington tried to get beyond the crisis by stating the erroneous targeting resulted from an old CIA map that did not show the correct location of the new Chinese Embassy. To calm the diplomatic hurricane, President Clinton apologized, and the United States paid $4.5 million to the families of the three Chinese diplomats killed in the ambassadorial structure and $28 million to China's government for damage to its Belgrade diplomatic mission. Months later, the CIA fired an intelligence officer for errors leading to the mistaken bombing. For its failure to protect the U.S. Embassy in Beijing, the PRC made a $2.87 million settlement to Washington. Despite U.S. conciliatory gestures and funds, the incident played havoc with Sino-American relations for months as the Chinese believed the United States deliberately attacked their embassy.

GROUND WAR VERSUS AIR WAR

The protracted bombing renewed debate on the effectiveness of American and NATO military power. Front and center in the debate was the narrowness of the instrument of power—air forces alone. On the first day of the air bombardment, the Clinton administration undercut even the plausible threat of a ground war. The president declared, "I do not intend to put our troops in Kosovo to fight a war."[23] Intended to calm domestic anxieties over casualties, the pronouncement no doubt induced a sigh of relief in Belgrade.

Britain's Tony Blair clashed repeatedly with Clinton over the Oval Office's unwillingness to consider ground forces in Kosovo.[24] The prime minister's passionate tone stirred unease. President Clinton's legendary apprehension for body bags arriving at Dover Air Force Base and the impact of casualties on his standing in the polls were well known in Washington power circles. Clinton telephoned Blair prior to NATO's fiftieth anniversary summit in Washington on April 23–24 and requested that he lower his strident rhetoric on the Kosovo war. In exchange, he pledged to reexamine the existing war plans as a quid pro quo to the British leader. All the while the Pentagon stuck to its public stance that the air war was working and that it was just a matter of time.

As the air operation ground steadily on, the president reversed his no-ground-troops stand. On May 18, he publicly stated, "[W]e have not and will not take any option off the table."[25] Then Sandy Berger began planning what was termed "Plan B-minus," in which a NATO force of 175,000 troops made up of 100,000 U.S. soldiers would invade in early September.[26] On June 2, the President's National Security adviser reaffirmed that Bill Clinton had not ruled out any option. Also on June 2, it was reported that Clinton had scheduled a meeting for the next day with the Joint Chiefs at the White House "to discuss options for using ground troops if NATO decides to invade Kosovo."[27] A land invasion never materialized because Milošević surrendered on June 3, 1999.

The threat to employ land forces was pivotal in ending the war, for it convinced Milošević that no easy way out existed.[28] A NATO ground attack would have destroyed a sizable portion of the Yugoslav army and police, the regime's strongest pillars. It would have made a coup possible, about which speculation existed since the early 1990s. After all, the presence of international foot soldiers in Kosovo is what Milošević feared most about the Rambouillet accord because they posed a definable danger to his rule. A possible ground war supplied the final impetus for Moscow to drive Milošević to the bargaining table. Otherwise, Russia would have been humiliated for not defending fellow Serbs and would have faced a formidable combat army in its former backyard. Neither prospect cheered Boris Yeltsin, always fearful of challenges from his extreme nationalist flank.

Washington and NATO's mistake lay in not initially applying enough power against the Belgrade regime. They should have deployed a credible land force to neighboring states before hurling GPS bombs and missiles on the FRY. Ruling out a ground invasion meant Milošević's generals could ignore the threat. In the end, Milošević, ever the artful dodger, accepted NATO's conditions to avert a land offensive and to retain power. The FRY agreed to a cease-fire, withdrawal of all Serb military and police units in Kosovo, return of refugees and displaced people, and the stationing of a NATO-organized peacekeeping force, and later its participation in a political settlement.

COALITION AND WARTIME DIPLOMACY

Diplomacy during any war is an important factor, but in coalition warfare it assumes a critical dimension. The Kosovo bombing was coalition warfare at its finest and at its worst. The roller coaster nature of the intra-alliance relations indicated a crack-up at times and encouraged Milošević to believe that NATO would fracture. Yet, the coalition, despite its intramural squabbling, held together. To be sure, it did not operate as smoothly as the American-run coalition in the Persian Gulf War. But America had been the prime mover of the earlier conflict and the predominant power. Whereas in the Kosovo conflict, collective decision-making and a consensus-seeking mode reined supreme, making the United States merely primus inter pares.

Tensions simmered among the coalition partners, particularly as hopes for a quick war dissipated. As the bombing dragged on, France and Germany joined Italy and Greece in their growing disenchantment with the NATO campaign. Always sensitive to American primacy, Paris became especially vexing as it looked for ways to constrain the "hyperpower" of the United States. Bill Clinton cajoled Jacques Chirac and enlisted Spanish President José Maria Aznar to smooth over relations with the prickly French president. But Clinton had to intervene himself so the French president would not walk out of the NATO summit in Washington in mid-April, lest it be seen as a sign of disunity.

Beyond NATO, diplomatic problems for the United States arose chiefly with Russia, threatening to redivide the two powers in a manner that smacked of the Cold War confrontation. Strobe Talbott, deputy secretary of state, whose portfolio dealt mainly with Russian-American relations, wrote later that the Kosovo bombing "was to be the most severe, dangerous and consequential crisis in U.S.-Russian relations of the post-cold war period."[29] Clinton's State Department and Vice President Al Gore had taken pains with Russo-American relations since coming into office. With Prime Minister Viktor Chernomyrdin, Gore cochaired the U.S.-Russian Bi-national Commission on Economic and Technological Cooperation to promote trade and investment with Russia. Known as the Gore-Chernomyrdin Commission, it focused on space exploration and energy enterprises in the Caspian Basin and Siberia. As a consequence, the Clinton government earmarked almost half a billion for Russian development by 1997, coming on top of the hundreds of millions already passed to the former foe. There was to be no Carthaginian peace for this new Rome. Clinton and his Russian team stressed the goal of making Russia a stabile and friendly power, if not a close ally.

Russo-American interactions hit a nadir after the bombing commenced. Protestors staged demonstrations at the U.S. Embassy in Moscow; Duma members demanded Yeltsin dispatch military aid and "volunteers" to Yugoslavia; and the Kremlin yanked its representatives from NATO. Yet, Russia never severed its ties with the alliance or the United States. It gained too much within the 1997 NATO-Russia Founding Act, which established a regular consultative channel between the Kremlin and the alliance's headquarters so as to alleviate frictions as NATO moved eastward. Yeltsin wanted to preserve the connections and the economic benefits that came from cooperation with the West, such as membership in the WTO and OECD.

The United States knew that Moscow was attempting to stop the bombing through separate appeals to the various capitals of the NATO members. But this beseeching came to naught. When the NATO allies did not fall out over the conduct of the Kosovo war at the transatlantic summit in April, Yeltsin and Clinton reopened the former Gore-Chernomyrdin channel to deal with Kosovo. This connection expanded to a troika when Russian and American officials decided to name a third partner to negotiate directly with Milošević. The Russians detested the Serb leader. His intransigence made it inevitable that NATO would garrison troops with the former Soviet orbit. Yet they feared a domestic backlash for pressuring him to capitulate. They wanted someone else "to accept the sword of surrender from Milošević," as Chernomyrdin colorfully put it.[30] Madeleine Albright accepted the suggestion of Finland's President Martti Ahtisaari, who hailed from a nonaligned and non-NATO country that was to take over the presidency of the European Union. Since Gore's presidential bid increasingly preoccupied him, Talbott stood in for the vice president.

The three—Talbott, Chernomyridin, and Ahtisaari—consulted several times to strategize on ways to persuade Milošević, who connived to forestall the two essential NATO demands—total withdrawal of some 50,000 Serb troops and paramilitary police and acceptance of a NATO "at the core" of Kosovo peacekeepers. Since only Russia had any influence over the Serbian strongman, it was left to Chernomyrdin to make repeated visits to Belgrade to convince Milošević about the wisdom of relenting to cut his losses before NATO invaded Serbia as well as Kosovo.

At Petersberg castle overlooking the Rhine, the diplomatic threesome met over the NATO-Russian dispute. The Russians pushed hard for a separate command and military sector in Kosovo. Washington held firm because it feared that the Kosovar

Serbs would migrate into a Russian zone, carving out a Serb-only enclave in the province. The Russian negotiators agreed at last to their troops reporting to an American officer and, therefore, only indirectly to the NATO command. Without Russian backing, the FRY president was isolated. The initial patriotic defiance of NATO's bombing had dissolved, and the popular mood in Serbia had shifted to war weariness, anxiety, and desire for peace. If it held out, the authoritarian regime expected unconstrained bombardments, feared a land invasion, and realized that no better terms were available.[31]

"WORLD WAR III"

Once the Talbott-Chernomyrdin-Ahtisaari settlement cleared approval in Belgrade and Moscow, these two capitals labored to gain favorable concessions on the actual implementation of the agreement. In other words, the final resolution of the conflict was still not nailed down. Attention shifted to the Military Technical Agreement that spelled out the procedures for Serb withdrawal and for NATO's occupation. Representing NATO, British General Mike Jackson met with Serb officers in Macedonia on June 2 while the bombing continued. The talks bogged down in a replay of some of the previous high-level diplomatic wrangles until agreement was signed a week later.

NATO suspended its air strikes on June 9, 1999, and the Security Council passed Resolution 1244. The resolution sanctioned the intervention of NATO troops into Kosovo and placed the province under UN supervision. Although the resolution postponed the final status of the province until the UN had put in place substantial self-autonomy, it left Kosovo's sovereignty in limbo indefinitely. This resolution also established the UN Interim Administration Mission in Kosovo (UNMIK), which oversaw the civilian administrative function, coordinated humanitarian relief, and facilitated the return of refugees.

A dicey incident unfolded two days after the Serbs signed the Military Technical Agreement. As the Serb military, police, and paramilitary units redeployed out of Kosovo, it looked like a time to celebrate. But a flap arose from unanticipated quarter—Russia. Moscow touched off a crisis by making an end run around the diplomatic settlement. On June 11, a contingent of 200 Russian soldiers, without the mandated four-month notice, departed from participation within SFOR in Bosnia and traveled overland in trucks and armored vehicles toward Kosovo. Russia's Foreign Minister Igor Ivanov assured Secretary of State Madeleine Albright that the troops were not bound for Kosovo. Hours afterward, the Russian battalion crossed into Kosovo and entered Priština, where thongs of jubilant Serbs gave the paratroopers a heroes welcome. Moscow now had more than a foot in the door and made a strenuous effort to hive off its own Berlin-like sector. It was a miniature replay of the Red Army dash to Berlin in 1945.

The Russian troops drove to the capital city's Slatina Airfield, where they took up a defensive perimeter. Next, Moscow decided to send airborne reinforcements from Russia, but Hungary, Bulgaria, and Romania repeatedly denied flyover permission to the Kremlin. How much the world had changed since the fall of the Berlin Wall was evident when three former Soviet satellites thumbed their noses at their erstwhile overlord. The three Central European countries clearly saw their futures tied to the West and perceived the United States a mightier power than Russia.

As the Russians had first approached the Kosovo border, General Clark organized a counterforce to block their passage to the airport. He was reliant on two companies of British troops and two French. In a blunder, the United States had pledged not to deploy its troops within Kosovo until the agreement was in place. Therefore, an American force was unprepared to enter the country on June 11. When France pulled out to avoid a confrontation with Russia, Clark fell back on the tiny British contingent to carry out orders from General Joseph Ralston, vice chairman of the Joint Chiefs of Staff, to obstruct the airport's runways to impede Russian reinforcements. Javier Solana, NATO's general secretary, concurred with Washington's plan to block the airport's use.

General Clark ordered General Jackson to seize the airport. After conferring with his London superiors, the British general told the NATO military chief, "Sir, I'm not taking any more orders from Washington." When Clark replied that he and Solana represented NATO, Jackson famously replied, "I'm not starting World War III for you."[32] The British officer's sensational statement ricocheted in world capitals before civilian officials calmed the furor. Washington and London resolved the standoff, and Jackson took control of roadways around the airport.

High-level diplomacy then took place between the United States and Russia. The old protagonists reached an agreement that denied Moscow its own Kosovo sector but permitted it a scaled-down force of 3,600 troops (from its original demand of 10,000 soldiers) to arrive at the contested airport outside Priština. Before these reinforcements arrived, the isolated Russians at Slatina begged food from the British soldiers, who gave them bread. Like a tropical storm, fierce but short, the airport crisis passed but while it lasted, the standoff gave one a déjà vu sensation of the Cold War crises, where one of the two superpowers crossed the threshold and triggered a counterchallenge by the other.

In July, a month after the bombing ceased, secretary of defense and chairman of the Joint Chiefs of Staff speeded up Clark's retirement for his insisting on a ground war and his political angling to achieve that strategy. The general's self-regarding manner, his outspoken comments to the media, and his direct appeals to the president irked his superiors. Thus, Clark's unmistakable victory elicited not gratitude but his early departure from the Army, even though he kept the war effort on track as commentators wrote about another Vietnam in the offing.[33]

The White House, for its part, took offense at Clark's forced early retirement. President Clinton reacted angrily to the news saying to an aide, "I'd like to kill somebody" over the decision.[34] Later, President Clinton awarded Clark the Presidential Medal of Freedom. Britain bestowed an honorary knighthood on the American general, and France the Legion of Honor. Years after leaving office, Clinton encouraged Clark to seek the presidency in 2004, which the four-star officer did without success.

America's resolution of the Kosovo crisis de-escalated the instability before it metastasized into a transregional conflict that endangered NATO and reignited a Cold War-type confrontation with Russia. The preservation of Euro-American unity brought Clinton international acclaim a year later when he was the first American president to receive the Charlemagne Prize, awarded by the German city of Aachen.

The grateful Kosovars named Priština's largest boulevard in his honor. Interethnic clashes between Kosovars and Serbs persisted but on a much reduced scale. Despite the strategic interests involved in the stabilization of Kosovo and Bosnia, Clinton got few accolades from politicians and pundits at home who faulted America for "strategic incoherence," global "care givers," and "social work" as foreign policy.[35]

Washington and allied NATO powers prudently accepted the Kosovar leadership, even if some had been tainted as terrorists. They made less effort to democratize and purify Kosovo according to Western standards. The war aims were narrow and doable. In fact, the U.S.-backed NATO occupation kept the peace by denying freedom to the Kosovars who wanted to breakaway officially from Serbia. The United States acted pragmatically, not overly idealistically in the turbulent Kosovo corner.

THE SIERRA LEONE AND EAST TIMOR HANDOFFS

The Balkan experience did chasten the United States about the difficulties of stabilizing interventions so much so that when violence exploded in West Africa's Sierra Leone and in Indonesia's East Timor during mid-1999, it strove to impart stability through other states' exertions rather than become directly involved.

Bill Clinton and his foreign policy experts recognized international and domestic hurdles to other peace-soldiering ventures so soon after the arduous Kosovo campaign, even if they had been inclined to intervene. Domestically, few clamored for another foreign incursion into a war zone. Quite the reverse: Congress and the Pentagon opposed it, and many commentators worried about wearing out the U.S. armed forces in one military venture after another. Internationally, the U.S.-spearheaded Balkan bombing campaign earned Washington enmity for its perceived unilateralism. But the president's humanitarian rhetoric tied to U.S. globalization objectives laid him open to accusations of hypocrisy, if he did nothing in Sierra Leone and East Timor to restore stability.[36]

When the long-boiling violence in the West African coastal country reached a critical mass, the United States brokered a cease-fire and then the short-lived Lomé Agreement, which established the UN Assistance Mission for Sierra Leone (UNAMSIL). The agreement bought only a hiatus in a vicious warlord's takeover of the nation's lucrative diamond mines. A year later, in June 2000, following the agreement's breakdown, British paratroopers intervened to put the warlord's drug-crazed teenaged militia to flight and imprisoned its leader Foday Sankoh. Things marginally improved but the neighboring Liberia underwent turmoil by Sankoh's mentor and abettor, confronting Clinton's successor with another regime-change and peacekeeping mission. In the interlude, Indonesian troubles beckoned Bill Clinton's attention.

The United States successfully encouraged the Australians to assume leadership of the UN-authorized International Force East Timor to restore order and to safeguard the Catholic East Timorese from the rampaging Muslim militias and regular Indonesia troops. It provided INTERFET with air and sea lift as well as communications support, while Britain, New Zealand, Canada, Thailand, and the Philippines dispatched troops, engineers, or medics to the ravaged sector. Clinton officials praised the hand off of peacekeeping duties as a case study in regional stability operations and a harbinger of future outsourcing to spare America from exclusive responsibility of being a global cop in the world's chaotic neighborhoods. In Sierra Leone and East Timor, the international powers quickly passed off power to the locals. They stayed clear of lengthy occupations to democratize the citizenry up to Western standards.

<h3>POSTSCRIPT ON THE BALKANS</h3>

Like the fabled sorcerer's apprentice, Milošević spent his remaining days in power trying to ride out the deluge that he had unleashed. He had incited Serb nationalism in Croatia's Krijina, Bosnia, and again in Kosovo only to betray it. Extreme nationalism bequeathed neither gain nor glory but only death and hardship for the Serbian people. A succession of wars left them impoverished and resentful of their unrequited sacrifices. The economic ruin and privation that followed in Kosovo's train sharpened the divide between citizenry and ruler. Serbian nationalism was the catapult that flung Milošević to his place in power, but it could not be sustain his survival there. Oblivious to the deep undercurrent of discontent, he called for a presidential election perhaps to highlight Serbian democracy and lessen the country's isolation.

Acting to stabilize the Balkans once and for all, this time Washington did not miss an opportunity for regime change, as had been the case when it failed to support the prodemocracy uprisings in late 1996. The United States, which had contact with anti-Milošević elements in neighboring states, provided instruction and funds for organizing political campaigns. Secretary of State Albright hammered away rhetorically that the United States wanted him "out of power, out of Serbia, and in the custody of the war crimes tribunal."[37] It is true that Washington pushed an opening door, but what counts in power politics is timing and gumption. But it did not militarily enter Serbia to set up its brand of democratic government; it left the governance to local figures. The Balkan experience should have served as a model for the Middle East.

On September 24, 2000, the opposition candidate Vojislav Koštunica overwhelmingly defeated the unpopular incumbent at the polls. Nevertheless, Milošević refused to accept the electoral verdict. Thousands of protestors took to the streets of Belgrade and other cities, paralyzing the country. Western governments called for Milošević to relinquish power. Only Moscow stood by him near the end, as his own police and many army units sat on the sidelines.

Finally, Milošević conceded on October 5 but hinted that his departure was only temporary. The new government soon ratcheted up political pressure on the former autocrat, looking into allegations that he diverted state funds. It ordered commandos to storm his residential compound in the capital and arrested him on April 1, 2000. Three months later, Belgrade handed him over to The Hague tribunal, which indicted him on charges of orchestrating genocide by Serb forces in the 1992–1995 Bosnian war. For Serbian ultranationalists, only Lucifer fell further from grace than the onetime demagogue. In 2006, they paid him homage in the thousands at his funeral.

Twice the United States led the Euro-Atlantic alliance in military interventions that saved Muslim populations in the Balkans from genocidal attacks, and twice it committed vast resources and put at risk its young men and women to secure peace and stability; however, neither instance made any significant dent in the implacability of the Middle East's hostility to America. If ever there was a failure of the positive ramifications of U.S. power to be recognized, it was during the 1990s. Indeed, the American beneficence occurred at a time of rising anti-U.S. sentiments and recurring violence directed at U.S. citizens beyond America's shores from the Muslim world. It was a warning about interfering directly in the Islamic Middle East domain no matter how high-minded the export of Americanized democratic stability might seem in Washington.

CHAPTER 7

CONTAINING NORTH KOREA, IRAQ, AND TERRORISM

Come the three corners of the world in arms,
And we shall shock them. Nought shall make
Us rue.

Shakespeare, *King John*

International politics, like all politics, is a struggle for power.

Hans Morgenthau

NOT ALL THE 1990S CRISES WERE AMENABLE TO INTERVENTIONS. Bringing stability and peace to Haiti, Bosnia, and Kosovo through military action proved not only necessary but also doable without undue expense in blood and treasure. Military power, or rather the cost of an armed intrusion, had its limits to address all threats to political equanimity, however. The United States prudently declined to bring democracy via armed intervention to hostile states like North Korea, Iraq, or Afghanistan. It relied on other tried-and-true measures to protect its interests and foster stability.

The United States clearly possessed the nuclear capacity to annihilate any adversary; but an atomic exchange with another thermonuclear power risked catastrophic losses. Therefore, America treated Russia and China differently. When Moscow sharply criticized the United States, Washington replied circumspectly. Even when Beijing provoked it by firing missiles into Taiwanese waters during the island republic's first direct presidential election in 1996 or forced down a U.S. reconnaissance plane and held hostage its crew on Hainan Island in 2001, it reacted with restraint toward the People's Republic of China. Russia and China's immense landmass, large populations, and well-stocked conventional armories also rendered the Russians and Chinese safe from U.S. invasion. Moreover, U.S. governments viewed both as commercial markets and stabile regimes, not as unstable, belligerent states. Globalization, trade, and economic progress would do far more to bring China and Russia around to being responsible global citizens than confrontation. Besides, threats to the

United States flowed more imminently from stateless terrorist networks and from nontransparent rogue nations with designs on weapons of mass destruction.

America turned to containing saber-rattling regimes rather than to military operations. "Containment and deterrence remain[ed] our only tested techniques for blunting regional foes such as Iraq and Iran," Walter A. McDougall wrote in the late 1990s.[1] Containment was about preserving the status quo, checking aggression, and deterring perils. It strove to contain rather than rollback a security threat. A containment strategy enjoyed much acclaim for bringing about the Soviet Union's collapse. The main elements of that containment enterprise were a robust military buildup, defensive alliances, economic aid to at-risk countries, arms control agreements, and clandestine measures to subvert Soviet advances. Containment's reputed victory made it the readymade fallback strategy for the United States during the 1990s, when confronted by unpalatable choices of war with or retreat from rogue states or shadowy terrorist networks, for which ground invasion costs looked disproportionate to shape and safeguard regional order.

Washington and allied capitals, long familiar with the set-piece confrontations of the Cold War, were initially caught off guard by the menacing conduct of unpredictable regimes. Rogue nations like North Korea, Iran, and Iraq defied international norms, repressed their own populations, behaved erratically, sponsored terrorism, flouted traditional diplomatic conventions, and, worst of all, sought weapons of mass destruction. History is replete with rogue polities from the ancient Gauls to Nazi Germany, which functioned outside the world community in their eras. Contemporary rogue states, on the other hand, date from the Cold War divisions. Moscow funded, trained, and armed client states as proxies to confound the United States. When the Soviet Union imploded, it left behind these pernicious endowments that like mythical dragon teeth sprang up as outlaw states. Once off the restraining Soviet leash, North Korea and Iraq gambled on overt risky behavior to advance their interests, while Libya, Syria, and Iran opted for secret sponsorship of terrorism or other activities inimical to the United States and its allies.[2]

These state-based dangers merged with the rise of a new and virulent strain of terrorism from small groups that espoused extremist Islam. Because each of these perils emanated from different quarters, they are best considered separately, although they shared vociferously anti-American sentiments and sometimes cooperated in providing arms transfers, training facilities, refuges, or financial assistance. Against each, the United States employed deterrent measures in the belief that time would bring genuine stability.

NORTH KOREA: THE QUINTESSENTIAL ROGUE STATE

Covenants, without the sword, are but words, and of no strength to secure a man at all.
Thomas Hobbes, Leviathan

The Democratic People's Republic of Korea (DPRK) drifted on and off of Washington's radar screen since the 1950–1953 Korean War, when America led a UN force to repel its invasion of South Korea. No peace treaty concluded the conflict that ended with an armistice. Technically, the combatants are still at war. Afterward, a time warp enveloped North Korea, which stayed frozen in a version of 1930s Soviet Russia, with its internal system of mass terror, prison camps, starvation, indoctrination, cult of personality surrounding its leader, and a guns-cocked propaganda against the United States. North Korea, however, was—and is—no carbon copy of the Soviet Union. Its signature ideology was devised by its own Great Leader, Kim Il Sung, not Marx or Lenin. Known as *juche*, it purports an extraordinary degree of self-sufficiency from the outside world, which has been honored more in the breach than in practice. In countless instances, Pyongyang has, in fact, accepted food, fuel, and other aid from the Republic of Korea, China, Japan, and even from the United States through the UN's World Food Program.

Despite the North's provocations along the Demilitarized Zone (DMZ) that divided the peninsula since the Korean War, it was Pyongyang's atomic weapons plans that put it on a collision course with the United States. The DPRK's quest for nuclear capability stretches back to the years after the Korean War, when Pyongyang reached out to the Soviet Union for technical assistance. Moscow trained North Korean scientists in its facilities and in 1965 transferred a small 2–4 megawatt reactor to Yongbyon, 60 miles north of the capital. Russian and Chinese engineers later lent a hand to their North Korean counterparts in their nuclear designs.

As orbiting spy satellites beamed images into the National Reconnaissance Office, evidence piled up on the DPRK's nuclear advances during the Reagan administration. It prevailed on Moscow to insist that its client enter into the Nuclear Non-Proliferation Treaty (NPT), which mandated inspections and controls to prohibit the forming of atomic arsenals while allowing for peaceful nuclear reactors. The Soviets pressured the DPRK, and Pyongyang became a signatory to the NPT in 1985. Signing the arms control treaty obligated the signatories neither to import nuclear arms nor to construct their own nuclear weapons. The NPT also legally bound signatories to open themselves to inspections from the UN's watchdog agency, the International Atomic Energy Agency (IAEA).

Amid the Soviet Union's disappearance, North Korean officials hinted ominously that they would no longer be bound by pledges to Moscow to abstain from developing nuclear weapons. The Cold War, despite all its tribulations, resulted in a containment of not just the two superpowers but also their proxy states. The United Stated checked the South Korean and Taiwanese nuclear arms programs in the 1970s. Although the Republic of Korea had built electrical-power-generating nuclear reactors, registering its atom-splitting expertise, it deferred to the United States and relied on its nuclear umbrella for protection.

The George H. W. Bush administration reacted to the North Korean nuclear threats by delaying the scheduled withdrawal of six thousand troops until uncertainties about the Pyongyang's nuclear program had been addressed. Uncommonly blunt, Chairman of the Joint Chiefs of Staff Colin Powell, expressed a thinly veiled threat during a background briefing: "If they [the North Koreans] missed Desert Storm, this is a chance to catch a re-run."[3] If ever there was an apt time to overawe North Korea, it was in the wake of the Persian Gulf War, when America's power looked omnipotent. Its devastating firepower wielded so effectively in the Persian Gulf War, no doubt, did awe the North Koreans and served to stabilize the Korean Peninsula for a short while.

The Bush government succeeded in getting the DPRK to accept international inspections as outlined in the NPT provisions. Director General Hans Blix, the former Swedish foreign minister, headed the IAEA's team in its visit to North Korea. After the Gulf War, Blix had been chagrined by the revelations of undetected nuclear plants in Iraq, despite IAEA inspections. He was determined not to have a repetition of this lapse in North Korea. He took his inspectors to Yongbyon in mid-May 1992 to make a physical assessment of the DPRK's nuclear plants. Among the documents turned over to the inspection team were inadvertent disclosures that the North had already reprocessed about 90 grams of plutonium in 1990. From this disclosure, the CIA concluded that North Korea had extracted even more plutonium from spent fuel, perhaps some 8–16 pounds, enough to manufacture one or possibly two atomic bombs.[4] The Blix disclosures set in train a sequence of doubts about North Korean veracity that exist to this day.

At South Korean urging, the United States acted with restraint and conciliation. President Bush pulled America's nuclear bombs and artillery shells from American bases below the DMZ. In addition, the Washington suspended the joint United States-South Korean military exercise, called Team Spirit, for one year and agreed to a high-level meeting with Pyongyang's officials. The purpose of these placatory measures was to facilitate North-South negotiations. In fact, Pyongyang and Seoul did enter into bilateral agreements banning nuclear weapons on the peninsula in late 1990.

Apprehension of North Korean nuclear aspirations, nevertheless, dramatically reemerged in the waning days of the Bush presidency. Satellites detected the reprocessing of plutonium in December 1992. The images confirmed the suspicion that North Korea was cheating on the NPT. The Bush administration passed the intelligence to the incoming Clinton administration.

RISING TENSIONS AND THE SEARCH FOR STABILITY

After settling into the White House, William J. Clinton, who had paid little attention to the DPRK on the campaign trail, encountered one of the gravest threats as the North's nuclear-arming politically destabilized the peninsula. The new government found itself hostage to events over which it had little control. Acting on the U.S. satellite findings, the IAEA's Blix asked inspections in mid-March to probe two questionable nuclear sites. To make matters worse for North Korea, the 1993 Team Spirit maneuvers commenced on March 8.

Combining the inspection demands and the U.S.-ROK military exercises was like the touching of two hot electrical wires together in North Korea. The voltage shocked Pyongyang's command circuits. The Great Leader's son and heir apparent, Kim Jong Il, girded the nation for conflict. The younger Kim put the military on a war footing in his newly assumed capacity as supreme military commander. His father acted on the international front by rebuffing Blix's request for inspections and by renouncing the DPRK's participation in the Nuclear Non-Proliferation Treaty, after passage of the mandatory 90-day grace period. The North's reaction took the world by storm.

Within American and South Korean policy establishments, factions either favored a tough line alone or a carrot and stick approach to reverse the North's decision to quit the NPT. The negotiating school won the bureaucratic battle but lost the antiproliferation cause. In retrospect, the Pyongyang regime's unbridled hostility toward the United States, its opaqueness, and its long-held desire for a nuclear program made a lasting settlement a forlorn hope. Washington, nevertheless, attempted fitfully to devise a policy to contain the DPRK's atomic program, even if it gave into blackmail for a semblance of normalcy on the Korean Peninsula.

The United States looked to Beijing for leverage with Pyongyang. China had much to lose if war erupted again across the Yalu River. Clinton officials also believed that China preferred to see Japan remain denuded of nuclear arms. If Tokyo went nuclear as a deterrent against North Korea, then Japan's weapons would challenge China's regional atomic monopoly and destabilize East Asia. China proved to be a weak reed on which to rest American policy. Beijing pleaded that it lacked leverage with its client regime in Pyongyang despite its lifesaving oil and food shipments southward. Yet, China constrained U.S. actions by its public statements against military options and calls for face-to-face discussions to resolve the nuclear standoff.

Washington responded to Pyongyang's threatened departure from the NPT by holding several bilateral meetings with North Korean diplomats in Beijing, New York City, and Geneva. Enough of an accommodation was reached with the DPRK regime so that on June 11, 1993, a day before its withdrawal from the NPT went into force, Pyongyang stopped short of abrogating the treaty. The dramatic brinkmanship epitomized the North Korean style of threats right up to the precipice that became, in retrospect, as predictable as Kabuki theater.

At the July 1993 meeting with U.S. envoys, the North Korean delegation refloated an idea to resolve the stalemate that the prior Bush government had rejected, because it rewarded Pyongyang's bad behavior and appeased its black-mailing. If the United States supplied modern light-water reactors (LWR), the DPRK offered to replace its old reactors with these new ones and stop constructing outmoded graphite reactors. Surprisingly the Clinton administration grasped the proposition as a way out of its dilemma. The offer served as the genesis of the Agreed Framework signed in Geneva 15 months later. Unlike the 1950-vintage heavy-water (using deuterium oxide) nuclear plants, the "proliferation resistant" light-water reactors used ordinary water, but these sophisticated nuclear-energy-producing mechanisms surpassed their comparatively primitive forbearers in electrical production.

The American negotiators seized the North Korean proposal because the LWR raised technical impediments to plutonium reprocessing that the old graphite models lacked. It must be noted that there were alternatives to LWR. Coal-burning generators would have been much more practical for North Korea with its rich coal lode. They are cheaper to build and maintain. They could have been scattered around the country, reducing costs of erecting new transmission power line. Experts warned that the surge of nuclear-produced electricity would vaporize the old power grid. What motivated the Northerners in this take-it-or-leave-it demand for only nuclear plants? Part of the explanation lies in the North's hunger for one-upmanship over South Korea because it possessed nearly a score of civil nuclear plants. Thus, the Northerners wanted their own nuclear energy to match their Southern rival as well as continue in the atomic game. And, of course, they wanted to stay in the nuclear game as a threat.

The U.S. interlocutors might have pressed harder against their DPRK counterparts' nuclear-only insistence by offering just goal-consuming alternatives. But then again, hardly anyone thought the pauperized Cold War relic would stave off collapse long enough to construct and bring online the LWR. The Soviet Union and its satellite regimes were just the first fallen dominoes. It seemed reasonable, at the time, to assume that the DPRK would also implode like the Warsaw Pact states.

The United States ruled out sanctions and military options because each had its drawbacks. The North Koreans often repeated their provocative admonition that sanctions, in their view, were an act of war. Neither the White House nor the Pentagon wanted a reprise of the destructive Korean War that had provoked China's military intervention to repel American advances toward its border. Clinton officials were also wary of embarking on economic quarantine without international authority. China's opposition to sanctions meant that the Security Council would not agree to a UN economic embargo.

The U.S. Defense Department did review military options in spring 1993. Mid-level staffers drafted a plan for surgical air strikes on the North's nuclear reactor. Bombing the facility prior to the removal of the spent plutonium fuel represented the optimum window for air attacks. But the draft was shelved. No one, however, was confident that a pinpoint bombardment would destroy all of the North's bomb-making capacity. The North Koreans had long constructed unknown numbers of fortifications deep within the country's mountainsides, which housed artillery and rockets. The mountain fastnesses also made for ideal secret nuclear bases. Even accurate bombings would generate radioactive dust that could spread over South Korea, Japan, and the region. Finally, Secretary of Defense William Perry and his military subordinates feared that a preemptive aerial attack would trigger a second Korean War.

The formidability of North Korean artillery and multiple rocket launchers along the DMZ gave military strategists second thoughts. These conventional armaments were poised to rain down tens of thousands of explosives on Seoul a mere 40 miles distant, inflicting as many as a million casualties within a matter of days. The Korean People's Army, the world's fifth largest, might also strike back across the DMZ. Ultimately, the United States and South Korea would prevail but at an estimated 50,0000 casualties among American troops and several hundred thousand ROK soldiers. Plus, the costs included tens of billions of dollars for reconstruction. The DPRK, therefore, possessed a powerful conventional deterrent to U.S. preemptive attack scenarios. First-strike options arose occasionally but each time succumbed to scary assessments of horrendous casualties.

The Pentagon concentrated intently on the North Korean threat during the first half of the 1990s. Military planners thought the prospects for war were highest with the DPRK and Iraq than any other potential trouble spots. Neither state kept the skeletons of war closeted. Post–Gulf War Iraq, as will be narrated below, was defiant toward its American conquerors by harassing the United Nations' weapons inspectors and assailing its Kurdish population in the country's north, which had been under U.S. military protection. On the other side of the globe, North Korea's nuclear weapons agenda and its bellicose propaganda stirred unease among the top U.S. military brass. The Department of Defense predicated their war game scenarios on handling simultaneous a "two-major-regional-contingencies situation."

Since the U.S. Defense Department underwent a 40 percent reduction in the years after Soviet Union's dissolution, a two-war strategy engendered intense debate. By the mid-1990s, warplanners hedged their two-war scenario by inserting the phrase "nearly simultaneously" to reflect the Defense Department's dwindling capability to fight two middle-sized wars at the same time. At the end of the Cold War, the U.S. Army boasted 18 active-duty combat divisions, the U.S. Navy approached a 600-ship fleet, and the U.S. Air Force possessed 28 Fighter Wing Equivalents (72 planes per FWE). After the cutbacks ushered in by the Bush and Clinton administrations, active American military forces shrank to 10 Army divisions, 357 Navy ships, and 13Air Force wings. In coming years, the Navy recorded another 100-ship decrease, as retired ships were not replaced. These sizable reductions raised doubts about the wisdom of wadding into two regional wars. Even the prospect of a single conflict on the Korean Peninsula caused anxiety in Washington. Containment seemed the best option for security and peace.

MOVING TOWARD THE AGREED FRAMEWORK

The year 1994 marked the worst for war worries on the peninsula than at any point since the Berlin Wall's fall. The simmering nuclear controversy reached a boil when a spate of incidents confronted governments in Washington, Seoul, and Pyongyang. The diplomatic efforts stalled when North Korean entreaties for light-water reactors temporarily fell from active consideration, and the IAEA calls for treaty-compliance inspections ran into belligerent North Korean defiance. Pyongyang dug in its heels at the IAEA demand for access to its installations. It reacted with warlike rhetoric to the U.S. deployment of Patriot antimissile batteries in South Korea as a defensive measure against projectiles from north. When the local U.S. commander, General Gary Luck, also requested an additional thousand troops for the 1994 Team Spirit exercises, the perception gained currency north and south of the DMZ that Washington intended to pursue a military course of action.

The bone-chilling steps and countersteps made many South Korean citizens panicky, who feared a dark cloud of shells and rockets raining down on Seoul from the North. This war phobia crested in mid-June, when former president Jimmy Carter traveled to Pyongyang to resolve the crisis, but during the three months prior to his visit things looked bleak. It was in the North-South dialogue that the most incendiary incident occurred. Around the quarrelsome conference table, the DPRK representative threatened the Southern delegates: "If a war breaks out, Seoul will turn into a sea of fire."[5] Since the exchange had been recorded on closet-circuit television, it could not be later explained away as a misunderstanding. It became a staple of commentary for months, unsettling the region.

For both sides, the light-water reactors ultimately became the silver-bullet solution. The Clinton administration wanted to avoid second Korean War and, at the same time, to bottle up the North's bomb-making efforts. Washington lacked the nerves for the North Korean version of roulette, played with a half-loaded revolver.

The Kim Il Sung regime needed aid to survive without undergoing the type of economic reforms taking place in China.

The Carter-Kim talks put the LWR deal front and center in the American-North Korean negotiations, thereby easing the nerve-wrenching tension. Washington and Pyongyang resumed the suspended third round of the U.S.-DPRK nuclear talks in Geneva. This led to the Agreed Framework, but not before the 80-year-old North Korean dictator died of a reported heart attack on July 8. Kim's death shook the Clinton White House about the agreement's prospects in the now-leaderless Democratic Peoples Republic of Korea.

American "Kim watchers" knew little about the Great Leader's mercurial son. Kim Jong Il came across to the foreign observers at first as enigmatic and decidedly different from his father, a mythic figure in the life of the North Korean nation. As he stepped out of Kim Il Sung's long shadow, the younger Kim's past extravagant lifestyle struck foreign observers as making him an ill-suited replacement for the communist world's first dynastic succession in a country known for regimented asceticism. Perhaps to atone for his misspent youth womanizing and indulging in Western films and liquor, he habitually wore his signature khaki Mao-like jumpsuit rather than Western business attire. Despite his playboy image, the younger Kim has been regarded as the mastermind behind the 1983 assassination attempt on South Korea's President Chun Doo Hwan that killed many in his entourage in Rangoon. Known as Dear Leader to the downtrodden masses, Kim Jong Il went along with the Agreed Framework negotiations to Washington's relief.

On October 21, 1994, two weeks before the U.S. congressional elections, the respective heads of the American and North Korean delegating teams, Robert Galluci and Kang Sok Ju, signed the five-page Agreed Framework in Geneva. Briefly, this nuclear-freeze deal called for the resolution of the crisis in three phases. First, North Korea pledged to abstain from refueling its now-unloaded graphite reactor, effectively mothballing it, and froze the construction of two larger graphite reactors. It also promised to store the eight thousand spent plutonium fuel rods in a cooling pond under IAEA monitoring. Furthermore, the DPRK affirmed that it would remain a party to the Nuclear Non-Proliferation Treaty and thus refrain from nuclear weapons activities, a pledge it later flagrantly broke.

In return, the United States agreed to establish a consortium to build a light-water reactor with a total of 2000 megawatts capacity for about $4 billion, based on South Korean models and financed mainly by Seoul and Tokyo. During the interim, the Clinton administration committed to substitute energy. Beginning in 1995, Washington agreed to supply 50,000 metric tons of heavy oil, an underused by-product of petroleum refineries, and to increase the annual amount to 500,000 metric tons starting in October 1996. Estimates placed the cost at $500 million for oil shipments from 1995 until 2003, when the first of two reactors was scheduled to come on line to generate power.

Not until the second phase, scheduled to take place before the completion of the first reactor, would the IAEA have access to the two nuclear waste sites to clarify questions about the amount of plutonium reprocessing. After full compliance with the inspection regime, the consortium was required to deliver key components to operationalize the first LWR reactor. The third and final phase obligated the North Koreans to dismantle all their old nuclear installations.

Washington along with Tokyo and Seoul founded the Korean Energy Development Organization (KEDO), which the South Koreans actually managed. KEDO preserved North Korean "face" by enabling Pyongyang to work ostensibly with an international entity, not directly with the hated South. For its part, the Kim Young Sam government resented being sidelined by the United States during its negotiations with the DPRK and denounced the United States for shoring up the tottering North Korean regime with the agreement. Seoul, however, placed its relationship with Washington over its reservations about the agreement and agreed to make available the bulk of the funding and expertise. In fact, the easing of the nuclear crisis helped clear the way for Seoul to lift restrictions on business dealings and economic cooperation with the North. The South's financial assistance and investment in the DPRK did more to stabilize the Korean Peninsula than any other single activity. It gave Pyongyang a stake in peace and demonstrated that negotiations brought rewards. The next South Korean government, under Kim Dae Jung, further engaged the North in its "sunshine" policy, paving the way for a de-escalation of peninsular tensions. Periodically, the Kim Jong Il regime vituperated against the United States with hair-raising taunts but these raised far fewer anxieties in the South, which gradually lost its fear of a Northern attack.

The United States stayed wedded to the agreement and its version of containment, despite North Korea's provocations. Pyongyang's 1998 test-firing of its long-range, multistage Taepo Dong missile over Japan temporarily rocked U.S.-North Korean interaction while speeding Japanese rearmament. But the Geneva accord steadied relations on the peninsula and between Washington and Pyongyang. Before leaving office, Clinton officials tried unsuccessfully to arrange a presidential visit to North Korea and to reach a missile-for-aid deal. Both initiatives lost out due to complexity, time constraints, and Oval Office priorities in the Middle East peace talks.

After President Clinton left the White House, evidence of the DPRK's cheating came to light. During the first years of the George W. Bush administration, intelligence accumulated that North Korea had embarked on secret uranium enrichment production. The credibility of these suspicions got a boost from two unexpected sources. First, a North Korean official owned up to the fact in October 2002 when confronted by American scientific evidence. Second, a Pakistani scientist, Abdul Qadeer Khan, disclosed in 2004 that he had been shown three nuclear devices five years earlier when he visited a North Korean underground nuclear plant. Known as the father of Pakistan's nuclear bomb, Khan sold Pyongyang know-how and equipment to produce nuclear weapons from uranium enrichment in the late 1990s. This second route to acquire a nuclear weapons capacity explicitly violated the Geneva agreement as well as the NPT.

In response, the United States suspended its oil shipments. Pyongyang counteracted by renouncing all its nuclear-freeze agreements. Despite theses developments, U.S.-DPRK relations never reached the 1994 fever-pitch tensions, because Washington looked to China to restrain its North Korean client and because friendlier North-South Korean political and economic interactions had progressed in the previous decade, making an intrapeninsula war seem unlikely, despite Pyongyang's record of brutality, duplicity, and blackmail. Enough political steadiness held that the George W. Bush's Pentagon could afford to stay focused on its war plans for Iraq.

The reawakened North Korean nuclear crisis did compete for Washington's attention as the United States geared up for the Iraq War. Pyongyang's October acknowledgment of its secret uranium enriching reannounced the Hermit Kingdom's intention to become a nuclear-capable power. The twin crises played off each other, heightened fears, and added to the Bush White House's political woes because it chose to handle the two threats with diametrically different approaches. Washington pursued containment and isolation of Pyongyang while at the same time it pushed for military intervention against Iraq. Politicians and commentators challenged the administration's priorities. The Oval Office marched to war against Iraq because the terrorists networks were far stronger in the Middle East, the Persian Gulf more unstable jeopardizing Western access to oil, the neighboring regimes more at odds with one another, and U.S. relations with friendly nations already troubled—none of these conditions pertained in Northeast Asia, where a rough quasi-homeostasis prevailed. Paradoxically, Pyongyang impelled the United States toward war against Iraq to prevent it from becoming another nuclear-armed North Korea. To do nothing about Iraq meant countenancing another rogue regime gaining nuclear arms. North Korea's nuclear program had the effect of intensifying Washington's scrutiny of Iraq, while protecting Pyongyang from a U.S. invasion. The United States repositioned a squadron of supersonic bombers across the Pacific but otherwise took no overt military action to jeopardize the peninsula's political equilibrium. Like Cold War relations with the Soviet Union, the United States relied on containment and deterrence; it astutely eschewed regime change or democracy implantation in North Korea.

Transfixed by the advent of the Iraq War, Washington could also take comfort in the budding reconciliation and economic ties between the governments of the new ROK President Roh Moo-hyun and Kim Jong Il that the Agreed Framework, for all its flaws, bequeathed to the thawing interpeninsula relations. America fell back on diplomacy by promoting the six-party talks (North and South Korea, China, Japan, Russia, and the United States) to deal with Pyongyang's missile and nuclear ambitions. It placed a premium on Beijing's help to pressure its erratic client, even after the DPRK tested a small nuclear device on October 9, 2006. For now, the North Korea regime seemed more stable and contained than it had been half a decade earlier, even if the agreement appeared as appeasement to critics. The same could not be said of Iraq, whose apparent ties to terrorist groups and WMD ambitions overhung the oil-rich Persian Gulf.

IRAQ: THE CONTINUING HEADACHE

Of all the headaches inherited by the Clinton administration, Saddam Hussein was the most persistent.

Madeleine Albright

Iraq's dictator resurrected himself back to political life from the ashes of the 1991 war like some malevolent phoenix to prey on the Persian Gulf region, which had emerged as one of the determining fulcrums in the global balance of power. With the bulk of proven oil reserves located in the Middle East, the United States attached immense strategic value to the stability of the Arabian Peninsula. Anything posing a threat to its security aroused Washington's interest. Saddam Hussein's reputation for mischief making, irredentist territorial claims, accumulating power, acquiring weapons of mass destruction, and cruelty to his subjects stood apart even in a precinct largely devoid of Western norms of conduct and jurisprudence. Hussein's nightmarish antics locked in Washington's worried obsession during the 1990s.

Containment of Iraq, as set down by George H. W. Bush, offered the incoming Bill Clinton administration a chance to pursue globalization and peace in the Middle East as well as tackle a spate of interventions. The Clinton foreign policy bureaucracy decided to stick with its predecessor's strategy of bottling up the Hussein regime. It retained the U.N. Special Commission weapons inspections. It kept in place the sanctions that deprived Iraq from commercial and diplomatic intercourse with much of the world. Like its predecessor, it also relied on aerial attacks on ground targets in reprisal for Hussein's provocations. Overtime, it termed this strategy as "containment plus," but it was old wine in new bottles. By mounting aerial attacks and fencing in the regime, the Clinton inner circle believed, like the Bush team, that Hussein would either fall to accumulating pressures or remain preoccupied with surviving. True enough, the Iraqi despot felt the check on his ambitions, faced plots, and endured economic troubles. But it was also true that at the end of the day, the various countermeasures failed to dislodge Hussein from power.

One Clintonian departure from previous U.S. foreign policy involved a so-called dual-containment strategy toward both Iraq and Iran. The Reagan and the Bush presidencies had worked to balance Iraq against what they perceived as the growing threat from the theocratic Iranian regime. After the 1979 ouster of the shah, the United States pitted itself against the revolutionary theocracy in Tehran and tentatively courted Iraq as a counterweight against the ayatollah regime. President Clinton did not take up the Persian Gulf balance-of-power prescription. He largely held both states at arms length, although he flirted with warming relations with Tehran.[6] These tentative feelers were never vigorously pursued, and U.S.-Iran relations stayed frozen. As for Hussein's Iraq, it never found itself courted again by the United States.

Checkmated by U.S. military might, Saddam Hussein's bid for weapons of mass destruction offered another avenue to realize his ambitions for dominating the Persian Gulf. His pursuit of biological, chemical, or nuclear arms in the early 1990s turned out to be his ultimate undoing, for it raised anxieties in many capitals. Defectors disclosed Hussein's clandestine manufacturing of the deadly nerve gas VX that kills within seconds of human contact, laboratories for biological weapons, and exertions to produce nuclear warheads. Hussein might have been able to continue to pull the wool over the eyes of the UNSCOM had it not been for the revelations of his own son-in-law, Hussein Kamel, who temporarily fled to Jordan before returning home in 1996 to death in a hail of bullets.[7]

General Kamel's revelations vindicated America's strident demands for arms inspections and stunned UNSCOM for the assessment that its investigation was nearing completion. UNSCOM's lapses conditioned the Clinton and later George W. Bush administrations to write off the UN weapons inspectors as ineffective. Washington's distrust of Saddam Hussein sharpened but it resolved to stick with its containing stance.

According to Warren Christopher the containment posture freed up the Clinton administration for more productive pursuits. By late 1995, it had brokered the Dayton Accord entailing U.S. peacekeeping in Bosnia. This meant two such enterprises, since the United States was still committed to minor-league nation-building efforts in Haiti. Most importantly, President Clinton by this time was engaging in what became an exceptional personal commitment to finding a peaceful resolution of the Israeli-Palestinian conflict. The nation's chief diplomat, who knew his boss's inclinations thoroughly, decided that an aggressive Iraqi strategy was a nonstarter. He and other top appointed officials, in fact, pulled the plug on a CIA-backed Kurdish revolt in 1995 rather than risk a repetition of the 1961 disastrous Bay of Pigs operation against Cuba's Fidel Castro, which embarrassed President John Kennedy.[8] Arms inspections, sanctions, and air patrols of the north and south "no-fly" zones remained at the core of Clinton's boxing-in strategy.

Just as the Cold War containment policy suffered setbacks, so too did Clinton's version against Iraq. Its dictator took advantage of political divisions among the Kurds to deploy his Republican Guards into northern reaches of the country in 1996. His armor and soldiers smashed Kurdish resistance, chased out CIA operatives, and executed some 200 members of a covert rebel group in Kurdistan. The brief incursions strengthened Hussein's hand internally and raised his standing in the Middle East for having dealt Washington a defeat by uprooting its covert operations.[9] The United States struck back by extending the southern no-fly zone northward to the thirty-third parallel, just below Baghdad. Then, it and Britain fired cruise missiles at radar and antiaircraft batteries in the enlarged southern zone, inflicting no damage on Hussein's northern attack.

These U.S. reversals alone, however, relate an incomplete story. The Anglo-American flights above the north zone during the course of the 1990s did enable Kurdistan to sprout fledgling democratic institutions and to develop economically. Washington's commitment fostered prosperity and democracy among 5 million Kurds in the mountainous area. This achievement must be added to other U.S. accomplishments of promoting democracy in postwar Germany, Japan, Taiwan, and South Korea. The Hussein-dominated portion of Iraq felt the lash of his power and enjoyed no similar decadelong period of growth and freedom, as did the Kurdish provinces.

Externally, the Hussein regime shrewdly took advantage of his country's newfound image as an underdog vis-à-vis an overweening American superpower in the second half of the 1990s. It played on the destitution of its subjects due to the UN-imposed embargo. Sanction exhaustion spread from sympathetic Arab governments to European capitals eager to reinstate commercial links with the oil-rich pariah nation. America tried in vain to prove through a bookkeeping approach that ample funds for food and medicines were at hand. Traveling to foreign capitals, Clinton envoys displayed declassified aerial photographs of Hussein's palaces, artificial lakes, and weapons plants. But they had to compete with graphic pictures and firsthand accounts of hungry and sick Iraqis from journalists or NGOs. Every fair-minded observer knew Hussein constructed huge residences at the expense of his countrymen, who suffered further at the hands of his cronies and black marketers; but they faced difficult odds.

Symbolically and politically, the United States, nonetheless, lost the containment campaign; Hussein won, garnering pro-Baghdad opposition to the sanction burden. Jordan reversed itself again, returning to Amman's former embrace of Iraq's strongman. Paris and Moscow also broke ranks with Washington. Baghdad reached out to France and Russia, countries that had enjoyed close political and economic ties with Iraq before the Gulf War and desired to resume their profitable business dealings. Lukoil, the Russian mega-oil company, signed a $3.7 billion development contract for a patch of Iraq's Rumaila field in 1997. The French pulled their aircraft out of participation in Operation Northern Watch at the end of 1996 and Operation Southern Watch at the end of 1998. Their departure left the policing of the no-fly zones to just American and British pilots. Solidarity on the Security Council for sanctions also flagged. France and Russia were becoming Iraq's advocates against the U.S. insistence that the Baghdad cooperate with the international arms inspections. At the same time, President Hussein paralyzed UNSCOM with seeming impunity as the 1990s wore on.

FIRMING UP CONTAINMENT

In his 1998 State of the Union message, President Clinton issued a stern warning to his Iraqi counterpart when he professed, "You cannot defy the will of the world."[10] But that is just what the Iraqi tyrant did. The sorry story of Iraq's cheat-and-retreat practices repeated themselves again in the new year. Baghdad refused to comply with UNSCOM searches or with the various Security Council resolutions. It demanded a lifting of the sanctions.

Kofi Annan flew to Iraq to defuse the escalating furor in early 1998. The UN's secretary general negotiated a Memorandum of Understanding on February 23 that pledged Iraq to accept all the Security Council "relevant resolutions," to cooperate fully with UNSCOM, and to "accord to UNSCOM and IAEA immediate, unconditional and unrestricted access in conformity with the resolutions." But Annan agreed to specific inspection protocols for eight of Hussein's palaces that raised fresh anxieties about off-limits stashes of WMD on the palatial grounds. Returning to his New York headquarters, he famously uttered that Saddam Hussein was a man "I can do business with."[11]

Still, the United States was frustrated by Baghdad's blockages of UNSCOM, which had the effect of deepening the fractiousness between the Clinton White House and the Republican-controlled Congress that had grown fretful about what it believed was the administration's vacillation and outsourcing of U.S. security to the United Nations. In reaction, Capitol Hill introduced and passed a bipartisan bill— the Iraq Liberation Act 1998—just before the midterm elections. The bill embodied four major components: (1) it called for a policy to remove Saddam Hussein from power; (2) it empowered the president to expend funds for a Radio Free Iraq; (3) it renewed congressional calls for an international tribunal to try Saddam Hussein and other regime officials as war criminals; and (4) it authorized $97 million in equipment and arms from U.S. military stocks and granted the president 90 days to designate Iraqi opposition movements for assistance. The Iraq Liberation Act passed 360 votes to 38 in the House and the Senate gave it unanimous consent. President

Clinton signed it on October 31 but he spent less than $3 million of the funds by the time he left office and those expenditures were for computer training and administrative costs. Neither his head nor his heart was committed to regime change, which had become the law of the land.

Events in Iraq once again conspired to compel the United States to react. Despite being beset by the brewing Kosovo crisis and the Monica Lewinsky scandal in 1998, Clinton took action when Saddam Hussein tossed out the American members on the UNSCOM team for being spies and refused any cooperation with the remaining inspectors. The Security Council denounced Iraq's noncooperation but once again declined to insert the "material breach" phrase in the resolution that would have trigged UN military action. Lining up a few Persian Gulf states as staging bases, the Clinton administration resolved to proceed unilaterally with only U.S. and British warplanes to strike at Iraq's installations for its noncompliance in mid-November 1998. Once again, Baghdad conceded at the last moment, and so the Pentagon recalled the in-flight planes before they crossed into Iraqi airspace. Hussein appeared more the marionette than a contained tyrant.

The Clinton government did mount a heavy air strike in mid-December 1998 in the wake of Baghdad's reneging on the so-called CNN promise made the prior month by Tariq Aziz, deputy prime minister and often Iraq's official spokesman. Asked by the television network in mid-November about letting the weapons inspectors pursue their work, Aziz gave his word. It was this pledge that prompted the White House and Downing Street to cancel the November air strike. Kofi Annan took this commitment of unrestricted access in good faith; but Hussein, once more, disrupted the inspections. Fed up with Hussein's on-again, off-again compliance, UNSCOM's chief, Richard Butler, pulled his inspectors out of the country because of the futility of further searches.

Exasperated by the Iraqi dictator's bob-and-weave tactics, Washington and London also unleashed the four-day Operation Desert Fox, the largest air offensive since George Bush's departing salvo in January 1993. U.S. Marine General Anthony Zinni, the head of Central Command, estimated that 74 percent of the 111 targets received significant damage. Anglo-American warplanes flew 650 sorties, and 325 cruise missiles pelted an array of military and security installations, including Republican Guard and Special Republican Guard barracks, airfields, communication nodes, and suspected WMD plants.

Addressing the nation from the Oval Office at the advent of Desert Fox, Bill Clinton explained his decision to bomb Iraq stemmed from U.S. support for UNSCOM. His words would echo right into the recesses of his successor's thinking when President Clinton argued that Baghdad sought biological, chemical, and nuclear arms, and Saddam Hussein "will surmise that he has free reign to rebuild his arsenal of [weapons of mass] destruction and someday, make no mistake, he will use it again as he has in the past." Clinton also touched on the regime-change theme by stating that the best way to eliminate Iraq's threat was "with a new Iraqi government."[12] The bombing and statement signaled a get-tough policy but it was signal only, no follow thorough came afterward. Clinton divined insufficient public tolerance for a sustained effort and lacked the personal commitment to rally the nation for such an all-out offensive.

The president did declare in a subsequent radio address that American policy now resolved to displace Saddam Hussein because his regime resisted compliance with UN resolutions and menaced the region. He held that determination, work with opposition groups, and global consensus would bring "Iraq a government worthy of its people."[13] Thus, the executive and legislative branches agreed on the necessity of regime change in Baghdad. Secretary of State Albright went so far as to pick a Special Coordinator for the Transition in Iraq. Described as the "czar for overthrowing Saddam," Frank Ricciardone, a career diplomat, soon ran aground on the shoals of exile politics from quarrelling anti-Hussein groups and opposition from Egypt and the United Arab Emirates. Despite the efforts of a few mid-level administration staffers and the moral backing of Vice President Gore (who did not want to be saddled with Iraq if he won the 2000 presidential race), the regime-change option never got off the ground.

There was a multitude of reasons for this inertia. The lengthy Kosovo air campaign was a coup d'grâce for a major assault on Iraq. The Balkan operation nearly required the commitment of ground forces to resolve, something the Clinton administration was loath to undertake. The prolonged bombing of Serbia during the first half of 1999 gave Clinton's senior officials second thoughts about commencing another aerial offensive in Iraq. Backing into a protracted and doubtful military engagement in Iraq never rose again to serious consideration during the remainder of the Clinton presidency.

Rather than pursuing a forward policy, the United States decided to return to square one and prod the United Nations to take a tougher tack toward Iraq. In mid-1999, Clinton appointees went back to the Security Council to reestablish a revised sanction policy that ensured unanimous consensus to be effective and enforceable, in what became the most arduous UN struggle for the administration. Other Security Council members bucked American initiatives.

Across the globe, goodwill toward the United States was drying up even before President George W. Bush launched his unilateralist policies. The waning years of Clinton's presidency registered international disenchantment with America's enormous power as well as with Washington's priorities. Whereas 32 nations rallied to the United States in the Gulf War, only Britain joined Washington 7 years later in the Desert Fox bombing.

On the home front, Bill Clinton also dueled with congressional opponents, many in his own party, over maintaining trading curbs on Iraq. Seventy members on Capitol Hill wrote an open letter in mid-February 2000, imploring the president to break the sanction ring because of the harm done to the Iraqi populations, including the UN estimate of 1 million deaths. The combination of domestic and international outcry increasingly rendered Washington's containment initiative politically untenable.

As the "fabulous Nineties" drew to a close, the world's economic expansion swelled the demand for oil, ensuring Baghdad a spiking crude price and underlining the global need for Iraq's political stability. Destabilizing the Iraqi polity through war, rebellion, or coup would send shock waves through the sensitive oil market. The United States was unwilling to risk an international rupture by interfering with Iraq's oil export. America's own need for oil also decreased its leverage over Baghdad, a vulnerability that the Hussein regime exploited. By summer 2000, Iraq's oil exports netted $7 billion a year, reflecting its sales of nearly 3 million barrels per day—a record since it invaded Kuwait in 1990.[14]

Washington, acting with London, kept up patrolling the northern and southern no-fly zones, although the Pentagon eased up on the air-to-ground strikes to protect aircrews and to spare civilian lives from errant bombs as the U.S. presidential election neared. One observer dubbed this de-escalation the "fire-and-forget foreign policy," after the modern munitions.[15] Baghdad authorities claimed that coalition jets penetrated their airspace 21,600 times and killed some 300 Iraqis in the 18 months following Operation Desert Fox. They also argued that the Anglo-American pilots deliberately courted ground fire so as to retaliate disproportionately and that warplanes intentionally strafed bystanders, farm animals, and mosques. Iraqi accusations aroused opposition in Saudi Arabia, Turkey, and European capitals to the Anglo-American air strikes. The costs of the air war were also nontrivial—$2 billion expended annually, 200 aircraft tied to the mission, and 25 ships offshore.

Despite its costs and drawbacks, the "hot containment" of Iraq offers a model, far cheaper in lives and money and far less destabilizing than democracy-transferring occupations, for confronting threats. Strategists would do well to study the precedent as an alternative to Western invasion, occupation, and lengthy counterinsurgency in the zeal to democratize hostile peoples.

As the clock ran out on the Clinton presidency, it treaded water on initiatives toward the Republic of Iraq. The White House not only ruled out showdowns but also set aside its previous insistence on arms inspections. In an extraordinary turnabout at the end of August 2000, the United States lined up with France, Russia, and China in declaring it premature to return any weapons inspectors to Iraq. The Security Council advised Hans Blix, the chairman of the UN Monitoring and Verification Commission (UNMOVIC), to cancel his announcement that his weapons team was ready to return to duty. The council had formed UNMOVIC to replace the defunct UNSCOM. In essence, a lame-duck White House put UNMOVIC inspections on ice until the next administration took office.

By the close of 2000, Iraq's isolation had lessened considerably. Earlier that year, Venezuela's populist President Hugo Chavez, the current OPEC chairman, thawed more than just the cartel's onetime frozen relations with Iraq by granting the pariah above-quota oil production during his two-day stay in Iraq in August. Chavez also breached the country's isolation. His planes' arrival at Baghdad International Airport inaugurated what became known as "air diplomacy," by breaking the logjam of flights to Iraq. Russian, French, and most Arab countries (except Kuwait and Saudi Arabia) next landed commercial jets in Baghdad to render the UN restrictions on aviation intercourse meaningless. The United States acquiesced to the new realities by permitting commercial planes to breach its exclusionary air zones.

Other Iraqi diplomatic breakthroughs ensued. Egypt and Saudi Arabia invited Iraq to attend a summit of the Arab League in Cairo on October 21–22, 2000. The Arab states convened the emergency session to address the outbreak of fierce Palestinian-Israeli violence after the breakdown of the Camp David talks. Arab unity was now more prized than holding old grudges against Saddam Hussein for invading Kuwait 10 years ago. Although Hussein did not travel to Cairo, his stand-in carried a presidential message proposing a jihad to liberate the Palestinians from the Israelis. Hussein's declaration and financial aid to the Palestinian cause burnished the Iraqi leader's prestige across Arab lands. He sponsored Palestinian terrorism against Israel and funded the Al Qaeda-linked Abu Sayyaf terrorist network in the Philippines as well. Inside Iraq, Hussein opened terrorist training camps for volunteers from the Arab Middle East.

Iraq's neighbors no longer even tried to ostracize the region's bully but tried to cozy up to Hussein. Most nearby states normalized diplomatic relations with Baghdad. Sanction busting became profligate. Turkey traded in Iraqi oil brought north to their joint border in miles of tanker trucks. Nor could the Gulf States be relied on to police their own nationals who smuggled oil out and goods into Iraq. So bold did the trade become that Baghdad demanded and received an illegal fee on each barrel of oil, the funds from which were deposited into accounts beyond the reach of the UN financial regulations. The Iraqi leader, it was feared by Washington, used these illicit monies to buy equipment for weapons of mass destruction. Even Syria, Hussein's arch nemesis, broke the UN ban and pumped Iraqi crude across its territory in a long-closed pipeline to get a rake-off in oil for its own use. With a regionwide tide flowing in his direction, Hussein was emboldened to demand only European euros, not U.S. dollars, in payment for the oil that the United Nations allowed Iraq to sell for food. Hussein would not stay contained.

Even the Cold War era containment policy recorded reverses in holding back communist expansion as the Soviet Empire's tentacles spread from seven countries in the late 1940s to more than 70 countries over the next two decades. In the case of Iraq, the United States lacked the will or imagination to move beyond its increasingly sterile and failing containment posture. Its in-the-box policy was bankrupt by the decade's end but that inconvenient fact was easier for a departing government in Washington to ignore than remedy. The fears coming from a reascending Iraq could not be magicked away by election-year politics or a roaring home economy. Hussein brimmed with confidence and, perhaps, hubris at his primary nemesis' retreat.

The story of Saddam Hussein's last years in power is incomplete without a brief note on the rising scourge of Islamist terrorism, even though his regime's full connections to Al Qaeda are still a matter of dispute. Iraq's reassertion of its sway in the Middle East coincided and interacted with America's apprehension of mounting terrorist incidents around the world. Terrorism represented a pernicious activity that manifested itself as an unmistakable peril at the moment when Iraq defied U.S. containment. The two anti-American strands became intertwined into a political Gordian knot that President Clinton's successor resolved to cut by invading Iraq and forcing a democracy conversion.

ANTECEDENTS TO THE AGE OF GLOBAL TERRORISM

We—with Allah's help—call on every Muslim who believes in Allah and wishes to be rewarded to comply with Allah's order to kill the Americans.
World Islamic Front fatwa, February 23, 1998

It is easier to resist at the beginning than at the end.
Leonardo da Vinci

Terrorism dates from antiquity. It has taken varied shapes but one constant is that it is used deliberately against noncombatants for political, religious, ideological, or nationalist causes. Sniper shootings or suicide bombs leveled at military forces, on the other hand, fall within the definition of insurgent warfare. Terrorism's contemporary anti-American appeal has been to individuals and networks utterly defiant of the United States, which lacked the conventional weaponry to confront directly its vast power. So, they chose asymmetrical means to hit American vulnerabilities.

Terrorists delivered many small but deadly attacks on Americans well before the Berlin Wall broke apart. For example, seven months after the Palestinian massacre of Israeli athletes at the 1972 Munich Olympics, the same terrorist organization, Black September, struck again at the U.S. Embassy staff in the Sudanese capital of Khartoum, killing the ambassador and the chargé d'affaires. Air hijackings also began prior to the 9/11 attacks on the United States. On September 6, 1970, the Popular Front for the Liberation of Palestine commandeered four commercial airliners within a 24-hour span. Afterward, three of the planes were flown to a desert airfield in Jordan and blown up. Beforehand, the hijackers had released the hostages. In subsequent aircraft incidents, the passengers did not fare so well, as terrorists turned to planting bombs aboard flights that exploded in midair. The United States as well as France and India had their commercial planes blown from the skies in the course of the 1980s.

During Ronald Reagan's presidency, assaults directed at Americans intensified. They took many forms from the kidnapping of Americans in Lebanon, bombings of U.S. embassies in Kuwait and Beirut, the murdering of Leon Klinghoffer (an American tourist on the Italian cruise ship *Achille Lauro*), air hijackings of American jets to the massive 1983 truck bombing of the U.S. Marine barracks in Beirut. None of these deadly occurrences was suitably dealt with by the United States. In the Beirut killing of the 241 troops, for example, evidence pointed to the radical Islamic group Hezbollah backed by Iran as responsible. Yet the United States never acted on a planned bombing mission against the group's training camps. Instead, it withdrew its forces from Lebanon early the next year. Some administration figures worried about the message of a cut-and-run tack. Secretary of State George Shultz called for action beyond "passive defense" to include "preemption and retaliation" in a speech at the Park Avenue Synagogue in Manhattan in October 1984.[16] The advice helped precipitate a limited counteraction in President Reagan's famed reprisals against Libya two years later. The combined U.S. Navy and Air Force nighttime attack in Operation El Dorado Canyon served as a model for future missions but they were a long time in coming.[17] By that time, Islamist terrorism showed itself even more menacingly.

One of the potent founts of this Islamic-derived terrorism is traceable to the stubborn resistance against the 1979 Soviet Union invasion of Afghanistan. Moscow marched into its neighbor to shore up a client regime but its incursion ignited a train of events that led to an international terrorist campaign, which has not yet run its course. The anti-Soviet fight rallied volunteers from the entire Islamic world who came to wage a jihad. These mujahideen (soldiers of God) were aided by Osama bin Laden, the scion of a wealthy Saudi construction family. Pious and ambitious, bin Laden went to Afghanistan where the experience radicalized him further away from secular life and traditional Arab nationalism. His piety and charitable contributions to Afghan widows and orphans elevated the Saudi's reputation among the combatants. After the Soviet retreat in 1989, the Afghan-Arab victory became a springboard for a global jihad against the United States. Bin Laden and his associates formed Al Qaeda ("the base"), an organization, which underwent a remarkable metamorphosis in Sudan from a ragged band of fighters to an effective terrorist network with offshoots worldwide.

Meanwhile, Afghanistan slipped into anarchy as the victorious warlord fell to fighting each other after the Red Army departed. Since at least England's fifteenth-century War of the Roses, demobilized soldiers have posed a danger to orderly society. At that time, knights returning from victories in Hundred Years War against France joined the dynastic dispute between the houses of Lancaster and York for the English crown. Twentieth-century Afghanistan similarly descended into blood feuds at the hands of rival bands, which no longer joined together to fight a common foe. Unlike the English dynastic battling, the Afghan turmoil spilled over into a brewing international firestorm.

Seeing no geopolitical stake in Afghanistan's slide into conditions of a failed state, the United States stood aside. Neither the outgoing Bush nor the incoming Clinton administrations lifted a finger to avert the mountainous country's descent into civil war and chaos. Unlike its concerns over Europe or the floundering Soviet Union, America did not understand at that time how instability in a distant Central Asia nation could adversely impact its security and interests, while destabilizing the Middle East.

Desperate times beget desperate measures in Afghanistan, and the Taliban ("the students") movement arose to stamp out the endemic lawlessness. Led by Mullah Mohammed Omar, a veteran of the Soviet war, the turbaned Taliban adhered to an extremely conservative interpretation of Islam, which they strictly enforced on themselves and others. Based mainly among the southern Pashtuns and nurtured by Pakistan, which wanted to influence events in Afghanistan, the Taliban accrued arms and marital skills from their Pakistani benefactors.[18] By the end of 1996, the Taliban prevailed over the northern Tajik and Uzbek warlords and seized the main cities including the sprawling, mountain-ringed capital of Kabul. Distraught by years of anarchy, Afghans embraced the Taliban as a necessary evil to restore civic order.

The United States fleetingly adopted the same logic and toyed with diplomatic recognition of the new rulers. American and European energy companies relished a return to political tranquility so as to route a natural gas pipeline from Turkmenistan across the land of the Hindu Kush to ports in Pakistan. Washington quickly recoiled at the Taliban's archaic treatment of women and brutal human rights abuses, including public executions and amputations for offenses against the Shari'a. Ruling from Kabul, the Taliban regime tried to take Afghanistan back to the tenth century when Islamic civilization reached an apogee. It banned music, weather forecasting, and kite flying. It required men to grow beards and women to clothe themselves head to toe. These reactionary practices beckoned to likeminded worshipers across the Muslim world.

After five years in Sudan, Osama bin Laden returned to Afghanistan in 1996, having fallen out with his Sudanese hosts. Once in Afghanistan, he turned the traumatized and impoverished land into the world's most deadly terrorist staging area for global terrorisms by building large camps for instructions in the deadly arts of aircraft hijacking, bombings, assassinations, and political martyrdom. From his mountain fastness, he also issued his first fatwa, or religious decree, that declared war against the "Americans Occupying the Land of the two Holy Places," calling on Muslims to expel the infidels from the Arabian Peninsula. Proclaimed on August 23, 1996, the statement marked the emergence of the genuine global Salafi jihad. Bin Laden focused on international targets in Bosnia, Chechnya, Saudi Arabia, East Africa, Yemen, and ultimately the United States. This proclamation heralded that bin Laden was about to unsheathe his sword. But other likeminded extremists acted first.

Terrorist incidents not directly attributable to bin Laden exploded from the same sense of grievances against the West and particularly the United States that the Saudi exile tapped to attract followers. Sheiks and terrorist facilitators railed against the sins of European colonialism, U.S. aid to Israel, American support of secular authoritarian rulers in the Muslim world, and the eclipse of Arab civilization by Judeo-Christian ascendancy since the fifteenth century.[19] A series of terrorist attacks took place during the 1990s that should have prompted the United States to shed its passive policy. Among these were the 1993 terrorist attack on the World Trade Centers, the shooting of two CIA employees outside their Langley, Virginia headquarters the same year, the Manila plot to blow up 12 American commercial jets over the Pacific, and the 1995 bombing of National Guard Headquarters in Riyadh that killed five U.S. soldiers and seven Saudis.

Almost a year later in June 1996, a massive fuel-truck bombing tore through the Khobar Towers in the Dhahran military base leaving 19 U.S. airmen dead and 500 wounded. Khobar's high casualties and the buildings' extensive blast damage generated political waves in Washington. The Senate Armed Service Committee held hearings and the ranking Republican senator, Virginian John Warner, berated the Central Command's head, Army General, J. H. Binford Peay, for inadequate safeguards at the quarters. General Peay, a product of the Virginia Military Institute, replied in what is now widely known about terrorism, "The terrorist . . . strikes at the target of his choosing, with any means, at any time." He added, "No amount of money or physical security upgrade alone can stop a determined terrorist."[20] In short, terrorism, as General Peay put his finger on it, cannot simply be contained defensively as was the Soviet Union because terrorism is a growing global phenomenon, not an identifiable state; thus, terrorism must be preempted whether by military, diplomatic, or other means.

Reacting, the United States turned to a number of defensive measures to contain the spread of terrorism. The Pentagon ordered greater "force protection" for U.S. armed forces. President Clinton called attention to the terrorist menace in some of his speeches. Terrorism rose higher in the minds of the FBI and CIA. Congress lavished more funds on counterterrorism programs. The Pentagon established the U.S. Joint Special Operations University. The Clinton administration also turned to the legal procedure of rendition, which entailed the apprehending of suspected terrorists in foreign lands and transferring them to the United States for trial. The FBI, for example, rendered from Pakistan both Ramzi Yousef, the 1993 World Trade Center bomber, in early 1995 and Mir Aimal Kasi, the CIA shooter, in 1997. A crime-and-punishment model alone against terrorism failed to arrest the upswing in jihadi violence.

For those paying attention, Osama bin Laden's February 1998 fatwa sent a chilling message. The Saudi terrorist financier-turned-emir issued a religious ruling of "Jihad Against Jews and Crusaders." Laced with Islamic references, the fatwa called for death to Americans and Jews everywhere in the world. Issued under the banner of the World Islamic Front for Jihad Against Crusaders and Jews, it proclaimed, "The ruling to kill the Americans and their allies—civilians and military—is an individual duty for every Muslim who can do it in any county."[21] The establishment of the World Islamic Front constituted a major achievement, for it provided "an umbrella to all organizations fighting the jihad against Jews and Crusaders."[22] Leaders of five terrorist movements submerged their differences to forge a worldwide front.

Tellingly, the Saudi millionaire's fatwas shed light on bin Laden's thinking and his contempt for America's toothless response to previous attacks. His reflections on the U.S. evacuation from Somalia after the 1993 Mogadishu street battle are most revealing:

> When tens of your soldiers were killed in minor battles and one American pilot dragged in the street of Mogadishu, you left the area in disappointment, humiliation, and defeat, carrying your dead with you. Clinton appeared in front of the whole world threatening and promising revenge, but these threats were merely a preparation for withdrawal. You had been disgraced by Allah and you withdrew; the extent of your impotence and weakness became very clear.[23]

This fatwa constituted a rollout for a campaign of bloody strikes. On August 7, 1998, Al Qaeda operatives conducted deadly bombings on American sites by the back-to-back blasts at U.S. embassies in the capital cities of Tanzania and Kenya. In Dar-es-Salaam, a suicide bomber drove an explosives-filled truck next to the embassy building blowing off one side of the structure. Nearly simultaneously and 450 miles away, another terrorist team detonated an explosive device alongside the embassy in Nairobi. The toll was high with 12 Americans and 212 Africans killed and some 5,000 injured, mostly Africans, by splintering glass and hurtling concrete.

Shifting into high gear, the Clinton presidency decided to strike back at the authors of the carnage, preempt additional onslaughts, and hold in check the spreading terrorism. It ordered cruise missile strikes on six Al Qaeda training camps in Afghanistan and a bin Laden-supported pharmaceutical plant in the Sudan, suspected of manufacturing VX nerve agent. The White House planning sessions eerily foreshadowed the post-9/11 deliberations about striking before being smote again by terrorists. Clinton's top aides debated the appropriateness of a preemptive attack on training facilities and a chemical factory as defensive measures sanctioned by the UN Charter's Article 51. While acknowledging the slender historical record either for first-strike assaults or for military action against another country based exclusively on secret intelligence evidence, they endorsed the missile salvos owing to fears of not halting additional terrorism. The reasoning was sound even if the application misfired.

Acting on intelligence placing Osama bin Laden and his inner circle at a camp near the city of Khost on August 20, U.S. naval vessels in the Arabian Sea launched

79 Tomahawk missiles that slammed into the Afghan terrorist installations and the al-Shifa plant near Khartoum. Operation Infinite Reach killed an estimated 20–30 people in the training camps and demolished the Sudanese chemical facility. The exhilaration experienced within government circles at hitting back against terrorism quickly dissipated as disappointing reports streamed in about the errant attacks. Osama bin Laden and his top lieutenants escaped the strike, perhaps being tipped off from Pakistani sources.[24]

Ayman al-Zawahiri, an Egyptian doctor who served as bin Laden' principal deputy, soon contacted friendly news outlets to gloat about the U.S. blows struck in the air. Exiled from his homeland for his terrorist activities, Zawahiri warned about more violence directed against the United States for its policies in the Middle East. The Western media were skeptical about the evidence for destroying the al-Shifa plant to boot. Public perceptions of the Clinton government's judgment sank, and it shrank from anymore rollback-type assaults. It was an augury of a much greater intelligence breakdown that came to light in postwar Iraq. Matters got worse in the interlude, however.

European political leaders were dubious about Washington's estimates of the threat posed by Al Qaeda. They believed that the United States was overreacting to the danger by firing the Tomahawks. They pointed to their own brushes with terrorist gangs. Germany's Red Army Faction (Baader-Meinhof gang), Italy's Red Brigades, and Spain's Basque separatist—all utilized the gun and the bomb for their political goals. The Irish Republican Army even detonated explosives in Margaret Thatcher's Brighton hotel in a near-miss attempt on the prime minister's life. The Europeans asserted that they never lost their perspective by staging huge attacks to combat terrorism. France's Foreign Minister Hubert Védrine even referred to the United States as a "hyperpower," as if to imply it needed a European counterweight. As such, the European mood represented a precursor to the Franco-German hostility to America's second war against Iraq when Washington moved beyond containment.

THE UNITED STATES PUNTS

On the heels of the cruise missile firing, President Clinton announced during an Oval Office address to the nation that he had ordered "our Armed Forces to take action to counter an immediate threat from the bin Laden network of terrorist groups." The commander-in-chief pledged, "We will meet it [the threat], no matter how long it may take," adding "there will be no sanctuary for terrorists."[25] But no further military attacks occurred.

Bill Clinton also signed a string of counterterrorism executive orders. One designated Richard Clarke the United States' first national coordinator for counterterrorism; he drafted the "Political-Military Plan Delenda." The head of the Counterterrorism Security Group adapted the Latin word *delenda*, meaning that something must be destroyed, to reinforce the goal to eliminate Osama bin Laden and his associates. The plan ranged from military actions to diplomatic steps and from covert operations to capture schemes. While the military route figured prominently in the secret paper, the Clinton administration never again fired cruise missiles or took any armed action against Afghanistan, Sudan, or other targets. Clarke proposed and the president authorized commando-type operations for the nation's elite Special Operations Forces (Delta Force, Green Berets, Rangers, and the Navy's SEAL teams) to disrupt terrorist plots. To destabilize bin Laden's Afghan hosts, Clinton officials also recommended supplying arms to the Northern Alliance, which was fighting an insurgency against the Taliban regime after being routed from Kabul. None of these preemptive missions was ever mounted. Why?

A picture emerges out of bureaucratic inertia, hidebound organizational culture, misplaced priorities, misjudgments, and risk aversion within the U.S. government. The Pentagon, for instance, was unenthusiastic about "cowboy" operations advanced by West Wing staffers. CENTCOM chief Tommy R. Franks wrote in his autobiography half a decade later that Richard Clarke never gave him "a single page of actionable intelligence" on which to mount a military operation.[26] Top military and civilian officials in the defense department looked askance at these cloak-and-dagger operations. Since the Vietnam War, the army generals closed their minds to the effectiveness of special forces operations, which they barely tolerated, if not actively disliked.[27]

To no avail, Washington did pursue diplomatic avenues with Afghanistan's Taliban rulers to expel bin Laden and to close down Al Qaeda's terror camps, which trained an estimated 10,000–20,000 militants from 1996 through the 9/11 attacks. Clinton officials prodded Saudi Arabia to negotiate with Mullah Omar to handover bin Laden in return for aid. Mullah Omar refused, and the desert kingdom broke diplomatic relations with Kabul. The United States also gingerly pressured Pakistan, the foremost backer of the Taliban's rise to power, to bring the bin Laden terrorist network to heel. The Pakistani government and its Inter-Services Intelligence Directorate (ISI) stuck by the Taliban regime, because they hoped to placate its large restive Pashtun population that spilled over the boarder into Afghanistan. Lobbying Islamabad came to naught; it simply shrugged of the U.S. importuning.

America likewise dispatched its representative to the United Nations, Bill Richardson, to Afghanistan in April 1998. When Kabul refused to surrender or oust America's chief terrorist suspect and his band, the United States convinced the Security Council to slap on UN sanctions. They proved ineffective against a subsistence economy, which relies on grazing sheep, cultivating small plots, growing poppy crops, and trafficking illicitly in opium for the profitable European market.

The U.S.-backed sanctions in 1999 did not budge the Taliban regime. Just prior to leaving office, President Clinton moved another resolution through the Security Council in December 2000. This UN resolution included an arms embargo on military goods to Afghanistan. By barring the transfer of weapons, the Clinton administration wanted to strike at the Taliban's Achilles heel because the fanatical Islamic regime was locked in a protracted war with the Tajik- and Uzbek-dominated Northern Alliance. The CIA did establish contact with the Northern Alliance as potential allies to grab Osama bin Laden. Its charismatic leader, Ahmed Shah Massoud, had been a genuine hero of the anti-Soviet war. He now waged an anti-Taliban struggle from his stronghold in northeastern Afghanistan, along the 70-mile Panjshir Valley that slices through the Hindu Kush Mountains. A CIA field agent recorded Massoud's disbelief when informed of President Clinton's preference for capture, not assassination, of bin Laden. He recalled Massoud's reaction as "You guys are crazy—you haven't changed a bit."[28]

Clinton officials lived in the shadow of history. During the 1970s, the CIA had been embroiled in controversy. Senator Frank Church, a Democrat from Idaho, headed a U.S. Senate committee investigation of the spy agency that revealed a series of outlandish plots to assassinate foreign leaders such as the Cuban leader Fidel Castro with exploding cigars. In 1975, the committee concluded that assassination was incompatible with American principles and that it should be rejected as a foreign policy instrument. As one consequence, presidential Executive Order 12333, issued by Gerald Ford and re-signed by subsequent presidents, outlawed political assassinations. Legal experts judged that the ban did not apply to military targets or to persons posing imminent threat to the United States in times of armed conflict. But executive branch officials still agonized over the precise language in Bill Clinton's secret legal authorizations to go after the chief terror suspect.[29] It is difficult to overemphasize Washington's immobility in regard to the lurking Al Qaeda threat. Risk avoidance carried the day. Nothing resulted from all the bureaucrats' meetings and memos.

Meanwhile, Al Qaeda proved less risk-averse. What it termed the "planes operation" moved from the planning to the execution phase as the second millennium neared. The terrorist movement selected, trained, and deployed its operatives. It put up an estimated $500,000 to plan and implement the 9/11 terrorism on the United States. By early 2000, when the CIA had abandoned proposals for putting U.S. boots on the ground in Afghanistan, Al Qaeda insinuated its conspirators into the United States. Before the 9/11 attacks, the United States, nevertheless, received another wake up call.

This warning came when two saluting men in a skiff pulled alongside the USS Cole, an Arleigh Burke-class guided missile destroyer, in Yemen's port of Aden for routine refueling on October 12, 2000. The small boat's crew detonated their explosives-filled craft, nearly scuttling the warship. The blast tore a 40-foot hole in the ship's side, killed 17 sailors, and wounded a further 39. It took 14 months and $250 million to repair the stricken vessel. The attack was, in effect, an act of war by Al Qaeda. But West Wing officials judged the episode as just another instance of the military's incapacity to take seriously the necessary safeguards against terrorism.[30]

The United States ordered no counterattack, even as bin Laden varied his residencies around Kandahar in anticipation of an air strike. It fell back on law enforcement practices. Secretary Albright telephoned Ali Abdullah Saleh, Yemen's president, to pave the way for the dispatch of FBI investigators to Aden. Neither the departing Clinton White House nor the new Bush government retaliated for the warship bombing. During the presidential debates between Texas Governor George Bush and Vice President Al Gore, the subject of the Cole blast came up just once. The candidates and the country had moved on to other issues. After leaving office, Clinton mused in his autobiography that his "biggest disappointment was not getting bin Laden."[31]

The incoming George Walker Bush government, in fact, initially retraced his predecessor's footsteps, when it came to responses to threats in the Middle East. In June 2001, three distinct terrorists plots produced a wholly unanticipated response from an administration that came into office deriding its predecessor's irresolution. Intercepted cell phone conversations indicated an impending attack on the FBI team investigating the Cole in Yemen. They hastily departed Aden. Next, American warships in nearby Bahrain, the headquarters of the U.S. Fifth Fleet, put out to sea on account of a warning about possible attacks. Finally, hundreds of U.S. Marines staging a joint training exercise in Jordan cut short their maneuvers, reboarded their amphibious vessels, and sailed away due to a terrorist alert. The incidents received scant media coverage and their recollection was lost in the uproar over the 9/11 strikes two months later. But their significance in the Middle East cannot be underestimated, for they reinforced the belief that America feared casualties, distrusted its local allies, and, most importantly, lacked a forceful answer to terrorism. It looked as if the new government adopted its predecessor's passive stance in an increasingly unstable arc from the Arabian Peninsula to the Hindu Kush. While containment no longer equated with stability and security, its polar opposite, the use of invasion, occupation, and U.S.-prescribed multiconfessional democracy was a worse option, as we will shortly see.

CHAPTER 8

ATTACKING
AFGHANISTAN

Hell is truth seen too late.

Thomas Hobbes

This place may be bombed, and we will be killed. We love death. The U.S. loves life.
This is the big difference between us.

Osama bin Laden, November 26, 2001

THE SEPTEMBER 11, 2001 TERRORIST ATTACKS DEALT A BLOW to the type of international stability so prized by post–Berlin Wall American governments. The plane crashes shattered complacency at home and assumptions overseas. The 110-storied Twin Towers, where some 50,000 people worked, collapsed less than 90 minutes after the first plane crash. Before the Manhattan skyscrapers' 12 million square feet of office floor space "pancaked" down into a fiery Ground Zero, another highjacked airliner slammed into the western face of the Pentagon just outside Washington, DC. Both sites were icons of America's paramountcy—one emblematic of economic power and the other the headquarters of military strength. Al Qaeda's turning commercial aircraft into missiles and killing nearly three thousand people in the time it takes to eat a leisurely breakfast astonished a country that believed for over two hundred years its bordering oceans made it a secure geopolitical island. The ramifications of such a devastating strike at America's heart had to be significant, and they were. Abroad, they transformed U.S. policy toward a crusading democracy agenda for unreceptive lands that historically fought "infidel" invasions and occupations.

It is the hypothesis of this book that America invested enormous effort and resources in stabilizing the world's turbulent patches after the Berlin Wall. The United States opposed Ukraine's independence from the dying Soviet Union, Yugoslavia's breakup into small republics, Iraq's invasion of Kuwait, North Korea's acquisition of nuclear weapons, Saddam Hussein's post–Gulf War provocations, and Al Qaeda's mounting terrorism. It used its military forces to stop aggression, maintain peace, and preserve order. It brought about regime-change to consolidate stability in Panama, Haiti, Liberia, and the Balkans. To check burgeoning threats, the United

States took its bearings from the Cold War's containment policy by backing authoritarian regimes, promoting multilateral alliances to share responsibilities, signing arms control agreements, and husbanding its armed forces for large conventional conflicts, like the Persian Gulf War. Disorder threatened its globalization agenda of stability through economic growth as well as American prosperity. Even worse, brush fires might turn into conflagrations necessitating a massive U.S. commitment to extinguish the flames. America fought neither for a landed empire, as Rome did, nor for colonies around the world, as did Britain. Even when oil figured in its calculations as in the Middle East, it paid the market rate, not a confiscatory price. It looked for stability in the access to this vital resource as it did for stasis in areas without energy for its cars, aircraft, and industries. Panama, Haiti, Bosnia, or Kosovo held no oil reserves but they needed stabilizing, lest they convulse their part of the world.

The 9/11 attacks briefly transformed America's fundamental assumptions, because they seemed flawed in their promises for stability. The fact that Afghan's theocratic dictatorship spawned terrorist attacks and that the 9/11 hijackers came from Saudi Arabia, Egypt, and other authoritarian countries led to a revaluation of America's worldview. Autocracies no longer guaranteed stability and security for the United States. America awoke to the truth that hell could come from authoritarian regimes, even friendly ones. Since autocratic regimes appeared not to ensure stability, the United States initially lurched to spread consensual government, which seemed to offer the prospect of peace, security, and stability, at least judging by the nature of the mature Western democracies. It dropped its reluctance to democracy-conjuring-up or nation-building endeavors in war-mangled or desolate areas so as to encourage development, intelligence gathering, and stability before Al Qaeda set up shop.

The United States no longer could afford to look away from desperate conditions in Africa, South America, or Asia, whose "ungoverned space" beckoned to Islamic terrorist networks. To wage the Global War on Terrorism, the U.S. Special Operations Command deployed special operators, channeled arms and equipment, and sleuthed out intelligence in a growing list of countries. Camp Lemonier in Djibouti, for example, served as the hub for a "pre-emptive strike on the hearts and minds of those living in the Horn of Africa."[1] Some 1,500 soldiers, sailors, airmen, and marines trained local forces, refurbished schools, opened clinics, dug wells, and created jobs in an effort to prevent terrorist cells from gaining a foothold in the desperately poor Horn. Half a world away, the GWOT required a $100 million assistance package and Special Forces to the Philippines, where they trained Filipino soldiers to route out the Abu Sayyaf terrorists who were linked to Al Qaeda.

Stability for a country eager to preserve its preeminent global position remained the primary goal. But the means to achieve it—national building and democratization—did change drastically from its prior semi-insular architecture. As was true of the containment doctrine, the Bush administration's so-called transformational diplomacy "to build and sustain democratic, well-governed states . . . [that] conduct themselves responsibly in the international system" was shot through with exceptions, as the cordial relations with the Egyptian autocracy or the Saudi Arabian and Jordanian monarchies attested.[2] The policy began with counterattacks after the 9/11 terrorist assaults. For organizational purposes, the Iraq War is dealt with in the next chapter. The U.S. alliances, invasion, and postwar Afghanistan pacification will be discussed here.

AMERICA PREPARES TO STRIKE BACK AT AL QAEDA

The hand of Al Qaeda was quickly discerned in the terrorist "Pearl Harbor" in New York City and Washington. Its "planes operation" bore all the hallmarks of the terrorist network's three trademarked "S" elements—suicidal, spectacular, and symbolic. Osama bin Laden's 1998 fatwa declaring war on the United States was now executed by large-scale destruction. America decided to strike back at his Afghan base. Intervening into Iraq or hitting the Bekaa Valley terrorist camps in Lebanon were quickly ruled out for now, as being diversionary and unlikely to garner international backing.

Following his initial lackluster television addresses, President Bush rallied the nation for war. His first speech was delivered at the memorial service for the terrorist victims in the National Cathedral where he designated the murderers as "the evil ones." Hours later he flew to lower Manhattan where fires smoldered and a toxic stench swirled from the charred ruins. Using a bullhorn to address the crowd of rescue workers, hardhats, and congressional delegates, Bush spoke about how the "people who knocked these buildings down will hear all of us soon."[3] His earthy, unscripted language resonated with his listeners. It was a high point of the Bush presidency.

The final speech in the trilogy of addresses that marked Bush as a wartime commander in chief was given before a joint sessions of Congress. Held nine days after the four plane crashes, Bush explained the case against Osama bin Laden, his Al Qaeda organization, and their sanctuary in the Taliban-ruled Afghanistan. He made clear that the fight was against the terrorists "who are traitors to their own [Islamic] faith," not "our many Muslim friends" or the greater Islamic world where the terrorists "want to overthrow existing governments in many Muslim countries, such as Egypt, Saudi Arabia and Jordan."[4] In fact, Washington reached out even to adversarial states such as Syria and Libya for intelligence about terrorist groupings.

Days before his speech to Congress, President Bush convened the members of his war Cabinet at Camp David. At the meeting, George Tenet got "exceptional authorities" that granted the CIA broad powers to eliminate Al Qaeda in Afghanistan and elsewhere. This type of authority was normally conveyed as an intelligence or presidential finding; the Bush version was labeled a Memorandum of Notification. Less than a week after the meeting, the president signed two memoranda bestowing legal sanction for covert operations to the CIA. Stripped to its essentials, the Bush approach departed from Clinton's law enforcement methods to combat terrorism by taking the fight to the terrorist headquarters in Afghanistan and to disrupt its global network.

The Camp David meeting also reviewed the Pentagon plans for Afghanistan offered by chairman of the Joint Chiefs of Staff, General Henry B. Shelton, who had been appointed by President Clinton. Shelton's cruise missiles or manned bombers alone were judged a version of Clinton's ineffectual "cruise missile" diplomacy and inadequate to the task of eliminating Al Qaeda. The conferees advocated a "boots on the ground" plan that called for commando-type incursion into Afghanistan to chase the Taliban from power. Plain and simple, they wanted regime change, a practice that saw frequent application in America's post–Berlin Wall interventions.

Yet, three days before the commencement of bombing on October 7 at a NSC meeting, the president's national security adviser was caught flat-footed about the composition of the next Afghan government. George Bush asked Condoleezza Rice,

"Who will run the country?"[5] No thought, let alone plans, had been laid on how to consolidate a victory.

Winning a war is one matter, governing a country quite another. Coming to office with an almost visceral contempt for the Clinton administration's nation-building efforts in Somalia, Haiti, Bosnia, and Kosovo, the Bush foreign policy team resolved not to engage in peacekeeping and government-building tasks. Candidate Bush, in fact, pledged never to stretch the military in peace-soldiering missions, and his soon-to-be White House security adviser bristled at the use of paratroopers escorting schoolchildren. American security soon dictated a revolutionary change from the 1990s reluctance for nation building to the wholesale espousal of rebuilding torn-apart societies for stability.

THE U.S. AGENDA AND GREAT POWER POLITICS

Before the United States overhauled its international posture, it had to corral allies for the coming Afghan War. George W. Bush reached out multilaterally in ways that had been unanticipated before the 9/11 attacks. He secured passage in the United Nations of a U.S. proposal to impede the flow of funds to terrorists. Making it illegal by international law to help terrorists was the easy part; it was another to get particular states, such as Saudi Arabia, Pakistan, and the Persian Gulf sheikdoms, to enforce the statutes on their own citizens. To this day, no one believes that terrorist funding has dried up from all the sources in the Muslim world.

As the Bush government reshaped American international ties, no more startling pirouette came than with China. Washington pushed the Hainan Incident of the past April, when Chinese warplanes compelled a damaged U.S. reconnaissance aircraft to land on the South China Sea island, to the recesses of its memory, as it befriended Beijing. A source of concern for Republican hawks during the 1990s, China went from what Bush described as a "strategic competitor" to virtually a cobelligerent against terrorism, as the United States asked Beijing to share intelligence on a common foe. Just as Russia had its rebellious Chechen Muslims, China suffered from terrorist violence in its western and largely Muslim-populated Xinjiang province, a hotbed of ethnic separatism from the Uighurs, a Central Asian people. Beijing delighted in America's overtures and recognition of their shared struggle, as it intensified its crackdown in the "Chinese Chechnya" and pushed Washington to ease up its support of the separatists on Taiwan.

The United States similarly reached out to Russia, although the U.S.-led NATO bombing of Serbia during Kosovo crisis had strained its interactions with Moscow. Now, Washington muted its criticism of the Russian Federation's human rights abuses in fighting the independence-minded guerrillas in Chechnya. This post-9/11 Russian-American cordiality gave birth to Moscow's acquiescence to U.S. bases in Central Asia, a belt Moscow held as its orbit. Russo-American cooperation on antiterrorism soon encountered the realities of a complex partnership. The United States criticized Russia's clampdown on an independent media and backpedaling on democracy. For their part, the Russians portrayed the United States as *glavny protivnik*, the main adversary, as during the Soviet era. Later, Kremlin hands resented Washington's bringing about peaceful regime changes in Georgia, Kyrgyzstan, and

Ukraine to promote democracy and undercut Moscow's influence. Just a few years after the 9/11 terrorists struck, U.S.-Russian relations fell far below the cordiality at the time of the American offensive into Afghanistan. Well before that, the United States was lodged in Russia's backyard.

FORGING THE OUTER AND INNER RINGS OF A COALITION

Secretary of State Powell pulled the laboring oar to assemble a coalition to combat global terrorism and to support the military invasion into Afghanistan. He met with Prince Saud al-Faisal, Saudi Arabia's foreign minister, for an expression against terrorism. The Saudis offered intelligence information on Osama bin Laden, an easy commitment since the House of Saud regarded the master terrorist like a bird does a snake. Riyadh demurred at U.S. requests to freeze the bank accounts of suspected Saudi financiers of Al Qaeda without ironclad proof, however.

Because 15 of the 9/11 hijackers were Saudis, the desert kingdom was put under intense scrutiny during the months after the terrorist assault. It came to light that luxury-loving Saudis hoped to buy off and divert Al Qaeda and other Islamic extremists. In bin Laden's mind, the ruling elite was guilty of apostasy for allowing infidel troops to be garrisoned on holy ground and for flouting the puritanical teachings of Islam. Members of the Saudi establishment, therefore, had entered into a Faustian bargain with the religious militants over many years. In return for personal survival, they financed terrorism abroad, funded the *madrassas* that inculcated their students with religious extremism, and hoped to export their problems with the religious zealots, who advocated terrorist operations against Israel, India, Western Europe, and the United States. Other Saudis embraced out of conviction, the intolerance of the Wahhabi sect of Islam, which loathes Christians, Jews, Hindus, and apostate Muslims, including Shias. The chickens came home to roost when Al Qaeda affiliates undertook a spate of terrorism within the desert kingdom on the heels of the 9/11 operation.[6]

To win support in the Middle East for an attack on Afghanistan, President Bush departed from his earlier hands-off policy toward the Israeli-Palestinian peace process. Now he gave clear voice to the conviction that a settlement could be reached only with the creation of a democratic Palestinian political entity. Before leaving office, Bill Clinton had quietly mentioned that peace could be achieved only by establishing a Palestinian state. But George Bush was the first president to make statehood a matter of U.S. policy in a speech before the UN General Assembly on November 10, 2001. Standing at the podium, Bush asserted, "We are working toward the day when two states—Israel and Palestine—live peacefully together with secure and recognized borders."[7] Designed to assuage Islamic hostility to the large-scale U.S. military intrusion into a Muslim country, the presidential foray actually languished after being launched. Periodically, the White House returned to the theme as in its endorsement of the "roadmap" to Middle East settlement in 2003 but it did not take matter until after Yasir Arafat's death and Bush's reelection to a second term, when it embraced the democratizing-for-stability concept.

Despite America's wooing, the Middle East generally opposed the U.S. invasion of Afghanistan. Oman first deferred U.S. requests for basing rights because its forces were involved in a training exercise with Britain. Qatar dissented from the coming war and refused Washington the use of its airport facilities. This aversion stands out in comparison to the first Gulf War, when the Arabian Peninsula kingdoms and the Middle East welcomed America's forceful expulsion of Iraq from Kuwait. Egypt, however, did back U.S. military action against Afghanistan. Once the battle started, its ambassador to the United States, Nabil Fahmy, expressed an "extremely positive" impression of the U.S. exertions "not to kill civilians."[8]

Many Near Eastern states adopted the American view on Afghanistan but not on any additional wars. The Arab League meeting of foreign ministers in Damascus nearly a month after the United States struck Afghanistan rebutted Osama bin Laden's televised statements that he spoke in the name of Islam or Arabs. At the same time, they warned that an expansion of the war to any Arab country would break the fragile alliance backing Washington against Afghanistan. This was a thinly veiled reference to an invasion of Iraq.

Washington's foreign policy also underwent pivotal shifts in orientation vis-à-vis several nations heretofore of marginal interest. For the actual military operation, Pakistan was the key country, for it geographically bordered Afghanistan. What made the approach delicate was the fact that Islamabad was a staunch backer of the isolated regime in Kabul. Pakistan's ISI, in fact, had materially aided the Taliban's capture of the country. With 2 million Afghan refugees still in its territory as a consequence of the Soviet invasion and then the civil war, Islamabad had an incentive to enlist the Taliban to establish order in the chaotic country. In addition, the puritanical Taliban enjoyed support from segments of Pakistani society. Convincing the military regime of Pervez Musharraf to desert its former proxy force was also a gamble if it succeeded. It might endanger the very regime Washington needed to pursue its offensive should the Islamic extremists turn their wrath against the Pakistani general.

George Bush's foreign policymakers had their work cut out for them, because the close Washington-Islamabad bond had gradually loosened after the disintegration of the Soviet Union, their common foe. A geopolitical realignment had also been furthered by the Clinton administration, in which India replaced Pakistan as America's main partner in South Asia. Bereft of its longtime ally after the Soviet Union's disintegration, India had reciprocated to American goodwill gestures. The world's largest democracy, India, in addition, shared with the United States a mounting uneasiness about the sudden economic rise of China, a state that had close ties to Pakistan. Terrorist attacks on India's occupied Kashmir territory by Islamic extremists after 1989 also formed another commonality in the Indo-American relationship. The bitter Pakistan-Indian rivalry meant that as ties warmed between Washington and New Delhi, they almost by necessity cooled between the Islamabad government and the United States. Thus, Washington wanted to enlist Pakistan in its Afghan campaign without endangering its budding relations with India.

President Bush's senior aides applied many stratagems to win over General Musharraf. Secretary of State Colin Powell spoke with Musharraf to facilitate Pakistan's cooperation. He worked to convince the Pakistani head to break relations with the Taliban, share intelligence, grant landing rights, and open his airspace to the United States. Later, President Bush credited the secretary of state for Pakistan's diplomatic reorientation for he "single-handedly got Musharraf on board."[9]

The United States rescheduled $379 million in Pakistani debt as well as waiving sanctions imposed on Pakistan and India after their nuclear tests. Other aid inducements later flowed to Islamabad. The country's surging economy, aided in part by U.S. largess, eased some political tension. By 2006, Pakistan's economic growth was second only to China's. U.S. policy, nevertheless, rested uneasily on the precariousness of Pakistan's continued stability. Washington acquiesced in Musharraf's amending the Pakistani constitution so as to prolong his presidency for five years and to have the power to dissolve parliament. The general's step away from democracy was predicated on a pledge to hang up his uniform but he reneged on the deal to his legislature, again with no real rebuke from Washington. This case of American pragmatism predated the democracy crusading that accompanied the Iraq invasion.

The Pakistani government duly swung toward the United States against its proxies now ruling Afghanistan—in part because Musharraf grasped the Bush administration's earnestness to sweep away Islamabad's client and in part because he realized that the Taliban were stirring up trouble inside Pakistan.[10] Islamabad lent the United States two bases—Pasni and Jacobabad for the U.S. invasion of Afghanistan. Cutting off Pakistani sponsorship of the Taliban was unlike turning off a faucet. Even after the U.S. struck inside Afghanistan, sympathetic ISI officials and businessmen smuggled weapons and ammunition in trucks filled with blankets and wheat through the Chaman border near the Pakistani city of Quetta.

To advance its interests, the United States also worked to smooth the long-standing political tension between Pakistan and India. In June 2002, President Bush directly involved himself with the Kashmir conflict, which is a prime source for the tension between India and Pakistan. The United States pushed both New Delhi and Islamabad for de-escalatory steps in their tense relationship. Over time, the flood of Islamic militants from Pakistan crossing the Line of Control into the Indian-controlled zone of Kashmir ebbed. The Indo-Pak tension lessened for a while, and both nations pulled back from the brink of war in an unheralded diplomatic breakthrough for Washington and unintended consequence of America's Central Asian campaign.

Afghanistan's western neighbor, the Islamic Republic of Iran presented less hostility to the American offensive than anticipated from its past tortuous relations with the Great Satan. As so often in the region, the enemy-of-my-enemy-is-my-friend logic temporarily overrode the clerical government's America loathing. Iran regarded Taliban-ruled Afghanistan as an enemy. Iran, like Russia, funneled weapons and supplies to the Northern Alliance to carry on its fight against the Taliban regime. It had ample reason to do so. The Sunni-dominated Taliban militias had murdered numerous members of Afghanistan's Farsi-speaking Shiite Muslim minority who were linked culturally and religiously with Iran. In addition, the Taliban turned a blind eye to the rampant drug smuggling across its border. Heroin addiction among Iran's youth had developed into a severe problem. None of these complaints against Kabul, however, made Iran friendly to Washington, but they restrained the Islamic Republic's opposition to the U.S.-led assault on the Taliban and later to the American and NATO efforts to defeat the insurgency that followed the invasion.

THE CENTRAL ASIAN BRIDGEHEAD

After getting a green light from Moscow for trespassing into the so-called Russian near-abroad, Washington struck out on an astonishing geopolitical vector that drove the United States into the Central Asian terra incognita, not unlike America's World War II drives into European and Asian lands to confront threats. President Clinton had extended feelers to the region for access to oil and natural gas reserves; these were largely for economic and energy purposes. Instead, the Bush offensive aimed at a geostrategic realignment with semipermanent bases for forward deployment of U.S. forces in a war.

Three Central Asian countries adjoined Afghanistan—Turkmenistan, Uzbekistan, and Tajikistan—of which Uzbekistan ranked as the most important since it backed up directly to the anti-Taliban resistance from the Northern Alliance. Uzbekistan, once a potential candidate for censure for torturing Muslim radicals, now drew unaccustomed courting from Washington, still in its pragmatic mode. Even before 9/11, the United States had negotiated an agreement with the authoritarian government in Tashkent to permit the CIA to operate surveillance UVAs, or unmanned aerial vehicles over Al Qaeda's Afghan bases in return for U.S. Green Berets training government troops against Islamic insurgents. From Uzbek territory, the spy agency also ran secret assets inside Afghanistan to gather intelligence about the Taliban. After the September attacks, it fielded covert paramilitary teams to mobilize the Northern Alliance and other anti-Taliban fighters throughout the country to provide information, commence sabotage operations, and generally prepare for an American invasion.

The war on terrorism brought the American-Uzbek collaboration closer. Washington got the Karshi-Khanabad airfield, known as K-2 to U.S. airmen, for Combat Search and Rescue (CSAR) to retrieve any pilots shot down lest they become political hostages. Once the fighting started, Washington also stationed nearly a thousand soldiers from the 10th Mountain Division in the country as a springboard for intervention into Afghanistan. President Karimov valued U.S. assistance, for he faced a danger from the Islamic Movement of Uzbekistan (IMU), a militant Muslim group. Since the IMU operated from sanctuaries inside Afghanistan, it would suffer a blow if the Taliban went down in defeat, a plus for Karimov and reason enough to ally with the United States.

Tajikistan, unlike its neighbor Uzbekistan, was thoroughly in the Russian camp. Fractured by a civil war in the mid-1990s and the poorest of the 15 former Soviet republics, Tajikistan relied economically and politically on Moscow for survival. Therefore, its cooperation with Washington hinged on the Kremlin's approval. Putin's intercession with the government in Dushanbe gained him diplomatic points with George Bush, who regarded the Russian leader in favorable terms at this time. Although Tajikistan shared a border with Afghanistan, its importance was secondary because the flight path to the Northern Alliance stronghold required navigating over mountainous terrain. The U.S. planes did flyover, refuel, and execute emergency operations from Tajikistan.

The third state in Washington's Central Asian line up was Turkmenistan, which bordered Afghanistan's northwestern quadrant and thus was less ideally placed for an air or land corridor to the pro-American Northern Alliance. Still, Turkmenistan's airport provided the United States useful contacts with the Shiite Tajiks, who clashed with the Sunni Taliban rulers. Turkmenistan, like Uzbekistan, served as land bridges for UN humanitarian relief supplies to destitute Afghans during the war and afterward.

Kazakhstan and Kyrgyzstan, which did not share borders with Afghanistan, joined with their sister Central Asian nations in cooperation with Washington for similar reason—to gain some leverage against the Kremlin's suffocating hug. Kazakhstan allowed coalition overflights during the invasion phase of the Afghan campaign. In addition, it joined with its neighbors in sending a liaison team to CENTCOM during the U.S.-led intervention and maintained its cooperation afterward. In order to strengthen its antiterrorist capabilities, Kazakhstan signed its first five-year military cooperation with Washington in September 2003. As a result, Americans and Kazakhs built a base on the Caspian Sea for training and reacting to terrorism on land or sea.

Kyrgyzstan opened its airfield at Mansas to U.S. aircraft to support the coalition attack on Afghanistan. Three years later, the American and European military tents took on a permanency with the erection of durable buildings for the 2,000 troops garrisoned in the Central Asian country. Outside the capital, Bishkek, U.S. forces set up Granci Air Base (named for the New York City fire chief who died in the World Trade Center attack) on a field next to the country's international airport. Years later some 1,000 U.S. personnel still resided at this logistical hub for Afghanistan.

The American move into Central Asia was largely defensive. Reactive as Washington's intervention was, it represented a replay of the need of powerful nations to secure their turbulent frontiers. The United States was not the first power to extend its sphere of interest to create a buffer zone to protect its vital interests. The Persian Gulf is a geopolitical hinge for the United States, which could not remain oblivious to the volatility of surrounding regions. From the Caucasian mountains to the Java Sea, militant Islamists made South Asia the epicenter of the "war on terror" before the September 11 strikes. Afterward, the United States counterattacked. At the risk of belaboring the obvious, America's incursion into this instable landmass will have profound consequences for the region in ways still obscure. The interplay of interests and power will transform the interactions among the states that stretch along the azimuth from Moscow to Manila.

THE ALLIES AND AFGHANISTAN

In the immediate 9/11 aftermath, Washington also laid the diplomatic groundwork with close allies for a military offensive against Osama bin Laden's lair. The terrorist assaults themselves facilitated coalition building for they evoked a rare upwelling of sympathy and support abroad for the United States. On September 12, for example, NATO invoked a mutual defense clause in its founding treaty for the first time. The alliance's ambassadors issued a statement after a hastily called meeting that stated, "If it is determined that this attack was directed from abroad against the United States, it shall be regarded as an action covered by Article 5 of the Washington Treaty."

Article 5, the cornerstone of the Atlantic alliance, made clear that "an armed attack" against any signatory "shall be considered an attack against all of them." The treaty committed NATO members to the use of force, if necessary, to restore security. The ambassador's statement acknowledged the 1949 treaty envisioned a different kind of aggression, presumably from the Soviet Union, but affirmed its validity "today, in a world subject to the scourge of international terrorism."[11] The call for collective security put NATO squarely behind the United States. In doing so, it afforded allied legitimacy to America's armed intervention into the Islamic Emirate of Afghanistan.

Three weeks later, NATO gave its final stamp of approval for an onslaught against Osama bin Laden, his Al Qaeda network, and the Taliban government in Afghanistan that harbored the terrorist organization. NATO took this action upon being presented with "clear and compelling proof" that Al Qaeda was behind the 9/11 terrorism. The U.S. classified evidence, according to press accounts, encompassed already known information as well as satellite reconnaissance photos and financial records of fund transfers to terrorist groups. It convinced NATO members that Al Qaeda was indeed behind the terrorism against the United States. Other NATO allies, particularly Germany, corroborated the American charges. George Robertson, the NATO secretary general, concluded that "its is now clear all roads lead to Al Qaeda."[12]

The United States asked for specific assistance from the North Atlantic Council, NATO's decision-making body, to include unlimited access to the member states' seaports, airfields, and airspace. NATO cut the United States some slack in the Balkans by replacing America's peacekeeping troops bound for Afghanistan. The most visible assistance, however, came as the Afghan campaign commenced in early October 2001 when NATO dispatched five European radar planes to patrol America's East Coast, taking over the responsibilities normally assumed by the U.S. Air Force. These airborne warning and control systems (AWACS) aircraft boasted advanced electronic devices to track intruders in American skies. The American AWACS fleet was stretched thin by the war in Afghanistan, patrols in northern and southern Iraq, and homeland defense. This had the practical effect of NATO pilots flying aircraft to protect the United States. Largely symbolic since the United States was prey to suicide hijackers, not conventional air warfare, the European gesture registered unity with Washington's Afghanistan intervention and heartened Americans, even though anti-U.S. demonstrators took to the streets in Athens, Berlin, and Paris to protest the approaching fighting in the Central Asian country.

Washington, for its part, treated some allies more equal than others. For many decades, Britain stood as the United States' staunchest ally. London and Washington often spoke of their "special relationship," cultivated since World War I. The fallen Berlin Wall left the relationship intact but more vulnerable during the halcyon 1990s. Bill Clinton did much to preserve the Anglo-American tie, for he and his British counterpart, Tony Blair, shared a mutual political commitment to lock conservatives out of power on both sides of the Atlantic. In addition, they worked closely on the Kosovo crisis and the Northern Ireland peace settlement.

President Bush and Prime Minister Blair were not political soul mates, since Bush was a Republican and Blair headed the leftist Labour Party. Fortunately for the United States, Tony Blair's commitment to the transatlantic alliance and his readiness to combat the terrorist threat concurred fully with the government presiding in Washington. Blair declared that fight against terrorism came down to "defeat or be defeated by it."[13] In time, these two unlikely political bedfellows became as united in a martial spirit as Achilles and Patroclus; their political destinies, as a result, became intertwined.

Her majesty's government, nonetheless, played Athens to Rome by appealing to Washington for restraint. Blair worried that the Bush administration, already "impatient with the perceived constraints placed on its national interests by international treaty commitments," would overreact and lash out on its own. He "decided to strain every fiber to persuade Bush of the merits of a multilateral response." Attending George Bush's joint congressional speech, the British prime minister was relieved that the U.S. president accepted his counsel. In response to Blair's concerns about a second front, the president said, "I agree with you, Tony. Afghanistan is the priority. We will come back to Iraq in due course."[14] Bush kept his word and a year on he staked America's response to global terrorism on war with Iraq.

By the close of September, several other NATO countries let it be known that they wanted combat assignments in America's antiterrorism operations in Afghanistan. But Defense's Donald Rumsfeld worried that an allied force might hinder the U.S. military effort, despite the obvious political advantages of a broad coalition, instead of the United States acting unilaterally. By this time the U.S. military organizing was leaping ahead for the Afghan offensive, but NATO's part in the conflict remained unclear at its early October Brussels meeting. American anxiety centered on NATO's unpreparedness for the agile, fast-moving warfare being drawn up by the Pentagon. Since the Atlantic alliance's founding, the European NATO members readied themselves for a conventional Soviet thrust across the Continent. Even those European forces were starved for adequate funds, culminating in eggshell defenses, reliant on American power. Paul Wolfowitz, the deputy secretary of defense, commenting about NATO assistance after the Brussels' meeting circumspectly said, "if we need collective action, we will ask for it."[15]

Washington also shied away from an operational role for NATO per se, remembering the unwieldy command structure during the Kosovo air campaign that delayed sorties or even excluded bombing targets while trying to reach consensus among factious allies. The Kosovo engagement taught the United States that reaching agreement among a 19-member organization was a cumbersome process at best. Consequently, Bush put together a coalition of allies instead of relying on a NATO-organized operation. His advisers ruled out any committee oversight on American power.

A month after the start of the bombing, European countries persisted in their desire to participate in the conflict. They chafed at what one French official alluded to as "washing up the dirty dishes" after the United States did "the cooking and prepare what people are going to eat."[16] The metaphor stuck and reinforced European feelings of second-class status toward their powerful ally across the Atlantic. This resentment broadened to other areas, posing huge diplomatic problems for the United States prior to the attack on Iraq.

For the Afghan war, the U.S. diplomatic exertions carried the day by the start of hostilities. George Bush could state, "More than 40 countries in the Middle East, Africa, Europe and across Asia have granted air transit and landing rights." Even though no Muslim governments joined the Afghan offensive, Bush still claimed, "we are supported by the collective will of the world."[17] Britain and Australia early on committed elite commandoes to the campaign. Italy pledged 2,700 combat personnel.

In late November, Poland, a new NATO member, announced its plans to field 300 soldiers, including 80 from its GROM commando unit. Later, France and Canada sent troops. By March 2002, units from Denmark, Norway, and Germany joined Operation Anaconda. Japan and the Netherlands stationed warships in the Arabian Sea. American diplomacy won over partners, neutralized detractors, and kept at bay its fiercest antagonists. Best of all, the Afghan alliance proved durable over the years. The U.S.-led effort's chief failing centered on its inability to serve as a diplomatic template for a far greater intervention two years later in Iraq.

FROM MANHATTAN TO MAZAR-I-SHARIF IN PURSUIT OF REGIME CHANGE

After the Anglo-Russian nineteenth-century duel, Afghanistan slipped again from much of the world's consciousness. The U.S. interest flickered briefly in the 1950s, under the country's last monarchy. It competed with the Soviet Union by awarding generous grants to build roads, airports, dams, and schools before the funds dried up in an atmosphere of neglect. The United States constructed a major airport at Kandahar, as a planned stopover for prop-driven planes. Jet airlines soon bypassed the passé runaways like superhighways sidestep rural villages. An irony could be derived from the obsolete Kandahar airport. An invading U.S. armed force decades afterward put it to good use as its logistical hub to subdue and pacify America's former aid recipient.

From a U.S. military planner's standpoint, it is hard to envision a more daunting challenge than an invasion of Afghanistan. Landlocked, underdeveloped, and distant from friendly ports and airfields, the Central Asian country was not easily accessible. It is desiccate, prone to icy winter winds, and deficient in roads and communication networks. Sprawling topography of dusty flatlands, steep forested valleys, and rugged mountains of scenic beauty presents treacherous terrain. Valleys crosscut craggy mountains that form an endless maze of ravines, outcroppings, and caves, some of which sheltered warrior bands for centuries.

The human topography was even more inhospitable. The defiance of its warring clans, fleeting alliances among fighters, and legendary treachery gave this bellicose land its epitaph as an imperial graveyard for Victorian Britain and Soviet Russia. Throughout history, the Afghans have suffered opening defeats from invaders only to rebound against their conquerors. Easy to penetrate but hard to hold might sum up its history. Once a passageway for traders and a crossroads for civilizations, this remote land became a buffer between the Russian and British empires in a Cold War–like confrontation that Rudyard Kipling made famous as the "Great Game."

Nominally governed from its 6,000-foot high capital in Kabul, no central government truly dominated the regional warlords or melded the disparate peoples into a homogenous folk. Estimates placed Afghanistan's population at 25 million inhabitants that were divided into a volatile mixture of ethnic groups, made up of approximately 38 percent Pashtun, 25 percent Tajik, 19 percent Hazara, 6 percent Uzbek along with smaller numbers of Turkmen and Baluch. Most of the population speaks an Afghan form of Persian called Dari or Pashto along with minor languages. Even the prevailing Islamic faith—itself split by Sunni and Shia sects—bestowed little unity among its peoples.

Having defeated the Soviet armed forces and seen Americans run from Beirut and Mogadishu, after being bloodied, the Afghans disparaged U.S. martial abilities. They were not alone in their dim estimate of America's prospects. American and European pundits also foresaw a U.S. defeat if it ventured into the Afghan killing fields. America's arsenal possessed supersonic jets and cruise missiles but on the ground it would run up against cunning tribesmen, long schooled in hide-and-seek gun battles. Unlettered and unaware of the world beyond their borders, the Afghans were no slouches when it came to fighting. History, terrain, and seasoned veterans—all pointed toward a catastrophe reminiscent of the Vietnam War, according to armchair generals.

Like Bronze Age warriors fighting an Iron Age power, however, the Taliban fought yesterday's war by which they defeated the Soviet military. They attempted to hold ground. By hunkering down to endure the aerial blitz, they prepared to reemerge to fire and hide, when the United States fielded a large ground army like the Soviets had done. By repeating their antiaircraft tactics, they would shoot down low-flying planes and helicopters. But U.S. jets dropped their ordinance from 15,000 to 30,000 feet above their targets, well beyond Afghan range. The electronically guided precision bombs landed unerringly on the Taliban earthworks, killing thousands. The Taliban anticipated positional, frontal warfare, not an information-age war machine. The weapons left over from the defeat of the Red Army—T-55 and T-65 tanks, MiG23 jets, and surface-to-air missiles—lent no protection against information-age technology.

The Afghan's technical backwardness did, in fact, present a paradox for a twenty-first- century military superpower. The Afghan theater was virtually bankrupt of military and industrial targets. So destitute of factories, power plants, water treatment systems, and communication nodes was the impoverished land that bombing, it was joked, would bring the country up to the Stone Age rather than reducing it to a Neolithic level. Expending high-end weapons against tents seemed futile. "Pounding sand," as Bush termed it, afforded the United States no gains. Target lists merely ran to a several dozen high-value installations, airfields, and command centers, entirely unlike the target-rich environment offered, by say, Iraq or World War II Germany and Japan.

From the start of war planning, the Bush administration realized the futility of an air-only operation. The Kosovo campaign had provided a useful reality check on the utility of bombing alone. Instead, the Rumsfeld Pentagon infiltrated Special Operations Forces together with CIA paramilitary teams into the Afghan countryside. They had two primary missions. First, these specialized operators would bribe with cash, instruct, arm, and coordinate the Northern Alliance and other anti-Taliban groups to hammer the regime. Second, they would call in precision air strikes against Taliban defenses and their roving bands of armed militia. Such a strategy relied on America's vastly superior firepower and on local manpower to crush the Taliban ground forces.

The Bush administration prized collaboration with the Northern Alliance for several reasons. Militarily, Washington needed allies on the ground inside Afghanistan to fight the Taliban, help track down bin Laden and the Taliban leaders, and pass targeting information to American warplanes. The anti-Taliban leaders had amassed an estimated 10,000–15,000 seasoned fighters. Their reliability, effectiveness, and general soldiering competency were matters of doubt right from start of the campaign but Washington had no other option unless it desired to deploy 50,000 American troops with all the accompanying logistical nightmares as the U.S. Joint Chiefs of Staff initially planned.

Politically, the United States also desired to package the conflict as one against Osama bin Laden, his confederates, and the government that harbored them. It was eager to shun the impression of a war against the Afghan people, let alone against Islam, just as bin Laden desired to paint the clash as a religious battle. In one of his videotaped speeches frequently broadcast by Al Jazeera, an Arab satellite channel with an anti-American bias based in Qatar, the terrorist mastermind posited that the American-led onslaught "is a matter of religion and creed . . . It is ideological, so Muslims have to ally themselves with Muslims against the Christian Crusade."[18]

The U.S. government also aspired to form a pan-Afghan coalition to govern and pacify the land after hostilities. For the postconflict governance, Washington contacted the exiled Afghan king, Mohammad Zahir Shah, who still lived in Rome. The 86-year-old former monarch, who was a Pashtun like the Taliban rulers, agreed to serve as a rallying point for the country's liberation but refused any restoration of his kingship. He met with representatives from the Northern Alliance and other anti-Taliban parties in the days preceding and following the advent of the U.S. military onslaught.

Another refinement of this new American way of war witnessed the United States dropping many thousands of packaged meals and medical supplies from the air to relive hunger and suffering among the internally displaced refugees. NGOs also trucked in relief supplies from Iran, Turkmenistan, and Tajikistan. The war struck a first of sorts in trying to feed people while destroying their government. This unique "guns and butter" game plan also entailed stepped up food supplies to Afghan refugees in Pakistan.

The bombs and cruise missiles started falling on Afghanistan on October 7, 2001, less than a month after 9/11 terrorist strikes. As the bombs fell, helicopter-borne Special Operations Forces landed and promptly went native by wearing local dress, growing beards, and mounting horses to gallop in picturesque cavalry charges, while punching bomb coordinates into their laptop computers. They skillfully fused the electronic age with the saddle era. With U.S. eyes and ears on the ground, Taliban forces were speedily targeted, even if they moved from one location to another. They could run but could not hide in large packs.

DOUBTS AND DEBATES ARISE

After three weeks of intense bombardment, measurable results were outwardly meager. No towns had fallen, and the Taliban reinforced their frontline units in Mazar-i-Sharif, the country's second largest city and the keystone in the defense of Kabul. Rather than being "degraded" by the bombing, the Taliban looked stronger. Appearances were deceiving but they fed the skeptics' opinion of the overall expedition. On October 27, six days after the Pentagon intensified the bombing of the Taliban trenches, Daniel Schorr, National Public Radio's senior commentator, pessimistically declared, "This is a war in trouble."[19] An international relations scholar, John J. Mearsheimer, wrote a commentary in the *New York Times* arguing that it made "little sense to continue the current bombing or to send American ground forces into Afghanistan" He recommended "bribery, covert action, dissemination of the American message by radio to Afghans and increased humanitarian aid . . . to break apart the Taliban."[20] This pessimism was premature.

Once the air war shifted from the preselected stationary targets to zeroing in on the Taliban trench works or truck convoys in coordination with the Northern Alliance ground offensive, the balance changed against the defenders. A primary refocus of the U.S. air campaign centered on the dusty city of Mazar-i-Sharif, set on a plain in the north some 40 miles from the Amu River separating Afghanistan from Uzbekistan. Capturing the city of 200,000 residents would establish a beachhead for a land-based resupply pipeline from the U.S. base in Uzbekistan. Mazar-i-Sharif's liberation would also shake the Taliban's rule and open the road to Kabul. The lethality and intensity of the U.S. bombardment did break the Taliban resistance, exposing the city to Afghan-American forces. Next Taloqan, Kabul and finally Kunduz fell in rapid succession to the Northern Alliance, which locked up the country's northern tier by late November. The sudden collapse of the Taliban stunned Washington, which had planned for a winter campaign and beyond. It also accelerated defections from Mullah Omar's regime.

Dissident Pashtun tribes, long estranged from ultrafundamentalist regime, now joined with U.S.-led coalition troops to lay siege to the Taliban's spiritual home, Kandahar, from which the former rulers took flight in early December rather than defend it. The ready CIA cash transfers and the inducement of sharing in power in a post-Taliban government accelerated the switching of sides in some cases. In other instances, moderate Pashtun had chafed under the theocratic regime's puritanical absolutism and now jumped ship.

After the fall of Kandahar, the locus of the fighting shifted to the mountainous Tora Bora region east of the city of Jalalabad. Retreating Al Qaeda forces of over 1,000 men, including presumably Osama bin Laden, holed up in the caves and then slipped southward into Pakistan. U.S. Special Forces and anti-Taliban Afghans chased the beleaguered elements and dynamited the caves. Bin Laden lived to fight on but one of his top deputies, Muhammad Atef, died in an air attack.

In early December 2001, the Taliban's ramshackle militia lay in disarray. It had been routed from all the major urban centers. It sustained around 10,000 battlefield deaths, about 20 percent of its former army. A further 7,000 had been captured. Many of Mullah Omar's tribal chieftains deserted his cause like Macbeth's thanes. Large cross-sections of the Afghan population said good riddance to the unpopular theocratic rule. They welcomed their liberation with clipped beards, unveiled faces, and loud music. U.S. military practices and precision-strike weapons kept civilian casualties unexpectedly low, with an estimated 1,000 deaths. As a consequence, the U.S.-led coalition started its occupation with a minimum of ill will among the civilian population.

The invasion phase lasted until late spring 2002 before the stabilizing operations began. U.S. forces inside Afghanistan—both CIA operatives and Special Forces personnel—at first numbered slightly over 400. As the Taliban disintegrated, the Pentagon deployed thousands of U.S. Army and Marine Corps troops. By then American combat casualties numbered less than a dozen, and financial expenditures reached merely $12 billion for fiscal year 2001. After the Operation Anaconda in the

Shah Kot Valley during March 2002, many of the Al Qaeda remnants melted quietly into Pakistan's semiautonomous tribal areas, where General Musharraf's government exercised limited authority. From these sanctuaries, they mounted cross-border forays into Afghanistan to inflict casualties on U.S. and NATO troops and their Afghan auxiliaries in the following years.

Overall, it is difficult to deny that Operation Enduring Freedom represented a lopsided military victory for the United States and its allies. Some analysts decided the integration of airpower and specialized ground troops constituted an "Afghan model" for future conflicts. Others refuted its uniqueness or replication.[21] The curious hybrid formed from marrying "Star Wars" weaponry with Civil War horse-mounted charges intrigued professional war planners and armchair strategists with the prospect of new models employing the extremes in what was thought to be postmodern war.

Osama bin Laden's escape was considered the only fly in the ointment. It was argued that the United States miscalculated by relying on Pakistani allies and Afghan irregulars to intercept the fleeing Al Qaeda head and his associates. If more U.S. troops had been deployed, so the argument went, they might have nabbed the terrorist chief as he stole across the Pakistan border.[22] More ground forces may or may not have captured or killed the elusive Saudi terrorist and his intimates, if they were, in fact, still in Afghanistan as the U.S.-led coalition swept over the country. Big fish often avoid the net, as did Ernesto "Che" Guevara and Carlos the Jackal (Ilich Ramírez Sánchez) who remained on the lam for years. Large bodies of friendly troops are no guarantee for the capture of suspects to wit: NATO troops crawled all over Bosnia for years without arresting Radovan Karadžić or Ratko Mladić, both indicted by the Hague for war crimes. In Iraq, tens of thousands of the troops missed capturing top Baathist generals or killing the elusive terror-mastermind Abu Musab Zarqawi for three years until tipped off by Jordanian intelligence.

A more relevant error stemmed from the Afghan campaign than bin Laden's escape. It influenced a similar low-troop density in the Iraq War, where it jeopardized the pacification effort. Minimal troop levels became the new gospel in the Pentagon's bible of war fighting. For the civilian leadership in the Defense Department, the new Rumsfeld doctrine supplanted the previous Powell strategy, which called for overwhelming force. Now, it was posited that the United States could rely on speed, mobility, and firepower to overcome land forces. Postinvasion Iraq sorely challenged that notion, as we shall see.

TO NATION BUILD OR NOT

The unexpected swiftness of the Taliban's downfall caught the United States by surprise. Beforehand, the new chairman of the Joint Chiefs of Staff, the Air Force General Richard B. Myers, mused about a conflict lasting a year or two. Now, Washington had to think quickly about a post-Taliban government, stabilization operations, and a host of civil-administrative issues. But the U.S. administration carried rhetorical baggage against nation building from its presidential campaign. A week into the fighting, President Bush announced, "I don't want to nation-build with troops" in one of strategy sessions with his advisers.[23] No concrete plans existed at the start of the conflict on what to do with the country once American power ousted the Taliban. In discussing impending fall of Kabul, Colin Powell declared, "We will turn it [Afghanistan] over to Brahimi and the U.N."[24] The Algerian diplomat, Lakhdar Brahimi, had been appointed by Kofi Annan to be the UN's special representative to Afghanistan. Pentagon officials spoke of a "division of labor" with coalition states assuming the burden of policing the country without much U.S. participation. As late as the end of November, Donald Rumsfeld thought it "highly unlikely" that U.S. forces would become "a part of a semipermanent peacekeeping activity in the country."[25] The United States was eager to palm off the job of nation building to others, preserving combat missions for U.S. forces rather than taking up the softer side of military operations in civic affairs ventures.

Two weeks after the seizure of Kabul but while fighting still raged in southern parts of the country, the key members of the Afghan opposition gathered at a UN-sponsored conference in Bonn to form a government. After several days of haggling, the attendees signed the Bonn Agreement on December 5, 2001, which mapped out a route for democracy and timetable for the interim government while setting up basic administrative functions. The participants also chose Hamid Karzai, an anti-Taliban Pashtun and former deputy foreign minister, who was acceptable to the Northern Alliance. Karzai also enjoyed the approval of Iran and Russia as well as the United States. The conferees doled out ministerial seats across ethnic groups, but the Northern Alliance Tajiks retained three of the most important portfolios—foreign affairs, defense, and interior. Karzai brought one of the most ruthless and powerful warlords into the fledging government, the Uzbek commander Abdurrashid Dostrum, in hopes of preventing his subversion. Although the conference process was not strictly democratic, it was inclusive of ethnic groups while recognizing local political realities.

The UN Security Council passed Resolution 1386 on December 20 that defined a framework for international assistance. It set up the International Security Assistance Force (ISAF) for security and peacekeeping missions with a rotating command. The ISAF enabled some 5,000 international troops to take up peacekeeping duties in Kabul, while the United States steadily increased its troop levels to nearly 20,000, most of whom were deployed along the Pakistani border to hunt for Taliban and Al Qaeda remnants. The Security Council passed Resolution 1401 on March 28, 2002 that established the UN Assistance Mission in Afghanistan (UNAMA), which integrated the UN activities in the country, including humanitarian and reconstruction efforts. To restore civic functions, several countries undertook the training of the police and judicial officials. Washington stepped up to the task of reconstituting a national army, known as the Afghan National Army.[26]

On December 22, 2001 in Kabul, Karzai took the oath of office as head of an interim government that presided over little else than the capital and its environs. Held in a cavernous Interior Ministry hall that was evocative of the ponderous Soviet architecture, the swearing in ceremony barely obscured the lurking threats not far beyond the walls. Outside the capital, the defeated Taliban, regional warlords, and bandits marauded through the countryside. Inside the assembly hall, Burhanuddin Rabbani, the internationally recognized president from the mid-1990s, transferred authority to the Karzai government, as orderly as any in the Western world. The

Bonn Agreement gave authority to the interim government for six months, when a *loya jirga*, or traditional council, was to be convened to establish a transitional government. It also imposed the drafting of a constitution and national elections within two years on the heirs of a new dispensation. A little more than three months after the 9/11 attacks, the United States clinched its regime-change goal in Afghanistan and moved to stabilize a truculent land.

The Bush government's diplomatic overtures brought together the neighboring protagonists to either cooperate or acquiesce in the subjugation of the South Asian nation. The prewar allies of the Northern Alliance—India, Iran, and Russia—joined the United States to install the alternative government. Their national interests coincided with Washington, which leveraged them into fashioning a postconflict arrangement in Afghanistan. Russia acquiesced in the American intrusion into its backyard. Iran, long an adversary, pledged $500 million for reconstruction and prevailed on its client, Ismail Khan (the key warlord in the west), to attend the Bonn conclave. India overcame its revulsion to Pakistan, which now stood in America's good graces for abandoning its former protégé in Kabul.

American allies partially filled the political vacuum, relieving the United States of the sole custodianship. It still did the lion's share of the fighting and nation building in rural areas. Because its partners at first shied away from expanding the ISAF countrywide, America introduced the Provincial Reconstruction Teams to implement its stability operations. Composed of 60 to 80 civilian experts and military personnel, the PRTs insinuated themselves in the fabric of village life. Officials from U.S. Agency for International Development and the Department of State worked at the grassroots level to fashion a benign civic institutions, promote cooperation with the Karzai government, and construct schools or wells, while U.S. and allied troops provided protection. Nation building and security had become one mission. In a sense the PRTs were the U.S. global policy writ on a micro-level: the need to install islands of stability in a violent countryside.

Recognizing the need for political order, the Bush government broke with its earlier disinclination to undertake nation-building enterprises by a presidential speech, although the turnaround on the ground came without adequate funds or enthusiasm in Afghanistan. In mid-April 2002, President Bush flew to the Virginia Military Institute to deliver a speech invoking the legacy of the military school's most renowned alumnus, George C. Marshall, "best remembered for the peace he secured" after World War II. Bush unequivocally attributed a restored Western Europe to Marshall's vision that raised "a beacon to light the path that we, too, must follow." The president added that the Marshall Plan known for "rebuilding Europe and lifting up former enemies showed that America is not content with military victory alone."[27] Neither the Marshall Plan analogy nor the aid matched the rhetoric, as Afghanistan remained starved for adequate assistance for years.[28]

Tactical shortcomings aside, the United States Afghan invasion phase succeeded beyond expectations. For relatively modest cost in money and lives, the United States ejected a brutal regime and denied the use of Afghanistan as a launching pad for anti-American terrorism—all within a 100 days-campaign. The U.S. intervention stunningly reordered the geopolitical landscape and entrenched America in middle Asia. Three months before, Afghanistan was tabula rasa on defense planners' maps. Now,

Washington stationed a sizable outpost along a new turbulent frontier. For its part, Afghanistan embarked on a shaky democratic path. Hamid Karzai won election as president against 17 other candidates in October 2004 as Afghanistan's first democratically elected leader with 55 percent of the vote. A year later in December 2005, the country's first democratically elected parliament in 30 years convened, completing the last milestone of the UN-sponsored Bonn accords 4 years earlier. American power came and quickly conquered but merely initiated political changes that sparked a fierce resistance. A resurgent Taliban struck back against a Western-imposed democratic order in the mountainous country at the very time the United States faced a far greater insurgency in Iraq.

CHAPTER 9

IRAQ: INVADED AND OCCUPIED

Carthago delenda est.

Ancient Rome's Senator Cato

American frontiers are on the Rhine and the Mekong and the Tigris and Euphrates and the Amazon. There is no place in the world that is not of concern to all of us. . . . [W]e are responsible for the maintenance of freedom all around the globe.

John F. Kennedy

You are flying in the face of four millenniums of history if you try to draw a line around Iraq and call it a political entity.

A missionary cautioned Gertrude Bell

THE UNITED STATES SETTLED ON THREE MAIN JUSTIFICATIONS to invade a reckless Iraq: first, the probable connection of Saddam Hussein to Al Qaeda's terrorism; second, the humanitarian impulse to liberate the Iraqi people from the grip of a tyrant; and third and mainly, the certainty that Baghdad possessed weapons of mass destruction (WMD). U.S. intelligence agencies unearthed contacts between Hussein and Osama bin Laden, but they have tried in vain to establish airtight complicity between the two figures in the September 11 terrorist strike. Thus, the Bush administration initially placed the bulk of its war logic on the third proposition that Saddam Hussein had developed—and was continuing to perfect—biological, chemical, and nuclear weapons, which he could either deliver on missiles hundreds of miles from their launching batteries or hand over to terrorist networks for their deadly use.

When the United States discovered no WMD stocks after invading Iraq, its main ex post facto rationale shifted from simple regime change to a mission of democratizing a rogue state to prevent it from becoming a terrorists' haven. In an astounding turnaround for American policy, the United States next decided on placing the advancement of democracy at the center of its international agenda for the Middle East, Central Asia, and elsewhere, in addition to Iraq. During the Cold War, it frequently backed autocracies as a bulwark against communist expansion or against instability that jeopardized regional peace. After the 9/11 attack, it pronounced democracy as the only means to ensure stability and its own security. The Iraq War provided the backdrop to the unfurling of America's "transformational diplomacy" for a global democratic conversion. But the democracy enthusiasts and the Iraq War brain trust never took into account the Middle East's historical resistance to non-Muslim interference and the warring sects' hostility to national cooperation.

AMERICA MARCHES TO ANOTHER WAR

Even as the Afghan invasion raged, Washington began planning to topple Saddam Hussein. Around the Thanksgiving holiday 2001, George Bush asked Donald Rumsfeld for an estimate on a war plan at about the same time as he called for a resumption of UN arms inspectors back into Iraq. Then the defense chief commanded the CENTCOM head General Tommy Franks to update and streamline the off-the-shelf Op Plan 1003, a Top Secret document that resembled the 1991 Gulf War script by calling for another 500,000 troops and a six-month logistical buildup within neighboring territories. Rumsfeld insisted on a revised scheme with substantially fewer troops.[1] Early in 2002, Rumsfeld voiced the concept of "shock and awe," for an overwhelming blitz of bombs and missiles to smash and stun the Iraqi defenders, that promised to reduce still further the need for a large invasion army.

In his State of the Union address on January 29, 2002, President Bush expressed his memorable phrase lumping together "rogue states" Iraq, Iran, and North Korea as constituting "an axis of evil, arming to threaten the peace of the world," which in retrospect was a call to arms against Iraq. Stating that "time is not on our side," Bush declared, "I will not wait on events, while dangers gather."[2] The White House's intention to regime change from early 2002 until the invasion itself was no secret. Its foreign policy bureaucracy spoke about Iraq in the manner of the ancient Roman Senator Marcus Porcius Cato who ended his speeches with the phrase "Carthage must be destroyed." After the Third Punic War, Rome indeed leveled Carthage and salted its ruins. Stories of war plans and military preparations were splashed across the front pages of American newspapers by spring 2002.[3] Not to be outdone by the Pentagon, the State Department held working sessions with experts and exiles on its "Future of Iraq Project" in July and August of 2002, which looked at post-Hussein government institutions and made recommendations for restoring civil society, eliminating corruption, and curtailing police abuse.[4] Its 13 volumes of reports identified many postinvasion problems but it was not a formal blueprint for rehabilitation.[5]

CENTCOM went about making preparations for a land and air assault on Iraq. It poured concrete, extended runways, constructed storage facilities, prepositioned supplies, and expanded bases in Kuwait, Oman, and the United Arab Emirates to extend the reach of American military power. It upgraded the landing strips and munitions depots at the Kuwaiti airbases in Al Jaber and Ali Salem. The Fifth Fleet, headquartered in Manama, Bahrain, geared itself for the coming engagement. But not every Near Eastern state welcomed U.S. plans.

Washington approached Qatar, when Saudi Arabia refused to allow its territory to be used as a springboard for another U.S. ground operation against Iraq. The friendly government in Doha spent millions of dollars to upgrade Al Udeid, a remote base on the shore of the Gulf. Then, the Pentagon transferred communications equipment, arms, and other military gear from its former command center at Prince Sultan Air Base. Aside from the tiny Persian Gulf sheikdoms, there was little, if any, public Middle East support for America's aggressive actions against Iraq. Unlike the first Gulf war, when Hussein's army invaded Kuwait, the regional players, such as Saudi Arabia, Egypt, and Syria, outwardly opposed an American-led intervention this time. They feared a long-term American presence in the region and the instability it would entail. Iran also dissented from Washington's war policy, although it stood to gain by the removal of Hussein. The United States additionally looked for allies beyond Middle East.

AMERICA'S TWIN-TRACK FORMULA

Washington pursued a dual-track approach toward its Iraq agenda, one military and the other diplomatic. The martial path included war planning, marshaling forces to the Gulf, and seeking partners for an invasion. The diplomatic posture embraced a no-plans-to-attack-at-this-time line. On his way to signing a treaty in Moscow with Vladimir Putin on May 24, 2002 that limited the numbers of deployable long-range nuclear warheads (between 1,700 and 2,200—a two-thirds reduction) by 2012, Bush stopped in Berlin. In the freshly reconstructed Reichstag, he replied to a question about regime change in Baghdad by repeating what he told the German Chancellor Gerhard Schroeder in private: "I have no war plans on my desk, which is the truth."[6] Because of rising antiwar protests and official European skepticism, Bush repeated his no-war-plans-on-the-desk formula in Paris when meeting with President Jacques Chirac a day later. The Bush statements hardly allayed German and French opposition, since American media buzzed with military scenarios to oust Saddam Hussein. So pervasive was the coverage of war preparations that a *Financial Times* editorial quipped in a Churchillian paraphrase: "Never in the field of human conflict has so much war planning been revealed to so many by so few."[7]

As diplomatic and military activities went ahead in 2002, the political ground was further cultivated for preventive war. In his West Point commencement address on June 1, George Bush lifted the curtain on his doctrine of preemption. Much more significant than the catchy phrased State of the Union message, his remarks high above the banks of the Hudson River unveiled a revolutionary departure from previous era's containment and deterrence formulas. Bush had Iraq in mind, if not in word, when he explained, "If we wait for threats to fully materialize, we will have waited too long." Instead, he announced that America would take "preemptive action when necessary." Bush first used the word *preemption* to the cadets on that sunny spring morning as he articulated a "strike first" strategy.[8] The speech's significance was overshadowed by Bush's announcement of the massive Department of Homeland Security, the first addition to the Cabinet departments in the security field since Harry Truman's proposal for the Defense Department in 1945, which combined the War and Navy departments.[9]

After Labor Day, the political pace quickened as the White House tightly trained its sights on Baghdad. Its West Wing rolled out a public relations offensive to convince Americans that Hussein must go so as to return geopolitical steadiness to the

Persian Gulf. Administration officials made repeated pitches about the WMD threat Iraq posed. Condoleezza Rice took to the airwaves, where the national security adviser uttered a memorable sound bite during a CNN interview: "We don't want the smoking gun to be a mushroom cloud."[10] On September 12, 2002, President Bush spoke in the soaring General Assembly hall, beseeching the United Nations to enforce its numerous resolutions against Iraq and hinting at U.S. military action if Baghdad did not tow the line. Speaking forcefully from the podium to the hushed diplomats gathered in the vast auditorium, the president said that UN resolutions ordering Iraqi disarmament "will be enforced—or action will be unavoidable." Bush retraced President Clinton's dark warning to Hussein four years before quoting his predecessor's 1998 State of the Union address: "You have used weapons of mass destruction before: we are determined to deny you the capacity to use them again."[11] Bush went further than Clinton and laid down a pointed threat: "If the Iraqi regime wishes peace, it will immediately and unconditionally forswear, disclose, and remove weapons of mass destruction, long-range missiles, and all related materials."[12]

Iraq was not an idle player. Saddam Hussein adapted to new realities after Bush's UN appearance. He announced Iraq's willingness to readmit the international weapons hunters. While Hussein's offer was seen as a cynical ploy, it afforded France, Russia, and China an opportunity to slow the American bid for a fresh, tightly drawn, Security Council resolution against Iraq. These countries stood to benefit economically from a peaceful resolution, since Hussein rewarded their citizens with business contracts. Moreover, they feared turmoil in the Gulf from a U.S. attack.

Before September ended, Washington's political offensive got a boost from the British government, which released a sensational intelligence assessment, "Iraq's Weapons of Mass Destruction," that maintained that Baghdad was working to break through international barriers to obtain WMD weaponry. The white paper, replete with photos and diagrams, concluded with the words of Prime Minister Blair that "the policy of containment is not working" against Iraq.[13] The dossier, in reality, reeked of half-truths and outright fallacies. Beset by media and political pressure in 2003, the Blair government divulged that its dossier amounted to a slapped-together case from secondary sources, including a paper by a graduate student living in California. But in fall 2002, the dossier buttressed findings in America's National Intelligence Estimate (NIE). The NIE, a summation of the U.S. intelligence community, assessed that Iraq had biological weapons and renewed production of chemical weapons with stockpiles up to 500 metric tons. Two and half years later, the presidential Commission on the Intelligence Capabilities of the United States Regarding Weapons of Mass Destruction concluded, "These assessments were all wrong."[14] In fall 2002, however, the two highly inaccurate intelligence estimates framed the debate toward a prowar outcome.

A DOCTRINE FOR STRIKING FIRST

Even though war rumors circulated for months, the White House's release of its National Security Strategy in September 2002 hit with a gale-force wind, for it put forward a doctrinal rationale for an Iraqi conflict. Contained within 31 pages, the landmark national security manifesto charted two broad muscular and momentous courses: one laid down the formula for preemptive attack, and the other established the benchmark for overwhelming U.S. military preeminence. Much of the document's language came from previous presidential speeches and owed its conceptual foreshadowing on preemption most directly to the president's West Point address. Against rogue states and terrorist actors, the document postulated the necessitating of a new offensive posture when containment and deterrence seemed to have failed:

> While the United States will constantly strive to enlist the support of the international community, we will not hesitate to act alone, if necessary, to exercise our right of self-defense by acting preemptively against such terrorists, to prevent them from doing harm against our people and our country. [We will deny] further sponsorship, support, and sanctuary to terrorists by convincing or compelling states to accept their sovereign responsibilities.[15]

The second major strategic prong (initially capturing less scrutiny) was no less high-voltage in its intent. Once more, it warrants a direct quote for the unchallengeable military ascendancy that it prescribes:

> The United States must and will maintain the capability to defeat any attempt by an enemy—whether a state or nonstate actor—to impose its will on the United States, our allies or our friends. . . . Our forces will be strong enough to dissuade potential adversaries from pursuing a military buildup in hopes of surpassing, or equaling, the power of the United States.[16]

The cultivation of preeminent American military power in the 2002 security strategy document had been foreshadowed by the 1992 draft of the Defense Policy Guidance (noted in chapter 1). Both statements marked the transformation from the former bipolar standoff with the Soviet Union to a world where America rose to ascendancy with enough power to reach for the stability that locked in a world favorable to itself.

Although the national strategy statement also listed traditional objectives—strengthening alliances, igniting a new era of global economic growth with free markets and trade, building the infrastructure of democracy, and even waging a war of ideas—its provisions for "acting alone and using preemptive force" coupled with its call for unrivaled military superiority riveted intense attention from pundits and academicians. Skeptics labeled the doctrine as dangerously provocative, unnecessarily hegemonic, needlessly boastful, strategically unwise, openly precedent-setting for rivals to follow, and utterly departing from traditional American diplomacy.[17]

Sailing against the storm of public outcry was Yale historian John Lewis Gaddis's influential book *Surprise, Security and the American Experience*. Professor Gaddis examined America's past, dispelling the commonplace accusations that the Bush doctrine, with its concepts of preemption, hegemony, and unilateralism, lacked historical precedent. Citing Britain's 1814 burning of the White House and Capitol, he plumbs President John Quincy Adams' articulation of a strategy to secure hegemony in North America through unilateralism and preemption.

Praising Adams as "the most influential American grand strategist of the nineteenth century," Gaddis identified America's sixth president as setting the strategic compass by which his successors steered. The United States' Continental expansion found inspiration from Adams' guidance in such episodes as Andrew Jackson's 1818 invasion of Spanish Florida, James K. Polk's annexation of Texas, and Theodore Roosevelt's preemptive strike against the Spanish fleet in Manila Bay. America's gunboat diplomacy in the Caribbean and its "preemptive interventions in Venezuela, the Dominican Republic, Haiti, Nicaragua, and ultimately Mexico derived justification on the grounds that instability" gave European powers a pretext for meddling.[18] In short, America sought stability first on its Western frontier and then on its boarders. Now as the planet's sole superpower, it looked uneasily at instability hither and yon for repercussions it might hold for its core interests.

The strategic tide flowed in another direction when Franklin D. Roosevelt devised a cooperative multilateral framework that played down more than a century of U.S. unilateralism and preemption in the pursuit of stability. At the end of World War II, Washington submerged its unilateral impulses within the profusion of international arrangements and institutions that came into being to contain and deter the Soviet Union. The Marshall Plan, World Bank, International Monetary Fund, and NATO were cooperative mechanisms designed to secure American hegemony. The United States locked out the Soviet Union from the world of commerce and finance and locked in the American preponderance of power. In that era, America adopted non-power devices, such as the rule of international law and international organizations, to ensure a world favorable to its interests.[19]

Therefore, President George Bush resurrected an earlier American approach rather than broke the mold of traditional policy. In fact, Cold War presidents also preemptively struck out for U.S. ends. Ronald Reagan intervened in Grenada to oust a fledgling communist government, and George H. W. Bush invaded and changed the regime in Panama. Later, Bill Clinton rolled U.S. forces into Haiti to restore order on the Caribbean Island. He also preemptively bombed the al-Shifa chemical plant in Sudan, a nation officially at peace with the United States. But America's forty-third commander-in-chief took the policy to extremes by forcing Americanized democracy on Iraq and even the greater Near East's inhospitable soil.

NAILING DOWN THE VOTES AT HOME AND ABROAD

September's rapid pace of events accelerated in the balance of 2002 as the United States moved toward a second Iraq conflict. The president picked up backing from self-selected coterie known as the "neocons," an abbreviation for neoconservatives. After September 11, the neocons came into their own, with an unabashed message of a *pax Americana*. Their calls for removing Saddam Hussein and other Mideast dictators through force of arms and implanting democracy to "drain the swamp" of terrorist-breeding conditions converged with new realities of stabilizing the region, as seen in George Bush's speech a month before the Iraq invasion. Speaking at the American Enterprise Institute, a major Washington "think tank" and home of many neocons, the president outlined an agenda for regime change in Iraq and democratization of the Middle East—recurrent neocon themes.[20]

The Bush administration surmounted two hurdles along its march to the Iraq War: one domestic and the other international. Domestically, the White House first went after congressional approval. It stepped up briefings to House and Senate members, and the president made the case in speeches to raise the poll numbers approving of a firm policy toward Iraq. Its campaign culminated with a presidential speech in Cincinnati that assured the public that "we will act with allies at our side" against an Iraq that "could have a nuclear weapon in less than a year."[21] At the start of Iraq War, one poll showed that 71 percent of respondents backed Bush's forceful disarmament policy.[22]

The U.S. House and Senate voted overwhelmingly to authorize George Bush the use of military force "as he determines to be necessary and appropriate" against Iraq.[23] The House voted 296 to 133 (six Republicans joined 126 Democrats and one independent to vote against Bush) and the Senate followed suit the next day with a 77 to 23 margin (29 Democrats joined 48 Republicans to back Bush) for the measure on October 11, 2002. Congress thus approved of the post-9/11 doctrine of preemptive war against Iraq, although later it contended that the president lied about the Baath regime's WMD stockpiles.

Next, the White House turned with renewed vigor to the second, far more difficult, obstacle, of lining up Security Council votes for its hawkish approach to the Iraqi regime. It proved to be devilishly hard, taking over seven frustrating weeks of tedious and bruising negotiations to overcome resistance from France, Russia, and China. Since it was almost an article of faith in allied capitals that Hussein's Iraq was progressing toward deployable biological, chemical, and, possibly, nuclear weapons, the debate concentrated on a course of action to take. Washington wanted one resolution that upon declaration of Iraq's "material breach" of the arms control provisions would trigger automatic authority for the United States and other powers to resort to "all necessary means" (meaning war) to enforce compliance. French Foreign Minister Dominique de Villepin, who spearheaded the Security Council opposition, rejected the "automaticity" of a single resolution; he demanded a second resolution to authorize military force.

Reluctantly, the Bush administration went along with the two-step approach after internal haggling. Vice President Dick Cheney and Rumsfeld argued that by opting for two resolutions, the United States was walking into a trap, in which one of the veto-wielding members on the Security Council could check American power. Colin Powell argued that the United States needed the Security Council's legal underpinning to escape diplomatic isolation and to secure international legitimacy in case of war. Powell convinced President Bush to go along with the compromise to get the French and others on board for a tough-sounding resolution, calling for "serious consequences" of Iraq's breaches. Secretary Powell's diplomacy succeeded beyond expectations. Not only the French accepted the American concession but also on November 18 the entire Security Council unanimously approved it. Thus, the final resolution passed unanimously with a 15 to 0 vote on November 8. Resolution 1441 entered the UN rulebook and the pages of history, for it was the last such convention against Hussein's Iraq.

A week after the advance party from the UN Monitoring, Verification and Inspection Commission entered Iraq on November 18, as part of the Security Council's disarmament resolution, the American president declared, "We're not interested in hide and seek in Iraq."[24] In his New York City headquarters, Kofi Annan countered Washington's skepticism saying, "[C]ooperation seems to be good."[25] Driven by the calendar, Washington gunned hard for an early negative finding from the arms inspectors so as to launch an invasion during December through March to avoid Iraq's torrid summer heat.

President Bush warned that "time is running out on Saddam Hussein," and fumed, "I am sick and tired of games and deception" early in 2003.[26] The White House interpreted Baghdad's actions as procrastination, an effort to run out the clock to the hot summer months or to avoid a U.S. attack entirely. Meanwhile, the military pipeline to the Persian Gulf delivered mountains of arms, munitions, fuel, and other war materiel. The first major troop deployment took place in early December 2002; at the same time, General Franks opened the doors of CENTCOM's new headquarters in Qatar, transferring his command of an Iraq conflict from Tampa, Florida, to nearer the frontlines.

International diplomacy recaptured center stage even before the January deadline for UNMOVIC's report on its search for prohibited weapons. At a Security Council meeting in Manhattan on global terrorism, France's de Villepin diplomatically ambushed Powell and the American understanding arising from Resolution 1441. The United States anticipated that debate about further action on Iraq would take place with the UNMOVIC findings. Instead, the French diplomat jumped the deadline and asserted, "We see no justification today for an intervention, since the inspectors are able to do their work."[27] Nothing justified war in French eyes, according to de Villepin.

Two days later, Donald Rumsfeld barked out a quotable sound bite that raised diplomatic temperatures on both sides of the Atlantic. He correctly attributed the dissent to France and Germany alone, not the entire Continent. But then before foreign journalists in Washington, the hard-hitting Pentagon chief let fly with his characterization about the two European states: "I think that's old Europe."[28] The "new" Europe was represented by the recently de-Sovietized nations in Central Europe. In Paris and Berlin, ministerial officials and the proverbial man-in-the-street bristled at Rumsfeld's "cowboy style" diplomacy. The new-versus-old-Europe comment sharpened rather than ignited the evolving split between the United States and Europe that dated from the fall of the Berlin Wall.

On January 27, 2003 Hans Blix delivered his first findings to the United Nations. The UNMOVIC chairman painted a broadly negative picture of Iraq's cooperation after two months of inspections.[29] The 15-page catalog presented the failings of the Iraqi regime to prove it had eliminated its chemical and biological weapons programs. Blix stated, "Iraq appears not to have come to genuine acceptance—not even today—of the disarmament which was demanded of it and which it needs to carry out to win the confidence of the world."[30] But UNMOVIC found no WMD. Next, Mohamed ElBaradei, the chief of the International Atomic Energy Agency, reported that his team uncovered no evidence that Baghdad attempted to restart its nuclear weapons program. Both chief inspectors requested more time to carry on additional inspections.

Another stride in the march toward invading Iraq came with President Bush's second State of the Union address the day after the Security Council received the weapons reports. He charged that U.S. intelligence estimated Iraq failed to account for nearly "30,000 munitions capable of delivering chemical agents" as well as large quantities of botulinum toxin and anthrax. Then, in a sentence that came back to haunt him, the president expounded, "The British government has learned that Saddam Hussein recently sought significant quantities of uranium from Africa."[31] For several months following the actual Iraq invasion, the Bush statement stood uncontested.

After the invasion, two factors clouded Washington's justifications for war. First, and most importantly, no nuclear or other banned weapons were uncovered following the U.S.-led invasion, except for some chemical shells dating from the 1980s. Second, revelations came to light from Joseph C. Wilson, the CIA investigator sent to the African nation of Niger, which undercut the president's assertion about Iraq's quest for yellowcake, a nuclear ingredient.[32] The former ambassador charged that no evidence could be found to substantiate the allegations that Hussein's agents tried to buy uranium in the landlocked Saharan country. His account cast grave doubt on Bush's State of the Union assertions, and no subsequent credible information arose to substantiate the president's claims.

THE TRANSATLANTIC DIVIDE AND QUEST
FOR A SECOND RESOLUTION

The divide that Resolution 1441 had papered over two months earlier reopened, complicated American diplomacy, and turned into one of the bitterest disputes in decades between Washington and a handful of other major players. Bush officials knew they faced an uphill struggle to convince the Security Council to take action. The White House deployed its most credible spokesman, Colin Powell, to make the case for action against Iraq. The secretary of state went to New York on February 5, 2003 to present the administration's brief at a specially convened meeting of the Security Council.

Secretary Powell's appearance commanded a worldwide television audience and rekindled recollections of a similar episode 41 years before when the United States and the Soviet Union lunged toward a nuclear apocalypse during the Cuban missile crisis. In 1962, Adlai Stevenson made a dramatic presentation at the United Nations. As the Kennedy administration's ambassador to the world body, Stevenson displayed U-2 reconnaissance photos of Moscow's secret installation of nuclear-tipped missiles on the Caribbean island. His performance and its impact were riveting, one of those high-powered moments, which are still enshrined in the nation's collective memory.

Colin Powell did not disappoint. The former soldier made a sober, straightforward, rapid-fire delivery of more than an hour long. He introduced radio intercepts, showed declassified satellite photos, played an audiotape, and offered corroboration by human sources to build a persuasive case that Iraq was hiding illicit weapons. Powell prodded council members by asking "how much longer are we willing to put up with Iraq's noncompliance before we . . . as the United Nations say: 'Enough. Enough.'"[33] A subtext of the speech also advanced a carefully drawn connection between Iraq and the infamous Al Qaeda terrorist network. Using circumspect language, Powell gave the impression that Abu Musab al-Zarqawi, a Jordanian-born terrorist and Osama bin Laden lieutenant, provided a link between Iraq and Al

Qaeda. He postulated, "[A]mbition and hatred are enough to bring Iraq and al Qaeda together."[34] This contention also fell to refutation and doubt from the 9/11 Commission. But more recent disclosures lend weight to Hussein's cooperation with Al Qaeda affiliates as well as his training some 7,000 recruits in terrorist camps for a wave of "martyrdom" operations against Western targets.[35]

France, as skeptic-in-chief, dug in its heels and demanded more time for the inspections before embarking on military ventures, after UNMOVIC made its second report that no WMD had been uncovered. Germany was decidedly against going to war. Moscow closed ranks with Paris and Berlin in a joint statement calling for "a substantial strengthening" of the "human and technical capabilities" of the weapons inspectors inside Iraq.[36] The transatlantic dispute sparked a war of words. Robert Kagan, a Washington-based writer, characterized the post-Wall relationship between the Americans and Europeans as increasingly occupying two different political universes that reflected their disparities in military power, historical outlooks, and global strategies. His much-quoted line "Americans are from Mars and Europeans are from Venus" found its way into the international debate.[37] The Euro-American disputes aside, the Bush administration won a crucial victory within NATO in mid-February 2003. The Atlantic alliance authorized the fielding of missile defense batteries and toxic-protection units to fellow NATO member Turkey to protect it in the event of a war with Iraq.

Turkey assumed a pivotal role in American military plans for regime change in Iraq. To compensate for lighter forces engaging the Iraqi army in the southern theater just north of Kuwait's border, the U.S. military wanted an attack from Turkey to confront Iraqi forces with a two-front war. The Bush administration ardently courted Turkey in late 2002 for passage of a U.S. Army division across its territory. The timing was inopportune for Washington, for in November 2002 the Justice and Development Party—an Islamic movement—had come to power in parliamentary elections. Only parliament possessed the legal authority to concede transit rights. The new religious government presented an obstacle for the United States unlike Turkey's secular rulers in the first Gulf War, which had granted air bases. On March 1, 2003, the Turkish parliament spurned a $26 billion aid package that America had offered for permission to pass through the countryside.

Back in New York, President Bush's adjutants futilely canvassed for Security Council votes among the members. Sensing defeat, the United States decided against pressing for a war authorization and held that Resolution 1441 alone justified the forceful disarmament of Iraq. The hardening opposition exposed George Bush to international criticism and led to Condoleezza Rice being quoted as telling associates in spring 2003 about her steely reaction: "Punish the French, ignore the Germans, and forgive the Russians."[38] U.S.-European relations hit another low.

On March 19, the president addressed the nation from the Oval Office. At 10:15 PM in Washington, the commander-in-chief announced the start of the Operation Iraqi Freedom about 45 minutes after the first strikes were reported against targets in and around Baghdad. After declaring the "opening stages of what will be a broad and concerted campaign," Bush was more prescient than he imagined when he predicted that combat in the days ahead "could be longer and more difficult than some predict."[39]

OPERATION IRAQI FREEDOM: THE CAKEWALK WAR

No battle plan ever survives the first contact with the enemy.

Carl von Clausewitz

War is the unfolding of miscalculations.

Barbara W. Tuchman

At just after 5:30 AM Baghdad time on March 19, 2003, the United States launched a surprise strike ahead of its long-anticipated second war against the Republic of Iraq. Two stealthy, radar-evading F-117A warplanes, flying from Qatar, released their satellite-guided bombs on the Dora Farms compound south of Baghdad, where informants pinpointed the Iraqi dictator's presence. The decapitation strikes missed their intended victim just as did subsequent bombings against other so-called high-value targets—army generals and prominent Baath Party officials. The thinness of U.S. intelligence on the location of Iraq's political and military elite portended a less than auspicious beginning to what became America's most contentious war since Vietnam.

The heavily armed columns of Operation Iraqi Freedom roused themselves into action on March 20 like some prehistoric herd of beasts. The Abrams battle tanks and Bradley Fighting Vehicles lumbered northward from the giant Kuwaiti staging areas. Accompanied by the "shock and awe" air campaign, the invasion resembled a Jurassic-era scene with hulking creatures roaring into action. Clouds of dust enveloped the steel-skinned mammoths as they rolled into Iraq from the temporary Camp Pennsylvania. Once up and moving, the U.S.-led computer-based offensive was anything but dinosaurian. Buttressed by state-of-the-art airpower, America's modern army proved mobile and lethal as it closed on Iraq's Republican Guard divisions.

In the tangled dramaturgy of warfare, it is easy to slight the basic plan of attack for the heroics, follies, and postmortem analyses as well as fascination with the latest instruments of battlefield death. One geographic fact must be recalled: Mesopotamia is Greek for "the land between the rivers," which is crucial to know for waging a war within Iraq. Hydrographic features mattered. Iraq's two main rivers and their offshoots had to be figured into the calculations on how to subjugate the country. River crossings by bridges, whether Iraqi-built concrete roadways or American-engineered metal spans, assumed critical dimensions for troops sweeping across the dun-colored landscape to Baghdad.

The American strategy was as simple to describe, as it was effective. The United States launched two pincer columns toward Baghdad, the nation's heart and nerve center. One thrust, led by 50,000 U.S. Marines, pushed up the plain between the Tigris and Euphrates rivers. The Army's Third Infantry Division made its famed "thunder run" into the capital to the west of the meandering jade-green Euphrates River. Its advance paralleled the U.S. Marine's route toward Baghdad. Before the United States stormed the capital, the 25,000-strong British force laid siege to the southern city of Basra, protecting the Marines' right flank. Their assault on Iraq's second largest city was coordinated with the Americans entry into Baghdad to further discombobulate the Iraqi defenders with simultaneous sieges.

Had Turkey opened its territory, U.S. forces would have pressed southward on Baghdad from a third front, splitting and dividing their adversary's defenses. The absence of the northern front meant, first and foremost, that fewer U.S. troops were on hand in the Sunni heartland to kill and capture the shell-shocked Iraqi units in the first days of the invasion. If the Rumsfeld Pentagon had anticipated a popular resistance in the Sunni region, the U.S. military might have strained to find a means to visit more death and destruction on it. Even before Baghdad fell, Saddam's Fedayeen initiated irregular warfare, signaling an incipient insurgency. This short fall in applied military might have furnished another example where America's formidability was not brought to bear in an active combat phase. In this case, it endangered its stabilizing operations soon after the invasion phase.

The air war started many months before the ground war. This explains why it was possible to commence the land phase without a monthlong prewar air blitz as in the first Gulf War. From June 2002 to March 20, 2003, Anglo-American pilots flew 21,736 sorties over southern Iraq and struck 349 targets, including air defense sites, command-and-control centers, and the networks of fiber-optic cables that transmitted military communications. During the war itself, some 1,800 allied aircraft carried out some 20,000 sorties, of which about 15,800 struck Iraqi ground units, smashing to bits Soviet-made T-72 tanks, armored personnel carriers, and artillery pieces. For the first three weeks of the war, coalition aircraft numbered as many as 1,000 a day over Iraq.

What went underappreciated at the time was the telltale fact that Iraqi officers and foot soldiers stripped off their uniforms and mingled among civilians. Following the ancient Greek statesman Demosthenes' advice about soldiers running away to fight another day, they fled the technological battlefield to fight asymmetrically months later as insurgents who hit, ran, and hid from their superiorly armed and trained enemies. Their hasting retreats, in the meantime, opened the gateway to Baghdad for American forces. The towns of Diwaniyah, Musayyib, Numaniyah, Kut, and Karbala fell by wayside in dust and debris as U.S. forces lunged toward Baghdad.

The opening days of the invasion phase went astoundingly well. Coalition troops easily seized Umm Qasr, the country's only deepwater port, turning it into a center for humanitarian relief supplies. The fear of burning Rumalia oilfields did not materialize, as saboteurs torched only six of about 1,000 oil wells due to coalition defenses. U.S. Navy SEALS and Polish GROM (Thunder) commandos secured the offshore oil platforms. Transport planes landed in Kurdish-controlled territory and unloaded U.S. troops to open a quasi-front in the north against Baghdad and Ansar al-Islam, a militant Islamic group with links to Al Qaeda. Special Operation Forces operating in the west took control of the H-2 and H-3 airfields and Scud missile sites preventing any launches against Israel that might have triggered Tel Aviv's involvement in the war, something that Washington wanted to curtail so as not to further agitate the Middle East.[40] The war in the West never completely wound down as jihadis, bent on establishing an Islamic theocracy, streamed in from Syria to feed the postinvasion insurgency to undermine U.S. stabilization efforts.

On April 7, the Third Infantry Division's heavy-duty Abrams main battle tanks and Bradley Fighting Vehicles brushed aside fierce Iraqi resistance, knifed into the heart of Baghdad, and occupied the Republican Palace, the seat of Iraq's government, and the smaller Sijood Palace, a gleaming residence in the spacious presidential compound on the Euphrates. From the east, the Marines blazed into the city, overrunning sandbagged positions, and knocking off pockets of outmatched bands of irregulars. Hastily dug trenches and dirt barricades hardly slowed the Leathernecks' drive into the city. Thus, the dreaded, climatic "Battle of Baghdad" never really materialized.

A scintilla of comic relief peaked through the plumes of dust kicked up from bursting tank shells. Mohammed Saeed Sahhaf, Iraq's minister of information, incredulously denied the U.S. Army and Marine offensive into Baghdad. At a news conference on the roof of the Palestine Meridien Hotel, he intoned, "[T]here is not any American presence or troops in the heart of the capital." Almost beyond belief to reporters present, he continued, "Let me reassure you that Baghdad is very secure, safe, and in control," as U.S. troops below moved into the main arteries and squares, smashing a 40-foot statue of Hussein on horseback.[41] Sharraf's Pollyanish predictions of Hussein's impending triumph earned him the nickname of "Baghdad Bob" among American GIs.

The sudden implosion of resistance inside Baghdad upended many military and civilian forecasts of an American Stalingrad. CENTCOM's Tommy Franks wrote in his account of the invasion that the only commentators surprised by the suddenness were "cable news folks, like al-Jazeera and CNN."[42] The surprising speed and awesome firepower, indeed, crushed Iraqi defense, saved the country's oil wells from sabotage, spared allied and Iraqi civilian lives, and thwarted deadly missile counterassaults on Anglo-American troops. The U.S. forces delivered an Armageddon to Hussein's conventional army in a high-tech, high-speed, and high-impact war.

America's "overmatching power" achieved unprecedented results in the major combat phase of the war. It seemingly confirmed the boasting of a "cakewalk war."[43] Not all had gone perfectly on the ground, with stressed supply lines, sandstorms, and sometimes-limited military intelligence; however, far more went right than wrong in the attack phase, which skirted urban areas as it fire-balled toward Baghdad. The rapid victory seemed to confirm the Rumsfeld's "shock and awe" strategy in subduing a California-sized nation. A relatively small land force of 137,000 U.S. soldiers and Marines scattered a 400,000-strong army fighting on its own soil in less than three weeks. The March–April campaign set a standard for the farthest advance at speed over distance ever recorded. The World War II Allied race from Normandy to the Rhine River took eight months, whereas the U.S.-headed coalition covered roughly the same distance in Iraq in half a month.

With invasion victories in Afghanistan and Iraq under his belt, Tommy Franks, the CENTCOM chief, retired from active service. John Abizaid, his deputy, assumed his new duties on July 7, 2003. An Arabic speaker, West Point graduate near the top of his class, holder of a masters degree from Harvard, and combat veteran, Abizaid came well prepared for what turned out to be the most difficult type of warfare for any army to wage, counterinsurgency operations against a determined foe willing, even eager, to die for his cause. The infantry general proved himself an able commander under arduous circumstances and an adroit diplomat amid the shoals of Mideast politics.

Major allied military operations virtually ceased on April 14. In Washington, Victoria Clarke, the Pentagon's spokeswoman, announced, "The regime is at its end and its leaders are either dead, surrendered, or on the run."[44] But the declaration of the end of major combat operations waited until the commander-in-chief made it. Six weeks after the start of the war, George W. Bush's photo op landing on the flight deck of the aircraft carrier *USS Abraham Lincoln* returning from the Persian Gulf was a made-for-television event. Behind the president fluttered a huge banner that read "Mission Accomplished." The Texan stood at the zenith of his presidency on the runway of one of the most powerful symbols of America's global reach. Off the coast of San Diego, California, on May 1, 2003, the triumphant chief lauded his troops about a victory that soon looked questionable. His detractors derided and mocked him for political grandstanding. Few still recall his words, but Bush spoke the plain truth when he uttered that "the war on terror is not over," accentuating the protracted nature of the conflict with militant Islam.[45]

All wars produce surprises, and the Iraq War had its share of unexpected events. For the troops, not getting attacked by deadly nerve and mustard gases or microbes was an unanticipated but welcome development. In the opening stages of the conflict, the young men and women on the front donned their hot, protective suits. The preparations proved unnecessary, even though the warnings had been ominous. In late January 2003, Egypt's President Hosni Mubarak and Jordan's King Abdullah II separately alerted General Franks that Hussein possessed WMD. Mubarak told him point-blank, "He has WMD—biologicals, actually—and he will use them on your troops."[46] Not finding WMD stocks, therefore, turned out to be the biggest surprise for the CENTCOM commander and his civilian bosses, who justified the invasion on intelligence about an alarming threat.

American casualties also defied expectations despite dire warnings of thousands dead and wounded by Washington-based experts.[47] They numbered 89 killed in action and 49 more deaths from accidents and other causes (including three from known cases of friendly fire) in the course of the war from March 19 to April 30. State-of-the-art medical care, with such innovations as blood-clotting bandages, one-hand tourniquets, and rapid evacuation of wounded to well-staffed field hospitals also explains the high survival rates.

Other casualties also stood at historic lows for large-scale military operations. British casualties numbered 42 dead, of which 19 resulted from accidents, by May 1. The exact numbers of Iraqi civilian and military deaths are unknowable. An Associated Press estimate placed the tally at 3,240 civilian deaths across Iraq during a month of war, including 1,896 deaths in Baghdad.[48] Other sources put the death toll higher, with estimates from 4,000 to 5,000 dead. Iraqi military casualties are also a matter of guesswork. One newspaper reported 2,320 military dead and 7,000 prisoners of war. It is more plausible to assume a much higher range from 5,000 to 20,000 dead.[49] As horrific as these figures are, they pale in comparison to modern warfare benchmarks.

For the coalition personnel, the grimmest shock arose from the postinvasion insurgency against them. Americans—troops as well as civilians at home—had been led to expect a grateful Iraqi people welcoming U.S. troops in a shower-of-flowers parade reminiscent of the Allied march down the Champs-Élysées in 1944 after the liberation of Paris. Unlike the formal German and Japanese surrenders, no Republican Guard generals or regime strongmen sat down with the victors to sign capitulation documents. Instead, Iraqi higher-ups went into hiding to oversee and finance a hit-and-run insurgency. When questioned about the adequacy of U.S. forces, Paul Wolfowitz told a congressional committee, "I am reasonably certain that they [Iraqis] will greet us as liberators and that will help keep requirements down."[50]

Initially, Iraqis did thank their liberators for ousting Hussein. But gratitude—the shortest-lived emotion—evaporated in the summer sun. Iraq degenerated into a hellhole for coalition troops who found themselves in a 360-degree battlefield in what was to have been a grateful country; instead, it turned fiercely to fighting its "infidel" occupiers, who seemingly carried in their knapsacks a democratic rule that enabled their sectarian rivals to gain the upper hand. Iraq's brief encounters with monarchy and dictatorship barely scratched its millennium and a half history of Islamic rule that governed all life, government and politics as well as religion. It was arid ground for transporting a Euro-American secular democracy into a country without hundreds of years of trial-and-error evolution of civil society, freedom of expression, and religious tolerance as in the Western tradition.

OCCUPATION, RESISTANCE, AND SOVEREIGNTY

I would like to thank the coalition, led by the United States, for the sacrifices that they have provided in the process of the liberation of Iraq.

Iyad Allawi, prime minister of Iraq

We should have had sovereignty from the day after liberation. But better late than never.

Barham Salih, deputy prime minister of Iraq

The toppling of Saddam Hussein's towering statue in Firdos Square in central Baghdad to cheering crowds on April 9, 2003 ended the autocrat's 24 years of ruthless, capricious, and venal rule. The fleeting images of the rope-pulled metal figure evoked memories of the Berlin Wall's collapse 14 years earlier. The two events markedly differed, however. While the destruction of the Wall brought freedom from fear, peace, and unification to Germany, the fall of Hussein's bronze-cast likeness cracked open a Pandora's box setting loose a phantasmagoria of violence, Islamic radicalism, and sectarian bloodshed amid Herculean exertions to stabilize and democratize a deeply traumatized society, after the spontaneous outpouring of relief in downtown Baghdad on that sun-splashed afternoon.

Deposing Saddam Hussein in the cause of democracy represented the revolutionary side of American power. No similar manifestation occurred during the 1991 Persian Gulf War, which, in fact, saw U.S. military force projected only to preserve the stabilizing status quo by expelling the Iraqi army from Kuwait and safeguarding the monarchies on the Arabian Peninsula. By comparison, the second intervention unraveled the status quo and introduced political revolution and democracy into an autocratic region.

Yet, Washington's yearlong direct governorship of Iraq was the most mismanaged postwar occupation in U.S. history since Reconstruction in the American South after the Civil War. Nobility of purpose and strategic necessity infused both wars, even if each of the postbellum landscapes brimmed with mistakes, corruption, and missed opportunities. As in the occupation of the Confederacy, a Republican administration in Washington went to the defense of a despised and powerless people, whose deliverance was also defied by a defeated elite, as it fought to reintroduce antebellum conditions through subversion, violence, and disenfranchisement. Like the twenty-first-century neocons, the Radical Republicans wanted to spread democracy in Dixie. The reactionary force in the nineteenth-century struggle was racism, whereas in twenty-first-century Iraq the resistance at first tapped into the Sunni minority's fierce resistance to the loss of its power and privilege and then the Shiite majority's sense of revival and revenge.

Despite a handful of similarities, modern-day Iraq is not an analogue to the nineteenth-century American South. Its history is the product of the Middle East's civilization, Ottoman and British rule, and a brutal dictatorship of a psychopath. Just as it is so different from the American experience, so also is it vastly divergent from the analogies that Washington officials looked upon for model and direction. The conditions in post–World War II Germany and Japan diverged greatly from Iraq after a 20-day war. Both prewar Germany and Japan enjoyed blushes with democracy and free markets. Whereas the war-weary Germans and Japanese welcomed their occupiers as a means of rebuilding and for protection against Soviet expansion, the Sunni Arabs shared no such predisposition.

Unlike the Germans and Japanese of the 1940s, the Iraqis escaped catastrophic defeat and the agony of a prolonged war. Their forces shamefully fled the battlefield before they were broken psychologically by U.S. power. America's precision weapons, network-centric warfare, city-skipping strategy, and effects-based bombing spared Iraqi lives as opposed to the blunt power used to crush Germany and Japan. And so, the Sunnis never tasted genuine defeated. They ran from the battlefronts. They raised their hands in surrender, but they never conceded defeat in their hearts. As General Eric Shinseki stated at his retirement, "We never broke the will of the enemy to resist."[51]

To expect Iraqis to be Germans or Japanese in reacting to foreign rule flies in the face of any reasoned analogy. Such thinking was worse than a mistake: it was hubris. Germany was broken and demoralized by the war, which claimed 4 million German lives and razed its cities. As the Führer shot himself to death, some 8 million American, Russian, British, French, and other troops marched on a vanquished German population of 60 million. Some 700,000 Allied troops took up a long-term militarized occupation, and these forces could draw on millions more nearby. Japan also felt the massive weight of American power. Two atomic bombs pulverized Nagasaki and Hiroshima, killing hundreds of thousands with blast or radioactivity. Other Japanese cities lay half-charred; Japan's war dead reached over 3 million; and its armies were thrown back on every front. Sealed off by the U.S. Navy, the island state boasted no sympathetic neighbors. Japan's revered emperor capitulated and indeed compelled his military to surrender, thereby ensuring a passive population to bow to America's half-a-million strong occupation.

The American-organized occupation of Iraq began auspiciously, with waving and happy crowds. Baghdadis poured into the streets to thank American troops. This euphoria gave way almost overnight to a spree of violence and looting in the capital's streets. The dispossessed, many of them Shias, turned on their former rulers with a vengeance. They ransacked the National Museum of Antiquities and broke into the luxurious mansions of Hussein's sons and their minions, lugging off paintings, furniture, refrigerators, almost anything movable. Marauding bands vandalized the unguarded German Embassy and French cultural center, because their governments led the international bid to derail the U.S. military operations against the Hussein regime. Iraqis also directed their ire at the UNICEF office, because they held the UN-administered oil-for-food program responsible for their hunger and malnutrition during the 1990s. Hardcore criminals joined the unruly crowds, thanks to Saddam Hussein's release of some 100,000 prison inmates the previous fall. Street crime, kidnappings for ransom, and homicide soared, adding to the unstable political dynamics.

Americans saw scenes of jubilation, but they should have seen scenes of Shiite revival after years of Sunni repression. They should also have noticed the fear and antipathy that the Shia's newfound freedom catalyzed among the Sunni, who had suppressed the Shiite for centuries in Iraq and across the Middle East outside of Iran. Both the revivalism and the foreboding were ominous signs missed by U.S.-led liberators of an impending clash between the two communities that would threaten the entire region.

As chaotic scenes swirled around them, U.S. servicemen stood on the sidelines, observing the looters and vandals. Asked by Iraqis why he did not intervene to halt the chaotic scene, a Marine officer atop a tank explained to a reporter, "I tell them the truth that we just don't have enough troops."[52] A sparse number of American troops had blasted through the Baghdadi defenders, but their lean numbers limited effective crowd control in Phase IV operations, the occupation stage after the major combat actions of the Cobra II plan—the official designation of the attack blueprint.

Larger forces present early on in the occupation phase might well have nipped in the bud the burgeoning instability before it blossomed into a rebellion, stanched the flood of arms pouring from unguarded armories, and reined in unruly crowds. A manpower-intensive occupation stood a good chance of suppressing early urges to rebel against the new authorities. It certainly could have immediately imposed a tight martial law. The Pentagon civilian brass was caught flat-footed in failing to plan for stability operations with adequate troops. In fact, Donald Rumsfeld "off-ramped" or canceled the deployment of the 16,000-strong First Cavalry Division as U.S. forces took Baghdad.[53]

Questions about troop strength, in fact, surfaced dramatically before the intervention phase. In a Senate Armed Services Committee hearing in February 2003, Eric Shinseki, Army chief of staff, responded to a question, "something on the order of several hundred thousand soldiers" would be needed for "posthostilities control" because of "ethnic tensions."[54] Despite 38 years of military service and a year of commanding peacekeeping forces in Bosnia, Shinseki found himself chastised by Pentagon political appointees. Paul Wolfowitz testifying before a House Budget Committee disparaged Shinseki's assessment as "quite outlandish" and "wildly off the mark." Defense's deputy secretary asserted, "It's hard to conceive it would take more forces to provide stability in post-Saddam Iraq than it would to conduct the war itself."[55] Soon afterward, Donald Rumsfeld fired back at a reporter's question in a Pentagon news conference about the postinvasion forces: "The idea that it would take several thousand U.S. forces I think is far off the mark."[56]

186 AMERICAN POWER AFTER THE BERLIN WALL

Compared to peacekeeping operations or insurgencies, U.S. forces were on the light side. With approximately 150,000 coalition troops in Iraq's population of 25 million, the ratio of security forces per inhabitants stood at about 6/1,000. For comparison, there were between 18–20/1000 in Bosnia and 16/1000 in Kosovo. In immediate post–World War II Germany, the ratio hit a high of 100/1000. The British counterinsurgent campaigns saw a 20/1,000 ratio, on average, in Malaya and in Northern Ireland. Two years later as American-trained Iraqi units came on line, the troop-population ratios improved approaching 12/1,000, although most indigenous soldiers fought well below the competency of U.S. platoons and companies.

The scarcity of soldiers on the ground permitted intransigent elements to stake out strongholds in the Sunni Triangle, a roughly triangular zone that stretched from Baghdad to the west of Ramadi then north to Mosul and southward to the capital. Most deadly attacks on U.S. troops took place within this geographical zone during the occupation phase until fighting picked up in Anbar province along the Syrian border as jihadis crossed into Iraq.

FROM CAKEWALK TO THE CPA AND COUNTERINSURGENCY

Suddenly, an aggressive, action-oriented military machine was turned on a dime from smashing through enemy fortifications to a civil constabulary. It now patrolled streets, secured arms depots, protected banks, and even stood guard at gas stations. Offensive forces underwent an immense transition with postconflict missions to ensure the delivery of drinking water, mend electric generators, pick up garbage, and reopen schools. In short, the small combat force by default assumed the functions of a civilian government.

At first, all went well. The uncovering of Hussein's mass grave sites, thought to hold some 300,000 victims, bolstered Washington's humanitarian justification for its invasion. The northern Kurdish provinces of Iraq remained calm and friendly to American forces, while demonstrators in the central and southern sections peacefully protested the coalition's presence. Local tribal leaders and aspiring politicians met under air-conditioned U.S. tents in Nassiriya to discuss the country's future political configuration. The early occupation stood in the eye of the hurricane, however.

Yet, the anticipated parlous conditions failed to materialize. The Pentagon's Office of Reconstruction and Humanitarian Affairs ([ORHA], only established two months prior to the invasion) to administer a liberated Iraq had planned on an outpouring of apocalyptic calamities akin to the Book of Revelations. ORHA expected the discharging of chemical, biological, and even nuclear weapons on troops and hapless civilians, resulting in massive deaths and gruesomely wounded in the thousands. As a consequence, it also envisioned WMD contaminated soil and pestilent no-go zones. An inferno of burning oil wells, plagues of typhoid and cholera, starvation among 2 million internal refugees—all loomed plausibly in the mind of ORHA's chief, former general Jay Garner. None of these horrific scenarios fortunately became reality. But other problems soon cropped up.

Shortly into ORHA's rocky tenure, Washington switched horses. In the first week of May 2003, the White House named L. Paul Bremer III as its presidential envoy and administrator of the Coalition Provisional Authority (CPA), granting him "full authority" over the occupation at his insistence.[57] He was an odd choice for the job. A 23-year foreign service officer in the Department of State and then chairman of a crisis-consulting business, Bremer possessed wide experience in advising, not in governing and management—a telltale lacuna. Nor did he have experience with large-scale construction projects. He was a Middle East neophyte to boot. The Bush government, in fact, miscast Paul Bremer for the pivotal role. Handsome, hardworking, and earnest, Bremer paled in comparison to the performance of General Douglas MacArthur, America's proconsul in post–World War Japan, who meshed with Japanese culture. Perhaps, a former state governor, like California's highly respected Pete Wilson, would have had the political experience for the job. Governors, after all, are used to working with obstreperous legislatures, balancing constituencies, managing budgets, overseeing infrastructure construction, and delegating authority to accomplish larger ends. Nonetheless, Bremer ensconced himself in the Green Zone, the 6-square-mile fortress-like compound in Baghdad where some 14,000 Iraqis lived encircled by 14-foot concrete blast barriers, coiled razor wire, and guarded by machine-gun-toting soldiers.

The decisions that Paul Bremer executed became a lightening rod for much of what went wrong during the Anglo-American occupation. Key among the early missteps was disbanding of the defeated Iraqi army. Rather than remobilizing the army into a sort of civilian corps to clear rubble, remove garbage, and restore civic services in return for wages, the CPA catastrophically misjudged the local conditions. The Bosnia intervention during the Clinton administration offered a lesson. There, the Stabilization Forces calmed the flames of ethnic hatred among the warring factions and their militaries. SFOR required all soldiers from the ethnic armies to report for duty each day and paid them for their service. As a result, most of the former combatants wiled away their hours playing cards and drinking the local slivovitz in their barracks. Unburdened by history and approved by the Pentagon chief, CPA Chief Bremer dissolved the Iraqi army on May 23. Suddenly, thousands of aggrieved men roamed the streets without jobs, pride, or money. Over time, this pool of militarily trained castoffs flocked to the insurgent ranks, pitching the country into strife, and ultimately calling into question America's global stability mission.

CPA Chief Bremer enjoyed much latitude according to Pentagon officials. Undersecretary for Defense Policy Douglas J. Feith contended that Rumsfeld "didn't want to use the five-thousand mile screwdriver" to micromanage Bremer.[58] But U.S. military officers in Iraq complained that the decision endangered coalition troops. It, moreover, markedly contrasted with actions in Afghanistan, where the U.S.-instituted Afghan Ministry of Defense put some 100,000 militia members on the payroll for over two years, even if the warlords' private armies numbered only about 60,000. While these chieftains pocketed the extra funds from the padded rosters, they kept the peace during the postinvasion period.

A second, no-less momentous decision occurred when CPA also ordered a de-Baathification policy. Likened to the de-Nazification measures adopted in postwar Germany, the decree was meant to purge upper-echelon Baath Party officials from holding office in the new Iraq. Bremer put in place the Iraqi De-Baathification Council of mostly Shiite and Kurdish advisers to identify party members. In principal, excluding senior Baath officials was necessary to reassure the Kurds and Shia that their Sunni tormentors were banished. The purging process, however, failed to distinguish properly the committed party members from the careerist and cowardly among the cardholders. It was also applied unevenly across different ministries, shedding thousands of employees in some and far fewer in others. Not until next January did the CPA overhaul its sweeping policy by instituting a new policy vainly designed to rationalize the tangled system.

Both CPA rulings politically emasculated the fiercely chauvinistic Sunnis. Although Sunni Arabs make up only about a fifth of Iraq's population, they traditionally dominated the officer corps and Baghdad bureaucracy—the backbone of the modern Iraqi state since independence in 1932. Sunni dominance, in fact, stretched back at least to 1638, when the Sunni Ottoman Turks consolidated their power over Mesopotamia and installed the Iraqi Sunni as a ruling minority. After World War I, the British rulers retained the Sunni as London's proxies to help govern their Mesopotamian acquisition. Iraq's royal family and military rulers who succeeded it, including Saddam Hussein, also came from the Sunni community.

Thus, the U.S.-led coalition ousted not only Saddam Hussein but also the Sunnis' centuries-long dominance of the Shia and Kurds, provoking a bitter backlash. Their anti-American fight attracted additional Islamic jihadis from other Sunni Muslim countries. The new arrivals crossed the Syrian border to engage American soldiers and Marines in a holy war. Many militants joined the Jordanian master terrorist Abu Musab al-Zarqawi (or AMZ to U.S. troops), who operated independently before swearing allegiance to Osama bin Laden in October 2004 and renaming his terrorist network Al Qaeda in Iraq. Both terrorists shared the teachings of the Salafi branch of Sunni Islam with its extreme hostility to the Western "crusaders," Zionists, and Shia, plus the goal of establishing a caliphate from Iberia to India under Shari'a law.

THE CPA ENTRENCHES ITSELF

Instead of putting an Iraqi face on the U.S. occupation, Paul Bremer held the governing reins himself. In mid-May, the CPA chief informed a group of Iraqi political figures that the coalition intended to remain in charge of Iraq for an indefinite period rather than forming a provisional government leading to rapid self-rule, as originally planned by civilian Pentagon officials. The White House sided with Bremer; it reasoned that a factious provisional government would heighten instability, and it threw doubt on its victory and policies. Thus, it immersed the United States in the nuts, bolts, and screws of Iraqi political life. Having passed up the opportunity to install an exile government at the time of invasion, this juncture was the last chance for the United States to turn over power to local officials after intercessions as in Haiti, Panama, Kosovo, and Sierra Leone, depart from a military occupation, and avoid a ferocious insurgency against America's exported democracy.

Bremer's decision also tossed out Jay Garner's guarantees to Ahmed Chalabi of the Iraqi National Congress, Ayad Allawi of the Iraqi National Accord, the two main Kurdish parties, and Abdul Aziz Hakim of the Supreme Council for Islamic Revolution in Iraq. Bremer decided on forming the Iraqi Governing Council composed of the leaders of the five movements and 20 others to advise him, not run the country. A forthright devolution of responsibility and power to Iraqi hands early on might have precluded much of the spreading rebellion. One on-the-spot observer concluded that the CPA's "obsession with control was an overarching flaw in the U.S. occupation from its start to finish."⁵⁹ It was the wrong prescription for building a stable polity in a volatile land.

For his part, Bremer was dismissive of the Iraqi political figures. Later in his book *My Year in Iraq*, the CPA chief wrote that the Governing Council members "couldn't organize a parade, let alone run a country."⁶⁰ Yet, many did end up running the country after being elected by their countrymen to the constitutional drafting assembly and then the parliament. By entrenching the United States in the protracted formation of an Iraqi government with an American face, Washington jumped from the frying pan into the fire.

Along with policy missteps, the American-engineered reconstruction also got off to a slow start with no realistic plan. Electrical power sputtered; gasoline supplies receded; drinking water dwindled; and the overall economy limped. Only frustrations grew. Iraq suffered from over a decade of UN-imposed sanctions, together with Saddam Hussein's misrule and underinvestment in infrastructure. Ordinary Iraqis, moreover, held unrealistic expectations that American power, so matchless on the battlefield, could attain miracles overnight in a long-neglected land. Restoring electricity, clean water, sanitation, and other essential services lagged terribly in the minds of a people who easily pegged every grievance to a single identifiable culprit, no matter how unreasonable it was to expect electricity-generating facilities or water treatment plants to be built in a flash. The same construction in the United States took years.

When things went right for Iraq's new caretakers, they often resulted from coalition troops rather than from the CPA. American soldiers and Marines served selflessly, endured hardships, and suffered wounds or death to lift a population out of neglect and privation. They performed far better than their small numbers and military training prepared them for nation building. In Karbala, a sacred city for Shiites, U.S. Marines stopped looting, restored electrical power beyond prewar levels, reopened an amusement park with free rides, and consciously respected religious sensitivities. In the northern areas around the city of Mosul, the U.S. Army's 101st Airborne Division quickly established rudimentary civil institutions while the U.S. civilian authority in Baghdad was still getting organized. Under Major General David H. Petraeus, who warmed to nation-building tasks, the paratroopers ran local elections, set up an Iraqi council for Mosul and the larger Nineveh province, established an employment office for former military officers, trained the local police, and temporarily reinstated professors at the university in Mosul.

The Commander's Emergency Response Program (CERP) vested a novel political instrument in the hands of U.S. military officers. CERP amounted to a decentralized aid program that started up shortly after the occupation began. Grants ranged from $1,000 to $30,000 for refurbishing schools or clearing irrigation canals of accumulated weeds. Funds initially came from dollars secreted in Hussein's palaces. Some 12,000 projects had been undertaken with about $80 million before funds ran out in October 2003. When the insurgency intensified in November and U.S. casualties spiked, Congress allocated $180 million in a supplemental spending bill, but it took until June 2004 for these funds to reach frontline units thereby suspending the program during a crucial period. Keeping Iraqis gainfully employed and out of the guerrilla ranks was critical to the counterinsurgency campaign.

With little or no CPA presence in the hinterlands, U.S. commanders engaged local authorities in a manner becoming the politically savvy Major Victor Joppolo, the fictional hero in John Hersey's novel *A Bell for Adano*, set in Sicily at the close of World War II. Their ingenuity and political skills built trust and restored a rough normalcy to vast stretches of territory beyond the reach of the civilian administration. The Coalition Provisional Authority, in fact, drew criticism in military ranks for its inefficiencies and delays, leading some GIs to quip that its acronym CPA stood for "Can't Produce Anything." Whereas the military culture placed a premium on quick action to repair hospitals, put locals to work, and improve infrastructure, the CPA fell far short of the same disciplined efficiency. American military prestige was so high by the end of 2003 that *Time* magazine picked the American soldier as its Person of the Year, putting a picture of three service personnel on its cover, an accolade not undertaken since 1950.

By late summer 2003, however, coalition troops ran up against an insurgency that showed no signs of abating. Deadly firefights exacted their toll, but roadside bombs, known as IEDs or improvised explosive devices (strapped-together landmines or artillery shells detonated by cell phones or garage openers) became the weapon of choice, killing or maiming over half of all U.S. combat casualties. Traveling in Humvees, the "thin-skinned" jeep-like vehicle afforded the soldiers and Marines no protection. The military "up-armored" these and other transports. But the adding of steel plates proceeded at a snail's pace and became an embarrassment for the Pentagon's Donald Rumsfeld in 2004.

The deaths of Saddam Hussein's two sons—Qusay and Uday—in an intense gun battle within an opulent stone mansion in Mosul in late July were heralded prematurely as a turning point. The elimination of the two sinister figures, likened to Caligulas to their father Nero, came about from an informant's tip in response to a $15 million reward for information. The insurgency barely hiccuped at their deaths. By the end of August, more U.S. soldiers had died since the end of major combat on May 1 than during the invasion.

Insurgents also struck at "soft" targets, such as undefended structure, oil pipelines, and ordinary citizens lining up for work. Worse, much worse, was to come. Iraqi insurgents dealt a severe blow to Washington and its bid to engage the United Nations in reconstructing the battered country. A suicide bomber exploded a munitions-packed cement mixer alongside the world agency's headquarters housed in a three-story hotel in downtown Baghdad on August 19, 2003, after the United Nations refused coalition protection. The blast killed 22 UN officials, together with the mission chief, the former UN High Commissioner for Human Rights Sergio Vieira de Mello. The bombing marked the deadliest assault in the organization's history. Fearful of another attack, Kofi Annan removed the international staff from Iraq in October, running UN operations out of offices in Amman until it returned a year later with a skeleton crew.

Initially, the Bush administration reacted erratically to the surge in violence. National Security Adviser Rice looked back to postwar Germany and exaggerated the resistance to the Allied occupation. In a speech to the Veterans of Foreign Wars,

Rice called for patience in rebuilding Iraq and then reflected that the "SS officers, called Werewolves, engaged in sabotage and attacked both coalition forces and those locals cooperating with them, much like today's Baathist and Fedayeen remnants."[61] After the German surrender in May 1945, the resistance to the American, British, and Russian overwhelming military presence, in reality, paled into insignificance in comparison to the post–May 1 Iraq insurgency.

For some time, it was believed that Saddam Hussein, who eluded capture, inspired and perhaps directed the anti-American attacks. But his capture dispelled that illusion. The U.S. Army dragged a disheveled and disorientated tramp cowering in an 8-foot spider hole at an isolated farm near Tikrit on the evening of December 13, 2003. Tracked down by Army intelligence, Hussein's arrest, trial for human rights crimes, conviction, and eventual execution in late 2006 did nothing to dampen down the spreading conflagration. His Sunni kinsmen fought for their political supremacy, not solely for his restoration.

Judged from the vantage point of major combat operations, the hit-and-dash assaults on the U.S. forces were minimal. No army or Marine platoon (roughly 40 troops) had been lost to the insurgent side. But low-intensity conflicts are about politics and perception, not victory on the battlefield. General Abizaid, the CENT-COM chief, grasped the political dimension of the insurgency and referred to it repeatedly in his meetings with the battalion-level officers or the press. He noted that "this not a military battle per se. It is going to be won on the political, economic, and information playing field, because there is no military contest."[62]

THE MIDCOURSE CORRECTION

Back in Washington, the somber realties dawned on the U.S. government by mid-November 2003. CENTCOM found itself so short of troops that the Pentagon extended the mobilization of National Guard and Army Reserve forces and called to duty additional standby units. The Pentagon also speeded its timetable for standing up a new Iraqi army of 40,000 troops in the Iraqi Civil Defense Corps by the next year to relieve overburdened U.S. forces from routine guarding assignments. The ongoing fighting diminished Donald Rumsfeld's reputation that towered in the invasion's immediate aftermath. The once-lauded secretary of defense came in for criticism about the costs, casualties, and paucity of forces in violent Iraq for calming the convulsed land.

In an about-face, United States decided overambitiously to end its Coalition Provisional Authority, elicit the drafting of a temporary constitution, form a caucus-selected transitional parliament, and restore Iraq's sovereignty by late June the following year. In addition, the CPA scrapped its ambitious plans to privatize the corrupted, state-socialized Iraqi economy. Paul Bremer and his aides wanted to dissolve the 48 companies owned by the Ministry of Industry. These government-run enterprises received state subsides to produce consumer goods; their inefficiencies made them noncompetitive in the world market. Now Bremer asserted it is an "issue for a sovereign Iraqi government to address."[63]

Putting the best face on the abrupt policy redirection, Washington stated that America was fulfilling its mission to extend democracy in the Middle East. President

Bush delivered a major speech on the twentieth anniversary of the National Endowment for Democracy. He stated his goal of spreading democracy to Iraq to facilitate a democratic transformation of the entire region: "Therefore, the United States has adopted a new policy: a forward strategy of freedom in the Middle East." The president concluded with the stability rationale for spreading consensual government: "As in Europe, as in Asia, in every region of the world, the advance of freedom leads to peace."[64]

Once again, the grim insecurity climate dashed the best-laid plans for the administration's overly ambitious plans for a new Iraq. Even before the surge of violence in April, internal wrangling among Iraqi politicians over the implementation of Washington's November plan rendered it a virtual dead letter. A blow-by-blow account takes us too far afield for this volume, however. Suffice it to note that the redoubtable Grand Ayatollah Ali al-Sistani, the Shiite Muslim communities most revered figure, denounced a caucus-selected transitional parliament for not being directly elected by the Iraqi population, which would ensure the Shiite majority a decisive governance role. But the CPA declared the impossibility of a popular election. Preparations for elections—the registration of voters, party formation, and open campaigning—appeared inconceivable to the CPA's Bremer given the rising level of insurgent attacks. Yet, to jump ahead, at the end of January 2005, the United Nations protected by coalition and Iraqi troops pulled off an overwhelmingly successful election.

By late 2003, the Bush government concluded that the road to Iraqi democracy passed through the United Nations. It asked for the secretary general's help in heading off Sistani's efforts to hold a popular election. In responding, Kofi Annan made an important concession to the American position by conceding that elections could not be organized in time for the creation of a provisional government. The U.S. initiative opened the door for the United Nations to help salvage the American-headed occupation of Iraq. This redirection was facilitated by the calming transatlantic discord, chiefly among Washington, Paris, and Berlin.

GOVERNANCE, CONFLICT, AND SCANDALS ON THE WAY TO IRAQ'S SOVEREIGNTY

The year 2004 ushered in a spate of problems that cascaded on the Bush presidency in an annus horribilis as it headed toward a November election. Its travails ran the gamut from reports on the government's ill preparedness for the September 11 terrorist attacks, to faulty WMD intelligence justifying the Iraq War, and finally to the ongoing challenges of Iraq's occupation in the face of scandals and declining international support for U.S. pacification of the Middle Eastern country.

A major scandal erupted in the treatment of Iraqi inmates in the Abu Ghraib prison facility outside Baghdad. Lurid photographs showing U.S. soldiers mistreating their charges ran on the front pages the world's newspapers in late April. Telecasted pictures and news accounts depicted Iraqi prisoners made to strip naked and pose in demeaning positions. Reports of physical coercion and abuse shocked and disturbed officials and average citizens. During the next several months, attention fell on seven reservists in the 372nd Military Police Company who behaved as a rogue element. It came to light that interrogating personnel at other detention facilities also used dogs and painful stress positions to elicit intelligence.

The hue and cry over the degrading treatment, but not torture, at Abu Ghraib compelled President Bush to apologize publicly for the misconduct by a band of renegade MPs and intelligence officers. Standing with King Abdullah II at his side in a Rose Garden appearance, George Bush revealed his private conversation with the Jordanian monarch earlier in the Oval Office: "I told him I was sorry for the humiliation suffered by the Iraqi prisoners, the humiliation suffered by their families."[65] The scandal briefly cast a dark shadow over the American effort in Iraq, sparking 10 major investigations and speeding the already planned reassignment of General Ricardo S. Sanchez, the highest officer, out of the command structure within Iraq. Army General George W. Casey Jr. took over in early July as the head of the 160,000 U.S. and allied troops.

A key investigative panel was chaired by James R. Schlesinger, former defense secretary under presidents Nixon and Ford. This four-person panel stated that there were about 300 reported incidents of mistreatment and 66 confirmed abuses as of its report (55 in Iraq, eight in Guantanamo, and three in Afghanistan). Unlike the military reviews held so far, the report assigned responsibility for the misconduct, at least indirectly, to the leadership high up the chain of command. The 93-page report of the Independent Panel to Review Department of Defense Detention Operations concluded, "The abuses were not just the failure of some individuals to follow known standards, and they are more than the failure of a few leaders to enforce proper discipline. There is both institutional and personal responsibility at higher levels."[66]

Even the United Nations did not escape being tarred by the scandal brush. During early 2004, the UN's oil-for-food program came in for public scrutiny. From 1996 to 2003, the world body's Office of the Iraq Program, headed by Benon V. Sevan, administered a relief effort that permitted Saddam Hussein to sell oil so as to purchase food and medical supplies for his desperate population. The $64 billion program was designed to prohibit Hussein from gaining conventional or unconventional arms, while alleviating the hardships of the ordinary Iraqi citizens that the 1990 sanctions imposed.

The United Nations collected and disbursed the oil revenues, and Iraq negotiated the contracts with foreign suppliers for approved goods. Saddam Hussein, however, engaged in nearly $11 billion in smuggling outside the UN-managed program. A yearlong independent UN investigation directed by Paul A. Volcker, former Federal Reserve chairman, was tasked with getting to the bottom of the charges of the program's mismanagement and corruption. The Volcker-led Independent Inquiry Committee on the Oil-For-Food Investigation issued its fifth and final report in late October 2005 that cited 2,400 companies and individuals from 66 countries for having paid bribes into Iraq's coffers to profit from the oil-for-food program. The wily tyrant received $1.8 billion in illicit funds from kickbacks and surcharges on the sales of oil and humanitarian goods.[67] The investigation accused the UN Secretariat of mismanagement but exonerated Kofi Annan from personal corruption charges.

The Iraq War also was accompanied by a domestic scandal with a Fortune-500 American corporation. Accusations swirled about no-bid contracts, overcharging for food and gasoline, and kickback schemes that favored Halliburton Company.

What gave saliency to the accusations against the giant Texas-based provider of oil industry products and services to the military was its connection to Vice President Cheney. After serving as secretary of defense in the first George Bush administration, Cheney took over the reins of Halliburton in 1995 as its chairman and CEO until returning to Washington as Bush junior's partner. Charges of abuse and corruption fed the perception that the Iraq occupation was spinning beyond U.S. control and that the costs exceeded the benefits for U.S. security.

The international scene also provided cold comfort to the U.S.-organized counterinsurgency. A massive terrorist attack in Madrid on rush hour commuter trains killed 197 people on March 11, 2004 just days before Spain went to the polls. The Moroccan terrorists accomplished their objective in swinging the Spanish election away from the conservative candidate to Jose Luis Rodriquez Zapatero's Socialist Party. Upon assuming office, Zapatero kept his preelection pledge to withdraw Spain's 1,300 troops from Iraq. Spain's troop extrication began an exodus from Iraq of tiny allied states, such as the Dominican Republic, Honduras, and the Philippines. Along with 10,000 British troops, the United States managed to hang on to small contingents from South Korea, Japan, Denmark, and Poland, whose forces were mostly in secure areas.

Coterminous with these scandals and thinning international support for the occupation was the U.S.-UN enterprise to fashion a return to Iraqi sovereignty. In mid-January Secretary General Annan dispatched Lakhdar Brahimi, the former Algerian foreign minister, to Iraq as his representative. Over the next months, Brahimi convinced Grand Ayatollah Sistani to drop his demands for an Iraqi-wide election. Without the elections or a caucus-picked assembly, the United States lacked a body to which it could return sovereignty. The divided Iraqi Governing Council did manage to draft an interim constitution, known as the Transitional Administrative Law (TAL). In addition to setting forth political rights for Iraqi citizens, the TAL called for elections not later than the end of January 2005 for a transitional assembly to draft a genuine constitution. Among other provisions, the formal constitution was to establish election procedures for an Iraqi parliament. But all that lay two years in the future. In the meantime, Iraq needed a caretaker government to accept back its independence from the country's occupiers.

HANDING OFF INDEPENDENCE BUT NOT THE WAR

With barely a month left before the transfer deadline, bruising negotiations took place for the composition of the caretaker government among Brahimi, Bremer, and members on the Iraqi Governing Council before they selected Ayad Allawi as Iraq's interim prime minister. An Iraqi neurologist and secular Shiite who enjoyed backing from Ayatollah Sistani, Allawi was well known to U.S. officials. As secretary general of the Iraqi National Accord, one of the exile opposition movements, Allawi had received CIA funding over the years.

Internationally, the United States made concessions in the United Nations to win unanimous backing for a resolution recognizing and endorsing transfer of authority to the interim Iraqi government, such as granting the new Baghdad government the right to order the exit of foreign troops, if it so decided. Sovereign Iraq also got authority to make political decisions, control its economy, and oversee the police forces. The United States preserved authority to wage offensive military operations as its commanders saw fit.[68]

Reaching for Security Council authority constituted a U-turn for the Bush administration in its dealing with the United Nations and represented a culmination of sorts in the narrowing of its differences with Paris and Berlin that had begun during the previous year. Washington's willingness to compromise demonstrated that the White House wanted to move beyond the bitter disputes over the U.S.-led invasion and regain European assistance to restabilize Iraq.

Back in Baghdad, matters moved swiftly toward the restoration of official self-rule. During the first days of June, the interim government assumed control of the ministries. Then the Coalition Provisional Authority transferred de jure sovereignty to the Iraqi interim government in a small ceremony in the heavily guarded Green Zone two days before the scheduled transition so as to elude terrorist attacks. Outgoing CPA Administrator Bremer and incoming Prime Minister Allawi signed the transfer documents around ten o'clock in the morning on June 28, 2004.

No marching bands, no flags lowered or hoisted, and no celebratory gunfire so characteristic of Iraq marked the improvised five-minute event held in a nondescript room with Louis XIV furniture that had served the Governing Council. Ambassador Bremer, who presided well-nigh dictatorially over Iraq for 14 months, left the same day with no broadcast farewell to his subjects. Later in the day, the Iraqi ministers were sworn into office, as Bremer boarded a plane to return to his Vermont home. All in all, it was an anticlimactic, even bland, event to relaunch a country's independence.

A new chapter opened in Iraq's history, but not a peaceful one. At its return of sovereignty, Iraq had become a radically destabilized society contrary to American plans. An election and transfer of power soon after the invasion might have spared the United States its greatest counterinsurgency imbroglio since the Vietnam War. But Washington's quest to democratize Iraq and to evangelize the larger Middle East with its brand of democratic values blinded it to America's best interests, Iraq's violent legacy, and the historical rebellion of the region against non-Muslim interference and Western occupations.

CHAPTER 10

STABILITY AND SECURITY THROUGH DEMOCRACY?

Make no small plans, for they have no power to stir the soul.
Niccolò Machiavelli

We are not to expect to be translated from despotism to liberty in a featherbed.
Thomas Jefferson

We must face the fact that the United States is neither omnipotent or omniscient—
that we are only 6 percent of the world's population; that we cannot impose our will
upon the other 94 percent of mankind; that we cannot right every wrong or reverse
each adversity; and that therefore there cannot be an American solution to every
world problem.
John F. Kennedy

TAKING THE OATH OF OFFICE FOR A SECOND TERM, George Walker Bush used the
inaugural podium to reinforce America's manifesto of global stability through
liberty. It was no longer messianic but necessary in his mind for the United States
"to seek and support the growth of democratic movements" because America's
security was linked with the stability that only democracy could ensure. Seeing "our
vulnerability" in "tyranny," Bush declared that now democracy around the world "is
the urgent requirement of our nation's security."[1] U.S. presidents have long championed freedom but America's forty-third chief executive went further than his predecessors. He dreamed of transplanting Americanized democracy first in Iraq and then
the greater Middle East, seemingly oblivious to the defiant rejection of the Arab-
Muslim host to this alien organ. In the White House's judgment, a U.S.-engineered
Westernized democratic stability replaced the earlier containment stance as
America's key doctrine for the post–Berlin Wall era. It was a shift that rankled the
Islamic world, major powers, such as China and Russia, and even most allied
nations. In the end, the policy brought neither self-sustaining democracy nor stabil-
ity to the invaded peoples. But this new manifesto first penetrated deep into the
U.S. military and civilian bureaucracies.

Implementing this stability-cum-democracy credo into military action was a little-noticed Pentagon directive. Announced in late 2005, the 11-page directive (Number 3000.05) placed stability operations on a par with combat missions: "They [stability operations] shall be given priority comparable to combat operations and be explicitly addressed and integrated across all DoD activities including doctrine, organizations, training, education, exercises, material, leadership, personnel, facilities, and planning." The Department of Defense's directive additionally asserted, "Stability operations are conducted to help establish order that advances U.S. interests and values." This blueprint, in one sense, was belated recognition of the necessity of postconflict stability enterprises in light of the bungled Iraqi occupation. But more significantly it signaled extensive preparations for future stabilizing ventures in forthcoming conflicts. Embracing stability operations signaled that the Bush Pentagon had made a 180-degree turn in its previous opposition to nation-building and democracy-constructing activities. The directive elaborated this new approach by listing the military's stabilizing tasks as developing "representative governmental institutions" and moving to "revive or build the private sector" as well as standing up homegrown security forces and judicial systems.[2]

In another shift toward a democracy-crusading agenda, the U.S. Department of State unveiled the Office of the Coordinator for Reconstruction and Stabilization. Dubbed with the acronym of S/CRS, the office became an active component of the U.S. "transformational diplomacy" initiative to promote stability through democracy as announced by Secretary of State Rice in early 2006.[3] The S/CRS charter outlined an ambitious global role in postconflict situations "to help stabilize and reconstruct societies." Nation building in broken countries became a State Department priority because the "security challenges" are "threatening vulnerable populations, their neighbors, our allies, and ourselves."[4] Small staffs and scanty funds hampered its start-up, but the sheer concept of using a civilian capacity within the State Department to democratize and reconstruct volatile states introduced a revolutionary way of doing business since the breakdown of the Berlin Wall. Backers of the new office noted the long-overdue recognition of the fact that the United States had wadded into more than 15 stability operations between the fall of the Berlin Wall and the invasions of Afghanistan and Iraq.[5]

THE DEMOCRATIC PEACE IMPERATIVE AND STABILITY

The United States held complex motives for attacking Iraq, but a political transmutation figured centrally in its preinvasion calculations and its democratic rhetoric afterward. George Bush and his advisers embraced the political theory that democracies are peaceful with each other. This hypothesis originated with writings of the eighteenth-century philosopher Immanuel Kant who famously argued in his essay "Perpetual Peace" that republics were less likely to go to war than monarchies because citizens of the former could object to bearing the hardships and financing the fighting. Subsequent academic researchers fleshed out the democratic peace theory to the degree that it has become a virtual article of faith in scholarly circles, although one with qualifications. Scholars agree that mature democracies do not fight one another; instead, they honor the international accords they sign, and they become economically interdependent. But experts emphasize that elections alone, without the full democratic panoply of an independent judiciary, free press, and viable political parties, constitute, in reality, illiberal democracies, which still menace their neighbors and destabilize their regions.[6]

Embryonic democracies, moreover, are more prone to belligerence, because politicians, spared the checks of genuinely independent institutions can, in fact, mobilize internal support by stoking grievances against outsiders. Elected demagogues, such as Venezuela's Hugo Chavez, can adopt ultranationalism and xenophobia to strengthen their domestic power and to cater to their own militaries out of fear about coups.[7] Ivory Towers denizens might cast doubt on the exportability and universality of democracy to unyielding places, such as the Middle East, but the Bush Oval Office maintained that democratizing Afghanistan and Iraq guaranteed a peaceful and terrorist-free Islamic epicenter. Western democracy and freedom hold universal appeal, but they require institutions derived from long fermentation periods to take root in uncultivated soil. U.S. policymakers, nonetheless, resolved to implanted Westernized democracy in series of actions that initially went well, abetting the notion that every political culture stood ready to embrace postmodern democracy and nonsectarian political movements. But the heart of the experiment, east of the Mediterranean Sea, remained violently resistant to non-Muslim interventions. Besides, the regions contained latent tensions between Shia and Sunnis or between Kurds and Turks that an outside force could activate with explosive consequences even with the best of intentions.

REGIME CHANGE, DEMOCRACY, AND STABILIZATION

In places as far afield as Liberia, Haiti, Ukraine, Kyrgyzstan, Lebanon, and the Republic of Georgia, the United States advanced its agenda by ushering out despotic regimes or protesting authoritarian power grabs in fraudulent elections to implement its democracy-for-stability doctrine. Soon after the Iraq invasion, it weighed in with stiff language, applied diplomatic pressure, dispersed democracy-enhancing assistance, or, in some cases, deployed military forces to the scene of instability to back democratic movements. Each case demonstrated, in vary degrees, America's reinvigorated commitment to democracy around the globe and its indispensability as *the* global guarantor of orderly change toward Anglo-Saxon freedom and political pluralism to strengthen its own security and international preferment.

One of the first tests for America's democracy initiative came from the former American colony of Liberia. Burdened by the mounting Iraqi insurgency, the United States hesitated to land troops in the seacoast capital of Monrovia, where AK-47 totting teens had unhinged the society in gunfire and bloodshed. Liberia had endured more than a decade of misrule and barbarity in a multisided civil war. Fueled by ethnically based rival rebel factions, the conflict engulfed the countryside until capped by an agreement in 1997. As part of the settlement, Charles Taylor, the biggest warlord, was engineered into the Liberian presidency by a dubious election. His ascension brought neither peace nor progress. Liberia soon slipped back into anarchy, as a smoldering second countryside civil war converged on Monrovia. By late summer 2003, the West African nation had become the archetypical failed state, chaotic and impoverished. Even worse, Taylor's continued rule all but ensured regional upheaval.

Wary of another Somalia where peacekeeping became urban warfare, the United States insisted on a cease-fire among the warring parties and the abdication and exile of President Taylor before deploying troops from a 2,300 U.S. Marine taskforce floating on three Navy ships offshore. American diplomatic pressure secured a shaky peace, and the deteriorating internal military balance convinced Taylor to seek refuge in Nigeria where he initially escaped prosecution for crimes against humanity by a UN-backed Special Tribunal in Sierra Leone until extradited in 2006. Just 200 Marines actually disembarked on August 14, 2003 to supply logistical support to a larger contingent of Nigerian peacekeepers.

The whole Liberian exercise represented a much less than overwhelming display of U.S. power. But it sufficed to change the regime and to secure stability that led the locals to hold a democratic election well after the U.S. armed forces departed. American power did not birth democracy; it simply served as a midwife by pushing out the dictator. The Liberians pulled off their own election two years later in which Ellen Johnson-Sirleaf, a former UN official, was elected as the first woman president in postcolonial Africa. Before that democratic outcome, the United States found itself again entwined with Haiti's recurring turmoil.

Like Liberia, the Republic of Haiti shared a tortuous history with the United States. Liberia had been an American colony, and Haiti, during its 19-year U.S. military occupation in the early twentieth century, had been an American colony in all but name. The Caribbean nation captured much more of Washington's attention during the 1990s, because of its propensity to flood the United States with asylum seekers, when conditions became especially onerous on the island republic. President Clinton's displacement of the junta to return Jean-Bertrand Aristide to the presidency, as related in chapter 4, did not bring a happy ending to the Haitian saga. The restoration of Aristide to power precipitated a return of all the baleful undercurrents within the Haitian body politic, as the reinstalled president reverted to the tactics of the country's past dictators. After winning a second term in a 2000 election, he incited mobs to intimidate and assassinate political opponents, politicized the police, and robbed the government coffers. Intoxicated with power, his behavior hollowed out his support over the next couple of years, even among the dirt-poor peasants in the countryside and the urban underclass living amid Dickensian grimness. His misrule also yielded a violent opposition from ragtag gangs led by former officers in the military that Aristide had disbanded. From the Dominican Republic, this rabble slipped over the border to sow chaos, captured towns outside the capital, and then spread violence to Port-au-Prince, as the country slid into anarchy. Inside the United States, Aristide had both detractors and adherents. Members of the Congressional Black Caucus rallied behind him as they had in the early 1990s, but other politicians expressed ambivalence about backing his sordid presidency, while voicing misgivings about letting a democratic leader in the Western Hemisphere fall to political enemies who were loosely allied to gunmen.

By early 2004, the United States had enough problems on its policy plate with the worsening insurgencies in Afghanistan and Iraq. The Bush administration cringed at that thought of a militarized humanitarian intervention into Haiti. It, nonetheless, grew apprehensive over deepening instability and the prospect of Haitian boat people washing up on Florida beaches as happened in past crises. When the month of February recorded over a hundred deaths from conflicts between rebels and Aristide loyalists, Washington intensified pressure on the defrocked slum priest to resign, sealing the fate of the National Palace occupant. On February 28, Aristide wrote out his resignation, boarded a U.S. military aircraft with his retinue and extensive baggage, and made a dawn departures initially for the Central African Republic. Compared to the violent regime changes of the Afghan and Iraqi dictatorships, Haiti was a velvet-gloved operation that many Bush officials favored.

The United States landed 200 Marines as the lead contingent of international peacekeepers from France, Chile, and Canada before a UN force arrived in June to calm a divided and volatile land and to unmake Clinton's regime change on behalf of Aristide. Administration detractors contended that the United States was "too willing to ignore democratic legitimacy in order to allow the removal" of the Haitian president, while acknowledging his faults.[8] In this instance, the United States prudently came down on the side of stability rather than a flawed but elected government. And yet again, it deposed a dictator, moved on, and let the indigenous politicians sort out the politics without the presence of U.S. bayonets.

Thousands of miles away American power, so it was argued, did not even have to be directly employed to bring about a change of heart, disarmament, and stability. Libya, a terrorist-sponsoring rogue state, decided to come in from the cold on the heels of the U.S. invasion of Iraq. The Libyan regime went public with its offer to pay compensation to the relatives of the bombed Pan Am Flight 103 and to abandon its secret nuclear and chemical arms programs. Prior to these breakthroughs, Libya's conduct placed it among the world's most egregious renegade nations. From the time of Colonel Muammar al-Qaddafi's deposing of the Libyan monarchy of King Idris in 1969, the North African state posed international problems. The Qaddafi regime confiscated Western oil-producing facilities, expelled foreign petroleum technicians, instigated a mob to sack the U.S. Embassy in Tripoli, and sponsored an array of terrorist fronts that shot or bombed innocents in Germany, Israel, Spain, and Northern Ireland. As a consequence of the Libyan-engineered downing of the Pan Am jet over Scotland in 1988, the United Nations imposed sanctions that compounded the country's isolation and its drastic fall in crude production.

At the time of the U.S. Iraq invasion, Libya quickened its secret discussions with Washington and London that had begun in 1999. Pressures on the Qaddafi regime had mounted over the preceding years as consequence of the sanctions, which diminished its oil revenues. Not unlike Iraq's Saddam Hussein, the Libyan dictator depended on oil money to buy the allegiance of influential figures and tribal chieftains as well as the complacency of the greater population with universal free education, urban improvement projects, and government-financed health care. The cost of this loyalty mushroomed, as did Libya's swelling population that by the second millennium reached over 5 million people, an increase of nearly 2 million from the two preceding decades. International sanctions stifled oil production as dilapidated equipment fell into disrepair and new technologies remained embargoed, jeopardizing Qaddafi's hold on power.

In December 2003, Libya agreed to give up its WMD and open its arms sites to international inspection, which revealed that Libyan scientists were "developing a nuclear fuel cycle intended to support nuclear weapons development."[9] Tripoli also disclosed that it had produced and stored 23 tons of mustard gas, aerial bombs, and Scud C-type missiles purchased from North Korea. It ratified the nuclear test ban treaty and opened its territory to monitoring teams to verify compliance with the terms of the treaty. It agreed to pay $2.7 billion in compensation to the families of those killed in the Pan Am explosion. The regime also renounced terrorism. Months later Tripoli released a statement that declared the country "accepts responsibility for the actions of its officials" for its hand in past terrorist attacks.[10] In turn, Washington and the United Nations dropped their respective restrictions on Libyan commerce and travel. The United States also moved to resume diplomatic ties with Libya.

How much impact of the ousting of the Taliban and Baathist regimes had on Qaddafi's Damascene conversion is an interesting question. In announcing the deal with the Qaddifi regime, President George Bush with Prime Minister Tony Blair at his side in the White House pressroom linked the Iraq War and the toppling of Saddam Hussein to the diplomatic breakthrough with Libya. Bush told the reporters, "In words and action: we have clarified the choices left to potential adversaries."[11] At the least, the unsheathed sword certainly did not hinder Qaddafi's decision to reengage with international society. The United States accepted the status quo by accommodating Qaddafi's continuance in power. Washington refrained from pressing for democracy or even regime change. It swallowed its democracy promotion rhetoric because deposing Libya's authoritarian rule might play into the hands Qaddafi's Islamic theocratic opponents, an outcome inimical to the United States. For American interests, it was a wisely pragmatic choice.

Elsewhere, America's diplomatic squeeze plays resulted in political changes that satisfied aspiring democratic populations within each of the countries but did not require a U.S. occupation. Far away on the Eurasian landmass, the three "color revolutions" in Georgia, Ukraine, and Kyrgyzstan offered positive outcomes for America's prudent nonmilitary tack. A first manifestation took place in the Republic of Georgia, 500 miles north of Iraq and six months after its invasion. As the Caucasus nation approached its November 2, 2003 elections, the U.S. government transferred its loyalties from President Eduard Shevardnadze, the defunct Soviet Union's last and most reasonable foreign minister, to the political opposition, because the ruling party's incompetence and cronyism that generated rebellious conditions. When the Columbia University-trained lawyer Mikheil Saakashvili disputed the election results as fraudulent, his followers took to the streets in protest and seized the parliament building in the so-called Rose Revolution. Eager to sustain its democracy-building initiative and head off instability that could invite Russian intervention, Washington sent Secretary of Defense Rumsfeld to Tbilisi in early December to meet with the fiery Saakashvili, issued demands that Russia withdraw its bases from Georgia, and hinted idly that the United States might send its own troops to the Black Sea country.

Russo-American tensions mounted over Georgia. Igor Ivanov, the Russian foreign minister, accused the United States of staging a coup against the incumbent. Expressing anger at his American-instigated removal from office, Shevardnadze resigned the presidency and defused the powder keg. Rescheduled elections ran in

January 2004, and the pro-Western reformer Saakashvili became president. He further irritated Moscow by demanding it dismantle Russian army bases, welcoming Western oil companies to construct a pipeline from Azerbaijan across Georgia to Turkey's seaports and by joining other Black Sea states in training exercises with a U.S. destroyer. These opening gains notwithstanding, Moscow persisted in pulling its former republic back in its gravitational field.

A few hundred miles northwest of Tbilisi a more significant democratic transition occurred with the United States' blessing. After a tainted presidential ballot in Ukraine in November 2004, the Bush administration staked out an assertive stance. Secretary of State Powell stated, "We cannot accept this result as legitimate because it [election] does not meet international standards."[12] The next month the East European nation's supreme court ruled to overturn the election results and to hold a revote after 17 days and nights of massive demonstrations during freezing weather in the capital's Independence Square. As in other onetime Soviet-occupied nations, the U.S. and European governments along with private groups sponsored democratic activities at the grassroots level. The street protests were a fruition of those efforts, which required no U.S. military force. It was American policy at its best, as a helping hand and not a blunt battleaxe.

The so-called Orange Revolution that ushered into the presidency the Western-leaning reformer Viktor Yushchenko in the second election during the last week of 2004 owed its nurturing, not its birth, to $58 million spent by the United States in the two previous years to train democratic activists, conduct public opinion surveys, maintain a Web site, and broadcast independent radio news that created a powerful effect in the closed society. Moreover, Ukraine's participation in the NATO-organized Partnership for Peace initiative contributed to the fact that the Ukrainian military, influenced by Western traditions, did not put down prodemocracy marches in Kiev. Washington's loud protestations over the corrupted election also steeled the demonstrators' nerve to confront the pseudo-winner after the balloting. Yushchenko's electoral victory scored another success for America's nonmilitary democracy campaign. But it also was a factor in Russia's deepening estrangement from the United States. As with Georgia, the Kremlin refused to accept the slippage of Ukraine into the American column.

In the Central Asian country of Kyrgyzstan, the United States joined with several European governments to fund and tutor the democratic opposition before the March 2005 parliamentary elections, which turned out to be a sham. Since the 1992 Freedom Support Act, Washington had targeted former Soviet republics to aid their economic and democratic transitions. Just the year before the disputed elections, Washington alone pumped in $12 million to underwrite civil society centers, which trained prodemocracy cadres, disseminated materials, and broadcast Kyrgyz-language programs by Radio Free Europe/Radio Liberty. It was small money shrewdly spent.

The Kyrgyz prodemocracy movement campaigned vigorously prior to the balloting only to be enraged by the fraudulent electoral results. It staged antiregime rallies around the arid mountainous country in what became known as the "Lemon Revolution" that ousted the repressive President Askar Akayev. After more than a decade in office, Akayev fled his landlocked state and wound up in Moscow, which had thrown its political weight behind the former physics professor by reminding

Western capitals that Kyrgyzstan was a Russian ally within its Collective Security Agreement. That a democratically mobilized population turned out its dictator in an Islamic country encouraged U.S. officials to take heart in their promotion of representative government in Afghanistan, Iraq, and elsewhere in the Middle East. But the real lesson was lost that the democracy arose from within the country, not from the imposition of a non-Muslim occupation army as in Iraq.

It was, in fact, in the Levantine country of Lebanon that Washington boasted of the first regional example of its touted "demonstration effect" for democracy promotion in postliberation Afghanistan and Iraq. The January 2005 elections in Iraq, according to this view, set off a "Baghdad spring" that rippled across the Near East, particularly in Lebanon. Syrian military and intelligence units had occupied the Mediterranean country since 1976. Damascus claimed it invaded Lebanon to snuff out the country's deadly civil war, which Syrian leaders held posed a threat to their country. Skeptics interpreted Syria's intervention as an attempt to restore Lebanon to Greater Syria as it had been under the Ottoman Empire. The Lebanese chafed under their neighbor's domination, which did, in fact, result in years of imposed political order after a bloody internecine conflict among Lebanon's fractured sectarian communities.

When a massive bomb blast killed former prime minister Rafik Hariri, an opponent of Syria's presence, in mid-February 2005, his countrymen staged huge anti-Syrian protests in Beirut. In the wake of allegations about Syrian responsibility for Hariri's assassination, the Lebanese marched and protested for a return of their sovereignty, genuine democracy, and freedom from Syrian hegemony in what the international media dubbed the "Cedar Revolution" but the street dissenters termed it the "intifada of independence."

Internationally isolated by the United States and Europe (especially France) and urged to withdraw by Saudi Arabia, Syria relented. It pulled out its 14,000 troops by late April 2005 and ostensibly its intelligence operatives. Parliamentary elections followed soon after the Syrian military's exodus, delivering a majority of seats to an anti-Syrian coalition. To official Washington, Lebanon constituted a Middle East example that the Bush strategy was bearing fruit. But they ignored the fact that Lebanese had elections and parliaments before the U.S.-led invasion of Iraq. Moreover, Lebanon's protest had much more to do with its independence-minded nationalism. Most significantly, months later Lebanon stood at the brink of civil wars, as Iraq's Shiite-Sunni violence was echoing among Lebanese sectarian communities. The Syrian- and Iranian-sponsored radical Shiite movement Hezbollah ("the Party of God") consolidated its political position as one player within the Lebanese government and then provoked conflict with Israel in July 2006. For Tehran, its proxy's actions deflected American and European pressure on Iran to step back from its nuclear weapons ambitions. The war with Israel aggravated Lebanese political and sectarian turmoil pointing toward civil war in early 2007.

Lebanon's largely passive ouster of Syrian rule marked a high point for the Bush White House's democracy campaign. At the American University in Cairo in June 2005, Condoleezza Rice delivered a direct political appeal to Egypt and Saudi Arabia, two of America's closest Arab allies, to democratize by holding genuine elections, empowering women, and tolerating free expression. The United States' top diplomat noted the shortcomings in America's decades-old policies: "For 60 years, my country, the United States, pursued stability at the expense of democracy in this region here in the Middle East. . . . Now we are taking a different course. We are supporting democratic aspirations of all people." Asserting that democracy does not lead to "chaos or conflict," she added, "Freedom and democracy are the only ideas powerful enough to overcome hatred, and division, and violence."[13] For the United States, universal democracy appeared to replace the former dependence on dictators for security against Soviet expansion. The secretary's claims went too far for democracy, however. It is not a panacea for all the world's violent and dysfunctional nations. Elections, referendums, and elected officials in Iraq and Afghanistan delivered neither peace nor security to their electorates.

A DEMOCRATIC DOWNSIDE?

A favorable report in late 2005 on the spread of freedom briefly boosted the standing of the U.S. democracy campaign, but the account glossed over its negative side, at least for American interests. Freedom House, an independent organization, released its annual global survey "Freedom in the World" that asserted, "The past year was one of the most successful for freedom since Freedom House began measuring world freedom in 1972." It singled out the Middle East for special attention because that region "experienced a modest but potentially significant increase in political rights and civil liberties in 2005."[14] Iraq, Egypt, and the Palestinian territories exhibited some competition in elections. The report also cited the introduction of women's suffrage in Kuwait and the improved "media environment in Saudi Arabia." Elsewhere in Ukraine, Kyrgyzstan, and Georgia, the study recorded notable improvements while recording retrogression of political liberty in Russia, Azerbaijan, Uzbekistan, and Belarus. As events soon showed, the report proved only provisional as a darker epilogue was soon written.

These democratic inroads irked Russia, which interpreted Washington's democracy expansion program in its "near-abroad" as a means to serve America's geopolitical priorities. Moscow pushed back by standing behind the dictatorial Aleksandr Lukashenko in his rigged reelection to the presidency of Belarus. The Kremlin also aggressively courted Kazakhstan and other former Soviet Republic in Central Asia with the aim of imposing a Cold War-style exclusion of the United States. Strikingly, it joined with China, a sometimes hostile neighbor, in forming the six-member Shanghai Cooperation Organization (SCO), a quasi-alliance. Along with Uzbekistan and Tajikistan, the seemingly pro-American governments in Kazakhstan and Kyrgyzstan also joined SCO, in which Beijing and Moscow promoted regional military cooperation and an "energy club" that invited no membership from the United States. Washington's democratization, in short, created a Sino-Russian backlash. There were other ominous clouds closer to the America's central front in its democracy offensive.

The Middle East witnessed a big shake-up in its political dynamics as Washington's democratic preoccupation persisted. The downside to this democratic reordering campaign was the realization that it enabled regimes hostile to U.S. interests to come to power through the ballot box. Democratization of the Islamic Middle

East was not a single-edged sword as American democracy proponents were to learn. Expanding political pluralism in some instances, in fact, cut against regimes allied closely with the United States.

Iraq's Kurdish population, whose representative governance had made long strides since the 1990s U.S. protectorate, reinvigorated the Kurds' guerrilla war in southeastern Turkey. Rather than bringing harmony to Turkey, a vital American regional ally, the autonomy of the Iraqi Kurds reinspired the Kurdish minority in Turkey to wage a fresh guerrilla war that in the 1980s had claimed 35,000 lives. Democracy thus gave rebirth to territorial conflict. Washington wrongly believed that democracy brought only peace and moderation. Ankara threatened reprisal raids into Kurdistan to crush the bases of its restive Kurds in what would contribute to Iraq's instability. Elsewhere in the Middle East, the U.S.-backed democracy push also agitated other countries and worked against American interests.

From Washington's perspective, Egypt's late 2005 election painted a worrisome picture. Its parliamentary contest produced substantial gains for the Muslim Brotherhood. Candidates associated with the Muslim Brotherhood won 88 seats in the 454-member People's Assembly, a fivefold increase from its previous showing, despite officially organized harassment of its candidates. The Muslim Brotherhood was far from taking power but it now had a sizable opposition bloc in light of the decline of secular antiregime parties and the increased Islamization of Egyptian society. Formed in 1928, the Muslim Brotherhood inspired even more radical offshoots such as the Egyptian Islamic Jihad (EIJ), which engaged in a wave of bombings and political murders including the 1981 assassination of President Anwar Sadat. One faction of the EIJ, led by Ayman al-Zawahiri, joined Al Qaeda. In recent years, the Muslim Brotherhood cultivated an image of civic honesty and community services to its constituents. But its ideological militancy and anti-Americanism confronts Washington's prodemocracy position with a dilemma that greater representative governments may lead to political victories for powerful Islamist movements, which would undermine American friends. Islamist regimes would in all likelihood open their territories to terrorists, as did Iran and Afghanistan.

In neighboring Gaza, another dramatic example of unintended consequences flowed from the Bush administration's democracy promotion efforts. Five months after Israel's disengagement from the pocket-sized territory, the parliamentary elections in January 2006 saw a democratically elected terrorist movement, Hamas, formally known as the Islamic Resistance Movement, come to power. As a spin-off from the Muslim Brotherhood, Hamas' political victory at the polls held enormous resonance for extreme Islam, for it defeated the secular nationalism of the Palestinian Fatah, the chosen partner of Tel Aviv and Washington. The United States and the European Union as well as Israel threatened to cut off their funding to the Palestinian Authority until Hamas recognized Israel and foreswore terrorism against the Jewish state. The Palestinian Authority's internal and external policies interjected uncertainty into the region as Gazan militants fought each other and fired rockets into the Jewish state, killing Israelis and disturbing the larger Middle East.

In reaction to the rise of Shiite political forces in Iraq and Lebanon and to the electoral gains by Islamic fundamentalists in Egypt and Gaza, other Middle East states either slowed their reform process or cracked down on democracy advocates. Qatar postponed parliamentary elections; Bahrain backtracked and imposed a constitution calling for a second appointed legislative house to curtail the elected house's power; Jordan placed democratization authority on the backburner; Yemen clamped down on the media; and Syria harshly suppressed the political opposition. The Arab Middle East indeed tested the theories of U.S. officials, who like Silicon Valley engineers, believed that their democratic software could operate on any cultural hardware. Coupled with intractable insurgencies in Afghanistan and Iraq, democracy promotion looked less than a peaceful cause to governments in the Near East.

Washington took note of these developments. Promoting elections or toppling regimes for democracy looked less appealing than the former authoritarian stability. Coercive regime change of Syrian ruler Bashar Assad, a consistent thorn in the American side, might toss Syria into a militant theocracy or the similar turmoil that engulfed the region. Nondemocratic stability and cooperation enjoyed a return in vogue. For example, the United States welcomed Ilham Aliyev, Azerbaijan's corrupt and autocratic but friendly leader, to the White House in spring 2006. The year before the United States had sent envoys to Aliyev and to Nursultan Nazarbayev in Kazakhstan pledging to elevate relations to a strategic level in return for honest elections. Notwithstanding some democratic trappings, neither nation held genuinely fair elections. And neither state was punished by Washington, which understood their importance as Iran made a bid for a nuclear arms capacity and Russia reasserted its influence in the Caucasus and Central Asia. Moreover, Azerbaijan and Kazakhstan export oil to foreign markets, a commodity vital to the West.

Stability, democracy, and energy had initially become intertwined in the high stakes of geopolitics with the American thrust into Central Asia during the first Bush administration. Well into its second term, stability and democracy were no longer cojoined everywhere. As a new "great game" dawns between the United States and Russia along with China for advantage in this crucial hydrocarbon zone, America has had less latitude to advance a democracy-driven enterprise. Instead, it has had to revert to its former policy of accommodating friendly dictators or risk losses to Russia or China, which seeks to influence Central Asian politics through the Shanghai Cooperation Organization. But in Iraq, the Bush government's democracy push empowered the Shia and disadvantaged the Sunni whose attacks on the Shiite majority set in train a cycle of revenge killings that by mid-2006 threatened to fragment the country along sectarian lines.

IRAQ: THE PURPLE REVOLUTION BRINGS NO PEACE

Neither electoral democracy nor the return of Iraq's sovereignty to the Prime Minister Ayad Allawi's interim government in June 2004 yielded a cessation in the intensifying insurgency. Iraqi and Arab nationalism fed on grassroots resentments against the non-Muslim occupiers. Jihadis crossed Iraq's borders to enflame anticoalition and anti-Shiite terrorism under Al Qaeda's banner. The Sunni insurgents fought to expel Westerners from Iraq, murder their fellow Shiite countrymen, and reassert their age-old dominance. Their bombings and execution-style murders propelled the Shiite's bloody reaction and powered Kurdish demands for independence. The Shia fought back with their own militias and their penetration of the central government's military and police forces, which carried on a "dirty war" with reprisal murders against the Sunni community, perpetuating retributive killings that coalition forces were unable to stop.

The Shiite-Sunni battles spurred a war-within-the-war phenomena that Thomas Hobbes might have characterized as a "war of all against all," with criminal gangs also kidnapping hostages for ransom interspersed with the political bloodletting. The distinct risk of a two-sided or even three-sided civil war loomed over Iraq after the return of sovereignty and in spite of the acknowledged success of the two political elections and one referendum. The promise of peace and order via Western democracy confronted the implacable realities of the Middle East. America looked quixotic for failing to take into account the regional legacy before clambering on an ill-advised occupation-enforced democratic train wreck.

Promoting democracy in the fractious society was to have accomplished two overarching objectives. First, an elected government would, according to the argument, gain political legitimacy among Iraqis. U.S. officials asserted that this legitimacy would take the edge off the anticoalition insurgency by giving the formerly disenfranchised populace a voice in their government. Second, a democracy would likely be pacific toward American interests and the United States. It would even recognize Israel and its right to political existence. Stability, democracy, and security were all linked in the official American mind. Yet unlike the earlier outcomes in Nicaragua, Bosnia, and Liberia, the Iraqi elections failed to restore peace. The Middle East stood apart from other arenas by its religious-based civilization and unremitting hostility to colonialism, Western cultural penetration, and non-Muslim occupying forces. Moreover, many of the states had existed only decades, being carved out of the defunct Ottoman Empire at the end of World War I, ruled colonially through League of Nations' mandate system and then subjugated ruthlessly by tyrants who never melded the disparate tribes, sects, or subregions into modern nations. In fact, dictatorial regimes often played one community off another to stay in power. Official Washington wrongly discounted these factors in Iraq as it clung for too long at the glimpses of voters going to the polls. An election in no way guaranteed an acceptable government strong enough to govern fairly and resolutely in the face of a deeply divided society.

On January 30, 2005, slightly over 8.5 million Iraqis, or nearly 6 in 10 eligible voters, went to the polls to elect a 275-member assembly that was to appoint a transitional government and write a constitution. Voters braved suicide bombings or gunmen as they voted for their own ethnic politicians, not as in an idealized red-state, blue-state U.S. election. Exhilarated, they waved their purple ink-stained fingers that proved they voted, except in the turbulent Al Anbar province where fear and Sunni Muslim clerics urged a boycott. By not voting, the Sunni Arabs marginalized themselves from nation's political workings because Iraqi voters cast ballots based on sectarian affiliation. A coalition dominated by Shiite Islamic parties, the United Iraqi Alliance, won 48 percent of the vote, not enough to rule without deal making with other factions, particularly a second coalition of the two main Kurdish parties.

The Shiite-dominated United Iraqi Alliance picked Ibrahim al-Jaafari, a formerly exiled physician who headed the Dawa Party and had served on the Governing

Council, to be the country's prime minister. To win the job and to form a government, Jaafari and his allies had to cut deals and make promises because Iraq's interim constitution, the occupation-period Transitional Administrative Law, effectively required a two-thirds majority in the newly elected National Assembly. The Kurds demanded recognition of their special autonomy within Iraq, control of the oil city of Kirkuk, and diminution of Islam's place in the new government. Adding to complicated negotiations was the necessity of accommodating the embittered Sunni minority, which held only six parliamentary seats. The die was already cast for a violent sectarian future.

Soon after the Jaafari-led governing body settled into its white and gilt offices within the Green Zone, top Bush officials pressed the new leaders to stop bickering and to complete the filling of government positions. America's prodding suffered from the absence of an ambassador on the ground. It took until late June for Zalmay Khalilzad to be confirmed by the U.S. Senate, three months after John Negroponte left to head up the newly legislated position of director of National Intelligence. Khalilzad badgered the transitional legislative body to complete a constitution by the August 15, 2005 deadline. The United States also threw its weight behind women's rights and inclusiveness of all religious and ethnic communities, even to the point of presenting its written version of key provisions. Even after the transitional National Assembly approved the document, it required further tweaking over the next month to placate the Sunni members enough to win passage of the draft constitution in the October 15, 2005 nationwide referendum that preceded the parliamentary election two months later.

The countrywide balloting to elect 275-seat National Assembly for a four-year term took place on December 15 in a poisonous electoral format that produced deadly antibodies in the state's political body. Voting for party slates rather than district representatives, Iraqis vested power in parties rather than in territorially defined constituents, a recipe for sectarian supremacists who pitched the country into enveloping violence. The Shiite-controlled United Iraqi Alliance captured 130 seats in the legislature, giving it the largest bloc but short of the two-thirds needed to name the prime minister without obtaining votes from Kurdish or Sunni officeholders. As happened following the election of the constitutional assembly eleven months earlier, the National Assembly bogged down in political bickering over the selection of the prime minister that reflected the deep sectarian division despite imposed democracy and an election. In late April, the parliament broke the logjam and endorsed Nuri Kamal al-Maliki, a Shiite Muslim and former exile.

Again, the insurgency recovered the momentum it lost in the wake of the successful election and death of Abu Musab al-Zarqawi, Al Qaeda's Iraqi leader, in June 2006. Indeed the reciprocal Sunni-Shiite violence engulfed Baghdad and environs in a sectarian civil war and local ethnic cleansing by mid-2006. The Sunni terrorist bombing of the Shia's golden-domed Askariya shrine in Samarra in February locked the two sectarian communities into deadly reciprocal retaliations. U.S. forces could not keep the peace no matter how many people voted.

Caught in the internecine crossfire, U.S. troops suffered steady casualties that hit 3,000 deaths as 2007 dawned. Financial costs reached $8 billion a month, with total direct expenditures at $450 billion. Sill, Iraq slid to the brink of disintegration with the prospect of regionalizing its sectarian fighting and drawing in the neighboring states. The unintended consequences of America's democracy fabricating were catastrophic for its own interests and the Middle East's political stability. The Iraqi failure undercut Washington's measures elsewhere to promote political cohesion and a burnished image around the globe through humanitarian aid.

HUMANITARIAN ASSISTANCE, INSTABILITY, AND THE U.S. MISSION

A series of catastrophic natural disasters demanded U.S. attention both to alleviate the potential for chaos and to refurbish America's reputation. The Iraq War tarnished America's standing in the greater Islamic world. Charges of atrocities, the Abu Ghraib prison scandal, and Iraq's messy postinvasion insurgency—all damaged America's standing among many Muslims. To redeem American prestige, the U.S. military responded with massive relief to the stricken tsunami victims in Indonesia and earthquake survivors in Pakistan. After the December 26, 2004 tidal waves inundated Indonesia's islands, killing about 130,000 inhabitants, Washington sailed a dozen warships to aid the tsunami-battered South Asian country. The Bush government also committed $350 million for aid along with a large military contingent, the only agency capable of delivering rapid succor. Off the coast of Aceh province, a U.S. flotilla rushed food, water, and medical supplies to the desperate islanders.

Nine months later and thousands of miles away, the Pentagon mounted similar operations on the wasted mountainsides of northern Pakistan. Only America's Chinook helicopters possessed the heavy-lift capabilities to ferry in relief supplies to Pakistan's remote Muslim-dominated Kashmir and evacuate the injured after the October 2005 earthquake. Islamabad lost much of its civil administration, roads, and, indeed, military forces in the inaccessible corner, where the 7.6 magnitude quake left some 80,000 people dead and 3 million homeless to face winter snows. Washington pledged $510 million for assistance and dispatched 1,000 troops to set up emergency operations, field hospitals, tent cities, and food distribution points.[15]

The twin relief efforts registered one of America's most monumental hearts-and-mind successes in the Muslim world. The television images of U.S. forces shuttling supplies and treating the injured became daily features on Indonesian and Pakistani television screens for months, where they helped to modify adverse sentiments toward the United States. In the world's most populous Muslim nation, 65 percent of Indonesians held a favorable opinion of the America as consequence of its post-tsunami humanitarian mission. In Pakistan, the number of people holding a favorable opinion of the United States jumped to 46 percent in November 2005 from 23 percent the previous May.[16]

Ameliorating local hardships was seen as contributing to political stability by denying terrorist networks grievances to exploit. In fact, the U.S. Joint Chiefs of Staff concluded in the 2006 "National Military Strategic Plan for the War on Terrorism" that humanitarian assistance is "often key to . . . mitigating problems that extremists exploit to gain support for their cause."[17] But relief efforts made little headway against intransigent foes. From bases in Pakistan, Taliban insurgents crossed the border into Afghanistan and stepped up their violence against American and NATO troops throughout 2006. They also attacked schoolteachers, policemen, and district chiefs to erode the political homeostasis that at first descended after the U.S.-led invasion five years earlier. Insurgent tactics applied in Iraq with devastating effectiveness found their way to a reenergized Taliban, threatening America's democratic experiment in Afghanistan.

THE INTERMEDIATE DESTABILIZER

As the Iraq War wound on with its potential for regionwide turmoil, other threats emerged to confront America's stabilization goals. Chief among the immediate destabilizing powers is Iran, which oddly enough benefited most from America's removal of Saddam Hussein and the Taliban regime. Instead of showing gratitude, the Islamic Republic worsened America's Iraqi predicament by bolstering Shiite insurgents. Since they pushed out the shah in 1979, the ruling clerics had confounded U.S. efforts to stabilize the region by backing terrorism particularly against Israel, meddling in Iraq and Afghanistan, and preaching against America as the Great Satan. Tehran escalated its threat level to another order of magnitude by its nuclear weapons designs. An Iranian opposition group revealed in 2002 that Iran had a secret uranium experiment facility in operation since 1985, a revelation that shocked the West.

Like the provocative North Korean nuclear test in October 2006 that roiled East Asia, Iran's growing nuclear capability and frequent threats to Israel through its president's ominous statements of annihilation and Hezbollah attacks from Lebanon unsettled the Middle East. And also like North Korea, Iran has threatened to respond to any international sanctions or preemptive military strikes on its nuclear facilities with a range of weapons from intermediate-range missiles, closure of oil shipments through the Strait of Hormuz, and terrorism inside Iraq, within the Gulf kingdoms, and against Israel.

As the world's fourth largest producer of oil, Iran presented a tough adversary for the United States and its European allies of Britain, France, and Germany to overawe. Its horde of petrodollars and its untapped crude reserves gave Tehran financial strength to resist international pressure and to fund proxy wars through terrorist-linked Hamas in Gaza and Hezbollah in Lebanon. The Israeli-Hezbollah fighting within southern Lebanon in mid-2006 confirmed rather than announced the trend in rising Shiite influence that stirred apprehension in the entire region. Jordan's King Abdullah warned that if Iraq fell to control of pro-Iranian parties, the result might be a "Shiite crescent" of dominant Shiite governments or movements stretching from Lebanon through Syria, Iran, and Iraq to the Persian Gulf, where, in effect, they would be a kind of fifth column challenging Sunni dominance in the littoral kingdoms. These facts also raised fears in Saudi Arabia, which has a sizable Shiite minority in its eastern oil-producing province. Riyadh worried about the Shiite political gains in Iraq's governance after that country's elections.[18] Iran's exalted sense of its Persian imperial history, militant nationalism, Shia revivalism, and vaulting aspirations for Gulf hegemony has made Islamic Republic a formidable adversary for the foreseeable future, which was made stronger by Washington's lengthy occupation that tossed Iraq into chaos and eliminated it as Iran's traditional balancer.

Another major destabilizing element radiating from the Middle East remains Al Qaeda and its clones or competitors. These terrorist networks subscribe to a major political and religious reordering that is transregional in scope. Through terrorist attacks and conversions to their cause, they aspire to establish an Islamic caliphate under Shari'a law that stretches from Southeast Asia, across Central Asia, the Middle East, North Africa into Europe. The loss of Afghanistan was a setback. But they have carved out safe havens in weak states such as Somalia, Sudan, and the anarchic belts along the Afghanistan-Pakistan border. In Europe, they have taken advantage of immigrant enclaves and open societies to launch bombings as in Madrid and London. Along with the objective of destroying Israel and putting an Islamic regime in its place, they seek to overturn apostate governments in Muslim countries such as Egypt, Jordan, Saudi Arabia, Yemen, Pakistan, and Bangladesh, whether through the ballot box or subversion. At this juncture, the Middle East and parts of South Asia look far less than secure, casting into doubt future U.S. exertions to achieve friendly, harmonious governments through the spread of democracy.

MANAGING THE PEACEFUL RISE OF CHINA

No country has more potential to upset America's democracy-promoting strategy than the People's Republic of China, an authoritarian state. It has the size, infrastructure, and ambition to challenge the United States in several arenas such as Asia, Africa, and the Middle East over the next 10–20 years. The economic rise of China is historically unprecedented. In the last quarter of a century, the PRC's gross domestic product has grown more than 9 percent annually. China's economy is now ranked fourth largest in the world, allowing ample funds for its annually mounting defense outlays. Its defense establishment is giving Beijing the capacity to project military power far from its shores. At a minimum, China offers an alternative pillar to anti-American states.

In Asia in the short term, China is more likely to seek dominance through a growing web of trade and bilateral military alliances with longtime U.S. allies such as Thailand and the Philippines, protection of Burma's military dictatorship, and a partnership with Indonesia than invasion or conquest. Its booming trade with Australia drives a wedge between Canberra and Washington, while Chinese pressure on tiny Singapore isolates a staunch American ally. How tightly it will draw a sphere of influence over East Asia is still to be determined. Its obsessive claims to the island of Taiwan as an internal province and envenomed disputes with rival Japan pose challenges to stability, which may even lead to military conflict.

Beyond Asia, its thirst for energy, second only to the United States, makes it a player in the Persian Gulf, where Beijing is cultivating commercial relationships with Saudi Arabia as well as Iran. Chinese arms transfers to these countries are part of this budding exchange for oil. Riyadh welcomes China's strategic interest and arms transfers to offset its dependency on the United States. Tehran sees China's courtship for oil as a political balance to American presence in the Persian Gulf and an ally in the United Nations. China has joined Russia in opposing U.S. lobbying for restrictive sanctions in the Security Council against Iran's economy for its nuclear weapons programs.

The People's Republic of China is too territorially vast, strategically significant, and distant—and so currently intertwined in financing U.S. trade and budget deficits—to contain as America did the Soviet Union. Mindful of the bloody half-century that stretched from the 1890s to embed an ascendant Germany into the international community, U.S. strategic planners know the importance of constructively integrating China into the comity of nations. Fears of pre-1914 Wihelmine Germany and the exclusion of the Weimar Republic after World War I compounded German isolation and resentment that burst forth in two world conflicts. Reasoning by analogy, Washington placed its bets on extensive trade, diplomatic engagement, and military exchanges to build trust and confidence with Chinese officials.

U.S. policymakers latched onto China's self-described "peaceful rise" to great power status. They urged China to become a "responsible stakeholder" in the international system.[19] The United States and the European Union have turned to coaxing China to become a good global citizen by allowing the market to set the value of its currency, cracking down on intellectual piracy, and tolerating religious freedom. But China's growing economic prowess and unrelenting arms buildup have resulted in the United States looking for ways to preserve the benefits of its strategic edge from China's bid to upset the status quo. By forging closer relations with regional powers such as Japan, Australia, Vietnam, and especially India, Washington is striving to counterbalance an ascending China. Will these policies succeed in integrating a powerful China into international society? The jury is still out until, perhaps, mid-century.

A TENTATIVE CONCLUSION

Nearly two decades after Soviet army boots reverberated across Moscow's Red Square in the last October parade before the Berlin Wall passed into history, the United States found itself facing a similar fate that befell the Red Army in South Asia. Like the Russian troops, America's modern army encountered suicidal resistance in Iraq as well as Afghanistan. Moscow fought nine years in Afghanistan to transfer Marxism, prop up an unpopular regime, and remake a Muslim society in its own image. American soldiers battled to impose an Occidental version of democracy and stability on Islamic countries. Passing over the Soviet lessons, official Washington pushed ahead confident of its beliefs and resources in its own revolutionary crusade.

American power was transformed by epochal fall of the Berlin Wall. No longer constrained by its deterrence and containment of the Soviet Union, the United States could afford a more expansive global role. Idealistic impulses flourished. At first, the United States acted with restraint in the export of democracy. Then its policies and actions aimed at a wider world democratically elected and friendly to American interests of free trade, globalization, and Washington's influence. Initially, things went well with its interventions to promote democracy in Panama, Haiti, Bosnia, Ukraine, Central Asia, and a handful of tiny African states. Encouraged by these small victories, its peerless military power, and, chiefly, a blinkered vision of its democracy-instigating capacity in a Arab-Muslim arena, the United States tried to transplant enlightened representative government in Afghanistan and Iraq. Here it ran up against the intransigent resistance of nationalistic and religiously fired insurgents.

Rather than birthing Westernized, secular democracy, Washington convulsed the vital Middle East, temporarily alienated European allies, and incensed the greater Arab-Islamic world. Its unilateral impulse to proselytize an American brand of multicultural democracy has also given rise to destabilizing threats among its allied states in the Near East.

The Bush government went from a policy of striking back at genuine threats to a far-fetched worldwide democracy crusade in span of four years. In the front-end section entitled "The Way Ahead" of the 2006 National Security Strategy of the United States of America, a clear emphasis is placed on the pursuit of stability through democracy promotion; its predecessor, the 2002 security document, differed substantially by announcing the preemptive attack doctrine when perils gathered. But the updated version propounded a democracy agenda: "Because democracies are the most responsible members of the international system, promoting democracy is the most effective long-term measure for strengthening international stability."[20] Six months later, Iraq's territorial integrity stood in jeopardy and rule-of-law civil society became unviable as all hell broke loose with the release of ancient tribal, clan, and sectarian blood feuds. The elimination of the dictatorial restraints gave vent to smoldering hatred and a desire of various communities to be free of one another, not joined together in a liberal democratic nation.

By 2007, two events raised doubts about U.S. democracy promotion east of the Mediterranean as unattainable. First, the surging violence in Afghanistan and particularly Iraq redefined American priorities from nation building and democracy building to getting out without too much chaos ensuing afterward. The everyday roadside bombings, sniper killings, and firefights took the lives of American troops who were trapped amid a Sunni-Shiite sectarian civil war as well as insurgent attacks. America's original purpose in removing Saddam Hussein from power was completed. It ascertained that no weapons of mass destruction existed in the Middle Eastern country. Its obligation of instituting democracy was at least fulfilled by protecting two elections and a referendum. But the American public had not signed on to keeping the peace amid a fierce religious civil war. Congress formed the bipartisan Iraq Study Group whose 79 recommendations left little political ripple in late 2006, as the panel advocated standing back and looking at Iraq in a larger sense within the Middle East. Its forty-second recommendation called for the completion of "the training and equipping mission" of Iraqi forces by the first quarter of 2008, pointing toward an American exit or at least a diminution of the U.S. military forces in the war-wracked land.[21] On the eve of his retirement as CENTCOM commander in March 2007, General Abizaid warned that "insurgencies are not easily solved by foreign troops" as if to reinforce the Iraq Study Group's conclusions and his own long-held views about the difficulties faced by an alien occupation in the Middle East.[22] Abizaid and other generals had concluded by late 2005 that a smaller U.S. military footprint would undercut perceptions of an occupation that generated anti-American attacks by insurgents and that sustained a "dependency syndrome" among Iraqi government troops, who would not engage the guerillas on their own.

Nothing the U.S. forces did could stop the Sunni-Shiite bloodshed. Midway through his second term, President Bush's justification for "staying the course" in the unpopular Iraq conflict had changed again. No longer was transferring consensual government to Iraq the primary objective; it was now how to deny terrorists a safe haven in the Sunni-dominated provinces and how to arrest Iraq's implosion opening a political vacuum and causing widespread instability in the Middle East. Less utopian than conjuring up democracy in Iraq, even these two agendas seemed beyond reach because of the intensifying sectarian- and insurgent-driven violence and especially because of the electoral results within the United States.

The second event impacting U.S. effort in the Middle Eastern country was the 2006 midterm elections, which in many ways constituted a referendum on the Iraq War. The outcome changed the political dynamics for the administration's war policy. The Democratic Party picked up 29 seats in the House of Representatives and six seats in the Senate that shifted congressional power to it after 12 years of Republican dominance. The new Democratic leadership challenged the White House's handling of the ongoing counterinsurgency in Iraq by steps to curtail congressional funding for the war. Feeling that their party's fate was tied to a pullout of American forces, the Democrats opposed and constrained the Bush government's conduct of the Iraq War and other international policies unlike its first six years in office.

President Bush rolled the dice once again by "surging" 28,500 additional troops into Baghdad to subdue the sectarian violence in a last-ditch effort to retrieve his war policy that enjoyed less than 30 percent approval among polled Americans.[23] From the White House library, he went before the country in a nationwide broadcast on January 10, 2007 to lay out his reasons for deploying five infantry brigades to Iraq's capital city and the scene of most of the bombings and murders. His plan also allocated $1 billion for reconstruction and job-creation projects to siphon off young men from the militia and insurgent ranks.[24] Seen as too little and too late by many experts, the approach relied heavily on the doubtful will and capacity of Iraq's Prime Minister Maliki to deliver a political settlement with the Sunni and to rein in Shiite militias.

America's lengthy occupation of Iraq turned into a strategic blunder. Rather than just penalizing the dangerous behavior of Saddam Hussein, the United States had become bogged down in a costly land war in the Middle East. Rather than installing an exile government or holding elections a few months after its invasion, the White House launched a lengthy occupation in a Muslim land, the type of military exercise that historically has met with unappeasable resistance in the region. Saudi Arabian King Abdullah, Washington's nominal ally, told a meeting of the Arab League in March 2007 that the American occupation was illegal.[25] Whatever the intermediate resolution of this conflict—withdrawal, lowered commitment, or unlikely status quo—American ends will suffer a setback. Because the United States failed to deny the insurgents and terrorists an opportunity to claim victory, its enemies—Iran, Syria, North Korea, and Al Qaeda—will declare it their own victory and gain converts or respite from an America fixated on Iraq. This outcome will embolden terrorists and hostile powers and prolong the struggle against violent Islamic extremism in the Near East, Southern Asia, and the Horn of Africa.

The Iraq setback can be overcome with other measures in what the Pentagon calls "the Long War" against militant Islam. The United States does not have to invade, occupy, and rebuild civic institutions to turn back every threat. It can resume its historic role as a beacon for democracy, speaking out for liberty and human rights. It can contain and deter, sanction and isolate, bomb and missile strike, or commando raid and punish its foes. At the close of 2006, Washington had swung tentatively toward a policy of containing Iran by exploring a regional alliance with Egypt, Jordan, and Saudi Arabia against their Shiite nemesis.

Where containment and deterrence cannot be applied to block threats, the United States will have to resort to offshore military strikes and covert actions that must sidestep a slippery slope into large-scale troop deployments that then "mission creep" into militarized democracy exercises. Providing diplomatic support, financial assistance, military and civic training, and arms to our allies or insecure nations are measures well short of lengthy occupations. Washington's assistance to Ethiopia's incursion into Somalia against the Islamic Courts Union in early 2007 is an example of this indirect approach. Our recent history of policing Iraq's no-fly zones with warplanes furnishes another illustration of a noninvasion form of hot containment. Already, the United States has behaved with circumspection toward Islamicist violence in Somalia, Sudan, and other African countries. In the Philippines, U.S. Special Operations forces train Filipino troops to wage counterinsurgency against Islamicist terrorists. At home and with allies, an array of human and electronic countermeasures can be strengthened to detect and disrupt terrorist cells before they can strike the American homeland. Above all, it can fashion a counterideological campaign to combat the jihadi exhortations to violence and martyrdom.

Like other floods, world terrorism will recede over time, leaving eddies where once there had been a deluge. But until that turn of events, the United States will face an arduous campaign against violent Islamic extremism. America's "unipolar moment" is far from lapsed.[26] But it must brace itself for a different kind of warfare, one unlike World War II battles, Cold War maneuvers, and, most of all, democracy crusades into areas politically unready for free institutions. It must transform its understanding of power to deal with a diffuse and elusive threat, while formulating a new grand strategy. By husbanding its strength, backing its friends, proclaiming an antijihadi message, hunting down terrorists, and keeping faith with humanitarian and democratic values, while avoiding massive military occupations to export democratic governance, America will prevail over Islamic extremism and see democracy sprout from its own roots across the Middle East.

NOTES

INTRODUCTION

1. John S. Galbraith, "The 'Turbulent Frontier' as a Factor in British Expansion," *Comparative Studies in Society and History*, Volume 2, Issue 2 (1960), pages 150–168.

CHAPTER 1   END OF THE BERLIN WALL AND THE AMERICAN COLOSSUS

1. Patrick E. Tyler, "U.S. Strategy Plan Calls for Insuring No Rivals Develop," *New York Times*, March 8, 1992, page A1.
2. Public Broadcasting System, "Excerpts from 1992 'Defense Policy Guidance.'" Downloaded from http://www.pbs.org/wgbh/pages/frontline/shows/ iraq/ etc/wolf. html (accessed May 14, 2007).
3. Barton Gellman, "Keeping the U.S. First; Pentagon Would Preclude a Rival Superpower," *Washington Post*, March 11, 1992, page A1.
4. Patrick E. Tyler, "Lone Superpower Plan: Ammunition for Critics," *New York Times*, March 10, 1992, page A1.
5. John Lewis Gaddis, *We Now Know: Rethinking Cold War History* (Oxford: Clarendon Press, 1997), page 284.
6. John Lewis Gaddis, *The Cold War: A New History* (New York: Penguin Press, 2005), pages 233–234.
7. Don Oberdorfer, "Thatcher Says Cold War Has Come to an End," *Washington Post*, November 18, 1988, page A1.
8. Timothy Garton Ash, *In Europe's Name: Germany and the Divided Continent* (New York: Vintage Books, 1993), pages 122–124.
9. George Bush and Brent Scowcroft, *A World Transformed* (New York: Alfred A. Knopf, 1998), page 128.
10. George Bush, Speech, Mainz, Germany, Federal News Service, May 31, 1989.
11. Bush and Scowcroft, *A World Transformed*, page 515.
12. Ibid., page 516.
13. Mitchell Reiss, *Bridled Ambition: Why Countries Constrain Their Nuclear Capabilities* (Washington, DC: Woodrow Wilson Center Press, 1995), page 98.
14. James A. Baker III with Thomas M. DeFrank, *The Politics of Diplomacy: Revolution, War and Peace, 1989–1992* (New York: G. P. Putnam's Sons, 1995), page 249.
15. Philiip Zelikow and Condoleezza Rice, *Germany United and Europe Transformed: A Study in Statecraft* (Cambridge, MA: Harvard University Press, 1995), page 352.
16. Stephen Sestanovich, "Not Much Kinder and Gentler," *New York Times*, February 3, 2006, page A27.

17. Mikhail Gorbachev, *Memoirs* (New York: Doubleday, 1995), page 533.
18. For a perceptive analysis of the coup, see John B. Dunlop, "The August Coup and Its Impact on Soviet Politics," *Journal of Cold War Studies*, Volume 5, Issue 1 (Winter 2003), pages 94–127.

Chapter 2   Intervention and Democracy in Central America

1. George Bush inaugural speech on January 20, 1989. Downloaded from http://bushlibrary.tamu.edu/research/papers/1989/89012000.html (accessed May 14, 2007).
2. Testimony of Leo Valladares Lanza before the House Committee on Government Reform and Oversight Subcommittee on Government Management, Information and Technology, May 11, 1998, page 1. Downloaded from http://www.fas.org/sgp/congress/hr051198/valladares.html (accessed May 14, 2007).
3. Gerald F. Seib, "CIA Participated in Nicaragua Raids in '83, Sources Say," *Wall Street Journal*, April 18, 1984.
4. Peter Schweizer, *Reagan's War: The Epic Story of His Forty-Year Struggle and Final Triumph over Communism* (New York: Doubleday, 2002), page 268.
5. For more on the Iran-Contra incident, see Martin Anderson, *Revolution: The Reagan Legacy* (New York: Harcourt Brace Jovanovich, 1988), pages 386–403.
6. Steven Hurst, *The Foreign Policy of the Bush Administration: In Search of a New World Order* (London: Cassell, 1999), page 22.
7. James A. Baker III with Thomas M. DeFrank, *The Politics of Diplomacy: Revolution, War, and Peace, 1989–1992* (New York: G. P. Putnam's Sons, 1995), pages 54–55.
8. Hurst, *The Foreign Policy of the Bush Administration*, page 49.
9. George P. Shultz, *Turmoil and Triumph: My Years as Secretary of State* (New York: Charles Scribner's Sons, 1993), pages 1075–1079.
10. Bill McAllister, "Bush Vows to Press Noriega; Delvalle Reassured of U.S. Policy," *Washington Post*, December 23, 1988, page A8.
11. George Bush, "Remarks and a Question-and-Answer Session with Reporters on the Situation in Panama," May 11, 1989. Downloaded from http:// bushlibrary.tamu.edu/research/papers/1989/89051100.html (accessed May 14, 2007).
12. Baker with DeFrank, *The Politics of Diplomacy*, page 183.
13. Colin Powell with Joseph E. Persico, *My American Journey* (New York: Random House, 1995), page 418.
14. Tom Kenworthy and Joe Pichirallo, "Bush Clears Plan to Topple Noriega," *Washington Post*, November 17, 1989, page A1.
15. Baker with DeFrank, *The Politics of Diplomacy*, page 189.
16. Powell with Persico, *My American Journey*, page 425.
17. Abraham D. Sofaer, "The Legality of the United States Action in Panama," *Columbia Journal of Transnational Law*, Volume 29 (1991), pages 284–285.
18. Lawrence A. Yates, "Operation JUST CAUSE in Panama City, December 1989," *Urban Operations: An Historical Casebook* (Fort Leavenworth, KS: Combat Studies Institute, Command & General Staff College, 2002), page 17.
19. Ibid.
20. Ibid.
21. Margaret E. Scranton, *The Noriega Years: U.S.-Panamanian Relations, 1981–1990* (Boulder, CO: Lynne Rienner Publishers, 1991), pages 207–208.
22. Lorenzo Crowell, "The Anatomy of Just Cause: The Forces Involved, the Adequacy of Intelligence, and Its Success as a Joint Operation," in *Operation Just Cause: The U.S.*

Intervention in Panama, ed. Bruce W. Watson and Peter G. Tsouras (Boulder, CO: Westview Press, 1991), page 95.

23. Powell with Persico, *My American Journey*, page 430.

CHAPTER 3   THE PERSIAN GULF WAR

1. William L. Cleveland, *A History of the Modern Middle East* (Boulder, CO: Westview Press, 2000), pages 395–397; and Charles Tripp, *A History of Iraq* (New York: Cambridge University Press, 2002), pages 167, 193–197.

2. Tripp, *A History of Iraq*, pages 250–252.

3. Joel Brinkley, "Israel Puts a Satellite in Orbit a Day after Threat by Iraqis," *New York Times*, April 4, 1990, page A3.

4. Amatzia Baram, "The Iraqi Invasion of Kuwait: Decision-Making in Baghdad," in *Iraq's Road to War*, ed. Amatzia Baram and Barry Rubin (New York: St. Martin's Press, 1993), page 12.

5. James A. Baker III with Thomas M. DeFrank, *The Politics of Diplomacy: Revolution, War, and Peace, 1989–1992* (New York: G. P. Putnam's Son, 1995), page 263.

6. Michael R. Gordon, "U.S. Deploys Air and Sea Forces after Iraq Threatens 2 Neighbors," *New York Times*, July 25, 1990, page A1.

7. George Bush and Brent Scowcroft, *A World Transformed* (New York: Alfred A. Knopf, 1998), page 311.

8. John F. Burns, "A Cadillac and Other Plunder," *New York Times*, December 30, 2002, page A1.

9. Bush and Scowcroft, *A World Transformed*, page 332.

10. Ibid., pages 346–347.

11. Rick Atkinson, *Crusade: The Untold Story of the Persian Gulf War* (Boston, MA: Houghton Mifflin, 1993), pages 81–85.

12. Margaret Thatcher, *The Downing Street Years* (New York: HaperCollins, 1993), page 824.

13. Bush and Scowcroft, *A World Transformed*, page 370.

14. George H. W. Bush, "Address to the 44th Session of the United Nations General Assembly," New York, September 23, 1991, George Bush Presidential Library. Downloaded from http://bushlibrary.tamu.edu/research/papers/1991/91092301.html (accessed May 14, 2007).

15. Patrick J. Buchanan, *A Republic, Not an Empire* (Washington, DC: Regenery, 1999), page 359.

16. Michael R. Gordon, "In Case of War, Congress Wants Right to Meet," *New York Times*, October 25, 1990, page A12.

17. The War Powers Act of 1973, Public Law 93–148, 93rd Congress, November 7, 1973. Downloaded from http://www.thecre.com/fedlaw/legal22/warpow.htm (accessed May 11, 2007).

18. Bush and Scowcroft, *A World Transformed*, page 429.

19. Anonymous, "Iraqi Scientist Discusses A-Bomb Effort," *New York Times*, January 28, 2005, page A8; and Dafna Linzer, "Arms Reports Names Western Suppliers to Nuke Program," *Washington Post*, December 18, 2002, page 13.

20. Colin Powell with Joseph E. Persico, *My American Journey* (New York: Random House, 1995), page 521.

21. Bush and Scowcroft, *A World Transformed*, page 489.

22. Powell with Persico, *My American Journey*, page 526.

23. Cited by George F. Will, "What to Ask the Nominee," *Washington Post*, November 17, 2004, page A27.

24. For more on the aftereffects of the war, see, e.g., Richard Leiby, "The Fallout of War," *Washington Post*, December 30, 2002, page C1; and John J. Fialka, "U.S. Debates Dangers of Depleted Uranium," *Wall Street Journal*, January 2, 2003, page 1. For the identification of some cases of Lou Gehrig's disease see Rita Rubin, "Studies Tie Lou Gerhig Disease to Gulf War Vets," *USA Today*, September 23, 2003, page 1.

25. Executive Summary, "The Wages of War: Iraqi Combatants and Noncombatant Fatalities in the 2003 Conflict," page 2. Downloaded from http://www.comw.org/pda/0310rm8exsum.html (accessed May 14, 2007).

26. Michael R. Gordon and Bernard E. Trainor, *The General's War: The Inside Story of the Conflict in the Gulf* (Boston, MA: Little, Brown, 1995), page 37.

27. Nicholas D. Kristof, "U.S. Cyclone Relief Forces Reach Bangladesh Port," *New York Times*, May 16, 1991, page A12.

28. "The President's News Conference on the Persian Gulf Conflict," Washington, DC, March 1, 1991, George H. W. Bush Presidential Library. Downloaded from http://bushlibrary.tamu.edu/research/papers/1991/91030103.html (accessed May 14, 2007).

29. "Remarks and an Exchange with Reporters Prior to Discussions with Prince Bandar sin Sultan of Saudi Arabia," February 28, 1991, George H. W. Bush Presidential Library. Downloaded from http://bushlibrary.tamu.edu/research/papers/1991/ 91022804.html (accessed May 14, 2007).

30. Gordon and Trainor, *The General's War*, pages 446–448.

31. John F. Burns, "Iraq's Thwarted Ambitions Litter an Old Nuclear Plant," *New York Times*, December 27, 2002, page A1.

32. Robert S. Litwak, *Rogue States and U.S. Foreign Policy: Containment after the Cold War* (Washington, DC: Woodrow Wilson Center Press, 2000), page 126.

33. Barton Gellman, "U.S. Attacks Industrial Site near Baghdad," *Washington Post*, January 18, 1993, page A1.

CHAPTER 4   GLOBALIZATION, SOMALIA, RWANDA, AND HAITI

1. Elizabeth Drew, *On the Edge: The Clinton Presidency* (New York: Simon and Schuster, 1994), page 138.

2. A transcript of the President Bill Clinton's Inaugural Address appeared entitled "We Force the Spring" in the *New York Times*, January 21, 1993, page A11.

3. Thomas L. Friedman, "Foreign Policy Cooks on Back Bruner," *New York Times*, February 8, 1993, page A5. For a close account of the Clinton administration's almost exclusive attention to domestic issues during the first year, see Bob Woodward, *The Agenda: Inside the Clinton White House* (New York: Simon and Schuster, 1994).

4. Drew, *On the Edge*, page 28.

5. James M. Goldgeier and Michael McFaul, *Power and Purpose: U.S. Policy toward Russia after the Cold War* (Washington, DC: Brookings Institution Press, 2003), pages 119–121.

6. George Friedman and Meredith Lebard, *The Coming War with Japan* (New York: St. Martin's Press, 1991).

7. Francis Fukuyama, "The End of History," *National Interest*, Issue 16 (Summer 1989), page 3; and Francis Fukuyama, *The End of History and the Last Man* (New York: Free Press, 1992).

8. Robert D. Kaplan, "The Coming Anarchy," *Atlantic Monthly*, Volume 273, Issue 2 (February 1994), pages 44–61.

9. Samuel Huntington, *The Clash of Civilizations and the Remaking of the World Order* (New York: Simon and Schuster, 1996).

10. Edward Mortimer, "Sights Set on a Wider World: The Imperatives Guiding America's Hesitant Foreign Policy," *Financial Times*, September 17, 1993, page 17.

11. Anthony Lake, "From Containment to Enlargement," Johns Hopkins University, September 21, 1993. Downloaded fromhttp://www.mtholyoke.edu/acad/intrel/lakedoc.html (accessed May 14, 2007).

12. Thomas L. Friedman, "Theory vs. Practice: Clinton's Stated Foreign Policy Turns into More Modest 'Self-Containment,'" *New York Times*, October 1, 1993, page A2.

13. Michael R. Gordon, "Christopher, in Unusual Cable, Defends State Dept.," *New York Times*, June 16, 1993, page A13.

14. Ibid.

15. Madeleine K. Albright, "Myths of Peace-Keeping," Statement Before the Subcommittee on International Security, International Organizations, and Human Rights of the House Committee on Foreign Affairs, June 24, 1993, cited in *U.S. Department of State Dispatch*, Volume 4, Issue 26 (June 24, 1993), page 46.

16. Mark Bowden, *Black Hawk Down: A Story of Modern War* (New York: New American Library, 1999), page 43.

17. Mark Bowden, "The Lessons of Mogadishu," *Wall Street Journal*, April 5, 2004, page A18.

18. Rowan Scarborough, "Mogadishu Lessons Help Foil Saddam's Strategy," *Washington Times*, April 8, 2003, page 1.

19. Marc Sageman, *Understanding Terror Networks* (Philadelphia, PA: University of Pennsylvania Press, 2004), page 48.

20. Drew, *On the Edge*, page 317.

21. Bowden, *Black Hawk Down*, pages 415–417.

22. Douglas Jehl, "Clinton Doubling U.S. Forces in Somalia, Vowing Troops Will Come Home in 6 Months," *New York Times*, October 8, 1993, page A1.

23. George P. Shultz, *Turmoil and Triumph: My Years as Secretary of State* (New York: Charles Scribner's Sons, 1993), page 339.

24. Drew, *On the Edge*, page 326.

25. Eric Schmitt, "Somalia's First Lesson for Military Is Caution," *New York Times*, March 5, 1995, page B15.

26. L. R. Melvern, *A People Betrayed: The Role of the West in Rwanda's Genocide* (London: Zed Books, 2000), page 26.

27. Ibid., page 190.

28. Michael Barnett, *Eyewitness to a Genocide: The United Nations and Rwanda* (Ithaca, NY: Cornell University Press, 2002), pages 149–151.

29. Holly J. Burkhalter, "The Question of Genocide. The Clinton Administration and Rwanda," *World Policy Journal*, Volume 11, Issue 4 (Winter 1994–1995), page 53.

30. Niall Ferguson, "A World without Power," *Foreign Policy*, Issue 143 (July–August 2004), pages 11–16.

31. Estimates of Haitian frozen financial assets in the United States ran between $30 million and $50 million. See Christopher Caldwell, "Aristide Development," *American Spectator*, Volume 27, Issue 7 (July 1994), page 35.

32. David Lauter, "Clinton Blasts Bush's Foreign Policy Record," *Los Angeles Times*, August 14, 1992, page A1.

33. UNMIH Fact Sheet, UN Department of Peacekeeping Operations. Downloaded from http://www.un.org/Depts/dpko/dpko/co_mission/unmih.htm (accessed May 14, 2007).

34. Madeleine Albright with Bill Woodward, *Madam Secretary* (New York: Miramax Books, 2003), page 156.

35. Robert Fatton Jr., *Haiti's Predatory Republic: The Unending Transition to Democracy* (Boulder, CO: Lynne Rienner, 2002), page 93.

36. Raymond A. Joseph, "Haitian Death Chamber Could Only Worsen with Aristide," *Wall Street Journal*, April 1, 1994, page A9.

37. Raymond A. Joseph, "The Haiti Imbroglio," *Wall Street Journal*, April 6, 2004, page A16.

38. David Malone, *Decision-Making in the UN Security Council: The Case of Haiti, 1990–1997* (New York: Oxford University Press, 1998), page 101.

39. Ibid., page 162.

40. Richard D. Lyons, "U.N. Authorizes Invasion of Haiti to be Led by U.S.," *New York Times*, August 1, 1994, page A1.

41. Doyle McManus and Robin Wright, "U.S. Tried Covert Action to Rid Haiti of Rulers," *Los Angeles Times*, September 16, 1994, page A1.

42. David W. Brady and Craig Volden, *Revolving Gridlock: Politics and Policy from Carter to Clinton* (New York: Westview Press, 1998), pages 123–135.

43. Douglas Jehl, "From Haiti, Images of a Foreign Policy Success," *New York Times*, April 11, 1995, page A4.

44. Bill Clinton, "1996 State of the Union Address." U.S. Capitol, January 23, 1996 Downloaded from http://clinton4.nara.gov/WH/New/other/sotu.html (accessed May 14, 2007).

CHAPTER 5   BOSNIA: WAR AND INTERVENTION

1. Noel Malcolm, *Bosnia: A Short History* (New York: New York University Press, 1994), page 20.

2. James A. Baker III with Thomas M. DeFrank, *The Politics of Diplomacy: Revolution, War, and Peace, 1989–1992* (New York: G. P. Putnam's Sons, 1995), page 636.

3. Michael Kelly, "Surrender and Blame," *New Yorker*, December 19, 1994, page 45.

4. Baker with DeFrank, *The Politics of Diplomacy*, page 651.

5. David Gardner, "EC Dashes into Its Own Backyard," *Financial Times*, July 1, 1991, page 2.

6. At least one observer concluded that Baker, in fact, gave Belgrade a green light to use force to stop the secessionist republics. Tim Judah, *Kosovo: War and Revenge* (New Haven, CT: Yale University Press, 2002), page 138.

7. Malcolm, *Bosnia: A Short History*, page 230.

8. Timothy Garton Ash, *History of the Present: Essays, Sketches, and Dispatches from Europe in the 1990s* (New York: Random House, 1999), page 161.

9. For an account of European diplomatic endeavors, see Stanley Hoffman, "Yugoslavia: Implications for Europe and European Institutions," in *The World and Yugoslavia's Wars*, ed. Richard H. Ullman (New York: Council on Foreign Relations, 1996), pages 97–121.

10. Don Oberdorfer, "A Bloody Failure in the Balkans," *Washington Post*, February 8, 1993, page A1.

11. Malcolm, *Bosnia: A Short History*, pages 218–219.

12. "U.S. Support for CSCE," *U.S. Department of State Dispatch*, Volume 3, Issue 28 (July 13, 1992), page 1.

13. Richard Holbrooke, *To End a War* (New York: Random House, 1998), page 23.

14. For a discussion of the Vance-Owen plan, see Laura Silber and Allan Little, *Yugoslavia: Death of a Nation* (New York: Penguin Books, 1995), pages 276–290.

15. Thomas L. Friedman, "Bosnia Reconsidered," *New York Times*, April 8, 1993, page A5.
16. Elizabeth Drew, *On the Edge: The Clinton Presidency* (New York: Simon and Schuster, 1994), page 153.
17. Colin Powell with Joseph E. Persico, *My American Journey* (New York: Random House, 1995), page 576.
18. Drew, *On the Edge*, page 156.
19. Silber and Little, *Yugoslavia: Death of a Nation*, page 274.
20. Statement by Secretary of State Warren Christopher before the House Foreign Affairs Committee, Washington, DC, May 18, 1993, page 4. Downloaded from State Department's Electronic Research Collection. Downloaded from http:// dosfan.lib.uic. edu/ERC/briefing/dossec/1993/9305/930518dossec.html (accessed May 14, 2007).
21. Michael E. Gordon, "Modest Air Operation in Bosnia Crosses a Major Political Frontier," *New York Times*, April 11, 1994, page A1.
22. Todd S. Purdum, "Clinton Vetoes Lifting Bosnia Arms Embargo," *New York Times*, August 12, 1994, page A1.
23. Tim Weiner, "Clinton Withholds Bosnia Data from Congress," *New York Times*, April 17, 1996, page 1A.
24. Bill Clinton, *My Life* (New York: Alfred Knopf, 2004), page 666.
25. Silber and Little, *Yugoslavia: Death of a Nation*, page 350.
26. P. W. Singer, *Corporate Warriors: The Rise of the Privatized Military Industry* (Ithaca, NY: Cornell University Press, 2003), pages 127–129.
27. Ibid., pages 213–215.
28. Robert C. Owen, ed., *Deliberate Force: A Case Study in Effective Air Campaign* (Montgomery, AL: Air University Press, 2000), pages 506–515.
29. Holbrooke, *To End a War*, page 106.
30. Ibid., page 214.
31. Strobe Talbott, *The Russian Hand: A Memoir of Presidential Diplomacy* (New York: Random House, 2002), page 186.
32. Richard Holbrooke, "America, a European Power," *Foreign Affairs*, Volume 74, Issue 2 (March/April 1995), page 40.
33. Anonymous, "The Road to 'Ethnic Cleansing,'" *Wall Street Journal*, June 11, 1996, page 18.
34. Holbrooke, *To End a War*, page 359, italics is in the original.

CHAPTER 6   KOSOVO: ROUND TWO IN THE BALKANS

1. Tim Judah, *Kosovo: War and Revenge* (New Haven, CT: Yale University Press, 2002), pages 25–31 and 53–54.
2. Noel Malcolm, *Kosovo: A Short History* (New York: New York University Press, 1998), page 348.
3. Warren Zimmermann, *Origins of a Catastrophe: Yugoslavia and Its Destroyers* (New York: Time Warner Books, 1996), page 20.
4. David C. Gompert, "The United States and Yugoslavia's Wars," in *The World and Yugoslavia's Wars*, ed. Richard H. Ullman (New York: Council of Foreign Relations Book, 1996), pages 136–137.
5. David Binder, "Bush Warns Serbs Not to Widen War," *New York Times*, December 28, 1992, page A6.
6. Judah, *Kosovo: War and Revenge*, page 127.

7. For example, see a letter to U.S. Ambassador Robert Gelbard from Serbian president Vojin Joksomivich, July 21, 1998, in the Balkan Repository Project. Downloaded from http://www.balkan-archive.org.yu/news/who_articles/suc73.html (accessed May 14, 2007).

8. For a scholarly and dissenting analysis of the Westphalian model, see Stephen D. Krasner, *Sovereignty: Organized Hypocrisy* (Princeton, NJ: Princeton University Press, 1999), especially pages 24, 129, and 155.

9. Press Conference by President Clinton and President Yeltsin, White House, September 2, 1998. Downloaded from http://www.fas.org/news/russia/1998/98090202_tpo.html (accessed May 14, 2007).

10. Strobe Talbott, *The Russia Hand: A Memoir of Presidential Diplomacy* (New York: Random House, 2002), page 301.

11. Ibid., pages 301–302.

12. United Nations Resolution, 1199, September 23, 1998. Download from http://www.un.org/peace/kosovo/98sc1199.htm (accessed May 14, 2007).

13. Judah, *Kosovo: War and Revenge*, page 183.

14. Talbott, *The Russia Hand*, page 302.

15. Tony Weymouth and Stanley Henig, *The Kosovo Crisis: The Last American War in Europe?* (London: Reuters, 2001), pages 87–88.

16. John Pilger, "What Really Happened at Rambouillet? And What Else Is Being Kept under Wraps by Our Selective Media?" *New Statesman*, May 30, 1991, page 1.

17. Wesley K. Clark, *Waging Modern War: Bosnia, Kosovo, and the Future of Combat* (New York: Public Affairs, 2001), page 421.

18. Jane Perlez, "Step By Step: How the U.S. Decided to Attack, and Why So Fast," *New York Times*, March 26, 1999, page A1.

19. Sidney Blumenthal, *The Clinton Wars* (New York: Farrar, Straus and Giroux, 2003), pages 632–633; and Madeleine Albright with Bill Woodward, *Madame Secretary* (New York: Miramax Books, 2003), page 406.

20. *PBS Frontline's* "War in Europe, Part 1," aired February 22, 2000. Downloaded from http://www.pbs.org/wgbh/pages/frontline/shows/kosovo/etc/script1.html (accessed May 14, 2007).

21. For the best analysis of the air campaign, see Benjamin S. Lambeth, *Transformation of American Air Power* (Ithaca, NY: Cornell University Press, 2000), pages 181–232.

22. Judah, *Kosovo: War and Revenge*, pages 258 and 264.

23. "In the President's Words: 'We Act to Prevent a Wider War,'" excerpts in *New York Times*, March 25, 1999, page A6.

24. Peter Riddell, *Hug Them Close: Blair, Clinton, Bush and the "Special Relationship"* (London: Politico's Publishing, 2003), pages 106–112.

25. Katharine Q. Seelye, "Clinton Resists Renewed Calls for Ground Troops in Kosovo," *New York Times*, May 19, 1999, page A10.

26. Blumenthal, *The Clinton Wars*, page 648.

27. Jane Perlez, "Clinton and Joint Chiefs to Discuss Ground Invasion," *New York Times*, June 2, 1999, page A14.

28. That the ground threat was *the* critical factor has been advanced by several experts. For example, see Clark, *Waging Modern War*, page 425; Benjamin S. Lambeth, *NATO's Air War for Kosovo: A Strategic and Operational Assessment* (Santa Monica, CA: RAND, 2001), page 76; and Ivo H. Daalder and Michael E. O'Hanlon, *Winning Ugly: NATO's War to Save Kosovo* (Washington, DC: Brookings Institution Press, 2000), pages 158–160, 214.

29. Talbott, *The Russia Hand*, page 297.

30. Ibid., page 314.
31. Stephen T. Hosmer, *The Conflict over Kosovo: Why Milosevic Decided to Settle When He Did* (Santa Monica, CA: RAND, 2001), pages 91–120.
32. Clark, *Waging Modern War*, page 394.
33. Bob Davis, "Clinton's Kosovo Policy Has Echoes of LBJ, Vietnam," *Wall Street Journal*, April 1, 1999, page A24; James Hoagland, "Shades of LBJ," *Washington Post*, April 7, 1999, page A 21; and James R. Schlesinger, "Idealism Won't End It," *Washington Post*, March 31, 1999 page A29.
34. Blumenthal, *The Clinton Wars*, page 652.
35. Jim Hoagland, "The Trouble With Playing Global Cop," *Washington Post*, September 2, 1999, page A39; Kay Bailey Hutchison, "The Case for Strategic Sense," *Washington Post*, September 13, 1999, page A 27; and Michael Mandelbaum, "Foreign Policy as Social Work," *Foreign Affairs*, Volume 75, Number 1 (January/February 1996), pages 16–32.
36. "Words of Clinton: 'Three Resolutions for the New Millennium,'" excerpts of Bill Clinton's United Nations General Assembly address in *New York Times*, September 22, 1999, page A 6.
37. Barry Schweid, "Albright Renews Anti-Milosevic Plan," Associated Press, June 29, 2000.

CHAPTER 7 CONTAINING NORTH KOREA, IRAQ, AND TERRORISM

1. Walter A. McDougall, *Promised Land, Crusader State: The American Encounter with the World since 1776* (New York: Houghton Mifflin Company, 1995), page 212.
2. For more extensive coverage of the rogue state phenomenon, see Thomas H. Henriksen, "The Rise and Decline of Rogue States," *Journal of International Affairs*, Volume 54, Issue 2 (Spring 2001), pages 349–373.
3. David F. Sanger, "Cheney, in Korea, Orders Halt to U.S. Pullout," *New York Times*, December 22, 1991, page A7.
4. Don Oberdorfer, *The Two Koreas: A Contemporary History* (Reading, MA: Addison-Wesley, 1997), page 269.
5. Michael R. Gordon, "U.S. Will Urge U.N. to Plan Sanctions for North Korea," *New York Times*, March 20, 1994, page A1.
6. Robin Wright, *The Last Great Revolution: Turmoil and Transformation in Iran* (New York: Alfred A. Knopf, 2000), page 292.
7. Kenneth M. Pollack, *The Threatening Storm: The Case for Invading Iraq* (New York: Random House, 2002), pages 76–78.
8. Robert Baer, *See No Evil: The True Story of a Ground Soldier in the CIA's War on Terrorism* (New York: Three Rivers Press, 2002), pages 215–218.
9. Charles Tripp, *A History of Iraq* (Cambridge, UK: Cambridge University Press, 2000), pages 272–273.
10. William J. Clinton, "1998 State of the Union Address." U.S. Capitol, January 27, 1998. Downloaded from http://www.washingtonpost.com/wp-srv/politics/special/states/docs/sou98.htm (accessed May 9, 2007).
11. Richard Butler, *The Greatest Threat: Iraq, Weapons of Mass Destruction and the Growing Crisis in Global Security* (New York: Public Affairs, 2000), pages 141–142.
12. A transcript, "Clinton's Statement: 'We Are Delivering a Powerful Message to Saddam,'" *New York Times*, December 17, 1998, page A16.
13. William J. Clinton, "The President's Radio Address," December 19, 1998. Downloaded from http://www.presidency.ucsb.edu/ws/index.php?pid=55434 (accessed May 14, 2007).

14. Tripp, *A History of Iraq*, page 278.

15. Thomas E. Ricks, "Containing Iraq: A Forgotten War," *Washington Post*, October 25, 2000, page A1.

16. George P. Shultz, *Turmoil and Triumph: My Years as Secretary of State* (New York: Charles Scribner's Sons, 1993), page 648.

17. Joseph T. Stanik, *El Dorado Canyon: Reagan's Undeclared War with Qaddafi* (Annapolis, MD: U.S. Naval Institute Press, 2002), pages 155–165.

18. Larry P. Goodson, *Afghanistan's Endless War: State Failure, Regional Politics, and the Rise of the Taliban* (Seattle, WA: University of Washington Press, 2001), pages 76, 106, 111.

19. Bernard Lewis, "The Roots of Muslim Rage," *Atlantic Monthly*, September 1990, page 56.

20. "Combating Terrorism in Saudi Arabia," *Defense Issues*, Volume 11, Number 59. Downloaded from http://www.defenselink.mil/speeches/speech.aspx?speechid=986 (accessed May 15, 2007).

21. Text of Fatwah Urging Jihad against Americans and Jews. Downloaded from http://www.fas.org/irp/world/para/docs/980223-fatwa.htm (accessed May 15, 2007).

22. Anonymous, *Through Our Enemies' Eyes: Osama bin Laden, Radical Islam, and the Future of America* (Washington, DC: Brassey's, 2002), page 175.

23. Osama bin Laden's 1996 fatwa, "Declaration of War against the Americans Occupying the Lands of the Two Holy Places." Downloaded from http://www.pbs.org/newshour/terrorism/international/fatwa_1996.htm.

24. Yossef Bodansky, *Bin Laden: The Man Who Declared War on America* (Roseville California: Prima Publishing, 1999), page 287; and Dan Eggen and John Mintz, "9/11 Panel Critical of Clinton, Bush," *Washington Post*, March 24, 2004, page A1.

25. Address to the Nation by the President, White House, August 20, 1998. Downloaded from http://www.pbs.org/newshour/bb/military/july-dec98/clinton2_8-20.html (accessed May 15, 2007).

26. Tommy Franks with Malcolm McConnell, *American Soldier* (New York: Regan/HarperCollins, 2004), page 227.

27. Richard H. Shultz, Jr., *The Secret War against Hanoi: Kennedy's and Johnson's Use of Spies, Saboteurs, and Covert Warriors in North Vietnam* (New York, HarperCollins, 1999), pages 267–277.

28. *The 9/11 Commission Report: Final Report of the National Commission Terrorist Attacks Upon The United States* (New York: W. W. Norton, 2004), page 139.

29. Steve Coll, *Ghost Wars: The Secret History of the CIA, Afghanistan, Bin Laden, from the Soviet Invasion to September 10, 2001* (New York: Penguin Press, 2004), pages 372–376.

30. Daniel Benjamin and Steven Simon, *The Sacred Age of Terror*, (New York: Random House, 2002), pages 323–24.

31. Bill Clinton, *My Life* (New York: Alfred A. Knopf, 2004), page 935.

CHAPTER 8   ATTACKING AFGHANISTAN

1. Charlie Coon, "Troops in Horn of Africa Hope to Keep Terrorists at Bay by Helping People," *European Stars and Strips*, November 21, 2004, page 1.

2. The quotation is from Condoleezza Rice, Transformational Diplomacy, Department of State Fact Sheet, January 18, 2006. Downloaded from http://www.state.gov/r/pa/prs/ps/2006/59339.htm (accessed May 15, 2007).

3. Bill Sammon, *Fighting Back: The War on Terrorism—From Inside the Bush White House* (Washington, DC: Regnery Publishing, 2002), pages 187–188.

4. George W. Bush, "Address to the Joint Sessions of Congress and the American People," September 19, 2001. Downloaded from http://www.whitehouse.gov/news/releases/2001/09/20010920-8.html (accessed May 15, 2007).

5. Bob Woodward, *Bush at War* (New York: Simon and Schuster, 2002), page 195.

6. Dore Gold, *Hatred's Kingdom: How Saudi Arabia Supports the New Global Terrorism* (Washington, DC: Regnery Publishing, 2003), pages 116–123.

7. Elisabeth Bumiller, "A Nation Challenged: The President; All Must Join Fight Against Terror, Bush Tells U.N.," *New York Times*, November 11, 2001, page A1.

8. Tom Carter, "Diplomat Says Egypt Backs Bush in Handling of War on Terrorism," *Washington Times*, November 9, 2001, page 1.

9. James Mann, *Rise of the Vulcans: The History of Bush's War Cabinet* (New York: Viking, 2004), page 342.

10. Stephen Tanner, *Afghanistan: A Military History from Alexander the Great to the Fall of the Taliban* (New York: Da Capo Press, 2002), page 292.

11. Suzanne Daley, "For First Time, NATO Invokes Pact With U.S.," *New York Time*, September 13, 2001, page A1.

12. William Drozdiak and Rajiv Chandrasekaran, "NATO: U.S. Evidence on Bin Laden 'Compelling,'" *Washington Post*, October 3, 2001, page A11.

13. Suzanne Daley, "Alliance Says It Will Fight If It Is Asked," *New York Times*, October 3, 2001, page A1.

14. Philip Stephens, *Tony Blair: The Making of a World Leader* (New York: Viking, 2004), pages 198 and 200.

15. Daley, "Alliance Says It Will Fight If It Is Asked," page A1.

16. Joseph Fitchett, "U.S. Allies Chafe at 'Cleanup' Role," *International Herald Tribune*, November 26, 2001, page 1.

17. Patrick E. Tyler, "U.S. and Britain Strike Afghanistan, Aiming at Bases And Terrorist Camps," *New York Times*, October 8, 2001, page A1.

18. Neil MacFarquhar and Jim Rutenberg, "Bin Laden, in a Taped Speech, Says Attacks in Afghanistan Are a War against Islam," *New York Times*, November 4, 2001, page A6.

19. Matthew Rose, "In War's Early Phase, News Media Showed a Tendency to Misfire," *Wall Street Journal*, December 24, 2001, page A1.

20. John J. Mearsheimer, "Guns Won't Win the Afghan War," *New York Times*, November 4, 2001, page A 28.

21. Stephen Biddle, *Afghanistan and the Future of Warfare: Implications for Army and Defense Policy* (Carlisle, PA: Strategic Studies Institute of the U.S. Army War College, 2002), pages 51–62.

22. Michael E. O'Hanlon, "A Flawed Masterpiece," *Foreign Affairs*, Volume 81, Issue 3 (May/June, 2002), pages 47 and 56; Ivo Daalder and James M. Lindsay, *America Unbound: The Bush Revolution in Foreign Policy* (Washington, DC: Brookings Institution Press, 2003), page 110.

23. Woodward, *Bush at War*, page 241.

24. Ibid., page 231.

25. Patrick E. Tyler, "U.S. Sees Limited Mission In Postwar Afghanistan," *New York Times*, November 28, 2001, page A1.

26. James Dobbins, John G. McGinn, Keith Crane, Seth G. Jones, Rollie Lal, Andrew Rathmell, Rachel Swanger, and Anga Timilsina, *America's Role in Nation-Building: From Germany to Iraq* (Santa Monica, CA: Rand, 2003), pages 132–134.

27. George W. Bush, "Remarks to the George C. Marshall ROTC Award Seminar on National Security," April 17, 2002. Downloaded from http://www.whitehouse.gov/news/releases/2002/04/20020417-1.html (accessed May 15, 2007).

28. For an illuminating study of the Marshall Plan's historical uniqueness, see Barry Machado, *In Search of a Usable Past: The Marshall Plan and Postwar Reconstruction Today* (Lexington, VA: George C. Marshall Foundation Press, 2007).

CHAPTER 9   IRAQ: INVADED AND OCCUPIED

1. Bob Woodward, *Plan of Attack* (New York: Simon and Schuster, 2004), pages 30, 81–82, and 98.
2. George W. Bush, "State of the Union Address," January 29, 2002. Downloaded from http://www.whitehouse.gov/news/releases/2002/01/20020129-11.html (accessed May 15, 2007).
3. Thom Shanker and David E. Sanger, "U.S. Envisions Blueprint on Iraq Including Big Invasion Next Year," *New York Times*, April 28, 2002, page A1; Eric Scmitt, "U.S. Plans For Iraq Is Said to Include Attack on 3 Sides," *New York Times*, July 5, 2002, page A1; and Thomas E. Ricks, "Timing, Tactics on Iraq War Disputed," *Washington Post*, August 1, 2002, page A1.
4. John Barry and Roy Gutman, "Rumors of War," *Newsweek*, August 12, 2002, page 36.
5. Eric Schmitt and Joel Brinkley, "State Dept. Study Foresaw Troubles Now Plaguing Iraq," *New York Times*, October 19, 2003, page A1.
6. David E. Sanger, "In Reichstag, Bush Condemns Terror as New Despotism," *New York Times*, May 24, 2002, page A1.
7. Editorial, "The Need for One Voice on Iraq," *Financial Times*, July 30, 2002, page 14.
8. George W. Bush, "Graduation Speech at West Point," June 1, 2002. Downloaded from http://www.whitehouse.gov/news/releases/2002/06/20020601-3.html. (accessed May 15, 2007).
9. The *Washington Post* almost exclusively did grasp the significance of the president's message toward Iraq. See its editorial "Taking the Offensive," *Washington Post*, June 4, 2002, page A16.
10. Julia Preston, "U.N. Spy Photo Shows New Building at Iraq Nuclear Sites," *New York Times*, September 6, 2002, page A1.
11. A transcript, "Clinton's Statement: 'We Are Delivering a Powerful Message to Saddam,'" *New York Times*, December 17, 1998, page A16.
12. George W. Bush, "Speech to the United Nations," September 12, 2002. Downloaded from http://www.presidentialrhetoric.com/speeches/09.12.02.html (accessed May 15, 2007).
13. British Dossier on Iraq. Downloaded from http://news.bbc.co.uk/nol/shared/spl/hi/middle_east/02/uk_dossier_on_iraq/pdf/iraqdossier.pdf (accessed May 15, 2007); and Patrick E. Tyler, "Britain's Case: Iraqi Program to Amass Arms Is 'Up and Running,'" *New York Times*, September 25, 2002, page A1.
14. Commission on the Intelligence Capabilities of the United States Regarding Weapons of Mass Destruction, Report to the President, March 31, 2005, page 22. Downloaded from http://www.wmd.gov/report/report.html#chapter1 (accessed May 15, 2007).
15. National Security Strategy, September 17, 2002. Downloaded from http://www.whitehouse.gov/nsc/nss/2002/index.html (accessed May 15, 2007).
16. Ibid.
17. Peter Slevin, "Analysts: New Strategy Courts Unseen Dangers," *Washington Post*, September 22, 2002, page A1; and Judith Miller, "Keeping U.S. No. 1: Is It Wise? Is It New?" *New York Times*, October 26, 2002, page A19.
18. John Lewis Gaddis, *Surprise, Security and the American Experience* (Cambridge, MA: Harvard University Press, 2004), pages 15–20.

19. Norman Graebner, *Foundations of American Foreign Policy: A Realist Appraisal from Franklin to McKinley* (Wilmington, DE: Scholarly Resources, 1985), page 354.

20. Stefan Halper and Jonathan Clarke, *America Alone: The Neo-Conservatives and the Global Order* (New York: Cambridge University Press, 2004), pages 154–156 and 224–231.

21. George W. Bush, "President Bush Outlines Iraqi Threat," White House Press Release, October 7, 2002. Downloaded from http://www.whitehouse.gov/news/releases/2002/10/print/20021007-8.html (accessed May 15, 2007).

22. Richard Morin and Claudia Deane, "71 % Of Americans Support War, Poll Shows," *Washington Post*, March 19, 2003, page A14.

23. Jim VandeHei and Juliet Eilperin, "Congress Passes Iraq Resolution," *Washington Post*, October 11, 2002, page A1.

24. Walter Pincus and Karen DeYoung, "U.S. Sets Late January Decision on Iraq War," *Washington Post*, December 19, 2002, page A1.

25. Betsy Pisik, "U.S., U.N. Spar over Iraq Report," *Washington Times*, December 13, 2002, page 1.

26. Serge Schmemann, "Bush Warns Hussein again but Sidesteps any 'Deadline,'" *New York Times*, January 15, 2003, page A1.

27. Julia Preston, "Threats and Responses: Diplomacy; An Attack On Iraq Not Yet Justified, France Warns U.S.," *New York Times*, January 21, 2003, page A1.

28. R. C. Longworth, "When Rumsfeld Speaks, Europe Bristles," *Chicago Tribune*, February 16, 2003, page A1.

29. Hans Blix, *Disarming Iraq* (New York: Pantheon Books, 2004), pages 178–179.

30. Julia Preston, "U.N. Inspectors Says Iraq Fall Short on Cooperation," *New York Times*, January 28, 2003, page A1.

31. George W. Bush, "State of the Union Address," January 28, 2003. Downloaded from http://www.whitehouse.gov/news/releases/2003/01/20030128-19.html (accessed May 15, 2007).

32. Joseph C. Wilson, "What I Didn't Find in Africa," *New York Times*, July 6, 2003, page 14.

33. "Powell's Remarks to U.N.," *New York Times*, February 6, 2003, page A6.

34. Ibid.

35. Stephen F. Hays, "Saddam's Terror Training Camps," *Weekly Standard*, January 16, 2006, pages 14–16; and Kevin Woods, James Lacey, and Williamson Murray, "Saddam's Delusions: The View From the Inside," *Foreign Affairs*, Volume 85, Number 3 (Volume 85, Number 3), page 16.

36. Craig S. Smith and Richard Bernstein, "NATO Members and Russia Resist U.S. on Iraq Plans," *New York Times*, February 11, 2003, page A1.

37. Robert Kagan, *Of Paradise and Power: America and Europe in the New World Order* (New York: Alfred A. Knopf, 2003), page 3.

38. Elisabeth Bumiller, "Bush's Tutor and Disciple: Condoleezza Rice," *New York Times*, November 17, 2005, page A1.

39. White House Press Release on George W. Bush's Address to the Nation, March 19, 2003. Downloaded from http://www.whitehouse.gov/news/releases/2003/03/20030319-17.html (accessed May 15, 2007).

40. Anthony H. Cordesman, *The Iraq War: Strategy, Tactics, and Military Lessons* (Washington, DC: CSIS Press, 2004), page 123.

41. Anthony Shadid and Rajiv Chandrasekaran, "U.S. Forces Seize 2 Hussein Palaces as Armor Reaches Heart of Baghdad," *Washington Post*, April 8, 2003, page A1.

42. Tommy Franks with Malcolm McConnell, *American Soldier* (New York: Regan Books, 2004), pages 39–93.

43. Ken Adelman, "Cakewalk in Iraq," *Washington Post*, February 13, 2002, page A27 and "'Cakewalk' Revisited," *Washington Post*, April 10, 2003, page A29.
44. Cordesman, *The Iraq War*, page 127.
45. George W. Bush, Remarks by the President from the USS Abraham Lincoln," May 1, 2003. Downloaded from http://www.whitehouse.gov/news/releases/2003/05/20030501-15.html (accessed May 15, 2007).
46. Franks with McConnell, *American Soldier*, pages 418–419.
47. Philip H. Gordon and Michael E. O'Hanlon, "A Tougher Target: The Afghanistan Model of Warfare May Not Apply Very Well to Iraq," *Washington Post*, December 26, 2001, page A31.
48. Niko Price, "AP Tallies 3,240 Civilian Deaths in Iraq," Associated Press, June 10, 2003.
49. Cordesman, *The Iraq War*, pages 228 and 247.
50. Thomas E. Ricks, "U.S. Troop Level in Iraq to Grow," *Washington Post*, December 1, 2004, page A1.
51. Albert R. Hunt, "What Might Have Been," *Wall Street Journal*, December 4, 2003, page A17.
52. John F. Burns, "Looting and a Suicide Attack in Baghdad," *New York Times*, April 11, 2003, page A1.
53. Michael R. Gordon and Bernard E. Trainor, *Cobra II: The Inside Story of the Invasion and Occupation of Iraq* (New York: Pantheon Books, 2006), page 461.
54. Hearing of the U.S. Senate Armed Services Committee, 108th Congress, 1st session, February 25, 2003; and Thom Shanker, "New Strategy Vindicates Ex-Army Chief Shinseki," *New York Times*, January 12, 2007, page A6.
55. Eric Schmitt, "Pentagon Contradicts General on Iraq Occupation Force's Size," *New York Times*, February 28, 2003, page A1.
56. Thom Shanker, "Rumsfeld Defends War Planning," *New York Times*, March 31, 2003, page A1.
57. L. Paul Bremer III with Malcolm McConnell, *My Year in Iraq: The Struggle to Build a Future of Hope* (New York: Simon and Schuster, 2006), page 11.
58. Jeffrey Goldberg, "A Little Learning," *New Yorker*, May 9, 2005, page 12.
59. Larry Diamond, "What Went Wrong in Iraq," *Foreign Affairs* (September/October 2004), pages 44–47.
60. Bremer with McConnell, *My Year in Iraq*, page 171.
61. Eric Schmitt, "2 U.S. Officials Liken Guerrillas to Renegade Postwar Nazi Units," *New York Times*, August 26, 2003, page A6.
62. Vernon Loeb, "Fighting a 'Battle of Perception,'" *Washington Post*, November 10, 2003, page A20.
63. Rajiv Chandrasekaran, "Attacks Force Retreat from Wide-Ranging Plans for Iraq," *Washington Post*, December 28, 2003, page A1.
64. "In Bush's Words: 'Iraqi Democracy Will Succeed,'" excerpts in *New York Times*, November 6, 2003, page A6. Downloaded from http://www.whitehouse.gov/news/releases/2003/11/20031106-2.html (accessed May 15, 2007).
65. Mike Allen, "Bush Apologizes, Calls Abuse 'Stain' on Nation," *Washington Post*, May 7, 2004, page A1.
66. Final Report of the Independent Panel To Review DoD Detention Operations, June 2004. Downloaded from http://www.defense.gov/news/Aug2004/d20040824finalreport.pdf (accessed May 15, 2007).
67. The Independent Inquiry Committee on the Oil-For-Food Program. Downloaded from http://www.iic-offp.org/story27oct05.htm (accessed May 15, 2007).

68. Press Release, Security Council Endorses Formation of Sovereign Interim Government in Iraq, Resolution 1546, June 5, 2004. Downloaded from http://www.un.org/News/Press/docs/2004/sc8117.doc.htm (accessed May 15, 2007).

CHAPTER 10   STABILITY AND SECURITY
THROUGH DEMOCRACY?

1. "President Bush Sworn-In to Second Term," January 20, 2005. Downloaded from http://www.whitehouse.gov/news/releases/2005/01/20050120-1.html (accessed May 15, 2007).
2. Department of Defense directive 3000.5, November 28, 2005. Downloaded from http://www.dtic.mil/whs/directives/corres/pdf/300005p.pdf (accessed May 15, 2007).
3. Condoleezza Rice, Transformational Diplomacy, January 18, 2006. Downloaded from http://www.state.gov/r/pa/prs/ps/2006/59339.htm (accessed May 15, 2007).
4. Office of the Coordinator for Reconstruction and Stabilization. Downloaded from http://www.state.gov/s/crs/ (accessed May 15, 2007).
5. Neil King Jr. and Greg Jaffe, "U.S. Sets New Mission for Keeping the Peace," *Wall Street Journal*, January 3, 2006, page A4.
6. Fareed Zakaria, *The Future of Freedom: Illiberal Democracy at Home and Abroad* (New York: W. W. Norton, 2003), pages 114–117.
7. Edward D. Mansfield and Jack Snyder, *Electing to Fight: Why Emerging Democracies Go to War* (Cambridge, MA: MIT Press, 2005), pages 9–11.
8. Editorial, "Shattered Democracy in Haiti," *New York Times*, March 1, 2004, page A28.
9. Patrick E. Tyler, "Secret Diplomacy Won Libyan Pledge on Arms," *New York Times*, December 21, 2003, page A1.
10. David Sanger, "Libya Thaw to Proceed; Guilt Is Reaffirmed," *New York Times*, February 26, 2004, page A6.
11. David E. Sanger and Judith Miller, "Libya to Give Up Arms Programs, Bush Announces," *New York Times*, December 20, 2003, page A1.
12. Steven R. Weisman, "Powell Says Ukraine Vote Was Full of Fraud," *New York Times*, November 25, 2004, page A10.
13. Condoleezza Rice, "Remarks at the American University in Cairo," June 20, 2005. Downloaded from http://www.state.gov/secretary/rm/2005/48328.htm (accessed May 15, 2007).
14. "Freedom in the World, 2006," Press Release, Freedom House, December 19, 2005. Downloaded from http://www.freedomhouse.org/template.cfm?page=70& release=317 (accessed May 15, 2007).
15. Bret Shephens, "Chinook Diplomacy," *Wall Street Journal*, December 22, 2005, page A14.
16. Husain Haqqani and Kenneth Ballen, "Our Friends the Pakistanis," *Wall Street Journal*, December 19, 2005, page A16.
17. Chairman of the Joint Chiefs of Staff, "National Military Strategy for the War on Terrorism," February 1, 2006. Downloaded from http://www.defenselink.mil/qdr/docs/2005-01-25-Strategic-Plan.pdf. (accessed May 15, 2007).
18. Daniel Williams, "Tehran Courts Support of Arabs," *Washington Post*, March 20, 2006, page A9.
19. Deputy Secretary of State Robert B. Zoellick in a speech to the National Committee on U.S.-China Relations, September 21, 2005. Downloaded from http://www.state.gov/s/d/former/zoellick/rem/53682.htm (accessed May 15, 2007). http://www.state.gov/s/d/rem/53682.htm (accessed May 15, 2007).

20. The White House, The National Security Strategy of the United States of America, March 16, 2006. Downloaded from www.whitehouse.gov/nsc/nss/2006 (accessed May 15, 2007).

21. James A. Baker III and Lee H. Hamilton, *The Iraq Study Group Report* (Los Angeles, CA: Filiquarian Publishing, 2006), page 87.

22. Quoted by David Ignatius, "Abizaid's Long View," *Washington Post*, March 16, 2007, page A21.

23. Susan Page, "Poll: Bush's New Iraq Strategy Fails To Rally Public Support," *USA Today*, January 15, 2007, page A1.

24. "President's Address to the Nation, January 10, 2007." Downloaded from http://www.whitehouse.gov/news/releases/2007/01/20070110-7.html (accessed May 15, 2007).

25. Hassan M. Fattah, "U.S. Iraq Role Is Illegal by Saudi King," *New York Times*, March 29, 2007, page A1.

26. Charles Krauthammer, "The Unipolar Moment," *Foreign Affairs*, Volume 70, Number 1 (Winter 1990), pages 23–33.

BIBLIOGRAPHY

Albright, Madeline, with Bill Woodward. *Madame Secretary.* New York: Miramax Books, 2003.

Anderson, Martin. *Revolution: The Reagan Legacy.* New York: Harcourt Brace Jovanich, 1988.

Anonymous. *Through Our Enemies' Eyes: Osama bin Laden, Radical Islam, and the Future of America.* Washington, DC: Brassey's, 2002.

Atkinson, Rick. *Crusade: The Untold Story of the Persian Gulf War.* Boston, MA: Houghton Mifflin, 1993.

Baer, Robert. *See No Evil: The True Story of a Ground Soldier in the CIA's War on Terrorism.* New York: Three Rivers Press, 2002.

Baker, James A., III, with Thomas M. DeFrank. *The Politics of Diplomacy: Revolution, War and Peace, 1989–1992.* New York: G. P. Putnam's Sons, 1995.

Barnett, Michael. *Eyewitness to a Genocide: The United States and Rwanda.* Ithaca, NY: Cornell University Press, 2002.

Benjamin, Daniel, and Steven Simon. *The Sacred Age of Terror.* New York: Random House, 2002.

Biddle, Stephen. *Afghanistan and the Future of Warfare: Implications for Army and Defense Policy.* Carlisle, PA: U.S. Army War College, 2002.

Blix, Hans. *Disarming Iraq.* New York: Pantheon Books, 2004.

Blumenthal, Sidney. *The Clinton Wars.* New York: Farrar, Straus and Giroux, 2003.

Bodansky, Yossef. *Bin Laden: The Man Who Declared War on America.* Roseville, CA: Prima Publishing, 1999.

Bowden, Mark. *Black Hawk Down: A Story of Modern War.* New York: New American Library, 1999.

Brady, David W., and Craig Volden. *Revolving Gridlock: Politics and Policy from Carter to Clinton.* New York: Westview Press, 1998.

Bremer, L. Paul, III. *My Year in Iraq: The Struggle to Build a Future of Hope.* New York: Simon and Schuster, 2006.

Buchanan, Patrick J. *A Republic, Not an Empire.* Washington, DC: Regnery Publishing, 1999.

Bush, George, and Brent Scowcroft. *A World Transformed.* New York: Alfred A. Knopf, 1998.

Butler, Richard. *The Greatest Threat: Iraq, Weapons of Mass Destruction and the Growing Crisis in Global Security.* New York: Public Affairs, 2000.

Clark, Wesley K. *Waging Modern War: Bosnia, Kosovo, and the Future of Combat.* New York: Public Affairs, 2001.

Cleveland, William L. *A History of the Modern Middle East.* Boulder, CO: Westview Press, 2000.

Clinton, Bill. *My Life.* New York: Alfred Knopf, 2004.

Coll, Steve. *Ghost Wars: The Secret History of the CIA, Afghanistan, Bin Laden, from the Soviet Invasion to September 10, 2001.* New York: Penguin Press, 2004.

Cordesman, Anthony H. *The Iraq War: Strategy, Tactics, and Military Lessons.* Washington, DC: CSIS Press, 2004.

Dobbins, James, James Dobbins, John G. McGinn, Keith Crane, Seth G. Jones, Rollie Lal, Andrew Rathmell, Rachel Swanger, and Anga Timilsina. *America's Role in Nation-Building: From Germany to Iraq.* Santa Monica, CA: Rand, 2003.

Drew, Elizabeth. *On the Edge: The Clinton Presidency.* New York: Simon and Schuster, 1994.

Dunlop, John P. *Russia Confronts Chechnya.* New York: Cambridge University Press, 2002.

Fatton, Robert, Jr. *Haiti's Predatory Republic: The Unending Transition to Democracy.* Boulder, CO: Lynne Rienner, 2002.

Franks, Tommy, with Malcolm McConnell. *American Soldier.* New York: Regan/ HarperCollins, 2004.

Friedman, George, and Meredith Lebard. *The Coming War with Japan.* New York: St. Martin's Press, 1991.

Fukuyama, Francis. *America at the Crossroads: Democracy, Power, and the Neoconservative Legacy.* New Haven, CT: Yale University Press, 2006.

———. *The End of History and the Last Man.* New York: Free Press, 1992.

Gaddis, John Lewis. *The Cold War: A New History.* New York: Penguin Press, 2005.

———. *Surprise, Security and the American Experience.* Cambridge, MA: Harvard University Press, 2004.

———. *We Now Know: Rethinking Cold War History.* Oxford: Clarendon Press, 1997.

Garton Ash, Timothy. *History of the Present: Essays, Sketches, and Dispatches from Europe in the 1990s.* New York: Random House, 1999.

———. *In Europe's Name: Germany and the Divided Continent.* New York: Vintage Books, 1993.

Gold, Dore. *Hatred's Kingdom: How Saudi Arabia Supports the New Global Terrorism.* Washington, DC: Regnery Publishing, 2003.

Goldgeier, James M., and Michael McFaul. *Power and Purpose: U.S. Policy toward Russia after the Cold War.* Washington, DC: Brookings Institution Press, 2003.

Goodson, Larry P. *Afghanistan's Endless War: State Failure, Regional Politics, and the Rise of the Taliban.* Seattle, WA: University of Washington Press, 2001.

Gordon, Michael R., and Bernard E. Trainor. *Cobra II: The Inside Story of the Invasion and Occupation of Iraq.* New York: Pantheon, 2006.

———. *The General's War: The Inside Story of the Conflict in the Gulf.* Boston, MA: Little, Brown, 1995.

Graebner, Norman. *Foundations of American Foreign Policy: A Realist Appraisal from Franklin to McKinley.* Wilmington, DE: Scholarly Resources, 1985.

Henriksen, Thomas H., ed. *Foreign Policy for America in the Twenty-First Century.* Stanford, CA: Hoover Institution Press, 2001.

Holbrooke, Richard. *To End A War.* New York: Random House, 1998.

Hosmer, Stephen T. *The Conflict Over Kosovo: Why Milosevic Decided to Settle When He Did.* Santa Monica, CA: Rand, 2001.

Huntington, Samuel. *The Clash of Civilizations and the Remaking of the World Order.* New York: Simon and Schuster, 1996.

Hurst, Steven. *The Foreign Policy of the Bush Administration: In Search of a New World Order.* London: Cassell, 1999.

Iraq Study Group. *The Iraq Study Group Report: The Way Forward—A New Approach.* New York: Vintage, 2006.

Judah, Tim. *Kosovo: War and Revenge.* New Haven, CT: Yale University Press, 2002.

Kagan, Robert. *Of Paradise and Power: America and Europe in the New World Order.* New York: Alfred A. Knopf, 2003.

Krasner, Stephen D. *Sovereignty: Organized Hypocrisy.* Princeton, NJ: Princeton University Press, 1999.

Lambeth, Benjamin S. *Transformation of American Air Power*. Ithaca, NY: Cornell University Press, 2000.

Litwak, Robert S. *Rogue States and U.S. Foreign Policy: Containment after the Cold War*. Washington, DC: Woodrow Wilson Center Press, 2000.

Machado, Barry. *In Search of a Usable Past: The Marshall Plan and Postwar Reconstruction Today*. Lexington, VA: George C. Marshall Foundation Press, 2007.

Malcolm, Noel. *Bosnia: A Short History*. New York: New York University Press, 1994.

———. *Kosovo: A Short History*. New York: New York University Press, 1998.

Malone, David. *Decision-Making in the UN Security Council: The Case of Haiti, 1990–1997*. New York: Oxford University Press, 1998.

Mann, James. *Rise of the Vulcans: The History of Bush's War Cabinet*. New York: Viking, 2004.

Mansfield, Edward D., and Jack Snyder. *Electing to Fight: Why Emerging Democracies Go to War*. Cambridge, MA: MIT Press, 2005.

McDougall, Walter A. *Promised Land, Crusader State: The American Encounter with the World since 1776*. New York: Houghton Mifflin, 1995.

Melvern, L. R. *A People Betrayed: The Role of the West in Rwanda's Genocide*. London: Zed Books, 2000.

National Commission on Terrorist Attacks upon the United States. *The 9/11 Commission Report: Final Report of the National Commission on Terrorist Attacks upon the United States*. New York: W. W. Norton, 2004.

Oberdorfer, Don. *The Two Koreas: A Contemporary History*. Reading, MA: Addison-Wesley, 1997.

Owen, Robert C., ed. *Deliberate Force: A Case Study in Effective Air Campaign*. Montgomery, AL: Air University Press, 2000.

Pollack, Kenneth M. *The Threatening Storm: The Case for Invading Iraq*. New York: Random House, 2002.

Powell, Colin, with Joseph E. Persico. *My American Journey*. New York: Random House, 1995.

Reiss, Mitchell. *Bridled Ambition: Why Countries Constrain Their Nuclear Capabilities*. Washington, DC: Woodrow Wilson Center Press, 1995.

Riddell, Peter. *Hug Them Close: Blair, Clinton, Bush and the "Special Relationship."* London: Politico's Publishing, 2003.

Sammon, Bill. *Fighting Back: The War on Terrorism—From Inside the Bush White House*. Washington, DC: Regnery Publishing, 2002.

Schweizer, Peter. *Reagan's War: The Epic Story of His Forty-Year Struggle and Final Triumph over Communism*. New York: Doubleday, 2002.

Scranton, Margaret E. *The Noriega Years: U.S.-Panamanian Relations, 1981–1990*. Boulder, CO: Lynn Rienner Publishers, 1991.

Shultz, George P. *Turmoil and Triumph: My Years as Secretary of State*. New York: Charles Scribner's Sons, 1993.

Shultz, Richard H., Jr. *The Secret War Against Hanoi: Kennedy's and Johnson's Use of Spies, Saboteurs, and Covert Warriors in North Vietnam*. New York: HarperCollins, 1999.

Silber, Laura, and Allan Little. *Yugoslavia: Death of a Nation*. New York: Penguin Books, 1995.

Singer, P. W. *Corporate Warriors: The Rise of the Privatized Military Industry*. Ithaca, NY: Cornell University Press, 2003.

Stanik, Joseph T. *El Dorado Canyon: Reagan's Undeclared War with Qaddafi*. Annapolis, MD: U.S. Naval Institute Press, 2002.

Stephens, Philip. *Tony Blair: The Making of a World Leader*. New York. Viking, 2004.

Talbott, Strobe. *The Russian Hand: A Memoir of Presidential Diplomacy*. New York: Random House, 2002.

Tanner, Stephen. *Afghanistan; A Military History from Alexander the Great to the Fall of the Taliban*. New York: Da Capo Press, 2002.

Tripp, Charles. *A History of Iraq.* New York: Cambridge University Press, 2000.

Weymouth, Tony, and Stanley Henig, *The Kosovo Crisis: The Last American War in Europe?* London: Reuters, 2001.

Wright, Robin. *The Last Great Revolution: Turmoil and Transformation in Iran.* New York: Alfred A. Knopf, 2000.

Woodward, Bob. *Bush At War.* New York: Simon and Schuster, 2002.

———. *Plan of Attack.* New York: Simon and Schuster, 2004.

———. *State of Denial: Bush At War, Part III.* New York. Simon and Schuster, 2006.

Zakaria, Fareed. *The Future of Freedom: Illiberal Democracy at Home and Abroad.* New York: W. W. Norton, 2003.

Zelikow, Philip, and Condoleezza Rice. *Germany United and Europe Transformed: A Study in Statecraft.* Cambridge, MA: Harvard University Press, 1995.

Zimmermann, Warren. *Origins of a Catastrophe: Yugoslavia and Its Destroyers.* New York: Time Warner Books, 1996.

INDEX

Australia, 119, 159
Austria, 83
Azerbaijan, 17, 203
Aziz, Tariq, 67, 136
  Bush's letter to Saddam, 46
  meeting with Baker, 46
Aznar, Jose Maria, 115

Baath Party, 191, *see also* Saddam Hussein
Baghdad Pact, 57
Bahrain, 170, 207
Baker, James A., III
  arms control, 11, 12
  Bosnia crisis, 44, 82, 87
  Nicaragua and the contras, 22
  Panama, 25–6
  Persian Gulf War diplomacy, 39, 42, 46
Bangladesh, 51
Barre, Siad, 63
Basque separatists, 144
Belarus, 12, 205
Belgium, 83
Bell, Gertrude, 169
Berger, Samuel R., 58, 114
Berlin Wall, 10, 12, 67, 79, 117, 176,
    183, 197
beyond containment policy, 13
Biamby, Philippe, 73
Biden, Joseph, 7
bin Laden, Osama
  anger at US troop presence in Saudi
    Arabia, 41, 142
  attacks on, 143–4, 162
  Bosnia appearance, 85
  contacts with Saddam Hussein, 169
  escape from Tora Bora, 149, 163
  fatwas, 140–3
  Iraq, 172, 177–8
  Mogadishu comment, 143
  Somalia, 143
  Sudan, 141
Black September terrorists, 140
Blair, Tony
  Iraq War, 174
  Kosovo, 109–14
  Qaddafi, 202
  ties with United States, 158–9
Blix, Hans
  Iraq, 138, 176
  North Korea, 126

Boland Amendment, 20
Bonn agreement, 165
Bosnia
  background, 80–1
  Clinton administration policy, 75
  Contact Group, 93, 96
  Dayton Accords, 85, 91, 96–7
  George H.W. Bush administration, 82
  Islamic extremism, 142
  Milošević, Slobodan, 81
  Muslims in Bosnia, 79–80, 86, 94
  Muslim-Croat Federation, 91
  NATO, 82, 85, 90, 95, 98
  Operation Storm, 94
  safe areas, 89, 93–4
  United Nations, 83
  Vance-Owens proposal, 88
Boutros-Ghali, Boutros, 63, 69
Brahimi, Lakhdar, 165, 194
Bremer, L. Paul, III, 186–7, 194–5
Brezhnev Doctrine, 9
Britain
  Bosnia, 83, 89
  Desert Fox, Operation, 53
  East Timor, 119
  German reunification, 14, 16
  Iraq War, 179, 194
  Kosovo, 108–9, 114, 117
  no-fly zones, 53
  Persian Gulf War, 48, 53
  relations with the United States, 158–9
  Sierra Leone, 119
  white paper on Iraq's WMD, 172
Bulgaria, 10, 93, 117
Bush, George H.W., 8
  achievements, 17–18
  address to joint-session of Congress, 151
  Afghanistan
  Bosnia, 82, 87
  Central Europe, 9–14
  China, 57–8
  coalition building, 42, 43
  decision not to topple Saddam, 52
  encouraging Iraqis to revolt, 52
  encouraging Europe to be whole
    and free, 10
  Haiti, 71
  Iran-Contra, 21–2
  Iraq, 38, 42, 49, 54, 133
  Kiev speech, 11

Printed in the United States
92642LV00002B/166-234/A